Bodies in Commotion

Corporealities: Discourses of Disability

David T. Mitchell and Sharon L. Snyder, editors

Bodies in Commotion

Disability & Performance

Edited by Carrie Sandahl
& Philip Auslander

THE UNIVERSITY OF MICHIGAN PRESS
Ann Arbor

2008   2007   2006   2005   4   3   2   1

A CIP catalog record for this book is available from the British Library.

Library of Congress Cataloging-in-Publication Data

Bodies in commotion : disability and performance / Carrie Sandahl and
Philip Auslander, editors.
  p.   cm. — (Corporealities)
  Includes index.
  ISBN 0-472-09891-8 (cloth : alk. paper) — ISBN 0-472-06891-1
(pbk. : alk. paper)   1. People with disabilities and the performing
arts.   I. Sandahl, Carrie, 1968–   II. Auslander, Philip, 1956–
III. Series.
PN1590.H36B63   2005
791'.087—dc22   2004022452

Acknowledgments

Bodies in Commotion was first conceived at the Association for Theatre in Higher Education's annual conference in Chicago nearly seven years ago. Our editor, LeAnn Fields, was an early champion of disability studies in the humanities, published pathbreaking books in the field, and foresaw that it was only a matter of time before disability studies would make an impact on theater and performance studies. She was right.

David Mitchell and Sharon Snyder, the Corporealities series editors, supported the project every step of the way, providing honest feedback and editorial guidance. David and Sharon's scholarship and activism have been touchstones in disability studies for nearly ten years.

Lisa Yaszek and Cole Hornaday gave us the title for the book; we couldn't have come up with a better one.

The Society for Disability Studies, Performance Studies International, and the Association for Theatre in Higher Education have been sounding grounds for many of the ideas in this book. We would also like to thank the following individuals and institutions for their unflagging intellectual and material support: Paul Longmore and Rosemarie Garland Thomson, who organized a National Endowment for the Humanities Summer Institute in Disability Studies in 2000; Florida State University's School of Theatre, especially Anita Gonzalez, Laura Edmondson, Stuart Baker, Mary Karen Dahl, and John Degen, for their invaluable encouragement and a summer grant in 2000; Jennifer Parker, Jennifer Knight, Jeannine Meis, Shannon Walsh, Jay King, and Jane Duncan for crucial logistical assistance; and Caleb Boyd, Ben Gunter, Jim Bell, Leah Lowe, Kyle Bostian, Donna Nudd, Jerrilyn McGregory, Delia Poey, Jean Graham-Jones, Gretchen Case, Alan Sikes, John Fletcher, and Shane Grant for their comments on early drafts of the introduction and other materials.

Disabled performing artists, especially Terry Galloway, continually inspire us. Victoria Ann Lewis deserves special recognition as a pathfinder of the disability theater movement. This book is dedicated in part to the memory of Spalding Gray (1941–2004).

Finally, we would like to thank our families, Randal Svea and Gregory Sandahl, and Deanna Sirlin, for their support.

Contents

Introduction

Disability Studies in Commotion
with Performance Studies

CARRIE SANDAHL & PHILIP AUSLANDER

*B*odies in Commotion is the first collection to explore *disability as perfor-mance* across a wide range of meanings—disability as a performance of everyday life, as a metaphor in dramatic literature, and as the work of disabled performing artists. It is important to address these myriad meanings in tandem because the depictions of disability embedded in dramatic literature always frame the performance of everyday life, and because the sense that disability in daily life is already performance is reflected in the content and form of disabled artists' stage practices. Considering these meanings together raises questions that productively disturb conventional understandings of disability, traditional performance aesthetics, and performance studies and disability studies. How does a disability studies perspective shed new light on readings of disability in dramatic literature? How is disability performed and transformed using new media? How does the work of disabled performing artists transform the artistic genres in which they work? What new genres are they creating? How does this work confront medical, charity, and freak-show models of disability? How do performance events contribute to disability "cultures," disability identities, and communication between disabled and nondisabled people? What do these performances reveal about who is on the inside of disability culture and who is on the outside? What collaborative strategies have disabled and nondisabled artists used to bridge the gap between their experiences? Are these collaborations equal exchanges between mutually consenting partners, especially when the disabled artists include those with cognitive impairments or the institutionalized? How does the disabled body challenge theoretical notions of "performativity"?[1]

Despite the fact that disability is a ubiquitous, even mundane, human experience, people with visible impairments almost always seem to "cause a commotion" in public spaces. An encounter with disability elicits surprise, attracting the attention of curious passersby.[2] The curious fight the urge to stare, to gather visual information that will help make sense of such startling physical difference.[3] Disability is considered out of the ordinary, separate from the everyday, a cause for pause and consideration. Disability theorists David Mitchell and Sharon Snyder explain that in Western literary, rhetorical, and visual traditions disability "inaugurates the act of interpretation" by functioning as a signifying difference—something out of place, in need of correction.[4] As in traditional representation, disability inaugurates the act of interpretation in representation in daily life. In daily life, disabled people can be considered performers, and passersby, the audience. Without the distancing effects of a proscenium frame and the actor's distinctness from his or her character, disability becomes one of the most radical forms of performance art, "invisible theater" at its extremes.

The notion that disability is a kind of performance is to people with disabilities not a theoretical abstraction, but lived experience. The dramaturgical metaphor of identity construction, first described by sociologist Erving Goffman as the "performance of everyday life" and more recently by philosopher Judith Butler as "performativity," is familiar to postmodern and poststructuralist scholars, but the notion that disability, too, is performed (like gender, sex, sexuality, race, and ethnicity) and not a static "fact" of the body is not widely acknowledged or theorized.[5] While scholars such as Butler argue that identity is performed unconsciously, disabled people talk about performing their identities in explicitly self-conscious and theatrical terms, as does playwright and wheelchair user John Belluso:

> Any time I get on a public bus, I feel like it's a moment of theater. I'm lifted, the stage is moving up and I enter, and people are along the lines, and they're turning and looking, and I make my entrance. It's theater, and I have to perform. And I feel like we as disabled people are constantly onstage, and we're constantly performing. We have to make the choice either to perform or not to perform. . . . There are times when it's fantastic to perform your disability, it's joyful, and it's powerful. Like when I enter on the bus, I love it. I really feel like it's an entrance, like, "I'm ready for my close-up, Mr. DeMille."[6]

Belluso echoes the experience of many visibly disabled people who become adept at turning disability stereotypes and narratives to their own ends. He transforms a potentially stigmatizing experience into an act of empowerment. When Belluso remarks that some disabled people may choose "not to perform," he is alluding to another tactic: the attempt to "pass" as able-bodied. Yet one could consider these efforts to deflect attention from impairment as another kind of performance, a performance of able-bodiedness, one rehearsed every day in rehabilitation hospitals, prosthetic and orthodic labs, speech therapy clinics, and surgery rooms.

The goal of both the self-conscious performer and the "passer" is to become an active maker of meaning, rather than a passive specimen on display. The late Ed Roberts (a founder of the independent living movement and a man with quadriplegia) told journalist Joseph Shapiro that making the choice to perform his disability was the starting point of his life as an activist. After years of bed rest and home schooling, Roberts fought hard to return to public high school.

> [Roberts's] first day back at school . . . had been a revelation. As he was lifted from the car, he had felt the staring eyes of his schoolmates. Staring was what he had most feared. But the stares that day were not looks of disgust. Those who were discomfited had averted their eyes. Instead, these were stares of fascination and excitement, as if Elvis Presley had suddenly descended upon the school. "It was like being a star," recalls Roberts. "So I decided to be a star, not a helpless cripple."[7]

Roberts marshaled a kind of charismatic celebrity status throughout his life to fight for disability civil rights.

Manipulating and transforming stereotypes are important tactics, since the available "scripts" of disability—both in daily life and in representation—are frustratingly limited and deeply entrenched in the cultural imagination. Mitchell and Snyder argue that physical or cognitive impairment serves narrative as "material metaphor," lending "a 'tangible' body to textual abstractions." Individual characters become metaphors that signify "social and individual collapse." Typical disabled characters are a familiar cast: the "obsessive avenger," who seeks revenge against those he considers responsible for his disablement; the "sweet innocent" (otherwise known as the "Tiny Tim"), who acts as a moral barometer of the nondisabled; the "comic misadventurer," whose impairments initiate physical comedy or whose body becomes the target for comic violence; the "inspirational overcomer," the extraordinary individual who excels despite her impairments; the "charity case," who elicits pity and allows others to mark themselves as nondisabled by bestowing goodwill; the "freak," the ultimate outsider; and the "monster," whose disfigurements arouse fear and horror.[8] The fates of such characters often include cure, death, or revaluation in the social order, a metaphorical quelling of the commotion that disability stirs up in narrative.[9]

Recently, disabled performers and theater artists have rejected these scripts and created work based on their own experiences, challenging both tired narrative conventions and aesthetic practices. Disability performance scholar and artist Petra Kuppers points out that the "physically impaired performer has . . . to negotiate two areas of cultural meaning: invisibility as an active member in the public sphere, and hypervisibility and instant categorisation." Kuppers goes on to explain that cultural narratives of disability preempt anything else the artist might be trying to communicate; in other words, audiences assume that the "disabled body is *naturally* about disability."[10] Scholar and performer Catherine Cole discovered this phenomenon for herself when she recently became disabled. In the artist's statement describing her dance-theater piece *Five Foot Feat,* she explains:

> I became disabled over two years ago when I lost my entire left leg to cancer. As I adjusted to my new body circumstances, I became interested in the public spectacle of disability. Going about on crutches with one leg, I became a walking performance art piece, with people stopping to stare or avoiding eye contact all together. But whether people looked or didn't look, I was a performer, a performer in a script I didn't write. So in creating *Five Foot Feat,* I was interested in working *with* that spectacle, the energy of people's visual interest in my body. I felt that by giving people permission to look, and to look on my terms, we could move beyond awkwardness to something more interesting. That's why I begin *Five Foot Feat* by taking off my prosthetic leg. The opening moment of the show is a way of saying, "Here's what my body looks like. Feel however you feel about that, and now let's move on!"[11]

Cole and other disabled artists confront cultural scripts and instant categories of disability before moving on to whatever else they want to communicate with audiences. In any performance medium, when disabled artists create work beyond the traditional roles provided for them, they necessarily challenge rigid aesthetic conventions. A dancer with one leg, for instance, upsets expectations that a dancer's body will be symmetrical and able to execute standardized choreographic movements.

Disciplines in Commotion

The essays in this collection conceive of the performing disabled body as a one that dances across artistic boundaries, questions the foundations of cultural theories, and agitates the divisions between academic disciplines. This presumes that a disability perspective is generative, challenging deeply held beliefs as well as newly emerging ones. In these essays, performance disrupts norms. Performance is a renegade term that describes bodies in a variety of contexts, from the overtly theatrical to the everyday.

Bodies in Commotion provides a platform for interdisciplinary conversations about disability and performance, conversations that have only recently begun to take place at academic conferences such as the Society for Disability Studies, the National Communication Association, the Modern Language Association, the Association for Theatre and Higher Education, and Performance Studies International. In the 1990s interdisciplinary essays began to surface in collections and journals devoted to disability art, literature, and culture. Important essays have appeared in anthologies in the series Corporealities: Discourses of Disability (of which our collection is a part): David Mitchell and Sharon Snyder's *Narrative Prosthesis: Disability and the Dependencies of Discourse* (2000); Susan Crutchfield and Marcy Epstein's *Points of Contact: Disability, Art, and Culture* (1999); and Helen Deutsch and Felicity Nussbaum's *"Defects": Engendering the Modern Body* (1999). Each of these collections includes essays devoted to disability in dance, theater, performance art, or dramatic literature. Other books, too, have explored disability performances. Kenny Fries' *Staring Back: The Experience of Disability from the Inside Out* (Plume, 1997) includes a section on theater. The journal *Contemporary Theatre Review* published a special issue entitled "Disability and Performance" (2001) edited by Petra Kuppers. And Thomas Fahy and Kimball King's *Peering Behind the Curtain: Disability, Illness, and the Extraordinary Body in Contemporary Theatre* (Routledge, 2002) combines dramatic criticism with interviews with artists and includes a full-length play by James MacDonald.[12]

It's not surprising that essays on disability and performance should appear in these collections, given the theatricality of disability and the centrality of performance to the formation of disability cultures and identities. Additionally, disability studies and performance studies share many qualities: academic-activist roots, interdisciplinarity, the body as primary object of study, an international scope, and an interest in the politics and dynamics of representation. Now a growing body of work by disabled performers and playwrights, especially those who make issues of disability central to their work, is bringing these two fields together. New interdisciplinary tools are needed to analyze the performances of artists such as Terry Galloway, Ron Athey, Angela Elsworth, Greg Walloch, the late Mike Lamitola, Cheryl Marie Wade, Mary Duffy, and the late Bob Flanagan; disability dance companies such as the Bay Area's Axis, London's CandoCo, and Seattle's Light Motion; theater companies such Joan Lipkin's DisAbility Project, the

National Theatre of the Deaf, the National Theatre Workshop of the Handicapped, and Joseph Chaikin's Disability Project; and disabled playwrights such as John Belluso, Mike Ervin, Lynn Manning, and Susan Nussbaum. These artists are prompting scholars to investigate how performance studies understands the disabled body and disability as an identity formation, how disability studies understands performance, and how the two fields might make common cause.

The bringing together of these two fields reveals each one's current limits and future possibilities. While the essays in this book apply disability perspectives to performance and performance perspectives to disability, they do not toe a party line, often reflecting different, or even opposing, positions on common issues. The aim of this book is to retain the radical (if ragged) edges of each field, even as they encounter one another. Because both disability and performance are intrinsically interdisciplinary concepts, the conversation between them inevitably includes other disciplinary voices as well. Contributors to *Bodies in Commotion* come from the fields of English, theater, dance, anthropology, sociology, music, arts education, communication arts, women's studies, physical education, and philosophy. Each discipline has its own historical relationship to the concepts of disability and performance, relationships that remain palpable in these essays. These traces of earlier disciplinary formations are important benchmarks, as they indicate the ways in which both disability and performance throw traditional fields into commotion.

Disability Studies and Performance Studies A Brief Genealogy

Disability studies has emerged only in the last twenty-five years or so, beginning as an interdisciplinary endeavor of the social sciences, humanities, and medicine. Only in the past ten years have the arts joined the conversation to any significant degree. Earlier scholars within disability studies looked askance at the arts, seeing them mainly as purveyors of negative images of people with disabilities. It seemed that most of those in the visual arts, dance, music, and theater who were involved with disabled people were the nondisabled interested in applying the arts as therapy. Art as therapy held little interest for many disability scholars who were diligently redefining disability as a minority culture, peeling away the label of pathology with its concomitant demand for cure.

Performance studies has likewise emerged as an interdisciplinary endeavor over the past twenty years. Performance studies arose initially from conversations among scholars whose primary affiliations were with theater studies, anthropology, communication, and sociology.[13] Although

certain American and British anthropologists and sociologists had used theatrical metaphors as ways of understanding their objects of study at least
since the 1950s, the field of theater studies had taken little notice of this
work, and the anthropologists and sociologists themselves had not examined in depth the implications of performance metaphors. Performance
studies was conceived as a cross-disciplinary platform on which these fields
could explore their common ground.

Performance studies has been informed by many other disciplines since
that initial formulation; the current turn is toward a model strongly
inflected by developments in cultural studies. It now provides a home for
the study of a wide variety of performative phenomena in the arts, everyday
life, popular culture, technology, and the media, using lenses provided by
performance theory, identity politics, psychoanalytical theory, and media
studies.

Partly because of the strong influence of feminist discourse, performance studies has long taken the performing body as one of its central
objects. Despite their concern with identity politics, however, performance
scholars traditionally paid little attention to people with disabilities as a
minoritarian identity. Performance studies has generally assumed the body
it studies is a normative one. Disability, unlike race, class, and gender,
escaped recognition as an important identity rubric for performance scholars. Whereas those involved in using the arts therapeutically have formulated a concept of disability, albeit a contested one, performance studies—
out of negligence rather than overt hostility toward disabled people or
disability studies—has had no such concept.

Since disability studies is implicitly conceptualized as the study of a
group of people (a very large group, since most of us are, or will be, disabled to one degree or another) and performance studies addresses a concept that transcends group identifications, the two fields are not based in
similar epistemologies. As emerging interdisciplines, however, both have
confronted problems of definition and distinction because of disciplines
out of which they developed. Medicine and the social sciences, for example, have considered the disabled a problem population who possess conditions needing amelioration and cure. To this received concept disability
rights activists have advanced alternatives commonly referred to as the
social-construction model and the *minority model*.[14] They are central to disability studies.

Activists developed and advanced these models during the Civil Rights
era in the United States, rallying to the cry, "Nothing about us without
us"—a demand for disabled people's leadership in anything having to do
with disability. Activists insisted that disability is not situated within pathological individuals in need of medical care and cure (the medical model)

but is a fundamentally social phenomenon. The social-construction model locates disability within a society built for nondisabled people. Disability is a disjuncture between the body and the environment. It is the stairway in front of the wheelchair user, or written text in front of the blind person, that handicaps an individual, not the physical impairment itself. Scholars using the social-construction model have demonstrated that disability's meaning and expression (i.e., discourses of disability) change over time according to cultural, religious, political, architectural, attitudinal, and economic factors.

The minority model extends the social-construction premise that disability is a mutable category by self-consciously crafting a new disability identity. In this view, the disabled become a distinct minority community that has been excluded from full participation in society because of discrimination in education, employment, and architectural access. This community is defined by shared experiences of discrimination and by its vital subculture, including the arts. Both of these models were deployed explicitly and implicitly in the passage of landmark U.S. civil rights legislation, beginning with Sections 501–4 of the Vocational Rehabilitation Act of 1973 and culminating in the Americans with Disabilities Act (or ADA) of 1990. These legislative coups would not have been possible without activists', artists', and scholars' insistence on new ways of considering disability.[15]

Although Deaf people have long considered themselves part of a separate world with its own language, history, and customs, people with disabilities have begun to think of themselves as a minority culture only in the past thirty years or so. Deaf culture (or DEAF-WORLD)[16] ardently rejects the notion that deafness is an impairment, and therefore members do not consider themselves disabled. Nevertheless, we have chosen to include essays about Deaf performance practices in this collection because they engage in important debates about the contingency of disability identity (especially considering that many hearing-impaired people do not use sign languages and consider themselves disabled), provide a model for alternative aesthetics based on somatic difference, and suggest methods of "translation" between cultures via various forms of interpretation.[17]

Like disability studies, performance studies in its initial formulation offered alternatives to the models of inquiry favored by its parent disciplines, particularly the understanding of theater and ritual put forth by theater scholars. Whereas the traditional view was that theater evolved out of ritual, which was implicitly posited as a less developed cultural form, Richard Schechner and Victor Turner, the main founders of performance studies, called for a revisionist approach that sees ritual and theater as related but different forms of performance, each with its own development.[18] This approach led to the investigation of many forms of performance; although theater and ritual remained dominant paradigms in this investigation, theatrical and ritual performances enjoyed no special privilege as objects of inquiry. Insights from sociologist Erving Goffman, who looked at everyday behavior as theater, were factored in, and the range of activities to be studied as performance expanded to include events outside the aesthetic realm.

Whereas theater studies, as exemplified by theater history, has been divided into subfields along traditional geographic, national, and, occasionally, ethnic lines, performance studies is inherently comparatist. In its quest for a "general theory of performance"[19] across these boundary lines, performance studies produced a supple paradigm that is applicable to many different human undertakings. That same quest initially de-emphasized the characteristics of performances that make them different from one another, in favor of those they have in common. Until the impact of feminism was felt on performance studies in the 1980s, it tended not to acknowledge the particularities of embodiment, implicitly accepting the assumption that the performer's body is a neutral "somatic support"[20] for the signifying practices of the performance in question. Since the 1980s, performance studies has become much more attentive to the relationship between performance and specific cultural identities, particularly in relation to feminism, queer theory, African American studies, and, more recently, Latino/a culture.

As this brief review suggests, developments in both fields have set the stage for the dialogue between disability studies and performance studies undertaken here. To think of disabled people as a minoritarian culture entails considering how that identity is performed both in everyday life and in theatrically framed events that contribute to the self-conscious expression of that identity. Performance studies provides tools for both levels of inquiry; to focus on disability culture through performance studies is also to raise questions asked all too infrequently.

At one level, the question of disability is a question of the deployment of bodies in space, the question of which deployments are normative and which are not, together with the articulation and enforcement of norms. At another level, because of their unique cultural and somatic experiences, disabled bodies relate to and define space differently than normative bodies. Performance provides a valuable conceptual model for the consideration of disability because it, too, is fundamentally about the deployment of bodies in space. The intellectual paradigm of performance that is evolving within performance studies can be applied as readily to representations of the disabled on stage as to the functioning of disabled bodies in daily life and the ways in which disabled people choose to represent themselves in both art and social action.

Similarly, to think of disability not as a physical condition but as a way of interacting with a world that is frequently inhospitable is to think of disability in performative terms—as something one *does* rather than something one *is*. This perspective is central to performance studies, which incorporated Goffman's notions of how identity and selfhood are performed in everyday life. Although performance studies has largely neglected disability as an identity category, its basic approaches are highly relevant to an investigation of how disabled identities are experienced and expressed.

Co-motion

While the word *commotion* denotes "disturbance" and "unruliness," a secondary meaning of the word is "moving together." Taken as a whole, the essays in this book suggest how an encounter between disability studies and performance studies might move both disciplines forward, together. The essays collected in *Bodies in Commotion* reflect both the range of performances to which a disability perspective may be applied and the wide variety of approaches and methods that contribute to disability perspectives themselves. The authors' objects of study range from canonical and contemporary dramas to everyday interactions seen as performance, to performances that articulate disability through technology and engage overtly with the politics of disability and representation, to performances not apparently thus engaged but interpreted afresh to bring out their connections to disability. The variety of methods and approaches reflects disability studies' and performance studies' development out of the arts, humanities, and the social sciences. The methods represented here include art production, case studies, literary analysis, performance criticism, rhetorics, ethnography, historical genealogy, and qualitative research.

Because *Bodies in Commotion* is the first collection to bring these two fields into sustained dialogue, we have opted to include the widest variety of perspectives possible.[21] We asked contributors to focus tightly on a central issue, as a means of raising the widest range of questions for future research. Part 1, "Taxonomies: Disability and Deaf Performances in the Process of Self-Definition," includes essays that map out current representational strategies and thematic trends in disability and Deaf performance. Part 2, "Disability/Deaf Aesthetics, Audiences, and the Public Sphere," explores the politics involved in shifting aesthetic practices for both mainstream and disability cultures. Part 3, "Rehabilitating the Medical Model," looks at how artists work both with and against medicalized notions of disability. The contributors to part 4, "Performing Disability in Daily Life," analyze performances of disability outside of artistic or aesthetic contexts. And finally, part 5, "Reading Disability in Dramatic Literature," engages the representation of in disability in drama from a disability perspective.

Notes

1. Carrie Sandahl addresses this issue in "Ahhhh, Freak Out! Metaphors of Disability and Femaleness in Performance," *Theatre Topics* 9, no. 1 (1999): 11–30.

2. These "passersby" are not necessarily able-bodied. Disabled people are not exempt from these cultural codes.

3. Our thinking about staring has been influenced by Rosemarie Garland Thomson's essay in this collection.

4. David T. Mitchell and Sharon L. Snyder, *Narrative Prosthesis: Disabilities and the Dependencies of Discourse* (Ann Arbor: University of Michigan Press, 2000), 6.

5. See Erving Goffman, *The Presentation of Self in Everyday Life* (New York: Anchor, 1959); and Judith Butler, *Bodies That Matter: On the Discursive Limits of "Sex"* (New York: Routledge, 1993).

6. John Belluso, interview by Carrie Sandahl, Los Angeles, July 2, 2001.

7. Joseph Shapiro, *No Pity: People with Disabilities Forging a New Civil Rights Movement* (New York: Times Books, 1993), 43.

8. We are borrowing terms and paraphrasing definitions of these stereotypes as laid out by disability film scholar Martin Norden in his book *The Cinema of Isolation: A History of Physical Disability in the Movies* (New Brunswick: Rutgers University Press, 1994); disability historian Paul Longmore in "Screening Stereotypes: Images of Disabled People in Television and Motion Pictures," *Social Policy* 16 (summer 1985): 31–37; and disability art critic David Hevey, *The Creatures Time Forgot: Photography and Disability Imagery* (New York: Routledge, 1992).

9. Mitchell and Snyder, *Narrative Prosthesis*, 54.

10. Petra Kuppers, "Deconstructing Images: Performing Disability," *Contemporary Theatre Review* 11, nos. 3–4 (2001): 26.

11. Catherine Cole, "Artist's Statement," http://www.fivefootfeat.com, accessed August 8, 2003.

12. Analyses of freak-show performance appear in Rosemarie Garland Thomson's *Extraordinary Bodies: Figuring Physical Disability in American Culture and Literature* (New York: Columbia University Press, 1997) and her edited collection *Freakery: Cultural Spectacles of the Extraordinary Body* (New York: New York University Press, 1996). In *Lend Me Your Ear: Rhetorical Constructions of Deafness* (Washington, D.C.: Gallaudet University Press, 1999), Brenda Brueggemann includes analyses of Deaf theater and performance art.

13. For a useful genealogy of performance studies, see Jon McKenzie, *Perform or Else: From Discipline to Performance* (London: Routledge, 2001), especially 29–53.

14. We specify that these models are U.S.-based, as similar terms are understood differently by U.K.-based disability scholars. For useful explanations of the differences between U.S. and U.K. models of disability see Lennard J. Davis, "The End of Identity Politics and the Beginning of Dismodernism: On Disability as an Unstable Category," in *Bending Over Backwards: Disability, Dismodernism, and Other Difficult Positions* (New York: New York University Press, 2002).

15. For full discussions of this paradigm shift and its relationship to the disability civil rights movement, see Simi Linton, *Claiming Disability: Knowledge and Identity* (New York: New York University Press, 1998); Shapiro, *No Pity;* and Doris Zames Fleischer and Frieda Zames, *The Disability Rights Movement: From Charity to Confrontation* (Philadelphia: Temple University Press, 2001).

16. This collection will comply with conventions that use "deaf" to describe anyone with a significant auditory impairment and "Deaf" to describe people belonging to a linguistic minority culture with its own language (American Sign Language in the United States), values, customs, artistic practices, and history. The term "DEAF-WORLD" refers to Deaf culture worldwide. In this collection, words or phrases appearing in all capital letters with hyphens between words are English glosses of American Sign Language (ASL). Because ASL is not a word-for-word translation of English and has its own syntax, grammar, and concepts, a gloss is the closest English word translation for specific signs. Thus, an English word in a gloss may only approximate a complex sign in ASL. The hyphen indicates a relationship between the signed concepts and makes apparent the grammatical and structural difference between ASL and English.

17. For more on Deaf culture, see Harlan Hahn's *A Journey into a DEAF-WORLD* (San Diego: DawnSignPress, 1996).

18. See Richard Schechner, "Approaches," in *Performance Theory* (New York: Routledge, 1988), 1–34.

19. This phrase is Jon McKenzie's in *Perform or Else*.

20. Wladimir Krysinski, "Semiotic Modalities of the Body in Modern Theater," *Poetics Today* 2–3 (1981): 141.

21. Our aim with this collection is to document current conversations about disability performance. A complete survey of contemporary disabled performing artists themselves is beyond the scope of our project.

PART I Taxonomies

*Disability & Deaf Performances
in the Process of Self-Definition*

This first part provides a wide sampling of performance strategies that artists with disabilities have deployed to construct disability and Deaf cultures. Historian and activist Paul Longmore explains that the disability culture movements reflect and feed the disability civil rights movement.[1] Longmore argues that both movements have critiqued "hyperindividualistic" American cultural values and coalesced around a set of alternative values derived from the experiences of disabled and Deaf people: "They declare that they prize not self-sufficiency but self-determination, not independence but interdependence, not functional separateness but personal connection, not physical autonomy but human community."[2] The contributors to this section demonstrate that disabled artists have been key to communicating this critique of hegemonic values and to embodying alternative values through performance. All of the artists under consideration in this part consciously attempt to articulate an alternative cultural identity for those on the inside of that experience as well as for those on the outside.

In her essay "Delivering Disability, Willing Speech," Brenda Jo Brueggemann argues that performers with disabilities primarily challenge notions of autonomy and what Longmore calls "functional separateness." Brueggemann contends that these artists challenge the "rhetorical triangle," which consists of three separate entities: the speaker, the audience, and the subject. The performers she considers—Neil Marcus, the Flying Words Project, and sign language interpreters—confuse the traditional rhetorical triangle by using cooperative communication tactics that muddle boundaries between individual performers and between actors and audience. Brueggemann ultimately argues that the field of rhetoric must adapt to take these alternative communication dynamics into account.

Rosemarie Garland Thomson analyzes performances by three artists—Cheryl Marie Wade, Mary Duffy, and Carrie Sandahl—whose work simultaneously tackles feminist and disability issues. In "Dares to Stares: Disabled Women Performance Artists and the Dynamics of Staring," Thomson argues that these artists must negotiate both the "male gaze" and what she calls "the stare" to claim a space for disabled feminine subjectivity. She explores how these artists confront the medicalization of both female and disabled bodies, take pride in their bodily difference, and turn "stigma management" into art. All three performances make apparent how identity is formulated through highly ritualized social exchanges.

The way in which identity is formed in communities is taken up by Jessica Berson in "Performing Deaf Identity: Toward a Continuum of Deaf Performance." Berson analyzes three performances: Shakespeare Theater's *King Lear,* Bruce Hlibok and Norman Frisch's signed performance art, and the Amaryllis Theater Company's *Twelfth Night.* She examines the role that language plays in defining Deaf cultural identity in practices ranging from "outside" performances, which explain Deaf culture to hearing audiences, to "inside" performances by and for the Deaf.

Finally, Jim Ferris's "Aesthetic Distance and the Fiction of Disability" describes how a group of college students at Southern Illinois University at Carbondale found community through the exploration of their disability experiences in a collaborative performance piece called *Do You Sleep in That Thing?* Ferris, who directed the project, describes how this group of performers experimented with calibrating various degrees of aesthetic distance to claim both affinity with, and difference from, their mainly nondisabled audience. Aesthetic distance also allowed the performers to explore disability as a "fiction" whose meaning is context dependent, a move that allowed them to rewrite the meaning of disability for themselves.

Declaring disability a "fiction"—or a social construction—is a significant thread running through all four of these essays. This declaration, however, is not meant to minimize or deny the very real experiences of disability and impairment. Instead, it allows people with disabilities to intercede in the meaning-making process by writing (and performing) their own fictions, fictions they find more truthful.

Notes

1. Paul Longmore, "The Second Phase: From Disability Rights to Disability Culture," in *Why I Burned My Book and Other Essays on Disability* (Philadelphia: Temple University Press, 2003). This essay was originally written in 1995 and is reprinted in this collection.

2. Ibid.

Delivering Disability, Willing Speech

BRENDA JO BRUEGGEMANN

We might start with Demosthenes, who, despite a stutter and "short breath," was the most celebrated of the ancient Greek orators. He was said to have worked to overcome his speech idiosyncrasies (they would now almost certainly be called "speech defects") and to have practiced, pebble-mouthed, projecting his voice over the roaring ocean. From Demosthenes, we can fast-forward two and a half millennia to Christopher Reeve's first major oration as a disabled citizen, stopping the track at his speech before the 1996 Democratic National Convention—delivered between the pulses of his respirator-regulated breaths (roaring, perhaps oceanically, in his own ears) and powerfully performed, yet gestureless and expressionless as it was, from his quadriplegic body. We can pause again at Reeve's speech delivered before thirty-eight thousand faculty, administrators, and graduating students with their family and friends at Ohio State University in 2003. From the center of the football field within the modern coliseum of one of America's largest stadiums, Reeve spoke in his characteristic measured tones and breaths on the subject of "integrity," while his newly shaved head reminded some of us of Patrick Stewart's portrayal as the mutants' center of integrity and master mind-melder, Professor X, in the X-Men films.[1] In these instances and infinitely more, disability delivers rhetoric.[2]

I will be concerned in this essay with how a disabled body, often existing and performing outside the typically narrowly prescribed boundaries of rhetorical "standards," performs successful political and persuasive discourse. I intend to expose the ancient rhetorical canon of delivery (variously known as *pronunciatio* and *actio*) as it has historically both prescribed and described "normalcy," delivering the norms of a rhetorical body—and therein, too, delivering the "norms of a rhetorical culture" (Farrell 1993). While I might locate my argument alongside Lennard Davis's own critique of "normalcy," both constructed and enforced (*Enforcing Normalcy;* "Constructing Normalcy"), I also want to push back disability's rhetorical "coming of age"—beyond his originary point of "the bell curve, the novel, and the invention of the disabled body in the 19th century"—to the development of the art of rhetoric from the ancient Greeks, and the historical march of rhetoric's descriptions and prescriptions for the canon of delivery, the performance of a speaker, and the normalization of speaker's bodies.

In pushing backward, I come to rhetoric as a practice, if not also a theory, of habilitation and rehabilitation. Through its more than twenty-five-hundred-year history, rhetoric has never been particularly friendly to "disabled," "deformed," "deaf," or "mute" people, the "less than perfect" in voice, expression, or stance. As Davis Houck and Amos Kiewe note in their introduction to *FDR's Body Politics*, "the relationship between rhetoric and disability, of course, did not begin with Franklin Roosevelt" (4). They cite, as an example, the way that Homer "effectively disabled Thersites and his speech of dissent" against Agamemnon and the siege at Troy.[3] In fact, without much injustice, one could define rhetoric as the cultivation and perfection of performative, expressive control over oneself and others. Though rhetorical theory has always devoted much, perhaps most, of its attention to the purely conceptual activities of inventing and arranging the "available means of persuasion" (Aristotle), it can never lose sight of the oral, performative communication of these means.

Patricia Bizzell and Bruce Herzberg, for example, begin their second edition of *The Rhetorical Tradition* (2001) with a bow to the complex and "overlapping meanings" of rhetoric, including, among its performative aspects,

> the practice of oratory; the study of the strategies of effective oratory; the use of language, written or spoken, to inform or persuade; the study of the persuasive effects of language; the study of the relation between language and knowledge; the classification and use of tropes and figures; and, of course, the use of empty promises and half-truths as a form of propaganda. (1)

I will work from essentially all of these definitions in this essay. For braiding together theory, practice, and analysis—as these definitions all do—is the pair of (rhetorical) hands that, on the one hand, require the cultivation and perfection of one's own performative, expressive self even as, on the other hand, they entail the similar cultivation and perfection of one's real, imagined, and potential audience.

Yet rhetoric has always been heavy-handed toward one of these two "hands," placing the responsibility for cultivating the speaking voice and performing body on the speaker-performer him- or herself, rather than looking to the audience to adapt in order to meet the ability of the speaker. I will argue, however, that when we put a disabled body/speaker into this rhetorical practice, then rhetoric—as the art of performing persuasion— must now play the "other" hand just as heavily. That is, when disability delivers rhetoric, the audience really matters.

While ancient rhetoricians almost never afforded the canon of delivery *(actio)* the same attention as they did *inventio* (invention), many orators— those who spoke in the assembly, the courts, or for ceremonial occasions— admitted that the performance was the most important aspect of persuasive speaking. In the second edition of *The Rhetorical Tradition,* Bizzell and Herzberg begin by sketching the five canons of rhetoric—invention, arrangement, style, memory, and delivery. Notably, while invention receives seven paragraphs and nearly two pages of attention, arrangement and style get three paragraphs and almost a full page. Even memory, often presumed gone from our rhetorical tradition, gets two thick paragraphs. Delivery tags along at the end with a seven-line single paragraph that, despite its puniness, packs a good punch:

> For Aristotle, delivery is an art akin to acting, which he despises. Like memory, delivery has often received rather perfunctory treatment, even by Quintilian and others who take a brighter view than Aristotle and acknowledge its importance. The Roman rhetoricians understand that voice, gestures, and facial expressions materially affect the impact of all that has gone into a speech. *Delivery is a system of nonverbal signs that has enormous power,* a power recognized by eighteenth-century elocutionists and by twentieth-century electronic media analysts, among others. (7; emphasis added)

This "system of nonverbal signs that has enormous power" is exactly the delivery that disabled performers-speakers-writers (rhetors)—and disability studies—can reinvent in the twenty-first century. For even Demosthenes called delivery the first, second, and third most important components of eloquence—a pronouncement upheld by the rhetorician, public statesmen, and consummate orator Cicero.

While the principles, rules, and proscriptions that make up the art of rhetoric vary from one age to the next, rhetoricians and orators have always taken for granted that those who hoped to control the will of an audience had first to control their own voice and body. Most important to the delivery of a speech was the energy and propriety of the orator's performance: it must convey the force of the speaker's passionate conviction *without* transgressing cultural codes of conduct and deportment. It must, that is, perform "normalcy" even as it incites and inspires some difference (otherwise, we would not be moved by, or remember, it). But disability can critique—can revise and reinvigorate and rehabilitate—the system of "normalcy." I will offer three examples.

Performing a Storm, Challenging Speech

Witness Neil Marcus, performer-actor and creator of an eighty-minute performance piece, *Storm Reading*. It opens with the challenge of—and a challenge to—speech. As the spotlight comes up on center stage, Marcus, sitting in his wheelchair, begins a monologue. His spastic muscles make his sitting barely ever that. His voice, punctuated by the same spasms, is difficult to understand—stuttering and heavy with hesitation as we wait for him to articulate tones, syllables, whole words, and to move us toward phrases, sentences, and fuller comprehension. For a full (very full) forty seconds, Marcus struggles to speak, and his audience struggles to comprehend. Then a female interpreter appears from side stage, gracious and flowing in a soft violet ballet dress. Her name is Kathryn Voice, though she doesn't voice. She signs. Voice works-acts-performs to deliver Marcus's speech, though she does not get its meaning through to those in the audience who do not know ASL (American Sign Language). An additional forty seconds goes by, and just as Marcus utters the final word, "h-h-h-human," a male interpreter, Matt Ingersoll, appears from the audience. As he approaches the stage, Ingersoll pronounces in a clear and mellifluous voice what Marcus has stammered out in two minutes: "People are always watching me . . . they're watching to see how well I do this thing called human."

I show a recorded performance of *Storm Reading*, especially this opening clip, often in classes I teach. I have always used it to open courses on representations of disability in language, literature, and culture. I use it first because Marcus begins with the central issue for disabled people: their position in relation to "human." In his opening line, Marcus articulates, "disability" as an antistrophe, a counterweight, to "normalcy"—much as Aristotle designated the relationship between rhetoric and dialectic. Occupying a place of opposition, designated as outside the limits of "normal," disability highlights the boundaries of the "human condition." Thus, disability is multifariously represented in our culture as *super*normal, *sub*normal, and *ab*normal. It is portrayed as essentially human; yet it is also portrayed as essentially not *human*.

I also like to show this opening clip from *Storm Reading* in my rhetoric-related classes because of these essential and yet antithetical qualities of disability, and because of its performance on the stage usually reserved for the "normal" subject. In such a class, we might focus on Marcus's delivery: the dissonance of a body whose gestures and expressions escape the prescriptions by elocutionists like seventeenth-century educator and rhetorician John Bulwer and eighteenth-century actor and orator Gilbert Austin.[4] Marcus's voice transgresses the boundaries of rhetorical propriety (and rhetoric is always concerned with propriety, with "taste," with prescription); it is a voice trained well beyond the rehabilitation most of us are likely to have experienced, and far beyond Demosthenes' own rehabilitation with pebbles and waves—and yet it is a voice still barely intelligible, hardly rhetorically rehabilitated. Yet Marcus's voice is somehow commanding, compelling, forceful—traits often ascribed to great orators in the rhetorical tradition.

In rhetoric classes, we turn to this paradox to examine delivery as located, not in the rhetor, but in us, the audience. In this audience-centered space disability can illuminate rhetoric, since audience, from Aristotle's *Rhetoric* forward, sits at the center of rhetorical theory and practice. I have never had a class—from Ohio freshmen to the most sophisticated of graduate students from places around the globe—that does not confess how enormously uncomfortable they felt in witnessing the opening of *Storm Reading*. A common descriptor of their emotional engagement at this point is *embarrassed:* they are embarrassed for Marcus as a spectacle on the stage; sheepishly but honestly, they also admit that they are embarrassed for themselves in feeling so embarrassed for Marcus.

They express frustration at being "forced" to watch and listen to this spectacle.[5] (Someone always admits to thinking, "Oh my god, will we have to listen and watch this struggle to speak for eighty long minutes?") The frustration, bordering on anger, often transfers to other rhetorical experiences. As one student wrote in a response to *Storm Reading*'s opening scene: "It brings back memories of all those times in school when a teacher would force someone to get up and speak in front of the class—and they just couldn't do it. All of us would hate it. Speaking like that was so hard to do."

At this point, they have put their fingers on the pulse of rhetoric—the "will to speech" that is desirable but anxiously gained. I invite my students to say more about the role of the two interpreters—who enable and "will" Marcus's speech even as all three performers challenge the will to speech. (The two interpreters play various roles in Marcus's "skits.") These three voices and bodies represent a powerful triangulated dynamic of disability, testing the will of speech, critiquing that will, and reinventing the systems of rhetoric. One is the silent female, the embodied, but voiceless, gesturing

interpreter (whose surname, with delicious irony, happens to be Voice)—
and the other is the male who voices *for* and *over* Marcus and occasionally in
the skits switches places with him. In fact, the triangulated positions of these
three performers rarely hold still.

For example, at one point Voice signs an interpretation of Marcus's own
reflective philosophical musings about who he is and how he affects others.
The stage features only Voice—signing—while a disembodied voice translates into spoken words what her hands and face are communicating. As
this scene develops, Voice's face begins to imitate the facial expressions we
have already seen from Marcus; she embodies, that is, his rhetoric. In a
scene called "Meditations on Dystonia," Marcus and Ingersoll switch places
while Ingersoll voices a meditation:

> *Matt:* When you walk into a room full of people
> and there is a disabled person in the room
> and she scares you
> or makes you want to avoid him
> or she mystifies you
> or you want to reach out and help
> but don't know how . . .
> when this happens, you are on
> the cutting edge of all liberation.
>
> *(Neil gets out of his chair and motions for Matt to sit in the chair. Neil stands next to
> Matt and puts his head close to Matt's head as if joined at the ear)*
>
> It is the experience of being different. It is the experience of living life from
> another point of view. It may be a contemplative or introspective experience.
> It definitely causes one to think.
>   People are curious about us. They wonder where we come from; what
> realm we live in . . . where we've been and where we're going.
>   Everyone wants to know what it's like.
>   See a disabled person clearly and chances are you'll see yourself clearly.
> That is when there are no limits. And there are no limits as to when that will
> happen.
>   It will probably happen now.
> *(Neil and Matt turn and look at each other—lights out)* (*Storm Reading*)[6]

In a third scene that my students always remember, Voice and Ingersoll
play a couple out for a romantic dinner. Marcus, it turns out, is their waiter.
In serving them, he must ask for their assistance; in their service to his service, the rhetorical boundaries of performative normalcy are again
expanded.

No man is a rhetorical island, and Neil Marcus's tripartite body and voice in *Storm Reading* makes this point as powerfully as anything in twenty-five hundred years of rhetorical tradition. We all rely on systems of encultura-tion, models (past performances), mentors, and even "helpers" in taking up and internalizing (making it into our own body) our will to speech. In *Storm Reading*, Marcus models and lays bare the (rhetorical) myth of the great individual speaker. Rhetoric loves a triangle, and Marcus's perfor-mance in *Storm Reading* triangulates the interdependent speaking, per-forming, political, and persuasive *human* experience fully and forcibly.[7] His performance cracks open the rhetorical front of a long-standing ideal, exposing the mask of the eloquent singular speaker and critiquing therein the methods and the ethics implicit in that ideal. Thus, in Marcus's perfor-mance of his disability—which is general dystonia, an all-over spasticity that makes his body "stormy"—and in the audience's reading of that storm (his performance), disability delivers rhetoric.

Flying Words (Subverting) the Order of Speech

Rhetoric can also deliver disability. For throughout its history, rhetoric has, paradoxically, *itself* been denounced as a disabling pursuit, often consid-ered a mask hiding the true ideal of philosophy, thwarting the "will to truth." To the degree that persuasion is worked on auditors (and now read-ers and viewers) through such nonrational avenues as stylistic figures, allit-erative diction, mellifluous tones, or emphatic gestures, it has often been seen as crippling the audience's ability to deliberate rationally or to follow the truth. In this crippling act, the audience does not typically enable the speaker, which is just what has to happen in Marcus's performance. Instead, the concern for rhetoric, from Plato forward, has been how the speaker "trips up" the audience. Thus, rhetoric's "will to speech" often stands both in line with (within the boundaries of) and in opposition to philosophy and dialectic's "will to truth."[8]

Deafness will help further my point about the "will to speech." Let me turn to a sign language poetry performance by the two-man team known as Flying Words Project.[9] This piece, titled "I Am Ordered Now to Talk," is delivered in three modes: a written (in "Deaf English") version of the poem placed in the hands of the audience; the garbled but arduously trained voice of the deaf poet, Peter Cook; and the rather clumsy signing of Cook's interpreter-collaborator, Kenny Lerner. Here are more of those triangles rhetoricians so love.

The subject of the poem is Cook's oral education; he was schooled at the (in)famous Clarke School for Deaf in Northampton, Massachusetts, where, "for more than 130 years our pioneering auditory/oral programs have

taught deaf and hard of hearing children to listen and talk" and where, bol-
stered by no less than rhetoric's "will to speech," great pride is taken in "our
results—independent young people prepared for a place in the world—
[who] speak for themselves."[10] Prefacing the poem-performance with an
explanation of how "at age three, I came down with a disease called spinal
meningitis" and then "recovered," Cook explains that he first thought that
"the dog's voice was broken, all the channels on the TV were broken, my
parent's voices were broken." Instead, he learned, "I was broken." His parents "didn't know what to do with me so they sent me to Clarke School, a
school where they teach you how to read lips and speak, so I could get along
in the hearing world." Here Lerner announces, "Peter will now sign something to the deaf audience only, and he will be focusing on hearing people,
so please—feel paranoid." The audience (hearing) laughs nervously.

Cook signs that he will be *voicing*—not signing (an act considered quite
inappropriate in DEAF-WORLD rhetoric)—in the next piece and that his
voice sounds lousy, "which is part of the point." Thus, the tables of the will
to speech are cleverly overturned; it is now the hearing members of the
audience who miss this pointed utterance. The performance then features
Cook, under one spotlight, delivering the poem in a voice that is off-key,
monotone, somewhat too loud, and sometimes unintelligible, while
Lerner, the "interpreter," signs—signs that are notably not as skilled or
"smooth" (the DEAF-WORLD equivalent of "mellifluous") as Cooks. The
poem is also printed in the program book placed in the hands of the audience, but written in "Deaf English" (a sign language gloss in English
words); it is not very smooth or articulate either. At one point in the three-
minute performance, Lerner stands directly behind Cook and, in a version
of "deaf ventriloquism," becomes Cook's hands, signing out the oral lessons
of spoken English consonants that are impossible to correctly lip-read: "SAY
'B' NOT 'P,' 'S' NOT 'Z.'"

I do not want to undertake a full rhetorical analysis of the poem here.[11]
But I do want to suggest that Cook plays, quite seriously, with the tradition
of rhetoric. It is this tradition, in its "will to speech," that has "ordered him
now to talk." He spent nineteen long years primarily in speech training,
longer than in the rest of his formal schooling—only to produce a voice we
are drawn to but don't much want to hear. Cook and Lerner (like Marcus
and Ingersoll) switch places—and they offer us writing too. Yet despite the
three linguistic avenues—speaking, signing, writing—things don't make
complete sense, and the will to truth and shared understanding still is
thwarted.

Or wait—maybe, in fact, it is enhanced? The paradox of both those possibilities—the thwarting and enhancing of rhetoric's will to speech—played
out in, on, and through Neil Marcus's and Peter Cook's bodies is the

moment of "delivering disability." This is the moment when disability critiques, even as it delivers, Western culture's nearly three-millennia-long emphasis on the will to speech. In fact, I want to suggest that their disabilities allow them a space to make these points even *more* persuasively. For if rhetoric is about the perfect spectacle—the ideal orator—disability can deliver rhetoric by offering, as well, the compelling antispectacle that, as one student wrote in response to the Marcus's *Storm Reading,* calls on the audience to look inward to its own fears and expectations about "the will to speech."

Interpreting Women, Willing Speech

I want to attend further to the thwarting yet enhancing, constructive yet critical capabilities of disability as it delivers rhetoric. Only now I want to turn more tightly to the ethical and political implications of that double-pronged possibility. These implications are also implicit in the Western rhetorical tradition that has insisted on interpreting selfhood in terms of speaking ability: in the rhetorical tradition, to be a "self," one must be able to "speak" for that self. Sign language interpreters—"speaking" for deaf "clients" (even the terms are telling here)—often bear ethical burdens from this rhetorically interpreted selfhood.

I am fascinated by sign language interpreters. Their work in what Mary Louise Pratt calls the "cultural contact zones"—right here in our own country as it occurs between deaf and hearing worlds and cognitions, between the radically different modalities and languages of visual-spatial, embodied ASL and print-centered, often disembodied contemporary English—is fraught with long-standing rhetorical tensions. I am also fascinated by sign language interpreters because their cultural space "working the hyphens" (Fine) reminds me often of my own "hard-of-hearing" doubly hyphenated existence in both deaf and hearing worlds.

Interpreters' work "in the hyphens," I argue, is the work of rhetoric—the work of delivering disability, trying to perform normalcy, willing speech. Recent books about (and for) sign language interpreters have just begun to explore the slippery space(s) of their hyphenated work/performance. For example, Melanie Metzger's *Sign Language Interpreting: Deconstructing the Myth of Neutrality* makes evident the rhetorical politics of interpretation in the act of interpreting. She concludes with subjectively oriented "participation frameworks" for the "role of the interpreter," thus ending far away from the "neutrality" (a "myth," as she declares in her title) that she opens with; these subjective orientations center over "the interpreter's paradox." And this paradox plays on the hyphen, the rhetorical space where a sign language interpreter is both/and—both informational conduit and inter-active participant, both "speaker" and "listener," both one who affects the discourse, as a full participant, and one who delivers it, impartially, like the U.S. mail.

Rhetoric, however, is never mentioned in relation to interpreting (so far as I have been able to uncover). The Registry of Interpreters for the Deaf (RID), one of the two principal certification and assessment organizations for sign language interpreting (along with the National Association for the Deaf, the NAD), defines interpreting as anything but rhetorical: "Interpret-ing, simply stated, is receiving a message in one language and delivering it in another. Not as simple as it sounds, interpreting is a complex process that requires a high degree of linguistic, cognitive, and technical skills."[12] The closest we can come to "rhetoric" in "the interpreter's paradox" (Metz-ger) or even the "art and science" of sign language interpreting (Stewart, Schein and Cartwright) is through "ethics." To be sure, rhetoric and ethics have a long kinship, having crystallized Plato's concern that rhetoric itself was not ethical, and even serving as the pivot for the anonymous (likely Sophistic) treatise, *Dissoi Logoi* (Opposing arguments) of roughly the same period.[13]

Yet perhaps the bridge between rhetoric and ethics is not as strong as it initially seems? Perhaps the hyphen-hopping rhetorical-ethical potential of interpreters as they deliver disability, as they carry out the will to speech—as both subject and object, participant and observer, "speaker" and "lis-tener," performer and audience, neutral and biased, obvious and invisible, spectacle and antispectacle—perhaps it is less about linking than it is (also) about upholding differences? (Imagine, for example, the linkage, yet sepa-ration, inherent in a term like *Asian-American*.)

Interpreters have a fieldwide code of ethics.[14] It exists to help them in: dealing with the murkier issues around the paradox of linking and yet also upholding differences; joining and yet still separating their deaf "clients" with the "hearing world"; pulling them through the muddy matters of "voice" and representation; assisting them in navigating their way through "the myth of neutrality"; and creating perhaps a thin blanket of comfort in the hyphen. This code of ethics attempts, I would argue, to reconcile their Western (hearing) rhetoric (inscribed as the "will to speech") with DEAF-WORLD ethics, and to help them perform some of the more powerful (and paradoxical) sides of their authority in the hyphens between this rhetoric and ethics—to try codifying their "caring" for their clients, and their repre-sentations of both self and client.

In the space of the classic rhetorical triangle (where speaker, audience, and subject occupy the points of the triangle) the interpreter complicates things considerably. In her "impartial" (in all senses of the word) rhetorical performance, she raises two very important questions. First, where should she place her own rhetorical complicity? Where should her own will to speech go in her performance between speech and sign—with the hearing member of the trialogue? with the deaf person? with herself? or with some-place possibly triangulated between the three?

Second, she forces the question: if the interpreting situation is a rhetor-ical triangle—here comprised of interpreter, deaf client, and hearing per-son/world—then who is *really* "the speaker" here? (The interpreter? The deaf client?) Likewise, who is the audience? (Since all three—interpreter, deaf client, hearing person/world—may perform that role in any given moment.) And where, by the way, did the "subject" go? Who then holds and makes manifest the "will to speech"?

What interpreters perform daily is the rhetorical power of *willing speech* that is often performed as "normalcy" in our culture—of speech that comes willingly, of the will toward speech, of willful speech. I have been trying to illuminate that will and articulate its delivery, especially as it relates to dis-ability. More work in the intersections of performance and disability—on stage, in media, in "real lives" and everyday encounters—will aid this artic-ulation. And it is a speech act I hope others will take up as well. For in this act disability can counterilluminate the long-standing performative tradi-tion of rhetoric in at least four ways that I have begun to illustrate in this essay: by critiquing codes of rhetorical, public, "normal" and "normalizing" conduct; by rebuilding the boundaries of rhetoric's long-standing trian-gle(s); by reinscribing the role of audience; and finally, by rearticulating its will to speech.

Notes

1. For a discussion of disability as/in performance, especially in relation to the comic strip (and later TV show and movies) *X-Men*, see Brueggemann et al., "Per-forming (Everyday) Exceptionalities: A Web-Text on Disability in Drama and Per-formance Art," http://english.ttu.edu/kairos/7.1/index.html.

2. These three brief culturally significant examples, spanning twenty-five hun-dred years, are meant only to bracket the perhaps infinite possibilities for the rhetorical space of "delivering disability" that I will attempt to plot in this essay.

3. The passage from Homer that describes Thersites before he speaks sets the stage for his ineffective rhetoric:

Here was the ugliest man who ever came to Troy.
Bandy-legged he was, with one foot clubbed,
Both shoulders humped together, curving over
His caved-in chest, and bobbing above them
His skull warped to a point,
Sprouting clumps of scraggly, wooly hair.

(*The Iliad,* trans. Robert Fagles, 106)

4. The elocutionists are a school (a long-standing and recurring trend, actually) of rhetoricians who focus on the canon of delivery by paying particular attention to the elements of oratory related to the performing of discourse—voice, gestures, expressions, bodily positions, etc.

5. Indeed, the whole point of rhetoric in ancient (classical) Greece was to make a spectacle of oneself—yet only in a culturally coded positive way that was deemed "manly" (see Fredal).

6. *Storm Reading* is based on the writings of Neil Marcus and was adapted for the stage by Rod Lathim, Neil Marcus, and Roger Marcus for Access Theatre (1993).

7. One of the most often taught elements of rhetoric—especially to student writers and speakers—is the rhetorical triangle. In this triangle, the *rhetor* (speaker/writer/performer) occupies one point, the *audience* another, and the *subject* of the discourse or communicative act the third. In creating (or analyzing) any rhetorical discourse, all three must be taken into consideration. Aristotle's classic treatise *Rhetoric* outlines considerations a rhetor must address in relation to these three elements. Likewise, Aristotle established three triangulated appeals that rhetoric often engages: logos (the appeal to logic or reason); pathos (the appeal to the emotions); and ethos (the appeal to character).

8. The "will to speech" is the dominant will that I ascribe to rhetoric at large, and to its relationship with deafness more specifically. See *Lend Me Your Ear: Rhetorical Constructions of Deafness*.

9. To date, there are no production-quality films of Flying Words Project's work. However, they are in the process of creating a video production of their performances. Several universities have demonstration videos of performances from the past. The Ohio State University Wexner Center for the Arts taped their one-hour performance during the April 1998 event "Enabling the Humanities: Disability Studies in Higher Education," and the University of California, San Diego has a webcast version of their performance at http://www.ucsd.tv/library-test.asp?showID=5756. The lack of taped productions of sign language poetry—from Flying Words Project and other sign language poets/performers—further illustrates its classical rhetorical-"oratorical" nature.

10. Http://www.clarkeschool.org/.

11. I discuss this poem, as well as other work by Flying Words Project and several other sign language poets, in the concluding chapter of *Lend Me Your Ear*. In that chapter, I offer a complete gloss of "I Am Ordered Now to Talk."

12. Http://www.rid.org/119.pdf.

13. Isocrates, a contemporary of Plato's, also took up the relationship between rhetoric and ethics, as did both Cicero and Quintilian in the Roman period (often in discussions of the relationship between rhetoric and poetics). In the Enlightenment, the Italian humanist Vico welded rhetoric and ethics, and the Scottish professor Hugh Blair also noted their affinities and reciprocal effects. In the twentieth century, influential rhetoricians such as Wayne Booth, Chaim Perelman, Richard Weaver, and Kenneth Burke have examined the intersections of rhetoric and ethics, often by considering rhetoric's relationship to interpretation, particularly of law or literature.

14. The *RID Code of Ethics* is available online at http://www.rid.org/coe.html.

Works Cited

Aristotle. *On Rhetoric: A Theory of Civic Discourse.* Trans. George A. Kennedy. New York: Oxford UP, 1991.

Bizzell, Patricia, and Bruce Herzberg, eds. *The Rhetorical Tradition: Readings from Classical Times to the Present.* Boston: Bedford/St. Martin's, 2001.

Brueggemann, Brenda Jo. *Lend Me Your Ear: Rhetorical Constructions of Deafness.* Washington, D.C.: Gallaudet UP, 1999.

———, with Wendy L. Chrisman, Angeline Kapferer, Marian Lupo, and Ben Patton. "Performing (Everyday) Exceptionalities: A Web-Text on Disability in Drama and Performance Art." *Kairos* 7.1 (spring 2002). Available at http://english.ttu.edu/kairos/7.1/index.html (accessed 6/28/03).

Clarke School for the Deaf/Center for Oral Education: http://www.clarkeschool.org/ (accessed 6/28/03).

Davis, Lennard J. *Enforcing Normalcy: Disability, Deafness, and the Body.* London: Verso, 1995.

———. "Constructing Normalcy: The Bell Curve, the Novel, and the Invention of the Disabled Body Nineteenth Century." In *The Disability Studies Reader,* ed. Lennard J. Davis, 1–9. New York: Routledge, 1997.

Dissoi Logoi. Anonymous. In *The Rhetorical Tradition: Readings from Classical Times to the Present,* ed. Bizzell and Herzberg.

Farrell, Thomas. *Norms of Rhetorical Culture.* New Haven: Yale University Press, 1993.

Fine, Michelle. "Working the Hyphens: Reinventing Self and Other in Qualitative Research." In *Handbook of Qualitative Research,* ed. Norman K. Denzin and Yvonna S. Lincoln, 70–82. Thousand Oaks: Sage, 1994.

Fredal, James A. "Herm Choppers, the Adonia, and Rhetorical Action in Ancient Greece." *College English* 64.5 (May 2002): 590–612.

Homer. *The Iliad.* Trans. Robert Fagles. New York: Viking, 1997.

Houck, Davis W., and Amos Kiewe. *FDR's Body Politics: The Rhetoric of Disability.* College Station: Texas A & M UP, 2003.

Metzger, Melanie. *Sign Language Interpreting: Deconstructing the Myth of Neutrality.* Washington, D.C.: Gallaudet UP, 1999.

National Association for the Deaf (NAD). "NAD Interpreters Code of Ethics." http://nad.org/openhouse/programs/NIC/ethics.html (accessed 6/28/03).

Pratt, Mary Louise. "Arts of the Contact Zone." In *Negotiating Academic Literacies: Teaching and Learning across Languages and Cultures,* ed. Vivian Zamel and Ruth Spack, 171–86. Mahwah, N.J.: Lawrence Erlbaum, 1998.

Registry of Interpreters for the Deaf (RID). "Code of Ethics." http://www.rid.org/coe.html (accessed 6/28/03).

Stewart, David A., Jerome D. Schein, and Brenda E. Cartwright. *Sign Language Interpreting: Exploring Its Art and Science.* Boston: Allyn and Bacon, 1988.

Storm Reading. "An Excerpt." http://www.newsun.com/StormRead.html (accessed 6/28/03).

Dares to Stares
Disabled Women Performance Artists
& the Dynamics of Staring

ROSEMARIE GARLAND THOMSON

We fear the visibility without which we cannot truly live. . . . And that visibility which makes us most vulnerable is that which also is the source of our greatest strength.

—Audre Lorde, *Sister Outsider*

Everyone knows that you are not supposed to stare. Yet everyone does. Both furtive and compelling, the staring encounter generates discomfort and provokes anxiety. So potent is staring that the Western imagination has persistently seized upon this formidable interchange as a source of vivid narrative. Medusa, for example, turned men to stone with her stare, and her severed head was a fount of power for those who appropriated it. The traditional curse of the evil eye pervades, as well, all European cultures, even into modernity.[1]

Staring is an urgent effort to explain the unexpected, to make sense of the unanticipated and inexplicable visual experience. A more emphatic form of looking than glancing, glimpsing, scanning, surveying, gazing, and other forms of casual or disinterested looking, staring starkly registers the perception of strangeness and endows it with meaning. Staring witnesses an intrusive interest on the part of the starer and thrusts uneasy attention on the object of the stare. At once transgressive and intimate, staring breaches the conventionalized anonymity governing visual relations among strangers in modernity. Staring is thus a kind of potent social choreography that marks bodies by enacting a dynamic visual exchange between a spectator and a spectacle. Staring, then, enacts a drama about the people involved.

The strongest staring prohibition surrounds people who are considered different, who are the most unexpected. Perhaps the most censured form of staring is looking at people with disabilities. Every mother at some point admonishes her child not to stare in an effort to minimize the rawness of astonishing visual confrontations. Yet, as anyone with a visible disability knows, persistent stares are one of the informing experiences of being considered disabled. If staring attempts to make sense of the unexpected, the disabled body is the paradigmatic form in modernity of the unforeseen. Modern culture's erasure of mortality and its harbinger, corporeal vulnerability, have rendered the disabled body extraordinary rather than familiar, anomalous instead of mundane—even though the transformations of bodily form and function that we think of as disability are so common to the human condition as to be the ultimate effect of living. Nevertheless, the disabled body is novelty writ large for the captivated starer, prompting persistent curiosity and launching a troubling tangle of identification and differentiation. For the person with disabilities, staring is an unwelcome exposure, a clumsy trespass into realms casual social relations forbid, and a tedious challenge to one's relational management skills.[2] Thus, encounters between the disabled and nondisabled are exemplary social dramas in which the contradictions and complexities of staring most vividly play out. Despite the ubiquitous admonitions not to stare, even children learn very early that disability is a potent form of embodied difference that warrants looking, even prohibited looking. Indeed, the stare is the dominant mode of looking at disability in this culture.

Staring thus enlists curiosity to telescope looking toward diagnosing impairment, creating an awkward partnership that estranges and discomforts both viewer and viewed. Starers gawk with ambivalence or abandon at the prosthetic hook, the empty sleeve, the scarred flesh, the unfocused eye, the twitching limb, seeking a narrative that puts their disrupted world back in order. Even "invisible" disabilities always threaten to disclose some inexplicable stigma, however subtle, that undoes the social order by its presence and attenuates the human bond based on the assumption of corporeal similarity. Because staring at disability is illicit looking, the disabled body is at once the to-be-looked-at and not-to-be-looked-at, further dramatizing the staring encounter by tending to make viewers stealthy and the viewed defensive. In this way, staring constitutes disability identity by visually articulating the subject positions of "disabled" and "able-bodied."

Many cultural critics have noted that modernity is ocularcentric. Although Western gaze theory is too complex to be adequately addressed here, three general, interrelated strands of critical analysis predominate the attempt to illuminate the workings of this hypervisuality. They can be classified as the psychoanalytic, the materialist, and the ethnographic models, all of which are sustained or shaped by Michel Foucault's formulation of the politics of surveillance.[3] The psychoanalytic underpins much of the robust theory on the patriarchal gaze that emerged from feminist film theory, but has roots as well in the work of such philosophers as Merleau-Ponty and Sartre, for example. Feminist gaze theory has articulated not only the normative heterosexual male gaze, but examined the complex identificatory tangle of how the female, Black, and lesbian gazes operate in patriarchal society.[4] Materialist theories of looking draw heavily as well from continental philosophy, tend toward historiography, and are often driven by a critique of consumer capitalism, as in the work of Guy Debord and Fredric Jameson.[5] Theories of the ethnographic or pathologizing gaze, extrapolated by critics such as Michel Foucault, E. Ann Kaplan, and Sander Gilman, examine the epistemological problematics of the colonizing gaze, whether it takes place in the imperialist, medical, or aesthetic arenas. Although my examination of staring is in dialogue with these theoretical registers, it approaches staring from a distinctly social model.[6]

If—as critics such as John Berger and Laura Mulvey have suggested—gazing is the dominant controlling and defining visual relation in patriarchy between male spectators and female objects of their gazes, staring is the visual practice that materializes the disabled in social relations.[7] The male gaze produces female subjects; the normative stare constructs the disabled. While both are forms of visual marking, gazing trades on a sexual register and staring traffics in medical discourse. Both visual exchanges prompt narrative. Gazing says, "You are mine." Staring says, "What is wrong with you?" Gazers become men by looking at women, and starers become doctors by visually probing people with disabilities.

This essay looks at—to use an appropriate metaphor—three disabled women who the appropriate power of the stare in their live art performances. Cheryl Marie Wade, Mary Duffy, and Carrie Sandahl purposively enlist and manipulate the staring dynamic to mount a critique of dominant cultural narratives about disability.[8] By boldly inviting the stare in their performances, they violate the cultural proscription against staring, at once exposing their impairments and the oppressive narratives about disability that the prohibition against staring attempts to politely silence. Staring unfolds in their work as a charged social exchange between active agents, not simply a form of exploitation or surveillance perpetrated by starers on victimized starees. In their sharp challenge to the prevailing ways of understanding disability, the disabled body becomes a critical aesthetic medium, rather than the object of charity, medical diagnosis, scientific evidence, or sideshow entertainment—the dominant discourses that frame disability in the Western tradition. Their performances thus unleash and realign the power inherent in the social transgression that is staring. Wade, Duffy, and Sandahl perform what Rebecca Schneider calls "the explicit body" as a form of cultural criticism that uses the body to explicate the bodies in social relations.[9]

Wade, Duffy, and Sandahl engage staring both as an oppressive social mechanism and as a visual interaction they seize to protest and to redefine disability. Each of these women's performances enlists a familiar visual genre and inflects its conventions with the stare by flaunting their extraordinary bodies to forge a fresh narrative of disabled female subjectivity. The artistic genre of performance lends itself especially well to the project of renarrating disability because the body is the artistic medium of performance. Thus, in these women's art, the body that performs disability in the social realm is the same body that is the instrument of artistic performance.

One might ask why these women who have bodies that so disrupt the expectations of the complacently normal would deliberately invite the stare in a public setting. Duffy, an Irishwoman who presents herself nude in performance, is armless, with delicate hands attached directly to her shoulders. Wade, an American, gesticulates from her wheelchair emphatically with hands that she describes as "gnarly." Sandahl, who uses a cane, fractures her own anonymity by going through her days in a costume that demands staring, foregrounding the impairment that polite interactions obscure. Each woman would be characterized as "severely disabled" by the standards of what my colleague Paul Longmore calls with great irony the "severely ablebodied."[10] The answer, of course, is that such performances are forums for profoundly liberating assertions and representations of the self in which the artist controls the terms of the encounter. These women's artistic engagement with self-display is a medium for social critique and positive identity politics. Simultaneously, these performances renarrate the scripts of both disability and femininity. They stage a dramatic encounter by inviting the staring that objectifies their bodies and then orchestrating that performance so as to create the image they intend to project. It is the task that all disabled people face writ large. Wade, Duffy, and Sandahl make serious art from the quotidian stuff of the daily stigma management all people with disabilities must master in order to survive and counter the oppressive assumptions about life with a disability.

The disability and gender systems inextricably intertwine in the performances of Wade, Duffy, and Sandahl. The staring relation is always gendered—as well as inflected by race and class, identity registers that the scope of this essay prevents me from addressing fully here. The perception of disability transforms the male gaze into the stare, thus altering the sexual dynamic of looking. The male gaze enacts normative heterosexual desire and constitutes a normalized feminine subject from a female body that is understood to be unimpaired. When the female spectacle is a disabled one, however, male heterosexual desire is no longer imagined as normative, but rather it becomes pathologized as deviant. Devoteeism, the term for heterosexual desire that issues from staring at the disabled female body, is almost universally considered to be pathological, often even by the women who participate in the sex work that capitalizes on this sexual practice. Almost all studies of or responses to devoteeism center on uncovering the etiology of what is assumed to be a pathological attraction to people with disabilities. Masculine fetishizing of female amputated limbs is taken as abnormal, while male fetishizing of female breasts seems completely unremarkable. The point is that the impaired female body is not imagined as the proper object of the male gaze. Wade, Duffy, and Sandahl exploit this transgressive potential in disabled female sexuality in order to renarrate a version of sexual subjectivity that is neither pathological, nor victimized, nor passive.

Cheryl Marie Wade's Hands

Wade works in the familiar genre of the poetry reading, in which the poet's body is a neutral instrument, an unremarkable and unmarked vehicle for the spoken poetic word the genre foregrounds. Wade's body, however, dominates her poetry readings. Capturing the cultural assumption that impairment is an inappropriate aesthetic sight, Wade enlists the power of the unexpected, the transgressive, by demanding that her audience look at what they have been taught is not to be seen outside the clinic. She appropriates the allure of the tawdry sideshow and the sentimental investment of the telethon, placing those urges to stare in the completely unexpected context of the poetry reading—one of the privileged rituals of high aesthetic culture.

Word and flesh, the aural and the visual, thus fuse in the poetic drama she stages. Her performance, like the body that enacts it, is an affront to social expectations. She forces her viewers to violate the staring taboo, refusing them the escape of furtive staring or visual avoidance that so often characterizes nondisabled looking. In "My Hands," for example, Wade parodically puts on the monster role she has been assigned, grabbing its potency and taunting her starers with it, hurling back the dominant culture's words for her body. Her performance foregrounds the particularity of her disabled body. From her wheelchair, she brandishes the hands that are usually hidden in polite society, their shape and function a bold affront to the delicate hands femininity fetishizes.

> Mine are the hands of your bad dreams.
> Booga booga from behind the black curtain.
> Claw hands.
> The ivory girl's hands after a decade of roughing it.
> Crinkled, puckered, sweaty, scarred,
> a young woman's dwarf knobby hands
> that ache for moonlight—that tremble, that struggle.
> Hands that make your eyes tear.
> My hands. My hands. My hands
> that could grace your brow, your thigh.
> My hands! Yeah!

With her invocation of "your bad dreams" and her truculent "Booga booga," Wade mocks her position as monster by conjuring up popular culture's formidable anxiety-turned-fear response to bodies like hers that has traditionally thrilled and titillated the nondisabled. The shockingly naked and visually unexpected hands she invokes verbally, she at the same time emphatically shoves in the audience's faces as she speaks, breaching both social and physiological rules.

Here, however, Wade controls the terms of the encounter. No victimized object of rude, intrusive, curious stares, Wade simultaneously rewrites the cultural narratives of the pathetic cripple and the pretty little lady. Instead, she claims empowerment, agency, and sexuality—the three aspects of personhood that have been denied the disabled subject. She overrides the normative ideal of the "ivory girl's hands," that commercialized image of feminine beauty, with a string of descriptors for her own hands that trounce its authority. Hers are "claw hands" that are defiantly "[c]rinkled, puckered, sweaty, scarred . . . dwarf knobby hands." Wade's hands do not look beautiful, indeed they are a sight so evocative as to "make your eyes tear," perhaps with shock, repugnance, or sympathy. Opposed to the soft static beauty of the "ivory girl's," these hands are the agents of Wade's subjectivity: they "ache," "tremble," and "struggle," exhibiting not loveliness but the evidence of a life of "roughing it." Moreover, these hands are sexual, not in the normatively feminine way of attracting and pleasing the male gaze, but rather as sexual agents. Wade's hands "could grace your brow, your thigh." *Could* here functions ambiguously as a proposition both threatening and tender, at once an offer of gentle love and a menacing "booga, booga" to the squeamish who imagine that the only legitimate caress might come from hands like the "ivory girl's." Wade avows a version of her hands as active rather than passive with her final line, "My hands! Yeah!" as she gazes admiringly and lovingly at her own hands with a sign of satisfaction reminiscent of sexual release. Here she reclaims the stare from her audience and transforms it into the look of love, a self-love here that is not narcissism but rather the affirmation of her own body as whole and right.

Mary Duffy, the Tableau Vivant Venus

Like Wade, Mary Duffy undertakes a project of redefinition, offering counternarratives to the prevailing cultural images of the disabled body. Whereas Wade enlists the genre of poetry reading to invoke the stare, Duffy appropriates the conventions of museum exhibition in her performances. The armless Duffy presents herself in the pose of the classical female nude, a startling tableau vivant of the *Venus de Milo.* Her performance exchanges the fleshly disabled body that has been hidden or sensationally displayed with the familiar marble body that is the icon of female beauty in the Western tradition. Such an ironic juxtaposition both shocks and compels her viewers. By making herself into an art object, she shifts the visual display of her body from the medical or freak-show context to the discourse of aesthetics. This is not the medicalized body stripped naked for diagnosis before the clinical gaze, nor is this the tawdry sideshow or dime museum exhibit hawked by barkers and gawked at by starers. Rather, this is a radical tableau vivant, a living, in-your-face Venus ready to provocatively challenge dominant notions about how we look—in both senses of the phrase.

Duffy's performance dramatically manipulates visuality by using light and darkness. Her exhibition begins with total darkness, the denial of visual gratification. After an uncomfortable time, enigmatic images and a rhythmic sound float up from the darkness. The visual and aural images soon clarify into a cluster of smooth stones that keep increasing in number, accompanied by a chugging sound. The suggestion of embryonic development and fetal heartbeat eventually emerge from this perplexing prolegomenon. Suddenly, the form of Mary Duffy appears out of the darkness, spotlighted from the front against a black background. The scene dramatically obliterates all visual alternatives except Duffy's ultrawhite form, forcing the audience to look at her completely naked body, posed as the Venus. Springing—like the mythological Venus—full-blown, full-breasted, and voluptuous, this living, armless Venus silently demands that the audience stare at her. Such arresting choreography hyperbolically fuses two opposing visual discourses: staring at the freakishly different body and gazing at the female body as a sexualized aesthetic object.

This image elicits a confusing combination of the rapt gaze and the intrusive stare, at once compelling and illicit, forcing her audience to stare, to violate the rules of proper bourgeois looking. Hers is simultaneously the sensationally different body glimpsed furtively in the tabloids, the pathological deviation from the norm sequestered in the asylum or the medical text, and the classical icon of beauty. This sideshow Venus invokes at once the degraded and the exalted bodies, the hidden and the canonical images, of Western visual culture. The understandings culture has supplied her audience are inadequate to this incarnate paradox. This art transforms consciousness, grants a new way of seeing the known world.

Having manipulated staring to upset any simple notion of disability identity, this work of art speaks, transforming from silent object of the stare to a speaking subject by narrating her own exhibition. Duffy's soliloquy flings the words, the questions, and the stares back at her lookers, rebuking the aggregate "you" who cast her as pathological specimen, freak of nature, or quintessential lack. "You have words to describe me that I find frightening," she accuses. Staring out at the starers she's created, she upbraids them for their intrusive "staring eyes and gaping mouths" and their questions about being "born like that" that made her feel "ashamed." Dismissing dominant perceptions of her body, she insists upon her own self-definition, asserting that "words" such as "congenital malformation" do not accurately describe her experience of herself. Her moves from exorcizing the oppressive language that defines her to voicing her own version of herself as "being whole, complete and functional."

Duffy's soliloquy repudiates the pathological narrative while her image insists on an aesthetic interpretation of her body. She refuses the reconstructed body completed by prosthetics that testify to the inventiveness of technology to standardize body. She asserts instead her wholeness, the beauty of her bodily particularities. Her Venus persona thus radically renarrates her supposed lack.

Carrie Sandahl's Medical Records & Daily Rounds

Both Wade and Duffy invoke the conventions of aesthetic genres—the poetry reading and the museum exhibit, respectively—to renarrate disability. Each seeks to move human corporeal variation out of the overdetermined discourses of the pathological, the sideshow, or the sentimental charity poster child, where disability almost exclusively abides, into a representational context where fresh meanings can be conferred. Following this pattern, Carrie Sandahl's performance invokes the interactive conventions of street theater and body art to stage her challenge to traditional understandings of disability. Sandahl's performance brings theatrical conventions such as costuming, props, roles, audience, and staging to her daily life activities, defamiliarizing these everyday encounters by disrupting the smooth social surface that subdues her disability status. Like Wade and Duffy, Sandahl unmasks the operations of disability identity formation and stigmatization that polite social prohibitions obscure in day-to-day social encounters.

Sandahl's performance materializes the objectification of her body by medical discourse. Her costume is a white suit upon which is traced the discourse of pathology that defines her particular body. Her scars, internal structures, such as her spine and pelvis, as well as clinical diagnoses and medical information about her private aspects such as bladder function and sexuality appear in red words on the white lab coat and form-fitting pants of her costume. Like Duffy and Wade, Sandahl's performance foregrounds the differences of her body. Her cane, her uneven gait, and her short stature shift from unmentionable to remarkable, loosing a dialogue both visual and verbal that social conventions usually proscribe. Words appear on parts of her body that are usually outfitted to deflect attention. She hands out prescription slips and medical definitions of her "condition," converting daily life into a theatrical space, passers-by and acquaintances into an audience, and herself into a living clinical text. Such theatrical conventions render her a tableau vivant X-ray and medical record. Whereas Duffy frames herself as a aesthetic object, inviting the gaze of the museum spectator, Sandahl frames her body as a hybrid of the patient, the doctor, the diagnosis, and the empirical evidence. She becomes an embodied, fugitive case study escaped from the clinic, loosed in public sphere from which medicalization has banished the disabled body. By performing in public the identity that is privatized and stigmatized by the discourse of what Michel Foucault calls "the case," Sandahl violates the norms of anonymous public encounters. She trespasses the cultural mandate of what William Ian Miller terms "disattendability," creating a relational space where the social codes and regulations dissolve. She makes, in short, a productive spectacle of her role as a specimen.[11]

Sandahl's performance thus authorizes any viewer to literally read her body. But where Wade and Duffy work in a formal theater space that restricts interaction between viewer and viewed, Sandahl must gather her own audience and transform the quotidian into the theatrical. The result is spontaneity rather than script, chaos rather than control. She transfers disability from the private, hidden, rationalized, impersonal discursive spaces of the clinic into the public ream of her daily life as a teacher, student, colleague, and anonymous citizen, conflating the mutually exclusive arenas of the clinic and the street by taking her medicalized body on the road, so to speak. Sandahl's performance allows her to engage the stares by confronting her starers with her own knowledge of what they think they know about her body, reversing the assumption that nondisabled people know something about people with disabilities by staring at them. Such an invitation to ask the inappropriate and to look at the forbidden creates a scandal and unleashes a torrent of attention that is unmonitored by the usual restrictions surrounding stigmatized identities. It undoes the skillful management by people with disabilities of discomfort surrounding conventional civility about disability that is so characteristic of Western culture. "Don't stare; don't ask; don't tell" breaks down, creating a transgressive space where conventional rules and relations are upset and subject to realignment. This space that Sandahl's performance opens up is neither inherently positive or negative, and once initiated, is no longer within her control, which produces a good deal of chaos, anxiety, and uncertainty. Whereas Duffy and Wade completely control the terms of the encounter between themselves and their audiences by creating one-way, one-woman shows, Sandahl performs a much more complex and risky act. The genie is out of the bottle; the staring encounter she's unleashed leads where it will.

Manipulating the Staring Dynamic

Drawing from varying established genres of performance art, Wade, Duffy, and Sandahl forge an autobiographical form of feminist disability performance art that unsettles cultural presumptions about humanity, femaleness, disability, and self. Wade's performance alludes to the Black Power movement of 1960s positive identity politics; Duffy's rendering of herself from a freak to a Venus draws on the 1970s deconstruction of high and low culture; Sandahl's choreographing of interactive theater space deepens the current art form of the installation. By merging the visual and the narrative, body and word signify together in an act of self-making that witnesses the liberatory potential of disability performance art.

These women make art from the daily experience shared by all disabled people of managing, deflecting, resisting, or renouncing stares. By manipulating the staring ritual so fundamental to disability experience, these performances mount a critique of the politics of appearance, the medicalization of human variation, the rationalization of the body in modernity, and the assumption that disability is embodied inferiority. Moreover, their performances unmask the dynamic of staring by forcing the audience to become starers, to violate the social proscription against being captivated by the desire to stare. If gazing exercises the privilege of disappearing as a marked body, staring marks the starer as the social transgressor. In short, these women cast the evil eye upon their audiences.

Disability, these performances assert, is to be expected. Indeed, the cultural narrative that imagines disability as unexpected, the hidden, the uncanny, is part of the oppression of the ability system. Wide human variation is the norm rather than the exception. It is the ideology of ableism that tells us we should all look the same.

Notes

1. Tobin Siebers, *The Mirror of Medusa* (Berkeley and Los Angeles: University of California Press, 1983).

2. Ann Cupolo Carrillo, Katherine Corbett, and Victoria Lewis, *No More Stares* (Berkeley: The Disability Rights Education and Defense Fund, 1982); Kenny Fries, ed., *Staring Back: The Disability Experience from the Inside Out* (New York: Plume, 1997); Fred Davis, "Deviance Disavowal: The Management of Strained Interaction by the Visibly Handicapped," *Social Problems* 9 (1961): 120–32.

3. Michel Foucault, *Discipline and Punish: The Birth of the Prison*, trans. Alan M. Sheridan-Smith (New York: Vintage, 1979).

4. Maurice Merleau-Ponty, *The Visible and the Invisible*, ed. Claude Lefort, trans. Alphonso Lingis (Evanston, Ill.: Northwestern University Press, 1968); Jean Paul Sartre, *Being and Nothingness,* trans. Hazel Barnes (New York: Philosophical Library, 1956). On feminist gaze theory, see Jill Dolan, *The Feminist Spectator as Critic* (Ann Arbor, Mich.: UMI Research Press, 1988); Jacqueline Bobo, *Black Women as Cultural Readers* (New York: Columbia University Press, 1995); Chris Straayer, *Deviant Eyes, Deviant Bodies: Sexual Re-orientation in Film and Video* (New York: Columbia University Press, 1996); Constance Penley, ed., *Feminism and Film Theory* (New York: Routledge, 1988).

5. Guy Debord, *Society of the Spectacle* (Detroit: Black and Red, 1973); Fredric Jameson, *Postmodernism; or, the Cultural Logic of Late Capitalism* (Durham, N.C.: Duke University Press, 1991).

6. Michel Foucault, *The Birth of the Clinic: An Archeology of Medical Perception*, trans. A. M. Sheridan Smith (New York: Vintage, 1994); E. Ann Kaplan, *Looking for the Other: Feminism, Film, and the Imperial Gaze* (New York : Routledge, 1997); Sander L. Gilman, *Difference and Pathology: Stereotypes of Sexuality, Race, and Madness* (Ithaca, N.Y.: Cornell University Press, 1985).

7. John Berger, *Ways of Seeing* (London: BBC and Penguin, 1972), chap. 3; Laura Mulvey, "Visual Pleasure and Narrative Cinema" and "Afterthoughts on Visual Pleasure and Narrative Cinema," in *Visual and Other Pleasures* (Bloomington: Indiana University Press, 1988).

8. Wade, Duffy, and Sandahl's performances are available in video on *Vital Signs: Crip Culture Talks Back*, directed and produced by David T. Mitchell and Sharon Snyder, Brace Yourself Productions, 1996. I have seen Duffy's and Wade's performances live; my readings of all these performances are influenced by the editing and thematic framing of Mitchell and Snyder's important film.

9. Rebecca Schneider, *The Explicit Body in Performance* (New York: Routledge, 1997).

10. Personal conversation.

11. Foucault, *Birth of the Clinic;* William Ian Miller, *The Anatomy of Disgust* (Cambridge: Harvard University Press, 1997).

Performing Deaf Identity
Toward a Continuum of Deaf Performance

JESSICA BERSON

A deaf couple on a cross-country trip stops for the night at an anonymous motel. Later that night, the husband has trouble sleeping, and decides to take a drive. When he returns to the motel, he cannot remember which room he and his wife are staying in. He ponders the problem for a while, and then, smiling, honks the horn for a solid minute. Lights come on throughout the motel, all the rooms illuminated but one. Oblivious to the protests of his neighbors, the man happily goes to the room not lit, where his wife remains peacefully asleep.

This joke is a standard one in the Deaf community,[1] and it reveals that community's keen sense of humor. Jokes like this one can be startling to hearing people, who are largely unaware that there is a Deaf culture, with its own language, mores, and comedic style. Performances in the Deaf community vary widely, extending from productions that employ "inside" jokes like the one above to signed translations of canonical works. Throughout this spectrum, performance functions as a means of constructing Deaf identity and staking out relationships between Deaf culture and the hearing mainstream. In this essay I will examine three examples of Deaf performance: the Shakespeare Theater's 1999 production of *King Lear;* a 1981 performance art piece by Bruce Hlibok and Norman Frisch; and a 2000 production of *Twelfth Night* by the Amaryllis Theater Company. Although these selections are by no means a representative sample of Deaf performances, they can be used to demarcate a range of productions, from those intended for "outside" spectators to those created for "inside" audiences. By exploring this range we can begin to develop a sense of the ways in which language has become a definitive and dynamic force in shaping the meanings of Deafness, for both Deaf culture and the larger hearing society.

The spectrum of Deaf performance can be described along a continuum that stretches from "outside" to "inside" performance. Outside performances can include interpreted theater and productions in which hearing actors "shadow" Deaf actors, and are intended for audiences that are both hearing and Deaf. I am defining inside performances as those by Deaf artists for Deaf audiences, or those that privilege the theatrical experience of Deaf viewers. My continuum of outside to inside complicates Dorothy Miles and Lou Fant's differentiation between "sign language theater" and "Deaf theater." According to Miles and Fant, sign language theater

> is based on the text of a play written by a hearing author, translated into sign language. It is performed by two casts, a signing cast in prominent position and a less-noticeable voicing cast. The work does not deal with deafness or situations involving deaf characters.

In Deaf theater,

> the work is based on situations unique to Deaf people and is generally performed in a realistic or naturalistic style. Often, the performance is presented solely in sign language, without voice narration. The theme or motif of the work involves issues of concern to Deaf people or conflicts between Deaf and hearing people. (Bangs, "Deaf Performing Arts Experience" 752)

Miles and Fant define both types of theater based on the cultural identity of the artists (Deaf or hearing), the language or languages used (ASL and spoken English), and the content of the performance (situations, mannerisms, and issues specific to Deaf culture). I would like to add to this list of criteria the intended audience, and to use Miles and Fant's bipolar model to imagine a broader and more flexible structure within which to examine Deaf performances. Some sign language theater, as defined above, is produced by Deaf directors and actors primarily for Deaf audiences, despite the inclusion of vocal elements; some Deaf theater, while reveling in Deaf culture, invites hearing audiences to partake in that culture as short-term guests. The boundaries between inside and outside performance are more ambiguous than those between sign language and Deaf theater, and allow an examination of performances that partake in aspects of both categories without necessarily belonging to either. However, performances across the continuum engage language as both form and content, and investigate language's power to shape personal and cultural identity.

Deafness occupies a unique position within the relatively new field of disability studies; while hearing-impairment is a disability, Deafness is a mark of a culture. The categorization and construction of deafness as a disability has competed for several centuries with the concept of deafness as one of the characteristics of Deaf culture, a linguistic minority group more in line with groups defined by ethnicity, religion, or sexual orientation than with many disabled populations. Members of the Deaf community, or what can be more directly translated from ASL as "DEAF-WORLD" (Lane, "Constructions of Deafness" 161), assert the latter notion, as British Deaf leader Paddy Ladd states: "We wish for the recognition of our right to exist as a linguistic minority group . . . labeling us as disabled demonstrates a failure to recognize that we are not disabled in any way within our own community" (159). The conflict between these two constructions of deafness has shaped Deaf culture, which has fought to maintain its integrity against educational and social policies that attempted to prohibit its language and "rehabilitate" its members.

Educational policy for deaf children is generally divided into two camps: manualism, a sign language–oriented approach, and oralism, which seeks to teach deaf children to speak and read lips. In his recent book *Forbidden Signs: American Culture and the Case against Sign Language,* historian Douglas Baynton frames this conflict in terms of wider nineteenth-century cultural and philosophical concerns:

> The debate over sign language called upon and expressed the central debates of the time, involving such fundamental issues as what distinguished Americans from non-Americans, civilized people from "savages," humans from animals, and men from women; what purposes education should serve; and what "nature" and "normality" meant and how they were related to one another. (2)

Rooted in evangelical Protestantism, the manualists saw sign language as a means of converting people who had previously been cut off from the word of God, and as a language more pure and "natural" than speech. They associated sign language with the pantomime of ancient Rome, and the syntactical structure of ASL with Latin and Greek, connections that appealed to their romantic fascination with the ancient world and furthered their admiration for the language. The oralists, on the other hand, aligned themselves with the principles of progress, rationality, and efficiency, arguing that sign language was a primitive means of communication, better suited to "the inferior races" or even "lower animals" (7). Much of the philosophy of the oralist movement was grounded in scientific naturalism, especially in contemporary evolutionary theory. Leaders of the movement, including Alexander Graham Bell, worried that manual education further isolated the deaf from the hearing world and allowed them "by their constant association with each other, to form a class of society and marry without regard to the laws of heredity" (31). Oralism dominated Deaf education for much of the twentieth century, and American Sign Language was often taught secretly by one child to another at residential schools in which signing was strictly forbidden. Though in retrospect the romanticism of the manualist approach seems somewhat paternalistic, at the time, deaf people in America enjoyed a higher level of education and professional possibility than they have since.

At the end of the twentieth century ASL began to be accepted as a legitimate language rather than a pale physicalization of English. In 1960, William Stokoe published the first linguistic study of ASL, and over the course of the next two decades ASL slowly became recognized as a language; however, the struggle between oral and manual education has not yet been resolved. ASL is not recognized for language credit at most colleges and universities, and New York City did not officially include ASL in its public school for the deaf until 1998 (Archer 5). Despite the endurance of attempts to suppress ASL, Deaf activists, like those who sparked the Deaf President Now protests at Gallaudet in 1988, adamantly assert the primacy of ASL in their lives as a legitimate, full language and a defining characteristic of American Deaf culture. Thus, the acceptance of a unique Deaf language is an important foundation for the struggle over the meanings and constructions of Deaf identity.

As in most cultures, performance has been an important site for the development of Deaf culture, as a means of strengthening communal ties, inscribing cultural history, affirming and exploring the expressive and communicative potential of ASL, and asserting the right to use ASL and define Deafness on its own terms. In "Toward a Poetics of Vision, Space, and the Body," Bauman and Dirksen write that "what many scholars would consider the marginal literary practices (if you can even call them literary) of 'disabled' persons is. . . of central importance to anyone, hearing or Deaf, who is interested in the relations of language and literature to culture, identity, and being" (316). Performance, as much as literature, is imbricated in these relations, and Deaf performance in particular illuminates ways that language constructs cultural and personal identity, both within the Deaf community and for the hearing mainstream. The Deaf community's struggle for self-determination of the borders and meanings of its language and culture is continually played out in a range of performances and productions, from ASL translations of Shakespeare to original "Deaf-centric" works.

The Shakespeare Theatre's 1999 production of *King Lear* in Washington, D.C., crystallized many of the issues involved in Deaf performance and troubled the borders between sign language theater and Deaf theater and between inside and outside performance. In her article "Shakespeare and the Limits of Language," Anne Barton writes, "In Cordelia's case, the inadequacy of language happens to express a true state of feeling. Her love for her father does indeed make her breath poor and speech unable" (24). Cordelia's insistence that she not betray her true feeling with words is an essential element of her character in the text: "What shall Cordelia speak? Love, and be silent" (1.1.57). Though pivotal, the role of Cordelia has few lines, and affords actors little opportunity to do much besides speak simply and die offstage. In the Shakespeare Theatre's production, the actor portraying Cordelia could not even speak: a Deaf woman, Monique Holt, signed her lines in ASL and was interpreted by the fool. This casting choice was made largely as a way of making literal the symbolic communication gap between Lear and Cordelia, but it had a host of other implications, both for the production itself and for a discussion about representations of deafness and disability on the mainstream stage. The Shakespeare Theater's *King Lear* presents one mode of Deaf performance among many, each of which offers alternative possibilities for the development and articulation of Deaf identity.

Some elements of *King Lear* point towards an inside approach. Director Michael Kahn and assistant director P. J. Paparelli chose to cast a Deaf actor, rather than a hearing or hearing-impaired actor who spoke ASL, and turned over the responsibility for translating Cordelia's lines to Holt herself (Paparelli). Rather than attempt to replicate Shakespeare's text word for word, Holt's speeches would adhere to ASL grammar and possess its kinesthetic logic. Holt herself describes the process of translating Shakespeare into ASL as challenging and rewarding. Often, especially in sign language theater, signing actors eschew ASL and employ manually coded English or other signing systems that utilize a syntactical structure more like spoken English in an attempt to match the pacing or rhythm of hearing actors. In her efforts to execute an ASL translation, Holt discovered that

> there were no models for actors to learn how to translate their own scripts nor do script analysis. Often, the deaf performers couldn't handle the vocabulary and that slows down the process. I am an impatient individual when things are not done or done properly. I often had to learn the hard way, but it was rewarding because I learned how to do it myself.[2]

Since the Shakespeare Theater's production of *King Lear* Holt has translated and performed monologues from *Othello, Much Ado about Nothing, As You Like It,* and several other Shakespearean works. Holt's translations of

Shakespeare's heroines into ASL demonstrate its potential as a performance language that can speak to both Deaf and hearing audiences.

Of course, creating a performance space for Deaf culture was not the primary motive for casting a Deaf actor as Cordelia. Rather, the Shakespeare Theater "disabled" Cordelia for metaphoric purposes. Disability as metaphor has a long history in dramatic and literary narrative;[3] Kahn and Paparelli borrowed from this tradition when they cast a Deaf actor for the texture that she and her disability would add to the play. For example, Kahn felt that by making Cordelia Deaf, he would reinforce the notion that she could not make herself heard by her father, and that the bond between Cordelia and the Fool would be strengthened through the act of interpretation. Holt's Deafness concentrated attention toward the ways in which the characters in the play communicate; Kahn has said that

> in the play's first crucial scene, people communicate by telling lies or use speech for power and manipulation. The only daughter who tells the truth is banished. So I thought it might be interesting if indeed it was a person who didn't speak—and how it would allow the Fool to speak for her and to comment on her. (Kuchwara)

Kahn's "disabling" of Cordelia calls into question the ways in which he perceives Cordelia's agency, and highlights some of the problematic assumptions that can undermine the seemingly progressive inclusion of Deaf performers in mainstream theater. In this production Cordelia's signing represents her innocence, romanticizing deafness in much the same way that the nineteenth-century manualists conflated signed language and purity. According to Paparelli, one goal of making Cordelia Deaf was to foreground her connection to the fool by making her dependent on the fool to communicate with her father (Paparelli). Later, the king of France assumes the duty of interpreting for his wife, a gesture that Paparelli believed demonstrated his affection; France loves Cordelia so greatly that he is willing to learn her language. But what this reading ignores is that until the very end of the play, when she signs directly to Lear, Cordelia is always mediated by a male voice—she is someone who doesn't speak, but is spoken for. Kahn and Paparelli believed that the fool's and France's ability to "speak for her and to comment on her" showed their love, but it also indicates that they position Cordelia as an object, rather than as a subject with her own, albeit visual, voice.

Holt has her own interpretation of the meanings created by the ways that Cordelia was presented in this production. When she was offered the role, she perceived difficulties not with her own assignment, but with Kahn's concept for the production:

Sometimes the characters do present more of a challenge than others. . . . I thought playing Cordelia was kind of easy. But with the new challenge that *King Lear* is not a Deaf production. Therein lies the problem: why would Cordelia sign if there were no one else to sign to? (A lot of directors, producers, and writers have done this.) In real life, I would not sign to a non-signer. (Holt)

Holt, Kahn, and Floyd King, who was playing the fool, devised an elaborate backstory to reconcile some of the pragmatic problems arising from the decision to make Cordelia a Deaf, signing character. In the history they constructed, Lear had abandoned his responsibility for Cordelia by hiring teachers to instruct her in sign language, while remaining too distressed by her deafness to learn to sign himself. The fool "sneaked in and learned how to understand Cordelia in her language. That's how the Fool was able to read signs," Holt explained. "Too bad, Shakespeare didn't write that part (haha!) . . . with that idea in my mind, I 'bought' it, and I went on stage and played it."

One reason that Holt "bought" this justification for her character's Deafness is that her story of Lear's relationship to his deaf child is a familiar one to those in the Deaf community; most hearing parents of deaf children never learn ASL. In creating this history for Cordelia, Holt inserted elements more characteristic of inside performance into what was otherwise a largely outside production. The use of a Deaf actor to forward a hearing director's vision of a mainstream play, the reliance on interpreters, and the largely hearing audience mark the Shakespeare Theater's *King Lear* as sign language theater, rather than Deaf theater, but like many such productions it resists easy categorization. Kahn imagined Cordelia's deafness as disabling, and the ways in which Holt was interpreted by the fool and France seem to rob Cordelia of the power to speak for herself. However, Kahn and Paparelli, along with Holt, insisted that the fool speak Cordelia's lines as if he were actually interpreting for her, rather than simply reciting them while she signed. These contradictory aspects, vacillating between inside and outside performance and different understandings of d/Deafness, illustrate the ambiguity of the categorization of Deaf performance.

Performance art offers another mode of performance for Deaf artists, a flexible, visually oriented form that has become an important site for non-mainstream discourses of culture and identity. Performance art is a relatively recent development within the field of Deaf performance, and one that may yield new opportunities to negotiate between inside and outside performance. Sally Banes described one such performance, *(More) Short Lessons in Socially Restricted Sign Language,* as "a parody of an academic lecture on 'dirty words' in sign language that was witty, instructive, and quite moving" (119). Created and performed by Bruce Hlibok and Norman Frisch for a festival of gay performance at P.S. 122 in 1981, *(More) Short Lessons* partook in several cultural traditions simultaneously. In an opening scene, a stuffy taped voice explained the difficulty that Deaf people experience trying to learn about sex, both because they cannot access information available through speech and because sexual vocabulary was suppressed in residential schools. As the voice continued, Tavoria Rae Kellam provided an ASL translation, demonstrating to the audience the ways that subtle changes in handshape or fingering can mean the difference between *testicles* and *well hung*, gesturing "voluptuously as the voice pedantically described the signs for sexual organs, acts, and positions" (119). The contrast between signed and spoken terminology highlighted the richness of ASL's visual, kinesthetic vocabulary, but also humorously pointed to a specifically Deaf way of constructing sexuality.

After the lecture Hlibok, Kellam, and Tom Schoenherr gathered to perform a signed version of a taped conversation between a married couple and a counselor. Kellam played the part of the male counselor, while the couple was portrayed by the two men. The act of translation desensualized the descriptions of arousal and pleasure, a sort of inversion of the effects of the first instance of interpretation. By the conclusion of *(More) Short Lessons*, the audience had realized the rich, evocative sexual vocabulary available in ASL: far from being restricted, sign language offers almost limitless, nuanced expressive possibilities. *(More) Short Lessons* resisted the perception of deafness as a disability by unsentimentally uncovering the sensual and communicative pleasures of ASL.

(More) Short Lessons was as much about language as sexuality. Hlibok and Frisch used a combination of signed and spoken texts to highlight ways in which language can be restricted and suppressed, and to explore ways in which those restrictions can be subverted and overcome. The performance commented on its own theatrical structure by reconceiving the relationships between speaker and interpreter, between speech and body. Scenes were repeated and reconstructed throughout the performance, so that the audience received a multitude of sign-speech interactions in which one mode of communication not only translated but critiqued the other. By utilizing the techniques and open-ended philosophy of performance art, Hlibok and Frisch found a way to make a work accessible to hearing audiences without taking a universalistic stance. The playful, self-aware intersection of language and sexuality undertaken by Hlibok and Frisch offered the potential for a different way of performing Deaf identity, one that was rooted inside Deaf culture and the Deaf community, but invited those outside into DEAF-WORLD without compromising that world's language, social codes, or aesthetic values.

The Amaryllis Theater Company's 2000 production of *Twelfth Night* at the Prince Music Theater in Philadelphia presents a new approach to creating Deaf performance. The processes of interpretation and analysis involved in this project provide a means of rethinking the continuum of inside to outside performances, and may create a kind of performance that subverts these categories as it generates new ones. Peter Novak, dean of Trumbull College at Yale, conceived of and directed the project, which involved an eighteen-month effort in "research, dramaturgy, and analysis" (Novak, email) as well as translation. On its surface, this production may appear similar to the Shakespeare Theatre's production of *King Lear*. However, though they share certain challenges of linguistic and cultural translation, the two projects represent very different methods of answering those challenges. The Shakespeare Theatre's *King Lear* incorporated a Deaf actor into a hearing production, while *Twelfth Night* pivoted on an exploration of ASL and its potential as a medium for Shakespeare from a DEAF-WORLD perspective, despite the fact that its director is hearing.

Unlike *King Lear* and many other sign language productions, Novak was primarily concerned with developing a cohesive, precise ASL translation, rather than allowing actors to translate their own lines or devising a non-ASL signed script to coincide with speech. Novak assembled a large company of Deaf artists and interpreters from the National Theatre of the Deaf and other Deaf theater companies, including Monique Holt, to work on the ASL translation and performance. The project hosted a website that offered not only detailed information about the translation process, but descriptions of Deaf culture and specific elements of ASL syntax and how these elements effected the translation. The website indicated the scope and depth of Novak's approach, and his own comments further reveal aspects that distinguished this production:

> I wanted to bring together a community of people to develop and translate this play with and through the community experience. . . . I was not looking for specific issues to bring out in the text. Rather, I wanted to see how ASL could match, and in some cases exceed, Shakespeare's use of language. . . . How is time and space structured in both English and ASL? Do class, gender, and socio-economic reality become visually inhabited? (Novak, email)

Rather than using Deafness to foreground a particular textual interpretation, Novak juxtaposed Shakespearean language and ASL, "so that both will be illuminated" *(Shakespeare's "Twelfth Night");* Deafness was not a metaphor, but a given condition of the production. Instead of looking for ways that *Twelfth Night* could articulate issues specific to Deaf culture, Novak and his company examined how language affects a matrix of social, sexual, and political questions. Working "with and through the community" *(Shakespeare's "Twelfth Night")*, Novak attempted a production in which an interrogation of ASL, and the ways that a visual-kinesthetic language can construct meaning, would take center stage.

This production was not simply "sensitive" to Deaf culture, but rather of that culture, in its language, dramaturgy, and staging. For example, Novak describes negotiating the apparent tension between Shakespeare's directives and the particular requirements of ASL in staging a scene in which Malvolio is imprisoned: "The stage direction from the First Folio, '*Malvolio within*,' indicates that he is most likely off stage, heard but unseen. Because ASL is a visual language, the spectators will not understand him if he is not seen . . . how to make Malvolio understood without being seen?" (Novak, email). The solution that Novak and his collaborators devised elegantly synthesized dramaturgical research with a Deaf-culture perspective. Novak writes, "It was Jacques Copeau who first staged the scene in a trap under the stage in a 1914 production, and the tradition has been prevalent throughout the century. The ASL translation stages the scene with Malvolio's hands and arms emerging through the trap door. . . ASL requires the body and face to produce meaning and so without them, Malvolio is trapped in a linguistic prison" (Novak, email).

Placing Malvolio under the stage and disrupting his ability to communicate heightened the poignancy of the character's desperation and highlighted the layers of deception and false identities that underlie his predicament. Because Malvolio's language was restricted by his inability to use his body or face, the ASL translation was forced to experiment with hybrid signs and gestures, finger spelling, and mime; "as a result, Malvolio's imprisonment was more devastating to watch . . . it clearly had a price for him" (Novak, email). A critic for the *Philadelphia Inquirer* noted the effect of this scene, writing, "a voice speaks what Malvolio is saying, but it isn't necessary. Those eloquently gesticulating hands need no words to express both the humor of the situation and the anguish of the character" (Keating, D02).

The Amaryllis Theater Company's *Twelfth Night* was advertised as "accessible to all audiences" and included hearing actors speaking alongside the signing actors. But unlike some performances in which signing is forced to conform to the rhythms and pacing of speech, this production privileged the theatrical experience of Deaf spectators, prioritizing the ASL translation of the text and asking the spoken performance to submit to the demands of its visual counterpart. However, although many hearing audience members felt that "the ASL helped them to understand Shakespeare more clearly because of the physicality of the actors" (Novak, email), at least one hearing reviewer wrote, "About an hour into the first act, I suddenly realized a deaf critic should have reviewed this show. . . . Facial gestures seem to be a part of that (ASL) vocabulary, so no recognizable emotions can be conveyed except in the broadest possible way. . . . All this creates an unnaturally static quality I found very disconcerting" (Zinman, 27). Part of this response seems to be based on a reaction to specific qualities of signed acting that are often different from those of spoken performance. However, *Twelfth Night* was neither sign language theater nor Deaf theater, as defined by Miles and Fant, and it belied categorization as either inside or outside performance. Spiraling from inside to outside and back again, Novak's production provided points of entry for hearing and Deaf audiences, and could be received as Deaf performance, interpreted theater, or experimental theater—or all of the above.

A number of performances by and for the Deaf doubtless created the space for the innovations of *Twelfth Night*. Interpreted theater made the presence of a potential Deaf audience known to theater practitioners, and companies like National Theater of the Deaf educated mainstream audiences about the expressive potential of sign language. Performance artists like Hlibok and Frisch explored ASL and its role in the Deaf community as both the form and content of their work, further testing the categories of inside and outside performance. Perhaps because of the work of so many previous artists who struggled to affirm ASL's legitimacy as a language and the construction of Deafness as a cultural characteristic, others like Novak can now begin to examine ASL and Deaf culture with a broader and deeper understanding, exploring not only the particularities of DEAF-WORLD but how that world both affects and is affected by a range of social, political, and artistic concerns. In an address to a group at the 1992 Deaf Way conference, Donald Bangs urged Deaf performers to move beyond Miles and Fant's model of sign language theater and Deaf theater, and to "join . . . in the birth of a new Deaf theatre, one that satisfies the needs of Deaf audiences and welcomes hearing audiences at the same time" (Bangs, "New Ideas" 134). Bangs' prescription for the creation of this new theater foreshadowed the Amaryllis Theater Company's production of *Twelfth Night:* he listed the development of unified translations and the inclusion of Deafness as "natural" as some of the key aspects of his vision. Although *Twelfth Night* represents a new direction for Deaf performance, it is part of an ongoing and diverse tradition of performances that examine ASL and an evolving Deaf culture. Examining performances by and for the Deaf, as they develop in relationship to continuing discourses on multiculturalism, linguistic integrity, and disability, allows us to explore an identity-driven theater that is still emerging, constantly staking out new ground.

Notes

1. Throughout this essay I will follow the convention of Deaf studies, in which capitalizing *Deaf* indicates persons who partake in Deaf culture, while using the lowercase *deaf* refers to persons with hearing impairment but not cultural identification.

2. ASL grammar differs significantly from Standard English, and direct quotations from Deaf performers in this essay may reflect that difference.

3. See, for example, Norden, *Cinema of Isolation;* Lane, *The Deaf Experience;* or Grant, *The Quiet Ear.*

Bibliography

Archer, Jeff. "NYC Gives Nod to Sign Language for Deaf." *Education Week,* March 18, 1998 http://www.edweek.org/ (accessed January 2000).

ASL Shakespeare. Website hosted by the ASL Shakespeare Project, Yale University: http://www.yale.edu/asl12night/ (accessed June and July 2000).

Baker, Charlotte, and Robbin Battison, eds. *Sign Language and the Deaf Community: Essays in Honor of William Stokoe.* Silver Spring, Md.: National Association of the Deaf, 1980.

Banes, Sally. Review of "Men Together." *Dance Magazine,* March 1981, 118–21.

Bangs, Donald R. "What Is a Deaf Performing Arts Experience?" In *The Deaf Way: Perspectives from the International Conference on Deaf Culture,* ed. Erting, Johnson, Smith, and Snider, 751–61.

Barton, Anne. "Shakespeare and the Limits of Language." *Shakespeare Survey* 24 (1971): 41–52.

Barton, Len. *Disability and Society: Emerging Issues and Insights.* London: Longman, 1996.

Bauman, H., and L. Dirksen. "Toward a Poetics of Vision, Space, and the Body: Sign Language and Literary Theory." In *The Disability Studies Reader,* ed. Davis, 315–31.

Baynton, Douglas. *Forbidden Signs: American Culture and the Campaign against Sign Language.* Chicago: University of Chicago Press, 1996.

Berge, Mark. "'My Poor Fool Is Hanged': Cordelia, the Fool, Silence and Irresolution in *King Lear.*" In *Reclamations of Shakespeare,* ed. A. J. Hoenselaars, 211–22. Amsterdam: Rodolpi, 1994.

Blanchard, Jayne. *Deaf Transitions.* London: Jessica Kingsley, 1996.

———. "Stark Staging Spells Doom for 'Lear.'" *Washington Post,* Sept. 25, 1999, D2.

Campbell, Jane, and Mike Oliver. *Disability Politics: Understanding Our Past, Changing Our Future.* London: Routledge, 1996.

Cohen, Hilary. "Theater by and for the Deaf." *TDR: The Drama Review* 33, no. 1 (spring 1989): 68–78.

Cohn, Jim. "The New Deaf Poetics: Visible Poetry." *Sign Language Studies* 52 (fall 1986): 263–77.

Corker, Mairian. *Deaf and Disabled, or Deafness Disabled?* Philadelphia: Open University Press, 1998.

———. *Deaf Transitions.* London: Jessica Kingsley, 1996.

————, and Sally French, eds. *Disability Discourse*. Buckingham: Open University Press, 1999.

Davis, Lennard J. *Enforcing Normalcy: Disability, Deafness, and the Body*. London: Verso, 1995.

————, ed. *The Disability Studies Reader*. New York: Routledge, 1997.

Erting, Carol J., Robert C. Johnson, Dorothy L. Smith, and Bruce D. Snider, eds. *The Deaf Way: Perspectives from the International Conference on Deaf Culture*. Washington, D.C.: Gallaudet University Press, 1994.

Grant, Brian. *The Quiet Ear: Deafness in Literature*. London: Andre Deutsch, 1987.

Harris, Jennifer. *The Cultural Meaning of Deafness*. Brookfield, Vt.: Ashgate, 1995.

Holt, Monique. Email correspondence, 1999–2000.

Horowitz, Jane. "'Lear' and Dear to the Heart; Kahn Seeks Relevance in a Difficult Classic." *Washington Post*, Oct. 5, 1999, C05.

Keating, Douglas J. "A Fine 'Twelfth Night' in Signing and Speech." *Philadelphia Inquirer*, Sept. 23, 2000, D02.

Kuchwara, Michael. "Playing Cordelia in 'Lear,' Acting Shakespeare She Can't Hear." *Associated Press*, Sept. 21, 1999. http://www.lexis-nexis-com (accessed January 2000).

————. "Rising to the Fierce Challenges of 'King Lear.'" *Associated Press*, Sept. 8, 1999. http://www.lexis-nexis.com (accessed January 2000).

Lane, Harlan. "Constructions of Deafness." In *The Disability Studies Reader*, ed. Davis, 153–71.

————, and François Grosjean, eds. *Recent Perspectives on American Sign Language*. Hilldale, N.J.: Lawrence Erlbaum, 1980.

Miles, Dorothy May Squire. *A History of Theatre Activities in the Deaf Community of the United States*. Unpublished thesis, Connecticut College, 1974.

————, and Lou J. Fant. *Sign Language Theatre and Deaf Theatre: New Definitions and Directions*. Northridge, Calif.: Center Deafness Publication Series, 1976.

Mitchell, David T., and Sharon L. Snyder. *The Body and Physical Difference: Discourses of Disability*. Ann Arbor: University of Michigan Press, 1997.

Muir, Kenneth, ed. *Aspects of King Lear*. Cambridge: Cambridge University Press, 1982.

Novak, Peter. Email correspondence, 2000–2001.

————. Unpublished manuscript, 2003.

Padden, Carol, and Tom Humphries. *Deaf in America: Voices from a Culture*. Cambridge: Harvard University Press, 1988.

Paparelli, P. J. Telephone interview, December 1999.

Parasnis, Ila, ed. *Cultural and Language Diversity and the Deaf Experience*. Cambridge: Cambridge University Press, 1996.

Phelan, Peggy. *Unmarked*. London: Routledge, 1993.

Reagan, Timothy. "American Sign Language and Deaf Cultural Studies." *Choice*, March 1994, 117–22.

Rose, Heidi M. "Inventing One's 'Voice': The Interplay of Convention and Self-Expression in ASL Narrative." *Language in Society* 25, no. 3 (1996): 427–42.

Rose, Lloyd. "'King Lear': Darkness Before Death." *Washington Post*, Sept. 8, 1999, C01.

Sacks, Oliver. *Seeing Voices: A Journey into the World of the Deaf.* Berkeley: University of California Press, 1989.

Salgado, Gamini. *King Lear: Text and Performance.* London: Macmillan, 1984.

Triplett, William. "Lear and Present Dancer; Ted van Griethuysen, Burning Bright for a Dark and Daunting Role." *Washington Post,* Sept. 5, 1999, G01.

Van Cleve, John Vickrey, ed. *Deaf History Unveiled.* Washington, D.C.: Gallaudet University Press, 1993.

Wilbers, Stephen, and Sherman Wilcox. "The Case for Academic Acceptance of American Sign Language." *Chronicle of Higher Education* 33, no. 42 (July 1, 1987): 27.

Wrigley, Owen. *The Politics of Deafness.* Washington, D.C.: Gallaudet University Press, 1996.

Zinman, Toby. "Rough Night." *Philadelphia Citypaper,* Sept. 28–Oct. 5, 2000, 27.

Aesthetic Distance & the Fiction of Disability

JIM FERRIS

Disability obscures the blurry lines that separate fiction and art from real life. Is disability "fictional," or is it "real"? Social models of disability contend that the oppression that accompanies disability is entirely a social construction—that the social implications of disability are made things that impose an unreal set of assumptions, interpretations, expectations, and restrictions on the lives of disabled and nondisabled people alike. Impairments do have real impact on how disabled people move through the world. But the negative social consequences that are larded on top of those functional limitations can claim their all-too-present reality only because too much of the dominant nondisabled world believes in the artifice called *disability*.

Awareness of fictionality is an essential component of aesthetic distance, a concept that provides some explanation for how we know the difference between what happens on the stage, for example, and real life. This is, of course, quite different from an awareness of the fictionality of disability. But disabled performers, through the management of aesthetic distance, may be able to expose the fiction of disability, transforming the closed look of the stare into a more open look that is both receptive and creative.

We can see this management of distance at work by looking at the public performance of a group of visibly disabled performers. *Do You Sleep in That Thing?* staged at Southern Illinois University, Carbondale, in 1992, explored a number of disability issues with a cast of performers with readily apparent physical impairments. The production featured solo and group performances of poetry, personal narrative, essays, fiction, and even a cartoon. Some of the texts performed related specifically to experiences of impairment and disability; others did not. As director, I assembled a pool of potential texts for performance but asked the performers to choose which ones to stage. Some performers generated their own texts; others brought in pieces that were not in the original pool.

A key tension in the show had to do with the degree to which it would mark disability as difference as opposed to stressing the commonalities of the human experience that we all share. Stress on differences is likely to increase the perception of distance, especially for nondisabled audiences. *DYS* called upon audiences to recognize that differences—in bodies, treatment, and experiences, for example—do not change our common humanity, and do not keep us from common needs, desires, goals, yearnings, and frustrations. But the fifteen performances that made up *DYS* tended to focus on either difference or commonality. Simply put, the performers could choose to actively remind the audience of their physical difference, could direct attention to the body and mark that difference clearly. Or they could choose not to, and allow, if not request, the audience to overlook their bodily faux pas to focus on what they shared. This essay explores aesthetic distance as a means of calibrating the relationship between commonalities and difference. To accomplish this, we will consider a few key performances, which situated themselves in different positions along this continuum.

Distance—both physical and emotional—is a factor in any relationship between people. The concept of aesthetic distance can illuminate the negotiations and implications involved in the management of physical space and interpersonal distance and show ways disabled people can manage their own performances to redefine the stare and present themselves as real people while not minimizing their experiences of oppression.

Aesthetic distance is a crucial element in consideration of disability and aesthetics. As performance scholar Beverly Whitaker Long explains, scholars have long been discussing ideas related to "distance,"[1] but the first and perhaps most influential formulation of the concept appeared in 1912 in Edward Bullough's essay "'Psychical Distance' as a Factor in Art and an Aesthetic Principle." "Distance is a factor in all art," Bullough argued (90), and he contended that art is fundamentally different from (though related to) reality. For Bullough, distance involves a detachment from practical needs and motives and from the "reality" of portrayed events—what Coleridge called "the willing suspension of disbelief"—which allows the audience an imaginative involvement with the art. In *Distance in the Theatre: The Aesthetics of Audience Response,* Daphna Ben Chaim adduces not only Bullough but also Sartre, Brecht, and film theorist Christian Metz to base this practical detachment in an awareness of fictionality, the recognition essential to the theatrical experience, that what happens on stage is art as opposed to life. This awareness of fictionality is "the first moment of distance in the process of aesthetic reception," according to Joanna Kot (6), who has studied manipulation of distance in modernist plays. Once audience members accept the fictionality of the work, they feel "emotionally cushioned and safe," which is thought to give them freedom to engage emotionally with the work. The awareness of fictionality, Kot argues, is predicated on two key sets of factors: the norms that develop within a particular culture, and the expectations generated by a given work of art. It is these expectations, Kot notes, that lead to the second type of distance, the positioning of the audience within and through the work. But Kot asserts that at the end of the process of aesthetic reception, at its heart, lies an emotional identification that "is premised upon distance" (9). Distance, an essential element of any aesthetic experience, is for Kot and for Bullough crucial to allowing audiences to emotionally engage with a work.

The various forms of aesthetic distance with which the cast of *DYS* experimented tended to mitigate nondisabled people's anxiety in the presence of disabled people. Disability studies scholar Harlan Hahn has described two kinds of discomfort that nondisabled people often feel around people with disabilities: existential and aesthetic anxiety. *Existential anxiety* refers to the perceived threat that a disability could interfere with functional capacities thought necessary for a satisfactory life (43). *Aesthetic anxiety* refers to fears of bodily difference, reflected in a propensity to shun those with unattractive bodily attributes, and in society's quest for what Hahn calls "supernormal standards of bodily perfection" (42). Aesthetic anxiety leads to discrimination against disabled people, who are devalued because they do not present conventional images of human physique or behavior. Both anxieties are deeply implicated in the treatment of disabled people in contemporary society. Not acknowledging people with disabilities in public, casting them in a "not fully human" role—these are ways to gain distance from the violation of cultural norms for bodies, ways to minimize the existential and aesthetic anxieties that can arise around people with disabilities. Analysis of performances from *DYS* illustrates how careful manipulation of aesthetic distance can quell, make apparent, or challenge existential and functional anxieties.

Aesthetician Oswald Hanfling identified five key kinds of aesthetic distance: (1) distance from the practical, (2) between the feelings of fictional characters and those of the audience, (3) between art and reality, (4) between the work and its audience, and (5) between the work and the artist. *DYS* experimented with all these forms of distance.

When audiences enter the theater, leaving what Hanfling calls "the practical," we cannot expect them to leave behind their own experiences of disability in the world. *DYS* was clearly framed as an aesthetic event, produced in a theater with a stage, rows of seats, tickets, programs, stage lighting. But because of its nature as a social issue production, framed as an evening of performance about experiences of disability, *DYS* offered a practical value in addition to an aesthetic one, to use Horace's terms, *utile* (usefulness, instruction) along with *dulce* (sweetness, entertainment).

The distances between the practical and the aesthetic, between art and reality, between the work and the performer, were all jumbled by the clash between cultural expectations for disabled people in the world outside the theater and those established inside. *DYS* overturned the stereotype-based cultural expectations that disabled people should stay out of sight, certainly stay out of the spotlight unless seeking a handout. But the key blurring had to do with the extent to which the performers were identified as actors performing fictional roles as opposed to disabled people telling their stories. Though the program identified the text in each of the performances, a tendency on the part of the audience to assume that the performers were narrating personal narratives seems inevitable. This blurring is valuable not just because it calls into question the conventional distinctions between character and actor but because it helps to focus attention on expectations that so often go unquestioned.

The first performance of *DYS* addressed both existential and aesthetic anxiety by stressing difference and exaggerating the distance between art and reality.[2] In "The Biped Lecture," Bob[3] wheeled onstage in a lab coat and bow tie to deliver a lecture describing the many personal trials and challenges people who walk upright face in a world built for those who use wheelchairs. Here are just some: traumatic head injuries and scoliosis caused by standard five-foot ceilings; humiliating biped jokes ("I hate talking to walkies; you look up and all you see are those disgusting nose hairs"); frequent "healings" attempted by religious fanatics; the indignity of the annual biped telethon; the necessity to carry their own chairs around with them wherever they go. The performance drew a lot of laughs, and was successful at provoking thought as well, according to feedback we received.

But at times during rehearsals and after the show closed, Bob voiced concern that the piece "separated people." "Sometimes the best way to [create understanding] is to switch tables on people," he said. "But I think you have to be fairly careful how you do that." He was concerned that "The Biped Lecture" made too much of the differences between people with disabilities and the nondisabled. "It set the tone for a we/they mentality," he said. "It was funny, it worked, it did what it needed to do, it sort of was an introduction to the agenda of the play. But, was it balanced? I'd have to say no." Bob's concern was that the emphasis on differences undercut the message of some of the later performances, that the exaggerated distance could have the effect of broadening the breach between disabled and nondisabled people.

"The Biped Lecture," as Bob recognized, focused on difference. It asked listeners to imagine a world that was not built for them, in which they did not fit and suffered for it. It positioned the audience—many of whom were disabled themselves—as outsiders, as Other, as object rather than subject. In "putting the shoe on the other foot," the piece sought to establish a significant degree of distance between the performer's perspective and the audience's perspective. This performance sought a high degree of distance from reality as well, an obvious and marked distance that gained much of its impact by calling attention to its degree of unreality. This great degree distance from social reality likely seemed to provide enough emotional cushion for the audience to relax and enjoy the humor. The performance explicitly positioned them as only bipeds, but it then invited them to consider the other side, and to compare the world that the performance was describing to the one we know outside the theater.

"The Biped Lecture" attacked both existential and aesthetic anxiety. The performance asserted a world in which the disabled people are not functionally limited; indeed, it is the nondisabled who are limited by the environment. The piece also demonstrated an aesthetic that negatively positioned walkies as unattractively outside the norm. The performance clearly stressed differences between moving through the world with a disability and without one. Despite Bob's concerns about being oppositional in relation to the audience, he made some similar choices to emphasize difference in the next segment of *DYS* we will consider, Bob's performance of Rilke's sonnet, "An Archaic Torso of Apollo."

In this performance, after clearly marking his physical difference, Bob invited the audience to decrease Hanfling's second kind of distance and join with the feelings of his character. He began facing away from the audience, looking at a wall lighted to suggest a museum. The audience heard a voice-over of a little girl asking, "Mommy, what's wrong with that man over there? He's all *crippled up.*" He shook his head slightly, turned toward the audience and moved downstage, then looked a moment at the imagined statue before he began to speak the poem.

That introduction indicated how clearly Bob wanted the poem contextualized by his disability; the introduction cued the audience to read the performance as motivated, at least in part, by the comment. But the introduction also directed the audience to read Bob's congenital amputee body, his missing and incompletely formed limbs, as essential to the performance. Bob did not take a tack common to many people with disabilities, allowing or even asking the audience to overlook his physical difference. Instead, he asked the audience to make an issue of his anomalous body, to make even more of an issue of it than they might otherwise have done in an evening of performance by and about people with disabilities. Instead of allowing the audience to minimize his difference, to forgive him the social faux pas of presenting a disability, he pushed the audience to make meaning of his body as they made meaning of his performance. In Hanfling's terms, Bob was distancing his body from its practical aspect and shifting to an aesthetic aspect, asking us to read his particular body as a key part of the aesthetic field—all the more important because the poem he was performing was about looking at an ancient statue of Apollo that was missing part of its body. Bob allowed the audience to identify with the persona he was performing, to move to some common ground between performer and audience as he invited them to join him in considering how this headless statue could be so moving. But he did this only after the importance of his own physical difference was clearly marked. After delivering the line "for there is no place here / That does not see you" (13–14), Bob moved away from the statue, then paused and turned back. But he looked straight at the audience instead of at the statue as he delivered the last words: "You must change your life" (14). Here Bob was making his challenge to the audience. He stressed the word *you* each time, pushing the audience to recognize that they were the true referent of the pronoun. By the last line, it was clear that this was not a case in which the speaker was saying "you" but meaning "me"; this was Bob's challenge to his audience: "*You* must change your life."

Bob told me in an interview after the production closed that his disability quickly becomes a non-issue in his relationships with nondisabled people.

I've been told, by a lot of people, that they see that my disability disappears real quick. In other words my *in*ability—not my physical difference, but the negative value that most people attach to that—vanishes somehow. Because I don't want my physical difference to vanish. I just want the negative associations to.

His introduction to "An Archaic Torso of Apollo" served to keep his physical difference from "vanishing." Bob's performance of "The Biped Lecture" certainly managed distance and marked difference; his concern about the piece "separating people" was that it set up a dichotomy between "walkies" and regular people (those who use wheelchairs) and then hewed unrelentingly to that dichotomy. "Apollo" marked difference as well, but not in the same way. In this performance he invited the audience to cross the line, but only after first reminding them that there was a line to cross, only after pointing out that by virtue of his difference, his body means differently than bodies within the norm do. Then, after inviting the audience to cross the line, he challenged them with the suggestion that to really cross the line would require changing their lives.

By contextualizing this performance in terms of his disability, Bob sought to reduce distance between work and audience by increasing accessibility. He was also seeking to reduce distance between character's and audience's feelings by making sure that they would read his performance of Rilke's poem in light of his particular anomalous body.

Those performances contrast with performances by Cal. Cal chose to perform Frost's "Stopping by Woods on a Snowy Evening" and ".05" by Ishmael Reed. In each case, Cal used the poem as starting point for personal narrative, an option all performers had but no others took. Cal used the apparent truth-value of personal narrative to shift different kinds of distance and negotiate a delicate balance between stress on difference and commonality.

In his first performance, the Frost poem and narrative, Cal significantly increased distance between the work and himself in order to decrease other kinds of distance, especially between the character's feelings and those of the audience. Stressing the physical barriers he so often encounters, Cal, who uses a power wheelchair, appealed, by means of his difference, to common needs and motives, particularly those related to existential anxiety and the desire for functional independence.

As Cal rolled onstage, he looked around himself and said, "Look at all those trees." After his recitation of the poem, his narrative began with trees. "I grew up in Chicago," he said, "and the only tree I ever saw was a very old, very diseased elm that was framed by my bedroom window." The woods on campus attracted him to the university: "They're the only completely accessible woods I've ever been in." He talked about accessibility elsewhere on campus and told a story about trying to get into one building for an exam. He could not open the door, even when he tried pulling it with his mouth. Nor was he successful trying to get help from passersby. "I have always relied upon the kindness of strangers," he said, evoking Blanche DuBois from *A Streetcar Named Desire*. He was about to quit and go back to his dormitory room when an African-American man felt "a kinship toward a member of another minority" and helped him out. The problem of inaccessibility is unfortunately common, he said, and he described the rest room outside the theater. No problem opening the door—"this time I used my hands"—

but getting to the stall proved enormously difficult. "It's not my intention to sit up here and rag on the university," he said. "But this university is my home. It's more my home than anyplace I've ever lived. I guess that makes you all my family. Christmas shopping is going to be hell this year. But like any good family member, I want my home to be the very best it can be." Ending the narrative with a reference to the Frost poem, he said the university has miles to go before it sleeps, in terms of accommodations for people with disabilities. "But then again, don't we all?" he asked.

Humor was important to Cal's narrative; he made many jokes, which were well received by the audiences. But in reflecting on his performance, he was happy to get away from the clown role he often takes on. Joking in his narrative "was different," he said, "because it wasn't making jokes because you wanted to hide behind them. It was making jokes because those jokes . . . helped to make your point." The overall thrust of his narrative was serious, he said. "It felt like I was telling people things I wanted them to know," he said, "and being serious, and allowing the jokes to take some of the sting away from the audience. Which is what I wanted to do. But they weren't jokes designed to hide behind." Unlike Bob's jokes in "The Biped Lecture," which played with the distance between art and reality, Cal's humor worked to diminish the distance between the feelings of the character onstage and those of the audience. While Bob's humor deliberately increased the distance between the performer's and the audience's perspectives, Cal's humor enlisted the audience to his perspective. The joke about using his hands instead of his mouth to open the rest room door, for example, suggested to the audience that Cal recognized the absurdity of having to open a door with his mouth, that he only used unusual methods in extreme circumstances, and that he is in most ways a regular guy going about his day, much more like them than not.

The family metaphor signaled Cal's complicated dance of difference in this piece. Cal's narrative stressed his physical difference. Note my difference, he was saying, that is why I have these problems with access. Marking difference increases distance, because the difference he marks lies between him and his audience. Cal was also making a minority group claim for disabled people in his narrative, which has a complex effect in relation to distance. On one hand, he was reminding his audience of the difference between his bodily experiences in the world and those of the majority. On the other hand, he claimed kinship with other oppressed minority groups, seeking both to make a statement to the majority and to reduce distance for members of other minority groups. But even when Cal was marking difference, he was doing it in an accessible way, through his humor and his open, friendly style. He implicated his audience in a gentle, funny manner, claiming them as family, bringing them in, reducing the distance between him and his audience. But he did not let them off the hook. He acknowledged that family relationships bring responsibilities: "Christmas shopping is going to be hell this year." Then, a little later, he called upon his audience to be responsible family members as well. He made no excuses for the people who refused to help him get in the door, and he implicated all of us in the university's failure to provide full access. The university has miles to go before it sleeps, but so do each of us.

Personal narrative as a genre is particularly open to management of aesthetic distance: it is presented with the expectation that it represents the performer's own personal experience, diminishing or even negating the distance between art and reality and between work and artist. And it was this "truth" value that helped to make Cal's performance so affecting. Yet to be effective such narratives must be carefully structured—they must be artful, even though their art may lie in how well they conceal their artistry. Cal felt that he had assumed a sort of "split personality" when performing, talking about his reality but stepping back and shaping his narratives. "It was sort of like knowing that yes, this is Cal up here, and yes, these stories he was telling were based on his life. But he also knows now, thanks to what they taught him, that he's got something he has to do with them . . . so that he can tell the story and watch what happens to the people around him. So that he doesn't get so wrapped up in the story he's telling."

The focus shifted to aesthetic anxiety and concerns about attractiveness and friendship in Cal's second personal narrative, the last performance of the show. Again Cal stressed his difference to appeal to common hopes, fears, and yearnings. The Reed poem "speaks about one of the most essential and common human conditions," Cal said. He said he chose to perform it because "it was a poem that I could use to express something that I'd been wanting to express to people." He has a problem sharing deep feelings without making people uncomfortable, he said, and he thought this performance might give him a way to do that.

The speaker in this short poem fantasizes that if he had a nickel "[f]or all the women who've / rejected me in my life" he would be the wealthy head of the World Bank. But with a nickel for all the women who have loved him, he decides he would be the "World Bank's assistant / Janitor", and "All I'd think about would / Be going home."

Cal began his nickel narrative with a confession:

As a kid, I was a pack rat. You name it: baseball cards, toy soldiers, comic books, TVs. . . . I had three TVs in my bedroom. It was really neat the year Dad gave in and got the satellite dish. I could watch three different reruns of *The Brady Bunch,* from three different countries, at the same time. I even learned how to say "groovy" in Spanish. Who says TV isn't educational?

He crammed all his stuff into an eight-foot by ten-foot bedroom. "Having all that stuff in such a small place," he said, "was the only way I knew to crowd out the loneliness I felt." When he got to the university, he was happy to see the "hundreds and hundreds of people . . . all those chances to make friends—all those opportunities." But he learned quickly that "society has its own special rules about friendship, and interpersonal contact in general. And that if you didn't know those rules, you were screwed." He spoke of disappointments in trying to make friends, for example, having people in his dormitory agree to socialize with him and then run away laughing, or being told to "go roll away like a good little boy" when he invited a girl to have coffee between classes.

Because of these experiences, he could understand the persona of the poem. "I could empathize with the speaker's sense of loneliness," he said. But Cal said he was very different from the speaker in a key way. The persona of the poem, Cal said, seemed to have "given up on the world around him. He'd given up on people in general. Most importantly, he'd given up on himself" and chosen to "close himself off in a little bubble"—something that Cal refused to do. He directed the audience's attention to the nickels we had taped to the backs of the programs.

> I spent a lot of years collecting nickels—collecting things—and being rejected by the people I most wanted to know. [This time] we thought we'd try something just a little different. We will never know what you decide to do with the nickels. . . . Like everything else, the choice is yours.

Appeals to common human nature tend to reduce distance, particularly between the audience's feelings and those of the character. Cal's narrative was full of such appeals, asking for recognition of common interests, needs, and humanity; acceptance; and friendship. We all yearn to feel loved, and most of us have felt stung by rejection, probably much more than once. But he sought that commonality by stressing difference, which seems likely to increase distance. He spoke of collecting things to soften the pain of being rejected by other people. However, Cal was speaking of being rejected because of his disability—because of his difference. In his performance Cal did not push the audience to consider his physical difference, as Bob did with the Rilke sonnet. But Cal's body was the ground on which his performance was figured. It would be nearly impossible for an audience not to read Cal's body as they read his performance, not only because of the frame for the show, not only because this was its last performance, but because of his earlier narrative about accessibility problems. Cal did not force the issue, as Bob did, but he did not have to; the body displaying a disability had already been problematized, clearly and repeatedly. A reading of Cal's body with its obvious impairments lent an added poignancy and enabled Reed's poem to work well in performance. And a big reason it worked well is because of Cal's disability, which particularized the poem in a way that allowed us to read the persona's experience as emblematic of a larger problem. Cal's physical difference was not incidental to his narrative; we had little choice but to read his body as we read his narrative.

In discussing accessibility problems on campus, Cal's first narrative focused on functional independence, the value fundamental to existential anxiety. But his second narrative focused much more on aesthetic anxiety and physical attractiveness. The power of the narrative was intensified by the nickels we taped to the programs. Instead of collecting nickels and being rejected, Cal gave out nickels in the hope of experiencing something better. Each nickel was a gift, an offer of friendship, a plea for acceptance. But it was also a token of responsibility, making the strong statement that each person shares responsibility for the treatment of disabled people. The nickel was a token, not only a symbol but a memento, a tangible reminder that each person has the power to make a change.

Or use the nickel as change. Cal, like Bob, was issuing a challenge to the audience, but he acknowledged that the challenge might go unheeded, the nickel spent on something fleeting. Also like Bob, Cal wanted to "turn the tables" on the audience. But he wanted to do more than ask the nondisabled to roll a mile in the chairs of disabled people. He certainly sought empathy, but by distributing the nickels he also took away a hiding place, making it harder for people in the audience to evade or deny a share of responsibility. Cal was not only seeking to reduce the distance between audience and character feelings; he was seeking to minimize distance on almost every front, but particularly the distance between art and reality. You have the power, he was saying; you see the fiction that is disability. The nickels "threw it back at them," Cal said. "We left it up to them, and tried to make them decide what they were going to do." As he said at the end of the narrative, "The choice is yours."

Whatever else it did, *DYS* prevented the distance that enables pity. Unlike the "normal" world, *DYS* allowed crips to control distance, to shine light on the fiction of disability. The nuanced ways that Bob and Cal negotiated aesthetic distance and the tension between difference and commonality both confirm and elaborate upon the contention that disabled people generally seek to manage their communication to shift attention from the impairment. Though such strategies can have positive effects, they also can allow the nondisabled to overlook the ways that society oppresses people with disabilities. Cal and Bob wanted not to let the nondisabled in the audience off the hook so easily. As Bob said, "I don't want my physical difference to vanish. I just want the negative associations to." This crucial distinction can perhaps best be maintained by refusing to conflate *impairment,* which addresses functional limitations, with *disability,* which some scholars use to refer only to the social implications of impairment. To pretend that the differences that impairments bring do not exist—or that they are insignificant—would be as big a mistake as pretending that those social implications have some natural basis, some reality other than the socially constructed one. Cal and Bob managed several different kinds of distance to give audiences a glimpse at the fiction of disability, but glimpses are fleeting, especially in a world in which the very language we have chosen blunts our awareness of fictionality. Are Bob, Cal, and so many others "people with *disabilities,*" or "people with *impairments*"? It is precisely where impairments become disabilities that the fiction of disability lies. Awareness of fictionality, which is the heart of aesthetic distance, is crucial to recognizing and remediating the damaging fiction of disability.

Notes

1. Aristotle discussed what he called "aesthetic disinterestedness"; Samuel Johnson argued that audiences recognize theatrical images for what they are, and later Samuel Taylor Coleridge contended that the pleasure we derive from theatrical performances is based on their unreal and fictitious nature.

2. The essay focuses on four performances that most clearly illustrate the issues at stake. These pieces were performed by men. Although it is beyond the scope of this essay to consider the role of gender in the performer's choices concerning aesthetic distance, questions related to gender could well help further illuminate this dance of difference, particularly in light of the compelling arguments that disability is a "feminizing" phenomenon.

3. In keeping with Southern Illinois University's requirements regarding research on human subjects, requirements that were current at the time, performers were promised anonymity regarding their reflections on their performances, so they are referred to here by pseudonyms.

Works Cited

Ben Chaim, Daphna. *Distance in the Theatre: The Aesthetics of Audience Response.* Ann Arbor: UMI Research Press, 1984.

Bullough, Edward. "'Psychical Distance' as a Factor in Art and an Aesthetic Principle." *British Journal of Psychology* 5 (1912): 87–118.

Frost, Robert. "Stopping by Woods on a Snowy Evening." In *The Poetry of Robert Frost,* 224–25. New York: Holt, Rinehart and Winston, 1969.

Hahn, Harlan. "The Politics of Physical Difference: Disability and Discrimination." *Journal of Social Issues* 44 (1988): 39–47.

Hanfling, Oswald. "Five Kinds of Distance." *British Journal of Aesthetics* 40.1 (January 2000): 89–102.

Kot, Joanna. *Distance Manipulation: The Russian Modernist Search for a New Drama.* Evanston: Northwestern University Press, 1999.

Reed, Ishmael. ".05." In *Chattanooga,* 51. New York: Random House, 1973.
Rilke, Rainer Maria. "An Archaic Torso of Apollo," trans. W. D. Snodgrass. In *After Experience: Poems and Translations,* 86. New York: Harper, 1968.
Whitaker, Beverly. "Edward Bullough on 'Psychical Distance'." *Quarterly Journal of Speech* 54 (1968): 373–82.

PART II Disability/Deaf Aesthetics, Audiences, & the Public Sphere

The essays in this part discuss the development of disability aesthetics by artists in dance and theater who set out to address and counteract the cultural marginalization of the disabled body and the invisibility of disabled people. One set of questions that arises inevitably in this context has to do with audience: who are the intended audiences for these performance practices? For whom are their representations designed? These essays also address the issues that arise when such representations are placed in the public sphere, where reactions and responses to them are shaped by the dominant discourses already in place.

As the authors included here show, the public sphere is a complex, heterodox realm made up of many voices and communities. Whereas the artists and those in the audience who consider themselves part of the disability community may respond positively to seeing non-normative bodies on stage, other parts of the public, including the critics, whose published assessments of the performances often carry considerable weight, may respond less favorably because of their (perhaps unconscious) ideological commitment to normative concepts of what a body should be, what kinds of bodies are appropriate to display in performance, what constitutes performance skill and "good" theater or dance, and so on. Clearly, there are benefits when disabled performers become visible to as broad an audience as possible, but these essays are as alive to the difficulties and pitfalls of that visibility as they are to its advantages.

In "Shifting Apollo's Frame: Challenging the Body Aesthetic in Theater

Dance," Owen Smith focuses on CandoCo, a British dance group made up of both disabled and nondisabled dancers. CandoCo wishes not to be defined solely in terms of its use of disabled dancers but to be seen as part of the general contemporary dance scene. As Smith shows, however, the critical response to their work often remains rooted in normative conceptions of dancers' bodies. Smith traces this deeply ingrained "exclusive corporeal aesthetic" back to the Renaissance, when ideas of nobility and bodily erectness came to be ideologically conjoined, and argues that disability will remain a critical absence until the work of performers like CandoCo have made sufficient inroads against the entrenched concepts of normative physicality.

Shannon Bradford also considers critical response as an important index of disability performance's relationship to the public sphere in "The National Theatre of the Deaf: Artistic Freedom and Cultural Responsibility in the Use of American Sign Language." Like CandoCo, the National Theatre of the Deaf employs both disabled (deaf) and nondisabled (hearing) actors, and seeks not to limit its audience to the d/Deaf community. Bradford points out that the theater, through its use of a performance style in which hearing actors speak at the same time as d/Deaf actors sign, may unintentionally be promulgating misunderstandings of deafness and of the relationship between American Sign Language and English. Much as the National Theatre of the Deaf's techniques may help to produce conventionally "good theater," they may be counterproductive in terms of the ways they make disability visible within the public sphere.

Dancer and choreographer Cathy Weis, the subject of Jennifer Parker-Starbuck's essay "Shifting Strengths: The Cyborg Theater of Cathy Weis," also does not see her work as belonging exclusively to the disability community. Rather, she sees disabled bodies (including her own) as part of a continuum of bodies with varying strengths and capacities from which she builds her choreography. Weis is the only performer discussed in this part to make extensive use of technology, including video and digital technologies, in her work. As Parker-Starbuck argues, these devices do not function as prosthetics for Weis, as ways of remaking the disabled body into a facsimile of a nondisabled body. Instead, they are tools for constructing new bodily configurations that both render disability visible and allow disabled bodies to perform in unexpected and unaccustomed ways. Weis thus inserts into the public sphere performed images that challenge conventional notions of the disabled body and its relationship to technology.

Like Bradford, Victoria Ann Lewis addresses the problematics of constructing a performance meant to appeal to multiple audiences. In "Theater without a Hero: The Making of *P.H.*reaks: The Hidden History of People with Disabilities*," Lewis shows that the choice of style for such a performance

raises immediate difficulties: whereas a realistic or "highbrow" stylized theatrical presentation would be more likely to garner critical favor, the use of
the broadly comic approach characteristic of "people's theater" yields a
production more accessible to multiple audiences and more conducive to a
collaborative production process meant to express a sense of community.
Lewis traces the development of *P.H.*reaks,* including the research and
artistic decisions that informed it, places it within the history of the modern
people's theater movement, and assesses the reasons why the project, spon-
sored by a well-known mainstream theater, was not developed further,
despite a positive reception from the disability community.

Shifting Apollo's Frame

Challenging the Body Aesthetic in Theater Dance

OWEN SMITH

When CandoCo emerged onto the British dance scene in the early 1990s, critics soon took note: they were new and they were different. At that time, Amici and Green Candle (both performing since the 1980s) were probably the most widely known dance companies in the United Kingdom that were not stuck in an aesthetic cul-de-sac characterized by corporeal exclusivity. Both worked with and included disabled and other "nontraditional" dance performers. However, these companies were not perceived in the same way as CandoCo; they were perhaps identified closely enough with the community and disability arts movements not to pose a threat to the dominant, mainstream aesthetic tradition: CandoCo was different.

From the company's birth, artistic directors Celeste Dandeker and Adam Benjamin presented professionally trained nondisabled and disabled dancers together: dancers who represented one particular kind of training and aesthetic tradition with dancers whose physicalities represented a challenge to this tradition. They consciously resisted the "disability dance" label, thereby questioning historically and socially constructed boundaries that attempted to define and secure what had been considered aesthetically acceptable by dominant social and cultural hegemonies.

The two founders had met at an integrated recreation center (funded through ASPIRE: the Association for Spinal Injury Research, Rehabilitation and Reintegration) in London. Adam was artist-in-residence; Celeste was on the management committee. He saw her in *The Fall* (1990), a dance film made for television, choreographed by Darshan Singh Bhuller, and was inspired. During the 1970s, while dancing with the London Contemporary Dance Theatre, Celeste had fallen awkwardly and broken her neck; paralyzed by the accident, Singh Bhuller's acclaimed film was her first public exposure as a dancer for over fifteen years.

Realizing that dance might be a vehicle for bringing disabled and nondisabled people together for physical recreation, Adam and Celeste began discussing the idea of developing an integrated dance program at the center. A visual artist who had also trained in dance, Adam had a strong interest in both "new" dance techniques and traditional Eastern techniques of movement.[1]

They began teaching together and soon built up a core of students. A year later (in 1992) they were performing, holding workshops, and teaching across the country. The following year they opened Dance 93 in Nottingham and the Spring Loaded dance season at the Queen Elizabeth Hall (one of London's prestigious performance venues) with a company that included three disabled and five nondisabled dancers. Their style was grounded in both contemporary and new dance techniques. They also sought a rigorous aesthetic quality with the wish that their work might be assessed according to the same criteria applied to any other contemporary dance company. Central to their creative ethos was the will to work in ways through which individual performers could complement each other's strengths and abilities, not to highlight any one individual's capacity—certainly not to create a frame in which disabled company members would be showcased and emphasized, simply because they were disabled people dancing. (Currently the company consists of two dancers who are mobility impaired through spinal injury and who use wheelchairs, one who has lost a leg below the midthigh, and three nondisabled dancers.)

The establishment's urge to place the company under the umbrella of "disability dance" was something the company had to struggle to resist. Their vision, to reinterpret dance in order to widen potential ownership of the art form, demanded that both non- and disabled people explore, work, and dance together; this would not happen if they were segregated within the category of the disability arts.[2]

The desire to pigeonhole and categorize the company, and an uncertainty about where to critically locate their work, represent a response to the challenge that they pose. Many critical reviews of their work during the 1990s appreciated their right to struggle for recognition and profile alongside other companies, perhaps acknowledging the inroads toward aesthetic heterogeneity that had been vigorously pioneered through various "post-modern" experiments within contemporary dance practice in Britain since the 1970s. However, other reviews expressed an unashamed conservatism in reaction to the company in defense of an assumed aesthetic integrity that appears to demand corporeal homogeneity and exclusivity. By placing themselves within the frame of contemporary dance's mainstream Can-doCo challenged that integrity through their rewriting of the dominant dance manual that insists on the exclusivity of a limited physicality.

Moreover, though conservative pronouncements from within the out-moded citadels of "high" art have been in the minority (in the predomi-nantly "liberal" arena of British contemporary dance performance), they do underscore institutionally entrenched, disablist attitudes that continue to influence relative degrees of participation and exclusion within perfor-mative dance. To counter the exclusionary tendency, CandoCo has not lim-ited its vision to contexts of public, contemporary dance performance (where the diverse styles and creative visions that have been represented by contemporary, performative dance since the 1980s have generated a rela-tively sophisticated audience, receptive to a degree of innovation). From its inception, the company recognized the need to champion the ethos of an inclusive aesthetic at both the level of professional performance and along the training and educational pathways that might lead to this level. Their emphasis on high-profile, inclusive performance practice and accessible training pathways for aspiring, disabled dance artists underscores their importance as a performance company and training organization. Adam Benjamin has acknowledged the need for a radical rethinking of the ways in which training is constructed and delivered, and also of the task involved in eliciting this reappraisal.[3]

Benjamin has used the term *new dance ecology* to describe the need for the dance establishment (including institutions involved in dance education and training) to assess its relationship with the wider world, a world that is not characterized by a uniform corporeality.[4] He draws attention to ways in which dance artists, challenging the dominant hierarchies of the contem-porary and classical dance establishment in Britain in the 1960s and 1970s (particularly dancers involved in the London-based X6 Dance Space), ques-tioned the numerous levels at which that hierarchy impacted on the ex-perience of dance and dancers. Often, these were politicized artists ready to challenge the social and cultural environments they inhabited and in which they worked, who acknowledged that these environments are constructed according to the imperatives of dominant sociopolitical hegemonies. Ben-jamin locates CandoCo on a trajectory he traces back to the creative radicalism of "new" dance during the 1960s and 1970s.[5] However, CandoCo has rejected the "alternative" label through its seizure of a position in contemporary dance's mainstream.

From this location, the company raises similar questions to those posed by artists who constructed an alternative dance culture in the latter part of the twentieth century, questions about relationships between the aesthetic codes that govern performance practice and the common prejudices that govern everyday social practice; about definitions of corporeal beauty; about access to, and denial of the right for, public, expressive, aesthetic self-representation; about the ways in which participation is delimited through the application of techniques of creative expression delivered in settings, and through teaching practices that are noninclusive.

CandoCo have made a significant challenge to the exclusive corporeal aesthetic that has traditionally dominated contemporary and classical dance. The history of the dominant Western theater dance tradition has reflected a particularly pervasive social coding of the body that enforces a corporeal hierarchy serving to invalidate differentiated, heterogeneous, and physically impaired bodies. According to this codification, disabled bodies are determined as insufficient and culturally invalid. Their entry into the performative spectacle of theater dance disturbs the ground on which the dominant history of mainstream dance has been developed. This history reveals ways through which a particular kind of body has been sanctioned, imbued with value, and invested as an emblem of corporeal desirability, fashioned to promote specific notions supporting widely pervasive and oppressive ways of reading bodies.

The ground from which the disciplining regimes of classical ballet emerged was established through discourses that constructed and conjoined definitions of the "honorable" and "upright" body. Both George Vigarello and Norbert Elias have used the evidence of early modern textbooks on "manners" to argue that the emphasis placed on carriage, as part of the promotion of particular codes of behavior, was predicated on a belief in the self-representational potential of the body.[6] The body was apprehended as both a sign of its individual being and its position in a social hierarchy, signifying a unique identity capable of demonstrating both material embodiment and representing an ideology that promoted distinction and difference to notions of "common" embodiment.

In 1530 Desiderius Erasmus published a treatise, *On Civility in Children*, dedicated to a young member of the nobility. It focused on "outward bodily propriety,"[7] with Erasmus claiming that "ordered and natural gestures give grace: if they don't eliminate faults, at all events they attenuate and mask them."[8]

The ideal of the graceful body entered the vocabulary of noble discourse. The ideal referred to the ability to achieve the appearance of effortless control and deportment: the naturalization of what is essentially an attempt to mask particular aspects of embodied experience.

In 1725 Pierre Rameau, the dancing master to the Spanish monarchy, published *The Dancing Master*. Rameau claimed that "if dancing do [*sic*] not completely eradicate the defects with which we are born, it mitigates or conceals them."[9] Rameau defined the balletic line as representative of what was described as "noble" deportment. Postural uprightness and verticality were imbued with connotations of nobility and moral conduct.[10]

As the dominant economies of western Europe shifted from a dependency on feudalism to the introduction of mercantilism, the European nobility attempted to reconstitute and distinguish itself according to discourses that aligned physical deportment with moral virtue. The erect, physically defined "Apollonian" form (privileged as the noble and honorable body in discourses that produced dance as a theatrical form) provided a representational trope that continues to reproduce a complex matrix of corporeal power relations.

Disabled dancers do not just break the chain of signifiers that might secure the Apollonian frame, they reconfigure the codes that inscribe and privilege a particular representation of corporeality within performative dance specifically, and indirectly within other dominant economies of cultural exchange, countering the tyrannical trajectory that fetishes a particular type of body within prevailing aspects of cultural life and representational practice.

The classical dance tradition emerged from the French Academie Royale de Musique et de Danse, established by Louis XIV in 1661. In support of an academy, a coalition of dancing masters had previously petitioned the king:

> The art of dancing has always been recognised as one of the most honourable, and the most necessary for the training of the body, to give to it the first and the most natural foundation for all kinds of exercises and amongst others those of arms: and as it is, consequently one of the most useful to our nobility.[11]

With entrepreneurial flair, dancing masters (themselves members of the emerging bourgeoisie) sold a pedagogical discipline to the aristocratic elite through the rhetoric of its application for martial and physical training. These "masters" were the individuals versed in, and entrusted with the teaching of the steps, positions, styles, and techniques of country (or "folk") dancing to noble families. Initially popular in Italy, they spread their pedagogy across Europe to style and train their patrons for the court balls. By

the mid–seventeenth century, with the increasing use of stage and proscenium to frame the techniques of dancing, a social and interactive event
became a performative and representational spectacle.

The French Royal Academy of Art and Sculpture had been founded earlier, in 1648. The academies were instrumental in developing the credibility of the various "arts" as specialist and professional practices. The academy
of art was established to displace the Guild of Master Painters and Sculptors
that had previously dominated the visual arts. Developing a pedagogy that
privileged the techniques of perspectivalism produced a distinction
between the works of the academy and other work; the notion of the specialized, "professional" artist emerged from this distinction. Paul Duro has
convincingly argued that the boundaries defining the form, and authorized
by the academy, were constituted to produce an ideological closure: that
which lay outside the frame of the sanctioned form would not be considered as "art."[12] In the art of dance we can see how the privileging of technical form, delivered in ways only accessible to bodies that reflect a particular
corporeal ideal, has operated as a tactic of exclusion, effectively defining
Apollo's frame.

For over three hundred years dominant forms of theatrical dance have
privileged a particular form of embodiment. Western classical ballet in particular continues to be limited by an exclusive, contained, and homogenous
body type. In Britain there are mainstream contemporary dance companies
who are challenging this formula, but the "normalized" body is still pervasive.[13] Despite being developed to counter the rigid formalisms of classical
ballet, contemporary dance has still tended to adopt classical codes and
structures governing the representation of aesthetic vocabularies and of the
training through which these are assimilated by individual dancers. Within
theater dance's frame of corporeal reference the failure of the dominant
aesthetic to acknowledge, include, and represent heterogeneous corporealities has aided and abetted the configuration of different forms of embodiment as inferior. This reflects an ideological mobilization of binary distinctions that values specific forms of corporeal embodiment while
discrediting alternatives. The inauguration of the Western classical dance
tradition occurred during a time, in the history of modern Western civiliza-
tion, in which relationships between disabled and nondisabled bodies were
being redefined.

Categorization, exclusion, and discursive organization did not inform
the individual and cultural experience of impairment until the late seventeenth century. The first institution with a particular remit for disabled people (initially, specifically soldiers and naval seamen), the Hotel des
Invalides, was established in Paris in 1674,[14] thirteen years after the inauguration of the first academy of dance and in a period when cultural mean-

ings, ascribed to the physical body and its organization, were facing transformation across the social body.[15]

Using the literature of Rabelais as a source of cultural history, Mikhail Bakhtin has also argued that the early modern period was marked by sociocultural transition. During this time, cultural forms emphasizing a notion of the human body as uncontainable and incomplete were subsumed by a tradition defining the individualized, isolated, and private body. This definition of the body was to become fundamental to bourgeois class-based society. Anathema to the body privileged in noble and bourgeois discourses were the collective bodies of "folk" culture. These are documented, in Bakhtin's reading of Rabelais, as representing "a material bodily whole" that "transgressed the material limits of their isolation," and in which "the private and the universal were still blended in a contradictory unity."[16]

The aristocratic body was disciplined in order that it might promote a universal ideology of nobility and distinction: an individual as opposed to a collective identity. The physically defined and contained body, emphasized in discourses that produced ballet as theatrical form, can be read in distinction to the collective body contained in Bakhtin's reading of premodern folk culture. And while Bakhtin can be criticized for essentializing and romanticizing the "folk" body, it is significant that other scholars also indicate the absence of sharp, divisive, corporeal categorizations that differentiate and single out specific groups for special attention prior to the early modern period.[17]

Bakhtin identifies Rabelais's celebration of the corporeal as representative of an aesthetic of "grotesque realism." Aspects of embodied experience that emphasize inconsistency, uncontainability, impermeability, and vulnerability (vilified within the nobility's discourses of propriety) were celebrated as positive representations of a collective, corporeal identity. While Bakhtin claimed the grotesque as an empowered category of popular subversion, Lennard J. Davis indicates how the term *grotesque* has come to serve as a signifier of undesirability. The term has been ideologically configured to operate as a visual marker that presupposes an idealized, desirable, "positive" form, particularly in relation to assessments of the body in the visual field. Davis indicates the associations made between the term grotesque and disabled bodies: reinforced and manipulated in visual media and serving to reflect and compound the designation of both as disempowering labels.[18] The tension between that which has been determined as corporeally desirable and that which is constituted as "grotesque" was successfully exploited in the nineteenth- and twentieth-century spectacles of the freak show and its forebear, the "human curiosity" show. In these, individuals with marked characteristics of physical impairment were displayed within the context of popular entertainment.[19]

A review of CandoCo by the dance critic Michael Scott, in which he describes the company as a "freak show,"[20] illustrates the reading of disabled bodies that Davis suggests, and supports my use of Bakhtin to highlight the challenge CandoCo pose to conservative and normalizing tendencies within the dance establishment. ·

> There is a horrific, Satyricon quality to CandoCo that heaves up in the chest—nausea at the moral rudderlessness of a world where we would pay money to watch a man whose body terminates at his ribcage, moving about the stage on his hands.[21]

The reference to Petronius's text highlights an elitist and exclusive perspective, committed to upholding the precepts of "high" art: betraying the fundamentally class-based origin of these precepts and the radical nature of CandoCo's presence on the stage traditionally claimed by the social elite.[22] Justin Lewis has argued that contemporary dance and ballet represent the most elitist of the performing arts.[23] Their limited appeal (and distance from "mass" or popular culture) adds weight to arguments that would claim them as purveyors of the "high" art tradition; CandoCo's position within this frame mounts a significant challenge to the class-based exclusivity that underwrites the precepts of the "high" art tradition.

The setting of Petronius's bawdy, comic fiction *Satyricon* is akin to the "common," public settings favored by Rabelais and celebrated by Bakhtin. Scott's allusion to the work seems to imply that, in the same way that the antiheroes of *Satyricon* had no place within Roman, aristocratic circles, CandoCo (and specifically its disabled members) have no right to a place within the elitist frame of contemporary dance. He also suggests that audiences buy tickets to CandoCo's performances to look at disabled people rather than to watch dance. Ascribing an absence of moral direction to this illuminates a contradictory dualism; while it might be considered bad manners to stare, discursive objectification (in which an iniquitous power relationship is engendered between the scrutinizing subject and those positioned as the object of study) has been promoted as the mainstay of a supposed impartiality and objectivity: the ivory tower that provides an assumed hermeneutic advantage to the professional critic. The medicalization of physical impairment, and its construction as pathology, has, since the inception of the Hotel des Invalides, served to position disabled people as objects for "specialist," "objective" scrutiny. However, this construction of impairment as sickness is challenged and undermined when disabled people are seen within a context inscribed with the culturally promoted "virtues" of health and fitness.

Joseph Roach has argued that aesthetic evaluation functions through the ruse of an inferred objectivity, behind which ideological processes construct social meanings. He uses the term *inscription* to describe how these meanings are applied to the body in order to promote "favoured representations."[24] The idealization of grace and corporeal verticality, and the subsequent establishment of the dance academy in which this idealization was codified in technical form, has inscribed these values onto the professional dance-artist. This has naturalized and normalized the "Apollonian" body within mainstream performative dance's frame of corporeal reference, demonstrating the occlusion of ideology within aesthetic discourse and illustrating why people might be challenged by the incursion of disabled dancers into the mainstream. Their apparently incomplete bodies are an affront to a "bourgeois" sensibility that would champion the contained, disciplined, and apparently complete body:

> As for those dancers whose limbs will never again be elegantly extended, what are we to think? Shall we pity them? Or accept their crabbed facsimile of dancerly motion as sufficient?[25]

In contrast to inscription, Roach applies the term *erasure* to describe the process by which representations with limited or no conferred social value are kept out of the frame.[26] Simi Linton has indicated how the normalization and privileging of particular types of appearance and behavior has organized individuals into groups within the social body. This organization corresponds to particular economic and sociopolitical imperatives. Organization according to these imperatives detracts from and denies value to specific groups of individuals, and essentially serves to limit and control them. In Britain, until relatively recently, this control and limitation effectively secured the almost total social "erasure" of disabled people, both in the public sphere and in dominant arenas of both popular and elitist representation. Linton argues that the visual presence of disabled people disrupts a social order defined by normalized and privileged appearances and behaviors.[27] Her elucidation helps explain and locate regressive reactions to CandoCo and the vision they represent. Their visual presence on the stage of contemporary dance disrupts the prerogative nondisabled dancers have enjoyed till now. It also disturbs aesthetic codes governing corporeal representation within dance practice, illuminating ways in which these codes, far from being impartial, serve specific ideological imperatives.

Other academics have also commented on the social status conferred on physical impairment. Robert Murphy argues that the impact of negative constructions of disability and impairment compromise both social and human status.[28] And Michael Oliver has illustrated how the historical, ideological construction of "able-bodiedness" (and the socially restrictive labels conferred on those who do not fit within this construction) ran concurrently with demands, made by industrial capitalism, for particular physical capabilities deemed necessary for profitable, economic production.[29] The normalization and naturalization of a standardized body type has precluded other body types from participation in the "normal" human pursuits of economic and cultural production. This has been reflected in the field of theater dance, where a particular representation of "able-bodiedness" has been emphasized and accentuated as a corporeal ideal.

Responding to Scott's attack on the company, David Toole (the company member referred to in the initial quotation from Scott's review) suggested the review indicated more about its author than it did about the company.[30] The review also emphasizes defensive presumptions about the tenability of class-based, aesthetic credibility that are not especially peculiar to Michael Scott.

In an earlier review of their work the British dance critic Alastair Macaulay described CandoCo as representatives of "victim art."[31] Using an epithet applied by Arlene Croce to Bill T. Jones's dance production *Still/Here* (1994), Macaulay questioned the aesthetic credibility of the company's work. Yet, by positioning the work within the value-laden frame of victimhood, Macauley betrayed the limitations of aesthetic criteria at his disposal, the ideologically determined boundaries within which professional criticism operates and his inability, as a consequence, to "impartially" and "objectively" appraise the work. Certainly, CandoCo's early work has been criticized for creating an aesthetic identity that was more concerned with "caring and sharing" than with dynamism; since then, work with "avant-garde" choreographers such as Javier de Frutos has helped dispel this image.[32] A critical appraisal of technical rigor and aesthetic limitations may well have been in order, but identifying work as "victim art" forecloses discussion about its broader significance and implication, and supports aesthetic stasis. It is not insignificant that *Still/Here* also challenged the illusory integrity of bourgeois culture through its multilayered, thought-provoking exploration of terminal illness, including that which is AIDS related.[33] By reducing work to the level of "victim art" (and/or suggesting it is uncriticizable, as Croce did about *Still/Here*) critics avoid confronting politicized issues that are either quite overt, or lie fairly close to the surface. The inability of aesthetic evaluation to encompass particular issues, or the refusal of particular critics to include certain issues within an aesthetic frame, supports the argument that aesthetic criticism and evaluation often operates as a form of rhetoric, normalizing the ideologies and interests of dominant social groups.[34]

The appearance of dancers with physical impairments demands the reappraisal (if not the deconstruction and reconstruction) of aesthetic evaluation so that it might effectively, and comprehensively, serve the interests of artists (similarly interested in maintaining standards and quality of work) who represent a plural vision of society and culture: the construction of aesthetic criteria that reflect the diverse and challenging realities of human experience. And of course, until more aspiring, disabled dance artists are able to access rigorous and extended training programs (delivered in ways that work inclusively with physical impairment), there will be a sharp difference between levels of technical proficiency and a distinct shortage of disabled dancers with vocabularies of movement (refined by training) through which to aesthetically articulate their embodied presence (and, through their choreographic statements, that of others), in a challenge to the established canon.

CandoCo's commitment to providing inclusive dance opportunities for novice and experienced, older and younger, non- and disabled dancers supports the exploration, development, and promotion of new aesthetic vocabulary. Their involvement in the development of inclusive pathways to and within professional training programs demonstrates their dedication to quality and "standards." This work will be supported by recently passed legislation, challenging disability discrimination in education, which suggests that institutional training providers will have to begin to rethink their delivery at all levels.[35] As a result, children, young people, and adults (disabled and nondisabled) are being, and will continue to be, exposed to an art of dancing that is stripped of those aspects of corporeal aesthetics that have served exclusion. For young, developing personalities the effect of this exposure makes potential what has previously been determined as intangible. In parallel to work in British schools undertaken by black and Asian dancers in the 1980s, young members of marginalized groups and communities are given the strong message that they too can dance, that participation can be a consideration if they choose. For the nonmarginalized, the culturally privileged and ideologically normalized, a formerly monochrome vision (delineating homogenized contours of participation) is given a rich texture that might inform an inclusive, egalitarian consciousness and subjectivity.

The movement to shift the aesthetic is under way.

Notes

1. M. Willis, "Britain's CandoCo: Celeste Dandekar and Adam Benjamin's Troupe of Performers in Wheelchairs Redefines the Meaning of Dance," *Dance,* January 1995, 76–81.

2. Adam Benjamin, "In Search of Integrity," *Dance News Ireland* (autumn 1994): 17–21.

3. From an interview conducted with Adam Benjamin at the London School of Contemporary Dance on November 19, 1997.

4. Adam Benjamin, "Unfound Movement," *Dance Theatre Journal* (summer 1995): 44–47.

5. Benjamin, "Unfound Movement."

6. Georges Vigarello, "The Upward Training of the Body from the Age of Chivalry to Courtly Civility," in *Fragments for a History of the Human Body,* ed. Michel Fehrer (New York: Zone, 1989); and Norbert Elias, *The Civilizing Process: The History of Manners* (Oxford: Basil Blackwood, 1978).

7. Elias, *The Civilizing Process,* 55.

8. Susan L. Foster, *Reading Dancing: Bodies and Subjects in Contemporary American Dance* (Berkeley and Los Angeles: University of California Press, 1986), 254.

9. Foster, *Reading Dancing,* 134.

10. Lincoln Kirstein, *Dance: A Short History of Classic Theatrical Dancing* (New York: Dance Horizons, 1969).

11. Kirstein, *Dance,* 185.

12. Paul Duro, "Containment and Transgression," in *The Rhetoric of the Frame,* ed. Paul Duro (Cambridge: Cambridge University Press, 1996).

13. DV8 and the Cholmondeleys are other British companies whose performers have included diverse body types.

14. Susan Reynolds Whyte, "Disability between Discourse and Experience," in *Disability and Culture,* ed. Benedicte Ingstad and Susan Reynolds White (Berkeley and Los Angeles: University of California Press, 1995).

15. Michel Foucault has focused on changes in social and cultural organization, and their impact on populations during the early modern period, in *The Order of Things: An Archaeology of the Human Sciences* (London: Tavistock Press, 1994) and *Discipline and Punish: The Birth of the Prison,* trans. Alan Sheridan (Harmondsworth: Penguin, 1986).

16. Mikhail Bakhtin, *Rabelais and His World,* trans. Hélène Iswolsky (Bloomington: Indiana University Press, 1984), 23.

17. Whyte, "Disability."

18. Lennard J. Davis, "Nude Venuses, Medusa's Body, and Phantom Limbs: Disability and Visuality," in *The Body and Physical Difference,* ed. David T. Mitchell and Sharon L. Snyder (Ann Arbor: University of Michigan Press, 1997).

19. For a comprehensive history, see Robert Bogdan, *Freak Show: Presenting Human Oddities for Amusement and Profit* (Chicago: University of Chicago Press, 1988); and Rosemarie Garland Thomson, ed., *Freakery: Cultural Spectacles of the Extraordinary Body* (New York: New York University Press, 1996).

20. Michael Scott, *Vancouver Sun,* May 20, 1999, http://web.lexis-nexis.com/execut . . . =a44b2bb612792e0ae5dda82529f088a9, viewed September 8, 2000.

21. Scott.

22. Andreas Huyssen explores the constitution of "high" art and its relationship with wider culture in *After the Great Divide: Modernism, Mass Culture, and Postmodernism* (Basingstoke: Macmillan, 1993).

23. Justin Lewis, *Art, Culture, and Enterprise: The Politics of Art and the Culture Industries* (London: Routledge, 1995).

24. Joseph Roach, "Theatre, History, and the Ideology of the Aesthetic," *Theatre Journal* 41 (1998): 159.

25. Scott.

26. Roach, "Theatre, History."

27. Simi Linton, *Claiming Disability: Knowledge and Identity* (New York: New York University Press, 1998).

28. Robert Murphy, "Encounters: The Body Silent in America," in Ingstad and Whyte, *Disability and Culture.*

29. Michael Oliver, *The Politics of Disablement* (Basingstoke: Macmillan, 1999).

30. M. McKeown, "Dance Reviewer Reveals Himself," *Vancouver Sun,* May 29, 1999, http://web.lexis nexis.com/execut . . . =e405bece53e62bd9757982e7 fbe8 bfff, viewed September 8, 2000.

31. Alastair Macaulay, "'Victim Art' Put through Its Paces," *Financial Times,* June 24, 1996, http://web.lexis-nexis.com/execut . . . =5f0667d457a7daa194ba210a9 8f6 47d8, viewed September 8, 2000.

32. Judith Mackrell, "CandoCo," *Guardian,* March 7, 2003, http://www .guardian.co.uk/arts/reviews/story/0,11712,909264,00.html, viewed June 12, 2004.

33. Croce's polemic on "victim art" and varied responses to it, can be read at http://canuck.com/Esalon/dance/Croce.html, viewed June 12, 2004.

34. An argument comprehensively postulated by Terry Eagleton in *The Ideology of the Aesthetic* (Oxford: Basil Blackwell, 1991).

35. The Special Educational Needs and Disability Act 2001 (SENDA) was introduced in 2002 with full implementation expected by 2005. Requirements of the act are summarized at http://www.ukcle.ac.uk/directions/issue4/senda.html, viewed June 12, 2004.

The National Theatre of the Deaf

Artistic Freedom & Cultural Responsibility in the Use of American Sign Language

SHANNON BRADFORD

The simultaneous presentation of theatrical works in English and American Sign Language (ASL), known as *sign language theater* or *theater of the deaf*, has been evolving in the United States since d/Deaf theatrical activity began at Gallaudet College in the late 1800s (Tadie 153). The Connecticut-based National Theatre of the Deaf (NTD), logging over seven thousand performances in national and international tours since its formation in 1967, not only stands as the world's most recognized theater of the deaf, but also retains the credit for popularizing this bilingual form, especially among hearing theatergoers who make up an overwhelming 90 percent of NTD's audiences (*NTD News* 1997–98; Tadie 107). This appeal is likely due to NTD's unusual performance style and choice of mainstream material (producing adaptations of works such as *Treasure Island, Through the Looking Glass, Hamlet, Under Milkwood,* and more recently *An Italian Straw Hat* and *Peer Gynt*).

Since NTD plays primarily for hearing nonsigners, what do the company's performance conventions communicate to the hearing about sign language and about d/Deaf people? While NTD promotes d/Deaf awareness through its educational programming (known as Little Theatre of the

Deaf), the company's touring fare of mainstream plays and literary adaptations is *not* designed to educate the public about the medical condition of deafness (defined as having no functional hearing) or about Deaf culture (defined as the group that chooses to be bound together by a particular sign language, social customs, and worldview). Instead, NTD strives to produce theater that "passes, without condescension the most exacting tests of the commercial theatre world" (Hays 590). NTD eschews labels like *Deaf theater* or *disabled company,* preferring to identify itself as a "visually stunning" *language* theater (*An Italian Straw Hat* program). I will argue that despite NTD's intent, its style inadvertently encourages the conflation of ASL and English, sometimes resulting in a belief that English subsumes ASL altogether. Further, I contend that the vast majority of NTD's mainstage works present nonhearing people as neither medically deaf nor culturally Deaf.

Such abstinence from treating d/Deaf identity has potentially profound implications for d/Deaf individuals and for the Deaf culture as a whole. Although the d/Deaf are frequently defined from the outside as lacking or "handicapped," they reject the sense of lack implied by the medical notion of deafness, instead seeing Deafness as social and political (Davis xiv). They believe "that their culture, language, and community constitute them as a totally adequate, self-enclosed, and self-defining subnationality within the larger structure of the audist state" (Davis xiv). "Audist" is employed here as *racist* or *sexist* would be, and denotes a bias toward auditory communication. If ASL is not understood to be an independent language, then it remains positioned as a subcategory of English, a sort of Braille for the deaf. And by extension, such a misperception invalidates the fundamental tenet of Deaf culture—its language, the hub around which Deaf culture operates, develops, and thrives.

My purpose is not to denounce sign language theater or this particular company, whose work has benefited both the d/Deaf and the hearing in several ways, including increasing the mainstream's exposure to d/Deaf people, generating rare professional opportunities for d/Deaf artists, making classic literature accessible to d/Deaf communities through performance, and encouraging theatrical activity in numerous d/Deaf cultures around the globe. Rather, as a hearing signer with ten years of experience as a researcher and an occasional practitioner of sign language theater, I believe that the conventions that have made NTD successful have potential resonances that have not been examined fully. I will outline these resonances, drawing examples from two of the company's mainstage offerings: *An Italian Straw Hat,* performed for the 1995–96 and 1996–97 seasons; and NTD's thirtieth-anniversary tour of *Peer Gynt* in 1997–98.

When attending an NTD production, hearing spectators can expect to see d/Deaf performers enact the main roles of the play in American Sign Language, while hearing actors, costumed as minor characters and frequently located on the periphery of the action, voice the lines for the main characters with timing and emotionality that seems to match the signing. A hearing, voicing actor faces the unusual demand of playing one character physically while enacting multiple other characters vocally. Since the main characters' voices do not emanate from the bodies that physically enact them, and since the bodies of the voicing actors usually remain still during speech (in order to give focus to the signing actors), the spoken lines of the play seem to hang in the air until one becomes accustomed to this convention. *Indianapolis Star* critic Marion Garmel said of this experience, "It takes a lot of concentration just to figure out where the voices are coming from." This central convention of NTD's work enables hearing audiences to see a production like *Peer Gynt* in sign language while they hear what seems to be a perfectly matched version of the play in English. Theatrical conventions in NTD's work such as lighting, costumes, and settings are roughly equivalent to mainstream practices, marking the company's use of sign language and the consequent foregrounding of the d/Deaf body as the most prominent features of NTD performance.

It may be difficult to contemplate the potential conflation of languages that operate in separate sensory channels (here, ASL in the visual channel and spoken English in the aural channel), or you may assume (as many hearing people do) that the signed language of a particular nation is simply a manual version of the spoken language of the region, and therefore that the two should match comfortably. In fact, signed languages are independent languages, and there are many *diverse* signed languages across the world, each with its own vocabulary, grammar, and linguistic features. ASL possesses a vocabulary and a grammar that differ radically from English. These two languages contain dissimilar idioms that are either extremely difficult to translate or are untranslatable. Concepts are organized and presented in divergent ways. For example: the English sentence, "Let's go to the store," when translated into ASL, would be glossed, STORE WE-2 GO. In this basic example, the ideas are presented in different orders; there is no one-to-one correlation between items such as the English *to* and *the* or the ASL directionality of the verb or specificity of persons involved. Five English words (six if the contraction is considered) are required to convey the concept of the sentence, while the ASL gloss needs three signed concepts to communicate the same content.

These linguistic differences illuminate the potential challenges of meshing these two languages for performance. The six-word sentence discussed above may require more time to utter than the three-sign gloss. The signer will sign the concept for "STORE" at the beginning of his/her sentence while the voicing actor will voice the word "store" at the end of his/her utterance, so a literal match between the two performers is impossible. NTD, striving for a temporal equivalent between ASL and English, negotiates such variances by compromising the delivery of one or both languages, thus enabling the signing and the speaking of a line or section to begin and end together. So complex are the nuances of ASL that Kenneth Albers, the (hearing) director of *An Italian Straw Hat,* constantly had an interpreter with him during the rehearsal process to assist him in communicating with the d/Deaf actors (Dodds).

As a language theater striving to illuminate the visual beauty of ASL, a great deal of rehearsal time is dedicated to developing the signed version of the play, which is typically a collaborative effort between the signing actors and the sign master (a Deaf individual considered by the company to have an exceptional command of ASL who is responsible for overseeing the translation of the play into ASL). For *Peer Gynt,* J Ranelli translated the 1867 text from Norwegian to English, making certain adaptations; then Ranelli's version was translated into ASL by three sign masters (Frank L. Dattolo, Susan Jackson, and Eric Malzkuhn) with the acting company (*Peer Gynt* program). The final step in the translation process involves integrating the English text with the ASL version and solving temporal dilemmas. This process of negotiation is not necessarily characterized by equal concessions in voicing and signing, for two reasons: (1) the NTD style positions the d/Deaf performers as the actors of the principal roles, in some ways relegating the voicing actors to the function of supporting cast; (2) it is easier for the hearing actors to adjust to the d/Deaf actors' choices since the hearing can see what the d/Deaf are doing while the deaf cannot hear the choices made in the voicing. Some NTD voicing actors describe their relationships with the signing actors as "symbiotic," but most concede that they base the majority of their vocal choices on the acting decisions made by the d/Deaf performers (Jennings; Mitchell; Scarl; Rhys). Often the voicing actor must speed up or slow down his or her lines to match the signing, but in some situations the opposite occurs. Voicing actor Brian Jennings explains, "Sometimes there are [lines in sign language] going by too fast for me to spit out or . . . too slowly . . . for me to make any kind of verbal sense out of them." In these instances, the signing actor might make adjustments in the delivery of the signed version to accommodate the requirements of the English utterance.

The complex process of negotiating ASL and English occurs in rehearsals, allowing the impeccable merging of these two languages in the performative moment. This carefully crafted seamlessness, while aesthetically riveting, inadvertently encourages the conflation of ASL and English. The hearing nonsigning audience experiences an aural enactment of the play, matched by the d/Deaf actors' inaccessible signing: gestures that seem to correspond both temporally and emotionally to the spoken lines. In this presentational style, the languages seem alike except for their contrary modalities. For the hearing nonsigner, these conventions can promote a belief that American Sign Language is not an independent language, but merely a gestural representation of English. This misunderstanding is furthered by NTD's ever-present marketing slogan (found on most posters and virtually all publicity materials), "You see and hear every word," which not only assumes a hearing audience, but also implies the impossible: a literal matching of ASL and English. *New York Times* critic Ben Brantley, discussing d/Deaf actor Robert DeMayo's portrayal of Fadinard in *An Italian Straw Hat,* attempted to describe DeMayo's acting in a particular scene by quoting a line from English text, writing: "Fadinard, (Robert DeMayo), the dapper bridegroom at the hub of the play's chaos, notes irritably, 'I'm talking to my uncle, who cannot see a word I've said.'" While Brantley may have observed rightly that DeMayo was exhibiting physical irritability, the critic quotes the hearing actor's line as DeMayo's utterance. In his next paragraph, Brantley states that DeMayo communicated in ASL, but he mentions no differences between the two languages. Printing an ASL gloss in a theater review is certainly not appropriate, but even written in English the quoted material could be more structurally similar to DeMayo's ASL utterance, as "My uncle. . . . I sign to him, but he can't see any of it." Brantley reveals no awareness of his conflated perception of the two languages. Certainly not all critics and audience members can be expected to arrive at an NTD performance with an in-depth understanding of the distinctions between English and ASL. But what responsibility, if any, does NTD have to distinguish the languages for their viewers? Beyond the separate sensory channels used in performance, there are no noticeable markers in the NTD style that indicate the intricate differences between ASL and English.

This simultaneous style may also engender a different misperception by hearing nonsigners: ASL may be read as an aesthetic stage language, akin to costuming or lighting rather than as a legitimate linguistic system. NTD's style of signing in performance is theatrical. Some signs are enlarged or slightly exaggerated for clarity and overall effect, so the signed interactions onstage are not representative of everyday conversations in ASL. This theatricality, combined with the hearing nonsigners' reliance on the vocal score of the play, may undermine the intended foregrounding of ASL. Hearing audiences, according to d/Deaf artist Peter Cook, "watch the actors signing for the first five minutes and then start to listen to the voice actor translating the signs," quickly losing their interest in ASL (5). This suggests that ASL is absorbed into the larger theater event, becoming one of many theatrical "languages" that interdependently support the "text," understood by the hearing audience to be the spoken words of the drama. Even director Albers acknowledges this phenomenon, "They [hearing audiences] seem to forget about the fact that people are signing and it simply becomes an element of the production" (Dodds).

Some reviewers, like the *Phoenix Gazette's* Christopher McPherson, identify aesthetic benefits to the inaccessible signing in *An Italian Straw Hat;* for example, it offered "funny sight-gags." McPherson seems compelled by the novelty of sign language and its noticeable difference from typical gestures. NTD's theatricality completely obscured portions of the ASL version of *Peer Gynt* because lighting designer Blu chose to silhouette the signing characters frequently, preventing the signs from being seen clearly. This transformed the communicative signs into a kind of abstract hand dance interspersed with patches of dialogue. According to d/Deaf members of the acting company, many d/Deaf patrons abandoned the show at intermission because of their inability to see the signing and, consequently, follow the story.

Design choices produced similar results in *An Italian Straw Hat,* where some of Charles Berliner's bright, farcical costumes were riddled with stripes and dense patterns that obscured the signers' arms and chests: key locations for effective communication since one must be able to see the handshapes, location, and movement of the signs in order to decode them. Fadinard's white hands periodically disappeared when backed by his light, vertically striped vest. Dr. Paign wore an eye-fatiguing and troublesome ensemble of three different tweeds: jacket in large pattern, vest in medium pattern, and neck scarf in a blurred combination of diamond shapes and stripes. Choices that compromise ASL to suit the larger aesthetic goals of production resonate in ways that diminish NTD's intended foregrounding of the signed language, and consequently, distort the presentation of d/Deaf people.

For NTD's hearing nonsigning audience, the d/Deaf performer's body becomes the site for potential understanding of deafness and Deaf culture, not only because of the prominence of the d/Deaf performer onstage, but also due to the *Other* of the d/Deaf individual. "Disability," Davis asserts, "is a specular moment. The power of the gaze to control, limit, and patrol the disabled person is brought to the fore" (12). As a producing organization, NTD has a range of representation options that may support or subvert the power of the hearing audiences' gaze. How the hearing see and read the d/Deaf body impacts how deafness and Deaf culture are constructed by the mainstream.

Most contemporary Americans assume when they see a person signing that the person is probably deaf. In the same way that sighted people associate red and white canes with blindness, sign language serves as the physi-

(Left to right) **Robert DeMayo, Ira Mitchell, Anthony Natale, and Camile L. Jeter in the National Theatre of the Deaf's production of** *An Italian Straw Hat.* **(Ivoryton Studio, courtesy of the National Theatre of the Deaf.)**

cal marker of deafness: it indicates that the person cannot hear. Generally, the mainstream population categorizes deafness with blindness and other *disabilities*. In NTD productions, the d/Deaf performers onstage do not acknowledge their deafness or comment on it; medical deafness is essentially absent in the characters. They are only marked as deaf by their use of sign language. Production sound design sometimes contradicts or denies deafness, as in *An Italian Straw Hat,* where a center stage one-man band sang and played instruments during scene transitions and sometimes within scenes as well. In this case, the majority of the music was played on synthesizer and thus had no substantial visual component that d/Deaf audiences might experience. The production designers attempted to compensate for this by using multicolored chaser lights when some of the musical cues occurred, but the resulting elements were not meshed effectively. NTD sometimes employs sound and music with visual components, such as drums and wind chimes played onstage by the actors during *Peer Gynt,* achieving a greater sense of equity between the d/Deaf and hearing audience's experience of the work. It should be noted that some deaf individuals can hear/experience a variety of sounds in particular registers, so I am not advocating an abandonment of sound altogether. However, when conventions such as sound or music are included largely for the hearing audience's enjoyment, the production text essentially ignores the fact that d/Deaf persons are in the audience and onstage, thus avoiding any acknowledgment or definition of deafness. NTD's mainstage repertoire rarely includes scripts that deal directly with Deafness or with prominent Deaf issues. One need only peruse the company's production history to realize that Deaf culture scarcely takes center stage in a topical manner. While American Sign Language does serve as the fundamental bond that constitutes Deaf culture, the fashion in which it is employed in NTD performances does not signify Deafness fully; it is an incomplete representation of the culturally Deaf.

The National Theatre of the Deaf's D/deaf body is a signing body, integral to achieving the remarkable style for which the company is world-renowned. Their productions are professional, intriguing, groundbreaking forays into the theatrical mainstream, yet embedded within their visually stimulating style are coded conventions that resonate outside of intended meanings and may fuel misperceptions about sign language and d/Deafness. Consider an Indianapolis critic's comments on NTD performers: "Most of these performers can neither hear nor speak" (Garmel). This statement reveals the critic's misunderstanding of medical deafness, as she assumes that to be deaf is also to be without speech (in antiquated language, to be *dumb* as well as deaf, when, in fact, this is not the case). Whether the critic arrived at the playhouse with this stereotypical assumption or formed it during the performance cannot be known. However, such a statement assures us that what she witnessed as an NTD audience member did not expose her successfully to the realities of deafness. Similarly, a *Los Angeles Times* critic's observation that Deaf audience members applaud "by raising their arms in the air and waving their fingers like so many rows of wheat," alludes to ASL as a sort of peculiar novelty rather than as a valid language (Collins). As long as such views are not challenged consistently and repeatedly, the d/Deaf will continue to be stereotyped, misunderstood, and marginalized. Thus, the National Theatre of the Deaf, and other companies like it, face a perplexing conundrum: where does the balance lie between artistic freedom and cultural responsibility?

Works Cited

Baldwin, Stephen C. *Pictures in the Air: The Story of the National Theatre of the Deaf.* Washington, D.C.: Gallaudet University Press, 1993.
Collins, Scott. "A Pretty 'Italian Straw Hat' Is Real Eyeful." *Los Angeles Times*, Oct. 21, 1994, Calendar: F30.
Cook, Peter. "Our Language Is Our Identity: American Sign Language and Deaf

Culture." *Critical Angles* (St. Paul, Minn.: Center for Arts Criticism), winter 1995: 3–6.

Davis, Lennard J. *Enforcing Normalcy: Disability, Deafness, and the Body.* New York: Verso, 1995.

Dodds, Richard. "Finding a New Language for an Old Farce." *Times-Picayune,* Mar. 28, 1995, third ed.: D1.

Garmel, Marion. "'Italian Straw Hat' Whips Up High-Speed Comedy." *Indianapolis Star,* Oct. 10, 1995, final ed.: D03.

Hays, David. "The National Theatre of the Deaf—Present and Future." *American Annals of the Deaf* 112 (1967): 590–92.

An Italian Straw Hat (program). By Eugene Labiche and Marc Michel, dir. Kenneth Albers, perf. National Theatre of the Deaf. Carver Center, San Antonio, Tex., Nov. 10, 1995.

Jennings, Brian. Personal interview. Nov. 10, 1995.

McPherson, Christopher. "'Straw Hat' Success a Good Sign for Company." *Phoenix Gazette,* Oct. 8, 1994, final ed.: E4.

Mitchell, Ira. Personal interview. Nov. 10, 1995.

Peer Gynt (program). By Henrik Ibsen, trans. J Ranelli, dir. Robby Barnett and Will Rhys, perf. National Theatre of the Deaf. W. M. Turner Auditorium, Nacogdoches, Tex., Mar. 28, 1998.

Rhys, Will. Personal interview. Nov. 10, 1995.

Scarl, Hilary. Personal interview. Nov. 10, 1995.

Tadie, Nancy Bowen. "A History of Drama at Gallaudet College: 1864–1969." Ph.D. diss., New York University, 1978.

Zachary, Samuel J. "The National Theatre of the Deaf and the *Teatr mimiki I zhesta:* Two Views on Theatre of the Deaf." *Theatre Topics* 5.1 (March 1995): 53–67.

Shifting Strengths
The Cyborg Theater of Cathy Weis

JENNIFER PARKER-STARBUCK

"I used to have a body," says the glowing face-within-a-television-monitor in front of a small audience at Dixon Place in NY. Just prior to this, audience members have been instructed to move "her" from out in the audience to where she can see: "Be careful, don't drop me," and "ouch, that pinched," "over there, more to the left," she directs, in a soft southern drawl. "He's beautiful" she sighs, of performer Scott Heron, who is trying in frustration to complete his dance. Heron finally storms off, leaving the embodied television center stage where "she" happily begins her story, "I used to have a body. Once, I was a dancer. I could run and jump and kick my legs high like the best of them."

—Cathy Weis, *Monitor Lizards* [1]

The live face in the monitor is New York–based dancer-choreographer Cathy Weis, who proceeds to physically enter the space and interact with her prerecorded self in her piece "Dummy," one-third of the 1999 *Monitor Lizards.* Weis's interrogations of the intersections between the body and technology exemplify what I call *cyborg theater,* technologically integrated performance that explores representations of the live body in conjunction with the mediatized image on stage. Cyborg theater uses technology not purely as a frame or aesthetic scenic backdrop for projected images, but as a mutually dependent component of a greater complex of social, political, and theatrical systems existing between the live and the technological.[2] For Weis, who has been diagnosed with multiple sclerosis, technology intersects with her body in performance, allowing for a freedom of movement no longer possible with her body alone. Her work reconfigures conceptions of the "dis/abled"[3] body in contemporary "posthuman" society.

As used by N. Katherine Hayles, the term *posthuman* defines an expansive condition that forces a reconceptualization of the notion of what it means to be human. Posthuman is not literally "after human"; instead, as Hayles explains, "it signals instead the end of a certain conception of the human, a conception that may have applied, at best, to that fraction of humanity who had the wealth, power, and leisure to conceptualize themselves as autonomous beings exercising their will through individual agency and choice."[4] The word *human* is embedded with constructions of what Rosemarie Garland Thomson calls the "normate . . . the constructed identity of those who, by way of the bodily configurations and cultural capital they assume, can step into a position of authority and wield the power it grants them."[5] In this essay I specifically engage cyborgean fusions between humans and machines within posthumanism as a means of escaping the normative/abnormal binary of current political thought regarding disability. Cathy Weis's body could be considered disabled, or abject—excluded from traditional privileging of the able-bodied, yet, through her technological performance strategies, her body disrupts "ableist" notions of what is considered "disabled." I explore Weis's cyborg convergences as an exploration of an alternate bodily presence on stage.

The cyborg—or "cybernetic organism"—is understood mainly through human-technological hybrids long featured in science fiction and metaphorized by social scientist Donna Haraway as "boundary creatures."[6] Haraway claims that the cyborg has the potential to "transform the despised metaphors of both organic and technological vision to foreground specific positioning, multiple mediation, partial perspective, and therefore a possible allegory for antiracist, feminist, scientific, and political knowledge."[7] However, as Peter Hitchcock writes in response to Haraway's idea of the cyborg as a political ontology, "it is irony that saves the formulation from crude technological determinism."[8] For Hitchcock, and I think rightly so, the cyborg also functions as a "symptom," and he reads Haraway's manifesto also to propose the cyborg "as a heuristic device: it is a way to learn about the forms of politics possible at the end of the twentieth century."[9] However, as Hitchcock also points out, the cyborg's boundary blurring, while allowing for metaphoric potentials, cannot be separated from its historical links to capital and to social and economic control. The questions of who controls the technology and in what context it is used are the factors that differentiate between negative examples of cyborg creations and the more metaphoric model Cathy Weis creates on stage. Weis refuses to let her body fully disappear behind the technology she uses, and instead controls the ways in which her physical presence extends into the live space.

The cyborg as metaphor has also been criticized for not accounting for actual bodies. Susan Bordo is astute in her caution of its whimsicality: "The spirit of epistemological *jouissance* suggested by the images of cyborg, Trick-

Cathy Weis, integrated seamlessly with technology in performance. (Photograph by Richard Termine.)

ster, the metaphors of dance, and so forth obscures the located, limited, inescapably partial, and always personally invested nature of human 'story-making.'"[10] Additionally, cyborgean couplings proposed to eliminate differences can suggest troubling and complicated prospects, as Jennifer González points out in her discussion of the term *e-race-sure*.[11] It is important to consider by and for whom the boundaries are blurred, and I agree with González's assertion:

> The image of the cyborg has historically recurred at moments of radical social and cultural change . . . imaginary representations of cyborgs take over when traditional bodies fail. In other words, when the current ontological model of human being does not fit a new paradigm, a hybrid model of existence is required to encompass a new, complex and contradictory lived experience.[12]

If this "hybrid model of existence" falls within the province of the posthuman, then instead of representing a cold disembodiment, the cyborg can emerge as a site to explore productive encounters (at least theoretical ones) between humans and machines. This is the space in which Weis works.

The cyborg, though it continues to reside largely in science fiction scenarios, film, and cartoons, is well applied in Weis's work, producing an expansive model of a diverse society in which there is no "norm." As Lennard Davis has said, "The application of the idea of a norm to the human body creates the idea of deviance or a 'deviant' body."[13] Certainly the body itself, flesh and weight, must be made manifest beyond metaphor, but perhaps, through an integration of the flesh with technology, an attempt can be made to "reverse the hegemony of the normal and to institute alternative ways of thinking about the abnormal."[14] To destabilize the problematic binary of able/disabled that Davis's reversal reinforces, I introduce the cyborg theater as a third possibility. When difference is embraced with as much acceptance as new technologies, the cyborg will have outlived its usefulness. For the moment, however, the cyborg can stand in as a site of resistance to illuminate the strengths of difference.

One site for the possibility of resistance is performance. In the work of Cathy Weis, the live claims technology as its "present absence." Weis's version of cyborg theater interrogates increasing absences. For example, in her piece *A String of Lies,* which she created shortly after her diagnosis with MS, she projected a juxtaposition of her upper body onto the moving legs of dancer Jennifer Miller, which allowed her to "finally do a ballet piece again."[15] Though professing a lack of awareness of the implications at the time, she later realized that the impaired mobility of her legs need not stop her from dancing—she simply dis/placed her body into the frame of video to create a new way to continue working. Weis never lets her body (or those bodies she choreographs) disappear completely behind her innovative uses of technology; instead technology merges with the live figure, projecting fractured, composite, and humorous images of this union. By creating a mosaic of bodies and body parts, Weis refigures traditional ways of seeing bodies, especially those Western society is trained (not) to see in/by mediatized representation.[16] Her work subtly comments on the media's obsession with an impossible ideal—a body too perfect, too thin, too fit to encompass the many actual varieties. Her work seems to seek a means of resistance to the hegemony of the supposed norm, and opens spaces for bodies that, although quite present, are either overlooked or oppressed to the point of invisibility.

Cathy Weis has been creating multimedia performance for the past fifteen years. She began her career as a teenage soloist with the Louisville Ballet and went on to Bennington College as a modern dance major. She has toured as a member of a bluegrass band, done street theater in San Francisco, and was once a self-proclaimed "disco queen." Weis began working with video in the 1970s after spending a period working with other mediums, such as stained glass, while recovering from a foot injury. After

Cathy Weis integrating her body with technology. (Photograph © Dona Ann McAdams.)

returning to dance and suffering recurring injuries, she was diagnosed in 1989 with MS, a disease that has progressively diminished the strength of her right side. Rather than give up dancing, Weis turned to a combination of video and performance in order to develop new sites for her own dance work. She does not see her work with technology as response to MS; it was an interest she had developed prior to her diagnosis. However, she does credit it as a way back into performance. Although she will freely discuss having MS, she pauses at the word *disability*. As she explains, "Over the years I've begun to feel that every time that word comes up, it has an attitude—'disability.'" It is a weak and victimized position. People who have had to really deal with physical problems and challenges understand that it is a shifting of strengths." To try to relate to the able-bodied, she uses the example of age:

As you get older, everybody loses things, and everybody understands the word *loss.* . . . For people with physical disabilities the changes happen either more quickly or more dramatically. . . . So I understand why that's a category, "disability," but there's something about the word . . . You have to really make a lot of choices and priorities and take a lot of responsibility for your life, and there are strengths that happen. Disability only looks at what you are losing, and not how you shift the balance for yourself. It only looks at what you've lost.[17]

Despite Weis's initial discomfort with the terminology, she does not let her "disability" disappear behind the images she creates. Her body is quite visible in her performance, and her project is to work with movement on all types of bodies. "Technology with imagination is a way of expanding voices so other people can listen to them. . . . It is important to break boundaries so things don't stay the way they are."[18]

In a *Village Voice* article titled "The Virtual Dancer," about the 1998 piece *Gravity Twins,* Deborah Jowitt comments, "Weis, the supposed spectator, is the actual choreographer in charge; yet her dancers are controlling her disembodied image . . . others 'dance' her."[19] Weis often elects to integrate her disability, rather than making it a focal point of her work. This absence, however, is no erasure. Her work speaks for itself; the presence of MS ghosts her work as she investigates alternate ways of envisioning bodies on stage. Weis's use of technology asks questions and seeks to find answers about her own changing body. In "Dummy" she emerges from backstage, introducing her "self" as opposed to her "head," who stays "focused on choreographed skills." "I know it is not easy without a body," the corporeal Weis says gently as she brings out a similarly dressed, two-foot-tall foam puppet body that attaches nicely to the monitor head. Weis's use of humor and movement transform the frightening Frankenstein tale into a powerful metaphor of visibility and presence, a cyborgean story to live with. Weis's newly formed cyber–alter ego seems to seek a friend when it remarks that "some people have a problem with sentient media . . . [It was] only a matter of time before we started interacting back." These are prescient words amid a societal debate over cloning and genetic engineering.[20] Although the puppet's head is Weis's mediatized own, and we are aware that the control and creation is also Weis's, she/it begins to take on a life of her/its own. The live Weis and her doppelgänger manikin do a little duet dance number, exchange witty repartee, and the piece is over. The cyborg in this performance is both a literal and a metaphoric manifestation, interrogating what it means to *have* a body, and what it means to have a body that does not entirely do what it is told.

Weis's cyborgean performance rehearses a new paradigm of bodily practices that makes visible—in an attempt to make understandable—the differing strengths bodies can possess. "All movement is interesting—it's how you deal with it. On crutches, in a wheelchair, or wearing a brace, this movement is as interesting as a ballet dancer's if it has its own voice."[21] In her attempt to make a larger variety of movement visible, Weis seeks out performers with strengths she wants to explore, regardless of race, gender, or ability. The differences from her own body are important to represent a heterogeneous space within which to work. In addition, there are many ideas she visualizes as a choreographer but cannot enact. Here too she depends upon technologies—video and drawings—to give her dancers ways to see what she wants.

Her awareness of the distance between choreography, writing dancing, and dancing is similar to the dancer with the broken hip in Peggy Phelan's "Immobile Legs": "As my feet tapped away under my chair and my fingers typed on the keys, I began to feel that the lack of direction in my feet might be cured by the mapping my fingers were making on the keyboard. I was transferring the hesitation in my feet to the plotting of my calmer hands."[22] Both Weis and this dancer desire to use technology as a means of "mapping" something no longer doable with their own bodies. Weis credits her interest in video as having given her the strength to emerge from the trauma of the diagnosis. Phelan's dancer goes on, "I lost the rhythm of my own limbs' utterance. Computing was an attempt to put that loss in my hands and head, to transfer the grief in my feet that formed the root of my own illness."[23] Like Weis's movements, which are in need their own voice, Phelan's dancer also searched for this resonance. It is through shifting their strengths from "pure" corporeality to the complex dance between embodiment and technology that both of these dancers are able to dance through trauma.

In the third piece of *Monitor Lizards*, "Fly Me to the Moon," Weis's integration of technology and the body directly addresses themes of bodily absence and presence. In this piece, an evocative technological foray aided by a narrative of love, loss, and the human body, Weis physically manipulates the camera, creating expansive depths within the small space around her. She enters pulling a camera on a cart, her body fixed in the eye of a camera, an effect that cascades her image back and forth endlessly. The flat wall suddenly seems to open up as the images reach backward as far as the eye can see. The melancholy mood of the piece is aided by grainy video, haunting sounds, and a sparse, compelling text. Dancer Scott Heron enters and speaks about Weis's character as he stands at a microphone: "Helen has left me and gone back to 1930." This thematic absence is contradicted by an extreme close-up of Weis's face directly behind him as he alternates between speaking and breaking into a twisted, contorted dance that resonates with a sense of pain and nostalgia. Heron's "able" body communicates loss through his movements, while the conceptually absent character Weis plays is made most present through the close-up projections, creating a complicated juxtaposition of the ideas of absence and presence. Weis also physically wheels the camera around on stage, controlling what is being captured and where it is projected. Her technological manipulations grant her an agency necessary for the disabled body on stage, an agency that resonates in Thomson's writing:

> I intend to counter the accepted notions of physical disability as an absolute, inferior state and a personal misfortune. Instead, I show that disability is a representation, a cultural interpretation of physical transformation or configuration, and a comparison of bodies that structures social relations and institutions. Disability, then, is the attribution of corporeal deviance—not so much a property of bodies as a product of cultural rules about what bodies should be or do.[24]

Weis's configurations of the body and technology propose alternate subjectivities—ones that do not attempt to be understood as the equivalent of able-bodied norms, but instead pose a challenge—to expand our cultural understandings of the body. Weis's slippage between the present and past allows us to imagine a future less marked by "cultural rules" about what bodies should be or do. Through her choreography Weis reinscribes both her character and her own physical body with empowering constructions of presence.

Performing Bodies in the Age of Global Technologies

Weis's Live Internet Performance Structure (LIPS) is a new direction in performance that allows culturally ideologically resistant work to emerge through the intersection and integration of the live and the technological on stage. LIPS may best be understood through the literal image of the acronym—two separate entities making up a whole: two simultaneous performance events linked and made one through a live Internet feed. Presently, a LIPS performance is based upon two groups of artists working from different sites but with the same technical "language"—the setup, mixer, screen, and monitors. Each performance space typically has several layers: a live audience watching live performers who "partner" remote performers, who are also performing live in their space across the world. The remote performers are projected into the other space onto a large screen. The ability to restore physicality to those out of reach is what attracted Weis to this work. The appropriation and development of the Internet as a performance tool (from its original development for militaristic purposes), serves to replace the global within local bodies in a performance site, while at the same time serving as what Jon McKenzie might call a "minor history"—functioning as a challenge to technological fetishism, globalized capitalism, and cultural imperialism.[25]

Weis sees these projects as long-distance connections—she has collaborated with performers in Prague, Budapest, and Macedonia. The performers in each space are choreographed to interrelate within the performance Weis designs, which varies in its narrative and improvisational content. The work has a fluidity based on the instability of the Internet link as well as the act of live bodies performing with projected ones. Additionally, live bodies are often projected onto the images of remote bodies, creating a third performance frame. Both sides are witnessed by audiences in the live spaces, but much of the mixing of images in one space is not seen by the audience in the other. The frames created by the screens give an awareness of dislocation and distance, especially as they reference ways of relating to television or film, but the live body in the mix and the ways the frames are used to bring global communities together create an expanded stage rich with connections. By using the Internet as a performance tool, Weis attempts a reengagement with the body made absent through technology—perhaps as a reaction to her own slowly declining body—by actively reinserting these virtual global bodies into a local space, by not letting them slip out of sight. The audiences become points of contact, witnesses to a piece of the performance rather than objective reporters of it as a whole. Weis maintains documentation through video of both sides, but no "whole" can ever be constructed from these dis-locations. Weis's own bodily trauma permeates her work. The work I have described represents a progression in Weis's "writing trauma." Dominick LaCapra differentiates between the idea of writing about trauma, which he thinks of as an act of historiography, and the more intangible "writing trauma":

> Writing trauma would be one of those telling aftereffects in what I termed traumatic and post-traumatic writing. . . . It involves processes of acting out, working over, and to some extent working through in analyzing and "giving voice" to the past—processes of coming to terms with traumatic "experiences," limit events, and their symptomatic effects that achieve articulation in different combinations and hybridized forms.[26]

For LaCapra, it is never fully possible to write trauma, because trauma itself cannot be localized or pinpointed in a fixed moment.

In January 2001, Weis premiered her program *Show Me* at the Kitchen in New York City. The first half of the program was made up of three multimedia pieces; the second half was the premiere of "Not So Fast, Kid!" Weis's

Internet collaboration with Phil Marden, based on a story told by Davor Petrovski, and using performers in both New York and Skopje, Macedonia. *Show Me*, as a whole, reflects a shift from Weis's initial resistance to the signs indicating that her body was changing, to a gradual listening to what these signs were telling her; from her traumatic experience immediately after her diagnosis with MS, to her ability to turn this experience out into the world and redefine the terms of her disability. Weis's use of a story from another culture addresses her own trauma as reflected through listening to another. Cathy Caruth explains this process:

> The inherent departure, within trauma, from the moment of its first occurrence, is also a means of passing out of the isolation imposed by the event: that the history of a trauma, in its inherent belatedness, can only take place through the listening of another. The meaning of the trauma's address beyond itself concerns, indeed, not only individual isolation but a wider historical isolation that, in our time, is communicated on the level of our cultures.[27]

Weis projects her work outward into the Skopje community and builds "Not So Fast, Kid!" upon a familial structure. The piece integrates a live "family" in New York, another in Macedonia, also live, and a third family of animated cartoon figures projected on a second screen in the performance space. In her program notes, Weis writes, "This piece is an attempt to connect with another culture. I went to Macedonia and asked artists there what story they would like to tell a New York audience. It could be anything. A fable. A war story. Something from the newspaper. The only rule was it could be no longer than one hundred and fifty words. This is our attempt to tell that story." The story they picked goes like this:

> I took off my shoe for the hundredth time, and checked to see if the little pebble was still there. Yes, it was. Every night, in the silence, my father, waiting for me to fall asleep, made an incantation to the little pebble so it would know how to prick me better. Today I have begun my 7,608th life. My foot grew and tore apart the shoe. The little pebble fell out. From the bridge, I watched it falling into the river, disappearing in the unfeeling waters. In the East began the new day. The wind brought the Dawn and with her came the gypsies. I was thinking what to buy from the bazaar, sandals or moccasins. Finally, I decided it would be best for some time to walk barefoot.[28]

The story might be a reflection of Weis's own symptoms—the nagging pain on her right side that grew greater and began to cause her to fall—and her coming to terms with her MS. Weis's "pebble" cannot fall out, but as she gives voice to her own trauma through her work, the work is strengthened, and as she listens to other voices, she listens more closely to her own. This story also reflects the politics of the place, freedom, growth, the fall of Communism. Each "family," the performers in the United States, those in Macedonia, and the projected animations, tells the story differently, and with different nuances. Each family performs on its own, and then the performers are integrated in a cross-cultural, hybridized exchange: Weis dances with "Robert" from Macedonia; another performer dances with an animated character; Ishmael Houston-Jones, the "father" figure in New York, dances with the "mother" figure from Macedonia. The tone of the piece varies from the comical, as animated eyes follow the live performer around the space, to the poignantly beautiful, as Houston-Jones begins to dance a "solo" in the New York space. A camera is fixed upon him, projecting his image onto the screen where the audience views it simultaneously interacting with the mediated image from Macedonia. In front of the screen Houston-Jones is aware of the interactions behind him and how his movement contributes to this complex picture. The images blur together at times, leaving a ghostly sweep of one's arm across the other's face, colors and textures blending into a cyborgean promise of crossed boundaries. The performers—live, animated, and remote—all interact with each other, creating densely layered images that represent connections between people and countries.

Weis is a pioneer with her video and Internet creations. Working against physical and financial odds, she has developed her work with small budgets and amateur equipment. It is a resonant echo of her body; she frames the fragmentations and textures that this technology grants her. Weis's interests are grounded in bodies, in the moments onstage in the present, but through her use of multimedia she also challenges the ways in which bodies are seen at both a global and a local level. Her work can be seen as a response to McKenzie's *Perform or Else,* which in conclusion states, "The challenge: not only to recognize that one experiences history from the perspective of the present, but to plug into emergent forces in order to generate untimely perspectives on this very perspective, perspectives that multiply and divide the present, rattling it to and fro."[29] With determination Weis questions boundaries of the body, technological frames, where the body begins and ends, how technology can augment the body, how to place the audience within technological frames, which frames to use, which bodies?

The cyborg has the potential to fill a space too often vacated by fears of the unknown, whether the fears relate to the loss of the live presence on stage, or are fears of what is societally abject or different. Weis's cyborg theater palliates an all-too-typical uneasiness of disabled bodies by uniting with technology to create a figure undiminished by the physical or psychological limitations placed on the living flesh. Her own physical limitations become evident when she, at the close of *Monitor Lizards,* puts a leg brace back on to greet her crowd. Her gradual acceptance of the brace after a period of self-consciousness peaked when she recently danced with it on in a piece by Scott Heron. "I wore this really tight sexy black dress and I had my brace on, I was in your face. . . . It was kind of liberating to do this, to wear something sexy and have this brace on—and it was still sexy!" In *Show Me,* Weis and Heron revived "Fly Me to the Moon" (now called "A Bad Spot Hurts Like Mad"), and Weis wore her brace throughout. This act strengthened the piece and reinforced the themes that seemed implicit in the original version. Weis's em-brace-ing of this feeling of sexuality empowers her image on stage. Watching her dance this revival, I was taken by the beauty of her movement; her body sweeping through the image-saturated space reconfigured negative tropes of the cyber-subject as bodiless and troubled stereotypical representations of disability. Weis's physicality converges with technology on the stages she occupies, creating a practical space that might otherwise be unoccupied by artists with disabilities.

Notes

1. This epigraph is my description of Weis's performance. The piece was titled *Lizard Monitors* when it was presented at Dixon Place, New York City, between April 9 and April 24, 1999. Weis has since changed the title to *Monitor Lizards.*

2. This essay is part of a larger project outlining forms of cyborg theater. Ideas in this essay were presented at the Association for Theatre in Higher Education conference, Toronto, 1999, and in "Performance Review: *Triangulated Nation* and *Lizard Monitors,*" review of *Triangulated Nation,* by George Coates, and *Lizard Monitors,* by Cathy Weis, *Theatre Journal* 51, no. 4 (1999): 445.

3. Although I will use the general configuration *disability,* I am tempted by Ann Cooper Albright's coinage *dis/ability,* which she uses to "exaggerate the intellectual precipice implied by this word." Her discussion of terminology invokes the ideas of many people writing in disability studies, and I will use *disability* carefully, acknowledging the word choices within the field. See Ann Cooper Albright, *Choreographing Difference: The Body and Identity in Contemporary Dance* (Hanover, N.H.: Wesleyan University Press; University Press of New England, 1997), 58–59.

4. N. Katherine Hayles, *How We Became Posthuman: Virtual Bodies in Cybernetics, Literature, and Informatics* (Chicago: University of Chicago Press, 1999), 286.

5. Rosemarie Garland Thomson, *Extraordinary Bodies: Figuring Physical Disability in American Culture and Literature* (New York: Columbia University Press, 1997), 8.

6. Donna J. Haraway, *Simians, Cyborgs, and Women: The Reinvention of Nature* (New York: Routledge, 1991), 2.

7. Donna Haraway, "The Actors Are Cyborg, Nature Is Coyote, and the Geography Is Elsewhere: Postscript to 'Cyborgs at Large,'" in *Technoculture,* ed. Constance Penley and Andrew Ross (Minneapolis: University of Minnesota Press, 1991), 21. There are differences in the versions of her manifesto that I cannot explicate in this essay.

8. Peter Hitchcock, "The Grotesque of the Body Electric," in *Bakhtin and the Human Sciences*, ed. Michael Bell and Michael Gardiner (London: Sage, 1998), 83.

9. Hitchcock, "Grotesque," 83.

10. Susan Bordo, *Unbearable Weight: Feminism, Western Culture, and the Body* (Berkeley and Los Angeles: University of California Press, 1993), 228.

11. Jennifer González, "Envisioning Cyborg Bodies: Notes from Current Research," in *The Cyborg Handbook*, ed. Chris Hables Gray (New York: Routledge, 1995), 277. González's term is a response to her experience of finding race a fraught issue in the literature of the cyborg. She writes, "Some see cyborgs and cyberspace as a convenient site for the erasure of questions of racial identity." Although this essay does not address racial theory, I hope to remain sensitive to her concerns.

12. González, "Envisioning Cyborg Bodies," 270.

13. Lennard J. Davis, ed., *The Disability Studies Reader* (New York: Routledge, 1997), 17.

14. Davis, *The Disability Studies Reader*, 26.

15. Cathy Weis, interview by the author, New York City, June 1, 2000.

16. I frame my argument within Western society and on modes of seeing that are promoted in Western media because this is my own personal perspective. This is not to say that the same argument could not be applied from other perspectives, only that I locate myself within a Western tradition.

17. Weis, interview, June 1, 2000.

18. Cathy Weis, telephone interview by the author, June 10, 2001.

19. Deborah Jowitt, "The Virtual Dancer," *Village Voice*, February 18–24, 1998, 145.

20. See Ray Kurzwell, *The Age of Spiritual Machines: When Computers Exceed Human Intelligence* (New York: Viking, 1999) for a thought-provoking examination of future human-machine interfaces.

21. Weis, interview, June 10, 2001.

22. Peggy Phelan, *Mourning Sex: Performing Public Memories* (New York: Routledge, 1997), 46.

23. Phelan, *Mourning Sex*, 68.

24. Thomson, *Extraordinary Bodies*, 6.

25. Jon McKenzie, *Perform or Else: From Discipline to Performance* (New York: Routledge, 2001). Although corporate video conferencing can be read in a similar way, I distinguish between the use within a corporate structure as a means of productivity and the use within a performance structure.

26. Dominick LaCapra, *Writing History, Writing Trauma* (Baltimore: Johns Hopkins University Press, 2001), 187.

27. Cathy Caruth, *Unclaimed Experience: Trauma, Narrative, and History* (Baltimore: Johns Hopkins University Press, 1996), 10–11.

28. *Show Me* program notes, story by Davor Petrovski.

29. McKenzie, *Perform or Else*, 255.

Bibliography

Albright, Ann Cooper. *Choreographing Difference: The Body and Identity in Contemporary Dance*. Hanover, N.H.: Wesleyan University Press; University Press of New England, 1997.

Bell, Michael, and Michael Gardiner. *Bakhtin and the Human Sciences: No Last Words.* London: Sage, 1998.

Bordo, Susan. *Unbearable Weight: Feminism, Western Culture, and the Body.* Berkeley: University of California Press, 1993.

Caruth, Cathy. *Unclaimed Experience: Trauma, Narrative, and History.* Baltimore: Johns Hopkins University Press, 1996.

Davis, Lennard J. *Enforcing Normalcy: Disability, Deafness, and the Body.* London: Verso, 1995.

———, ed. *The Disability Studies Reader.* New York: Routledge, 1997.

González, Jennifer. "Envisioning Cyborg Bodies: Notes from Current Research." In *The Cyborg Handbook,* ed. Chris Hables Gray, 267–79. New York: Routledge, 1995.

Gray, Chris Hables, ed. *The Cyborg Handbook.* New York: Routledge, 1995.

Haraway, Donna. *Simians, Cyborgs, and Women: The Reinvention of Nature.* New York: Routledge, 1991.

Hayles, N. Katherine. *Chaos Bound: Orderly Disorder in Contemporary Literature and Science.* Ithaca, N.Y.: Cornell University Press, 1990.

———. *How We Became Posthuman: Virtual Bodies in Cybernetics, Literature, and Informatics.* Chicago: University of Chicago Press, 1999.

Hitchcock, Peter. "The Grotesque of the Body Electric." In *Bakhtin and the Human Sciences,* ed. Michael Bell and Michael Gardiner, 78–94. London: Sage, 1998.

Jowitt, Deborah. "Embodying the Invisible." *Village Voice,* February 18–24, 1998.

Kurzweil, Ray. *The Age of Spiritual Machines: When Computers Exceed Human Intelligence.* New York: Viking, 1999.

LaCapra, Dominick. *Writing History, Writing Trauma.* Baltimore: Johns Hopkins University Press, 2001.

McKenzie, Jon. *Perform or Else: From Discipline to Performance.* New York: Routledge, 2001.

Parker-Starbuck, Jennifer. "Performance Review: *Triangulated Nation* and *Lizard Monitors.*" Review of *Triangulated Nation* by George Coates and *Lizard Monitors* by Cathy Weis. *Theatre Journal* 51, no. 4 (1999): 445.

Phelan, Peggy. *Mourning Sex: Performing Public Memories.* London: Routledge, 1997.

Thomson, Rosemarie Garland. *Extraordinary Bodies: Figuring Physical Disability in American Culture and Literature.* New York: Columbia University Press, 1997.

Weis, Cathy. Interview with author, New York, June 1, 2000.

———. Interview with author, New York, December 20, 2002.

———. *Monitor Lizards,* dir. Cathy Weis. Dixon Place, New York, April 16, 1999.

———. *Show Me,* dir. Cathy Weis. The Kitchen, New York, January 6, 2001.

———. *Show Me* (program notes), dir. Cathy Weis. The Kitchen, New York, January 2001.

———. Telephone conversation with author, June 10, 2001.

Theater without a Hero
The Making of P.H.*reaks: The Hidden History of People with Disabilities

VICTORIA ANN LEWIS

Finch McComas: We're old-fashioned: the world thinks it has left us behind. There is only one place in England where your opinions would still pass as advanced.
Mrs. Clandon: (scornfully unconvinced) The Church, perhaps?
Finch McComas: No: the theater.
—George Bernard Shaw, *You Never Can Tell*

Come, I beg you, come and find your souls again in the people's theater, in the people themselves. . . . On the stage of that theater give them their own legends, and show them their own deeds. Nourish the people with the people.
—Jules Michelet, *L'Etudiant*

Before this workshop you couldn't get me in a room of disabled people. I thought they'd start passing out matching jackets.
—Vince Pinto

This essay chronicles the development and production of a play about "the hidden history of people with disabilities" by a group of disabled writers and actors[1] in Los Angeles from 1991 to 1994. The project's particular—perhaps peculiar to some readers—ambition was to tell the unknown, invisible history of disabled people. Challenging the dominant dramatic narrative of disability, the individual's heroic triumph over a personal tragedy, the writers issued a call for community.

In offering this case study of a theatrical process, I intend to connect this self-identified disability theater to a larger project of reform in Western theater, to people's theater, and to dramaturgical strategies that have been employed by past (and present) progressive theater artists invested in bridging the gap between the world of the stage and the world of social change and crisis. After establishing the extent and importance of the modeling provided by the practice of people's theater to early disability theater, a practice that has historically defined itself against the established theater and the avant garde in content, form and function, I will investigate one specific genre of people's theater, the history play, and the development and production of *P.H.**reaks: The Hidden History of People with Disabilities. Throughout my analysis I will be concerned with the narrative determinism, to use David Mitchell and Sharon Snyder's helpful term, of the disabled figure in the theater, understanding theater to exist as both as a literary and a performing art, and the possibilities for change given the intractability of the art form that George Bernard Shaw correctly characterizes as more old-fashioned than the church. And although I agree with Rosemarie Garland Thomson that a "disability politics cannot at this moment . . . afford to banish the category of disability according to the poststructuralist critique of identity,"[2] and although *P.H.**reaks was to designed to function as a people's theater play, that is, to heal wounded identity and create community, I do not intend to forget Vincent Pinto's fear of matching jackets. As I hope my analysis establishes, the boundaries of disabled identity explode, shift, and realign throughout the play, which is, after all, only make-believe.

Why Theater?

Most Americans are not theatergoers. . . . if you insist on sticking with a preindustrial art form in postindustrial society and still want to make it count politically, you must either content yourself with speaking to a narrow audience, or find a way of popularizing theater.
　　　　　　　—Joan Holden, playwright, San Francisco Mime Troupe

Other Voices is a revolving group of disabled actors and writers under the direction of a disabled theater artist. The writers of Other Voices set themselves the task presenting a social-construction model of disability, disability as an historically determined, collective identity, in a genre that privileges the individual narrative. There are other genres available in which to reimagine the disabled experience—television, film, poetry, the novel, creative, nonfiction, wheelchair dance, solo performance, the Internet—any one of which is more pliable than the creaky, old-fashioned, "preindustrial art form" of the theater. Even when theater flourished as a dominant form of cultural expression, as in ancient Greece and Elizabethan England, it was still a conservative institution, subject to regulating energies—dramaturgical, governmental, ecclesiastical, economic, technological, and physical. Displaced in the nineteenth century by the novel and in twentieth century by film and television, theater is today, if not a backwater of the main current of cultural energy and interest, not more than a tributary.

This demotion of cultural influence affects both the talent available for the theater and the forms that theater takes. In Elizabethan England a surplus of educated young men found an outlet for their talents and a economic living in the newly emerging commercial theater. Today, similarly talented young men and women seek out careers in television and film. Though the point is beyond the range of my discussion here, it should be mentioned that the institutional, not-for-profit theater depends upon and defines itself by the voice of the individual playwright. Since the 1960s, the theater establishment has expended a good deal of energy and money in "new play development." Virtually every playwright who has risen to national attention, including August Wilson, David Henry Hwang, Tony Kushner, Jose Rivera, and Anna Deveare Smith, has received grants, commissions, residencies, and workshops that have enabled them to develop a body of work. While I do not begrudge these artists their good fortune, it is fair to suggest that the new play development network has not robustly supported theater artists with disabilities, especially if we measure by the discrimination that disabled people experience at every developmental level on the path toward a career in the arts.[3]

But to return to the difficulty of pursuing a preindustrial art form in a postindustrial era and representing a social construction of identity in a medium that privileges the individual narrative: why not just change the genre, update it to fit the times? The modernists attempted just that. At the turn of the century theatrical experiments were undertaken to revitalize the theater through a disruption of conventions. In 1896 symbolist Maurice Maeterlinck repudiated plot, proclaiming,

> I have come to believe that an old man sitting in his armchair, simply waiting by his lamp, listening unconsciously to all the eternal laws which reign around his house . . . is living in reality a deeper more human and more universal life than the lover who strangles his mistress, the captain who wins a victory, or the "husband who avenges his honor."[4]

By 1904 Maeterlinck had retreated from this position, acknowledging that what is possible for a "lyric poet" is not available to the dramatist. Now he declared, "The sovereign law, the essential exigency of theater, will always be action."[5] Other movements such as futurism refused to bend to the "exigencies" of the theater and, rejecting every previous theatrical convention or genre, reveled in "the pleasure of being booed." This suspicion of, and dismissal of, the popular audience, is reflected in Arnold Schoenberg's famous epigram: "If it is art, it is not for all, and if it is for all, it is not art."[6]

People's theater, on the contrary, seeks to expand cultural enfranchisement by increasing and diversifying audiences. Romain Rolland, an early-twentieth-century theorist of people's theater, for example, had no interest in an elite audience, the "cultured few" who took pleasure "sucking melancholy as a weasel sucks an egg." In the twentieth century people's theater endeavored to create a "theater for the 98%," that being the portion of the American populace who had never attended a live theater event.[7] John McGrath of Scotland's 7:84 Theatre Company voiced his impatience with the mystery and ambiguity favored by Royal Court Theatre, and his own preference for the "directness" of working-class theater.[8] Joan Holden, playwright for the San Francisco Mime Troupe, criticized so-called serious theater artists for narrowing the audience, contending, "Their aversion to simple truths, the high value they place on complexity and difficulty, and the emotional flatness of the postmodern aesthetic not only confine the audience to economic and social elites, but tend to depoliticize our theater."[9] The people's theater agenda for reform, the changes necessary to revitalize the theater, differed radically from those of the modernists.

People's Theater Version of Dramaturgical Reform and Disability Theater

In process, form, and function, the dramaturgy of people's theater proved more useful to early disability-identified theater artists, including the writers of *P.H.*reaks,* than that of the modernists. The project of a people's theater was first articulated by the Jacobins during the French Revolution, resurrected by historian Jules Michelet in response to reaction and oppression in postrevolutionary France, codified by novelist and theater visionary Romain Rolland in *Le Theatre du Peuple* in 1903, and reappropriated in the 1960s and 1970s by a number of political, popular theater companies.

Early theorists valorized the personal experiences of the silenced, marginalized people. "Give them [the people] their own legends, show them their own deeds," Michelet urged. "Nurture the people with the people." Michelet urged writers to gather the stories of the people, to "go into the fields and chat with a peasant." Much early performance in the disability community incorporated personal storytelling. For example, Other Voices' first presentations consisted of autobiographical monologues, interspersed with original songs about the disability experience.[10] Cumulatively the single narratives functioned as an exorcism of a shared, negative disabled identity characterized by infantilization, invalidation, and de-erotization.

In terms of form, people's theater offered alternative constructions for the basic elements of drama such as character and plot construction. Early theorists were interested in reforming the depiction of working people. Plays, Rolland insists, must no longer be "servants' literature," where lower-class characters are only portrayed as "skulking valets."[11] In the later manifestations of people's theater, the construction of character was informed by Bertolt Brecht's epic theater, in which "man [*sic*] is a process," and "social being determines thought,"[12] and by Erwin Piscator's theories of political theater. Piscator wanted to get "beyond the *purely individual aspect* of the characters and the fortuitous nature of their fates . . .[and] to show the link between events on the stage and the great forces active in history."[13] This was a dramaturgy that lent itself to an understanding of disability as "part of a historically constructed discourse, an ideology of thinking about the body under certain historical circumstances,"[14] as critic Lennard Davis has explained. Dan Chumley, founding member of the San Francisco Mime Troupe, describes the function of character and collective identity in his company's dramaturgy: "You are incredibly unique, and that goes without statement. Having said that, you haven't said enough. What you need to say is: what's the commonality, what's the thing that connects us, because that's where social action takes place."[15]

In another formal innovation, people's theater disrupted the traditional heroic narrative with an episodic, review-like structure that mixed comic sketch, music, and dance-movement. Putting a high value on "entertainment," these companies presented work that was varied, quick, and funny. The beginnings of disability drama gravitated toward accessible, comic, and exaggerated theatrical forms.

Perhaps most important for these isolated artists with disabilities was the commitment of people's theater to the creation of community within the ensemble and between the actors and audience. As Terry Eagleton proposed in *Nationalism, Colonialism, and Literature,* collective identity in oppressed minorities is initially the acknowledgment of a shared negative status, an exclusion from the dominant culture in terms of participation, representation, education, and employment. Once this shared negative status has been consciously acknowledged, it can be countered. As Eagleton notes, "Nobody can live in perpetual deferment of their sense of selfhood, or free themselves from bondage without a strongly affirmative consciousness of who they are."[16] People's theater offered tools to fashion such a culture, to free the alienated and stigmatized. Comparing a production of the great director Max Reinhardt to the rough-and-tumble review of a people's theater troupe, a German reviewer commented:

> Reinhardt might spread heaven at our feet with *Twelfth Night* . . . and yet when you stepped out into the city after the show, it was a jungle and you are lost. . . . But after a review like this you felt as if you have had a bath. You had new strength. You could swim and row in the streets. Traffic and lights, the roar and the machines all made sense.[17]

Joan Holden makes an argument for the centrality of the function of healing and creation of community not just to people's theater but to all theater: "I believe that what most people seek, beyond entertainment, in the theater is still exorcism and affirmation."[18]

Authors before Actors

Like the institutional theaters of today, the early promoters of a people's theater privileged the playwright. Like the modernists, the initial impulse of the people's theater was to erase all previous dramaturgy and start anew. Rousseau set the task for the new dramaturgy when he proclaimed in *The Letter to D'Alembert on the Theater*, "We should have authors before we have actors."[19] But the mandate for a new dramaturgy foundered in 1789 and would continue to falter during subsequent periods of political crisis and revolution. As Brecht famously observed, "Petroleum resists the five-act form; today's catastrophes do not progress in a straight line. . . . Even to dramatize a simple newspaper report needs something much more than the dramatic technique of a Hebbel or Ibsen."[20] Revolutionary Russia director Vsevolod Meyerhold found nothing of interest in the social realist dramas that came his way and instead presented innovative adaptations of the classics. In Germany, the Freie Volksbühne, organized in 1890 to bring good theater with a social content to ordinary workers, at the height of its success had fifty thousand subsidized memberships (subscriptions).[21] It presented by default a classical repertoire. Socialist dramas were most often rejected by the Volksbühne administrators on the grounds of "artistic quality."[22]

This cursory survey provides two relevant insights for discussion of the development of *P.H.**reaks. It is difficult to write plays with a historical materialist perspective. (As both the liberal theater establishment and the revolutionary theaters discovered, it is difficult to write plays period.) The second lesson for the development of *P.H.**reaks, applicable to much disability-identified drama, lies in the Volksbühne's rejection of socialist dramas on the grounds of inferior "artistic quality." The twentieth-century revival of the people's theater suffered a similar fate at the hands of the established liberal theaters. The rousing, comic, exaggerated slapstick of the political alternative scene lacked the moral ambiguity and serious tone favored by the temples of high art.[23] Since so much of the early disability drama shared a similar dramaturgy and in addition rejected the familiar dramaturgical tropes of victim and villain, it is not surprising that many of the irreverent playwrights speaking out of a politicized disability experience in a comic and accessible voice lacked access to the new play development network that has proven so essential to the development of multicultural theater.

Background to P.H.*reaks

Since 1982, Other Voices had developed theater that questioned the stereotypes of disability prevalent in dramatic literature, a process that created ensemble and community among the group's members and audience and opportunities for the professional development of disabled theater artists. A workshop process, drawn from feminist and alternative theater practice,[24] was the core of Other Voices' practice for its first years. The group explored expressive movement, improvisation, and personal storytelling. The liberating physical work coupled with the exchange of stories of discrimination fostered a collective identity capable of effecting social change.

In 1993 Other Voices presented the collaboratively written play *P.H.*reaks: The Hidden History of People with Disabilities*, which argued for a collective identity for persons with disabilities across time and history—an epic sweep that included court dwarfs in the seventeenth century, sideshow freaks, Franklin Delano Roosevelt, Henri Matisse, and disabled civil rights protestors from the 1930s till today. A variety of forces pushed the project in this direction, not the least of which was the growth of a disability culture outside of the world of theater.

The History Play

In the 1980s disabled cultural historian Paul Longmore published two influential articles, "The Life of Randolph Bourne and the Need for a History of Disabled People" (1985) and "Uncovering the Hidden History of People with Disabilities" (1987).[25] Their mandate—to recover and fashion a history for a collectively imagined disability community—served as the catalyst for the Other Voices History Project workshop at the Mark Taper Forum Los Angeles that resulted in the 1993 production *P.H.*reaks.* Unknowingly the group had hit upon Romain Rolland's preferred genre of people's theater, the history play. For Rolland, "History is the source of a people's art."[26] History, he reasoned, teaches us that we are members of a community and that we posses a "spirit of fraternal solidarity" with all the members of our nation. This secure sense of a communal past and future provides the individual with sufficient strength and the most "urgent reasons for action."

As the project director I decided to take up Longmore's challenge and write a history play, a history of the construction of disability through time. In the process of creating *P.H.*reaks,* we (re)discovered many people's theater dramaturgical strategies: first, a process of collaborative playwriting or collective creation that served as a metonym of the identity we were endeavoring to construct; second, the inclusion of documentary, found materials to reconstruct historical events and recover forgotten history; third, exhuming known and unknown persons with disabilities from the past and absorbing them into the modern social construction of disability, what Benedict Anderson in his influential study *Imagined Communities* calls history as ventriloquism; and fourth, fictional elements including a frame story, comic parodies, and love scenes.

The Process Collective Creation and Research

COLLECTIVE CREATION

Many of the early people's theater companies, such as the Blue Blouse troupes in revolutionary Russia and the Red Riot Revue in Germany in the 1920s and 1930s,[27] gravitated toward an alternative model of playwriting—collective creation, a theatrical process in which a group of people work together to develop a production. In the 1960s and 1970s collective creation was adopted by many people's theater companies as a protest against the individualization, specialization, and hierarchy of the traditional theater. Although we had employed de facto collective creation in earlier review pieces,[28] in *P.H.*reaks* Other Voices used a more deliberate and directed collaborative process.

Drawing on the model of collective creation, we engaged in research and study as a preliminary step in our writing process. The first workshop of the Other Voices History Project was August 3, 1991. Paul Longmore joined us in Los Angeles for a two-day seminar of performance, lecture and discussion, to present a rapid overview of the course he was then offering at Stanford, "The History of Human Differences: The Disability Minorities in America."[29] We began with rehearsed performances by professional actors of scenes illustrating the dominant depictions of disability in dramatic literature: *Of Mice and Men* by John Steinbeck (the moral model) and *Sunrise at Campobello* by Dore Schary (the medical model). Also presented was a scene from Caryl Churchill's *Top Girls* to suggest deconstructed theatrical strategies. All the writers received a copy of the recently published study of carnival freaks by sociologist Robert Bogdan, *Freak Show: Presenting Human Oddities for Amusement and Profit*, which positioned disability as a social construct.

The scene presentations provided Longmore with a launching pad for his discussion of the dominant myths of disability in Western culture, the moral, medical and minority (what we would call "Movement" in the final script) models familiar to most students of disability studies. Longmore shared his most recent research with us, including the life story of disabled social critic Randolph Bourne, which would bear dramatic fruit nearly ten years later.[30] The scenes, lectures, and discussions were critical to the workshop process, for although the fledgling playwrights had some experience of both writing and civil rights advocacy, most had not reflected on the intersection of those worlds, and many had unconsciously internalized dramaturgical strategies that propagated negative depictions of disability that in their role as activists they would have taken to the streets to discredit.[31]

Response by the playwriting initiates to Longmore's presentation was positive but concerned. How to reconcile the dramaturgical reforms Longmore called for with the demands of good storytelling? Paul Ryan, a sit-down comic and humorist, could acknowledge that monsters and villains "are obviously not doing the disabled community good," but what, he asked, do you use in their place for a dramatic device?[32]

> You couldn't very well do *Friday the 13th* with Pat Sajak in the leading role. ...The same thing for the standard disabled story—the victim or hero—if you cut all those [characterizations] out, you're left with someone who just pushes the story around. So I don't really have any ideas as to what this is going to look like.

Leslye Sneider offered a tentative response, observing, "It's not going to be interesting if we try to show them we're 'normal.' But if we turn the tension back on society, and show that's where the tension comes from. . . ?" Ben Mattlin agreed: "Showing a person in a wheelchair or a blind person getting up in the morning and brushing his teeth and going to work—big deal, it's boring. What's interesting is confronting the obstacles that are put in front of us." The group had agreed—the task was to find a way to situate disability identity in a sociohistorical context.

The collaborative process was essential to the creation of *P.H.*reaks*. Not only did the writers get ideas from the brainstorming environment, but they also experienced their own disabilities as part of a larger construct. The process served as a metonym of the identity we were endeavoring to construct. Writer and actress Tamara Turner's response was typical.

> [From] being part of this group I think I learned that I have to find who I am first, my disability, our culture, where we came from and then take that to the abled-bodied world and ask them into that world. I loved our discussions. I learned other people are thinking this. I wasn't the only one.[33]

The Documentary Impulse

The second strategy employed in the fashioning of a socially constructed disability identity was the use of documentary materials, a strategy employed in past Other Voices work and now expanded. Theater historian Attilio Favorini employs the term *documentary impulse* to emphasize the form's emergence as an impatient response to the theater's inability to react to pressing historical conditions.[34] Piscator complained that theater "lagged behind the newspapers" and was "never quite up-to-date."[35] The documentary impulse is often associated with periods of actual revolution and war but also emerges at times of cultural crisis, such as the Great Depression and the movement against the Vietnam War.

Documentary materials gathered for *P.H.*reaks* included the text of state laws, photographs, newspaper clippings, television and radio coverage, interviews, and images from the history of Western art—medieval to modern—depicting the impaired body. The photos for the most part documented acts of civil disobedience beginning in the 1930s. For example, during the New Deal recovery, people with disabilities were denied employment under the WPA, their applications stamped with *P.H.* for "physically handicapped" and routinely rejected.[36] A group of disabled persons, the League of the Physically Handicapped, came together to protest this discrimination. Paul Longmore shared his research on the league, including oral histories from surviving members, rare snapshots of the group at political protests and social gatherings, and a surprising amount of contemporary print coverage of the group's demonstrations.[37] Two additional periods of protest were included—the 1977 takeover of the Health Education and Welfare (HEW) offices in San Francisco to force the implementation of Section 504 of the Rehabilitation Act, and the actions of the militant group ADAPT in the 1980s and 1990s. We interviewed key players in the twenty-eight-day HEW occupation and were given access to activist Hale Zukas's extensive audio files of radio and television coverage of the siege. I also conducted a number of phone interviews with members of ADAPT and gained access to their rich photo documentation.[38] Of the sixty-odd slides used in the final production, approximately forty were photos of actual events or images of existing works of visual art, with the remaining twenty created to support fictional elements. Some interview texts were transferred verbatim into the script; for example, leader Kitty Cone's stirring account of the HEW takeover became a group choral piece. Mike Auberger's and Stephanie Thomas's recollections of ADAPT street battles from Denver to the Capitol steps in Washington, D.C., were similarly altered in production. Some audio records were played during the final production, among them television coverage of the HEW occupation and excerpts from Franklin Delano Roosevelt's radio chats.

The Playwright as Ventriloquist Creating a History

In the mid–nineteenth century French historian Jules Michelet first described the role of history in cultural reform as speaking for the voiceless. As Benedict Anderson explains, "Michelet is always concerned with the exhumation of people and events which stand in danger of oblivion."[39] Michelet, promising to give the forgotten *misérables* of the past a second life, proclaimed:

> Yes, each dead person leaves a little fortune, his memory, and asks that it be taken care of. For those who do not have friends, the magistrate [history] must make up for that deficit. . . . I have exhumed them for a second life. . . . They live now with us who feel we are their parents, their friends. So we make a family, a common city between the living and the dead.[40]

This recovery of a lost voice is characterized by Anderson as ventriloquism because Michelet not only takes on the role of spokesperson for all those who are dead and forgotten, but offers to explain their experience to them. In this fashion he is able to construct a "common city between the living and the dead." Significantly, for our project here and for Michelet, this linkage did not require a shared genetic pool, but instead a shared experience, a common objective or intention, in Michelet's case, a revolutionary tradition uniting the oppressed serfs of feudal France with Michelet's contemporaries—fishermen, tradesmen, and women—in a struggle across time against royal and aristocratic classes.

Michelet was not interested in just *any* story from the past, but rather one that supported his own political necessity. Longmore defined his search for a history of disabled people similarly in his 1985 essay:

> Historians must apply a minority group analysis to the historical experience of disabled people. Past social practices and public policies affecting them require reexamination from this perspective, and the history of eugenics needs revising from the viewpoint of its primary victims, people with handicaps.[41]

This is a history designed to claim community, a history that establishes over time and across nations a "shared fact of oppression" as Eagleton put it, a "common set of stigmatizing values and arrangements" in Longmore's formulation.[42]

In *P.H.*reaks* we manipulated time and space in order to assign to disabled figures in the past a sociohistorical awareness that would not be articulated until the late twentieth century. The play encompasses three time dimensions corresponding to the division of moral, medical, and movement (minority or social) constructions of disability. The moral encompasses ancient and medieval times; the medical in our version centers on the late nineteenth and early twentieth centuries; and the movement begins in the 1930s, picks up again in the 1970s, continues into the 1990s. By manipulating theatrical time and place, and by doubling and tripling the roles that each actor assumed, we were able to construct characters with multiple manifestations through historical time, whose accumulated experiences of discrimination and prejudice justified their giving voice to an oppressed status.

For example, the sideshow exhibit Princess Angie, a dwarf, was first presented as a character in the frame story of the backstage life of a carnival sideshow and was played by Shari Weiser, an actress of small stature. However, in her sideshow act Weiser appears not as Princess Angie, but, as we learn from the barker, Eugenia Martinez Vallejo, nicknamed "Monstrua" or "monster," an actual dwarf in the Spanish court who was the subject of several portraits by the Baroque artist Carreño de Miranda. Weiser, dressed in an opulent, seventeenth-century red brocade gown, dances a slow court dance to a plaintive Spanish air. Above her a slide projects her sideshow banner, "The Tempest in a Teapot." As the barker reviews the superstitions attached to the physically impaired body in ancient times, slides of medieval woodcuts of various "monsters," real and imaginary (dwarves, Siamese twins, human cyclops), appear above the slowly turning actress. A woman's voice-over intercuts with the barker's spiel, saying, "It is better to be in the court than on the streets begging for food scraps. I am not as feeble minded as they make me out to be. . . . For a meal, a bed and free-flowing wine I will be [pose] for you." This voice represents the inner monologue of the seventeenth-century "monster," the court dwarf Eugenia, the text written by Other Voices workshop member Leslye Sneider. The woodcut images give way to richly colored portraits of contemporary court dwarves, including Eugenia, as the barker titillates the audience with references to the erotic cult of the dwarf in the seventeenth century.

Then an incongruous slide appears, a black-and-white photograph, a signed publicity shot of Lia Graff, a little-person celebrity of the 1930s. The barker pretends to be surprised but then reveals another dark fact: Lia Graff made an unfortunate visit to her homeland Germany in 1935, was arrested as a useless person in 1937, and was sent to Auschwitz in 1944, where she was murdered as part of the Nazi campaign to eliminate disabled persons.[43] Out of this atmosphere of danger tinged with eroticism the final visuals emerge—two Carreño portraits of Eugenia, one in elaborate court dress, and the other of her in the nude. In this latter painting, Carreño has adorned his model's head with a laurel wreath and covered the genital area with leaves. Eugenia's round belly protrudes, minimizing her small breasts sufficiently to make her sexuality ambiguous, allowing Carreño to present her as the male god Bacchus. As the barker leeringly reminds the audience that Bacchus is "the well known god of the drunken orgy," Eugenia's voice-over protests: "I am not Bacchus, I am a woman." The barker entices the rubes into the tent with promises of even more titillating entertainment ("no pregnant women or children under twelve allowed"), while the actress onstage portraying Eugenia brings her stately dance to a close and the voice-over finishes: "Look at me as long as you like. You won't see me smile." The play conflates time and place to expose the predatory nature of the moral model, the use of the physically different body as a surface on which to project sexual fears and anxieties and, in Eugenia's inner monologue, asserts a resistant counternarrative.

Fictional Elements

The fourth strategy for presenting disability as a social construct in *P.H.*reaks* was the use of dramatic fiction—including a frame story, comic parodies, and love scenes—to destabilize the received constructions of disability. Although this strategy contain elements that are closer to naturalistic dramaturgy, in aggregate they thwart any attempt to reduce the play to a

Shari Weiser as sideshow attraction Eugenia/Princess Angie performing a seven-teenth-century court dance in *P.H.*reaks: The Hidden History of People with Disabilities,* adapted by Doriz Baizley and Victoria Lewis, created and developed by Other Voices, produced by the Mark Taper Forum's 1992–93 New Work Festival. (Photograph by Jay Thompson.)

unified plot organized around one central character and thus the domi-nant narrative of disability in Western drama as the individual triumph over a personal tragedy.

FRAMING DEVICE

The play's framing device is a fictional plot involving a group of sideshow exhibits (loosely based on Bogdan's book) whose livelihood is threatened by concerned citizens who want to ban the freak show. The reformers decry the exploitation of the poor unfortunates who are not entertainers but vic-tims of disease. Despite the freaks' indignation at such a depiction, when we next see them, some scenes later, they are in line at the unemployment office. A bureaucrat, ignoring their claim to job skills, their right to collect unemployment insurance and to receive job counseling, puts them on welfare and sends them to institutions. The next and last time we see the freaks they are dressed in hospital gowns and on medical display. The freaks, conventionally individualized dramatic characters that inhabit highly unique and disparate bodies, find themselves subject to a shared fate of invalidation, infantilization, and institutionalization. Dramaturgically the freaks move us from a predominately moral to a predominantly medical societal construction of disability. The freak framing story is also an essentialist argument for the superiority of the disabled over the nondisabled body: being a sideshow oddity is better than being "normal."

COMEDIC PARODY: DEFLATING THE "GREAT OVERCOMER"

In Vincent Pinto's comic scene, "Changing of the Guard," inspired by *FDR's Splendid Deception*,[44] two secret service officers practice walking a life-sized dummy, a stand-in for Franklin Delano Roosevelt. The older officer explains to the new recruit that their job is to make the public believe Roosevelt can walk. The men drop, toss, and shove a life-sized dummy, a stand-in for the real FDR, who can be heard in the background speaking to a crowd.[45] The scene combines broad physical comedy, larger-than-life characters, and funny dialogue. Pinto manages to deconstruct stigmatized identity through comic exaggeration of efforts to conceal it, releasing an explosion of laughter that dispels pity and fear.

LOVE SCENES: RE-EROTICIZING THE DISABLED BODY

In addition to comic parody and manipulations of stage time and space, *P.H.*reaks* incorporates one of the standard tropes of traditional dramaturgy, the love story, even managing to end with a successful pairing, the triumph of eros, and thus earning the play the label of comedy. But the love story is fractured and does not follow the plot line of one pair of lovers and is unified only in the sense that it tracks a progression from sexual rejection to sexual acceptance, loosely paralleling the three-part structure based on the moral, medical, and movement models. The play opens with in medieval times (the moral model) and pits a sanctified, beatific disabled woman against a demonized, disabled male. The disabled woman rejects the disabled man in favor of able-bodied protection.

Next the "Tempest in a Teapot" sideshow exhibit Angie is visited backstage by a small-town doctor, who disguises his sexual curiosity as medical concern. This scene inverts the medical model by reversing the normal rela-

Two Secret Service officers, the Old Guy (*left*, Barry Schwartz) and the New Guy (*right*, Lisa Dinkins), practice walking an FDR substitute in order to hide his disability in *P.H.*reaks*. (Photograph by Jay Thompson.)

tionships of patient and doctor, man and woman, disabled and nondisabled, through Angie's skillful manipulation of the doctor to her own profit.

The re-enactment of the 1930s protest of the League of the Physically Handicapped is followed by a love scene involving one of the protestors. A young woman has watched the demonstrators from her window and invites the handsome young man on crutches in for a glass of lemonade. Their mutual attraction cannot overcome the girl's discomfort with the boy's disability, and, unlike the dramas of adjustment we are familiar with from the mass media, the young disabled man manages to bring the embarrassing situation to a close. In the penultimate scene of the play, two disabled people make love for the first time. We witness an attendant, a paid personal assistant, preparing the two unmarried adults for lovemaking in a rented motel room. The scene represents the triumph of the new depiction of disability in the disabled persons' recognition of each other's bodies as love objects. In addition the characters are played by the same actors who played in the opening medieval scene as well as two characters in the freak frame-story; in fact, they carry the same names as the freaks, Joey and Beth.

This time-travel, *Orlando*-like approach to character and plot construction that moves from self-hatred to sexual reclamation allows us to experience the evolution of the historical construction of disability aesthetically and emotionally. As the only successful sexual relationship depicted in the play, the scene also serves an essentialist argument that privileges sexual partnering between two disabled people over a mixed relationship.

The response of the disability community to the workshop production was strong.[46] Paul Steven Miller, then serving in the White House Personnel Office, sent a typical response:

> As a disability civil rights lawyer and a person with a disability . . . the play had an immense impact on me. It was one of the few pieces of theater that I can relate to—which talks about me and my people. The combination of documentary material, comedy and drama made it unique. It was a good night of theater notwithstanding the fact that it addressed disability issues. But given the fact that it addressed disability culture, it was quite remarkable. Instead of just pulling on the traditional heart strings, the play addressed real issues of discrimination and prejudice. The audience had to think as well as feel.[47]

Epilogue

Despite the excitement in the disability community about the performance of *P.H.*reaks,* the Mark Taper Forum, citing economic and aesthetic reservations, chose not to continue development of the play, not an unusual fate for original plays in the not-for-profit American theater. Plays, as I have argued, do not exist independently of historical-materialist conditions.

Did this production change the theater? Did we dislodge the narrative determinism of the disabled figure in the theater? In an art form that is not only old-fashioned but ephemeral, it is hard to know. The people's theater theorists of the turn of the century are forgotten now, but their visions persist. The diversification of the not-for-profit theaters in America is a successful example of the implementation of one of the people's theater central mandates, to decentralize the performing arts and dislodge the cultural domination of cities like New York and Paris. But it was not the first attempt.

In the early twentieth century the charismatic actor-director Firmin Gémier took up Michelet's call to bring the theater to the countryside, to the people, and founded the Théâtre Ambulant. In 1911, eight fifteen-ton,

steam-driven tractors pulled thirty-seven rolling cars containing a collapsi-
ble, seventeen-hundred-seat playhouse around rural France. The strange
caravan struggled to cross cornfields and rivers where the railway could not
go, and a crew of seventy stagehands, twenty-six actors, and several musicians would install the theater on an open plot of land, perform one or
three times, and then pack up the playhouse and rumble on to the next village. This is the particular world of the theater—a combination of hard
labor, technology, tedium, most assuredly quarrels, all animated by a vision,
which manifests itself for a few hours in the night. Getting the actual disabled body on the stage, representing the lived experience of disability in
modern drama, finding new theatrical metaphors that release instead of
confine the disabled body, is a task as challenging as Gémier's dream of taking theater into rural France. The creation of *P.H.*reaks* was and is one leg
of a longer journey.

Notes

1. Contributing writers: Isaac Agnew, Doris Baizley, Victoria Ann Lewis, Mary
Martz, Ben Mattlin, Peggy Oliveri, Steve Pailet, Vince Pinto, John Pixley, Paul Ryan,
Leslye Sneider, Bill Trzeciak, Tamara Turner.

2. Rosemarie Garland Thomson, *Extraordinary Bodies: Figuring Physical Disability
in American Culture and Literature* (New York: Columbia University Press, 1997), 23.

3. Further information on this topic is available at http://artsedge.kennedy-
center.org/forum. In June 1998 a National Forum on Careers in the Arts for Persons with Disabilities was convened in Washington, D.C., under the joint sponsor-
ship of the National Endowment for the Arts, the Department of Education, the
Social Security Administration, and the Kennedy Center. The website provides full
text versions of several position papers and presentations.

4. Marvin Carlson, *Theories of the Theatre: A Historical and Critical Survey, from the
Greeks to the Present* (Ithaca, N.Y.: Cornell University Press, 1984), 296.

5. Carlson, *Theories of the Theatre*, 297.

6. As quoted in Alex Ross, "Ghost Sonata: What Happened to German Music?"
New Yorker, March 24, 2003, 70.

7. Maxine Klein's title, *Theatre for the 98%* (Boston: South End Press, 1978),
emphasized the elite constituency of regional and Broadway theater. A recent survey by the National Endowment for the Arts shows a small improvement by 1997.
According to NEA figures, 85 percent of Americans have never attended a live theater event.

8. John McGrath, *A Good Night Out: Popular Theatre: Audience, Class, and Form*
(London: Eyre Methuen, 1981), 3, 54.

9. Joan Holden, "In Praise of Melodrama," in *Reimagining America: The Arts of
Social Change,* ed. Mark O'Brien and Craig Little (Philadelphia: New Society Publishers, 1990), 280.

10. These open workshops proved highly successful, so much so that two of
these presentations were refined into "documentary musicals" featuring the origi-

nal workshop members and produced for national television, while another made a tour of local independent living centers (ILCs).

11. Romain Rolland, *The People's Theater*, trans. Barret H. Clark (New York: Henry Holt, 1918), 115–16.

12. Bertolt Brecht, *Brecht on Theatre: The Development of an Aesthetic*, ed. and trans. John Willet (New York: Hill and Wang, 1992), 37.

13. Erwin Piscator, *The Political Theatre*, trans. Hugh Rorrison (London: Methuen, 1963), 9; emphasis added.

14. Lennard J. Davis, *Enforcing Normalcy: Disability, Deafness, and the Body* (London: Verso, 1995), 2.

15. Interview by the author, February 2000.

16. Terry Eagleton, Fredric Jameson, and Edward Said, *Nationalism, Colonialism, and Literature* (Minneapolis: University of Minnesota Press, 1990), 37.

17. Piscator, *The Political Theater*, 97.

18. Holden, "In Praise of Melodrama," 283.

19. Jean-Jacques Rousseau, *Politics and the Arts: Letter to M. D'Alembert on the Theatre*, trans. Allan Bloom (Ithaca, N.Y.: Cornell University Press, 1960), 120.

20. Bertolt Brecht, *Brecht on Theatre*, ed. by John Willet (New York: Hill and Wang, 1964), 30.

21. Raphael Samuel, Ewan MacColl, and Stuart Cosgrove, *Theatres of the Left, 1880–1935: Workers' Theatre Movements in Britain and America* (London: Routledge and Kegan Paul, 1985), xviii.

22. Richard Bodek, *Proletarian Performance in Weimar Berlin: Agitprop, Chorus, and Brecht* (London: Camden House, 1997), 9.

23. At the close of the twentieth century some people's theater artists have created work for the regional, not-for-profit theaters. Joan Holden's adaptation of Barbara Ehrenreich's best-selling memoir *Nickel and Dimed: On (Not) Getting By in America* was produced in regional theaters in both Seattle and Los Angeles. Joan Schirle of Dell'Arte Players directed original productions at the San Diego Repertory Theater. The Cornerstone Theater has collaborated with a number of regional theaters, including the Arena Stage and the Mark Taper Forum. In 1997 the Nobel Prize for literature was awarded to Italy's Dario Fo, a comic writer and actor working in the popular people's theater tradition.

24. The project's director, this writer, was a member of two people's theater ensembles prior to founding Other Voices: Family Circus in Portland, Oregon, and Lilith, a Woman's Theatre.

25. Paul Longmore, "The Life of Randolph Bourne and the Need for a History of Disabled People," *Reviews in American History*, December 1985, 581–87, and "Uncovering the Hidden History of People with Disabilities," *Reviews in American History*, September 1987, 355–64.

26. Rolland, *The People's Theater*, 98.

27. F. Deak, "Blue Blouse," *Drama Review*, 17, no. 1 (March, 1973): 35–46; Piscator, *The Political Theater*, 81.

28. *Tell Them I'm a Mermaid* (1982), *Bionics Anyone?* (1984), and *Growing Pains* (1986).

29. Irving Zola also generously shared his syllabus with me.

30. Playwright John Belluso adapted this material for his full-length drama *The*

Body of Bourne, which received its world premiere in June 2001 on the main stage of the Mark Taper Forum.

31. I had learned this earlier in a workshop I offered to a group of disabled ILC (Independent Living Center) workers, when an improvisatory storytelling exercise produced unexpected results. One person begins a story and each member of the group adds to the evolving narrative until an end is reached. I provided the inciting incident—a woman incurs a spinal cord injury in an accident. By the time the story had made it around the circle of nine activists, the main character had been cured three times.

32. The following comments by Paul Ryan, Leslye Sneider, and Ben Mattlin were made during a roundtable discussion at the Mark Taper Forum's Other Voices history project workshop on August 2, 1991.

33. Tamara Turner's comments are from a post-mortem discussion following the first workshop presentation of *P.H.*reaks* on October 8, 1991, in Los Angeles.

34. Attilio Favorini, ed., *Voicings: Ten Plays from the Documentary Theater* (Hopewell, N.J.: Ecco Press, 1995), xx.

35. Piscator, *The Political Theater,* 48.

36. This historical incident is the origin of the eccentric spelling in the title *P.H.*reaks,* and the contribution of participant Bill Trzeciak.

37. Paul K. Longmore and David Goldberger, "The League of the Physically Handicapped and the Great Depression: A Case Study in the New Disability History," *Journal of American History* 87, no. 3 (2000): 888–922.

38. I am grateful to ADAPT photographer Tom Olin's generosity over many years and projects.

39. Benedict Anderson, *Imagined Communities: Reflections on the Origin and Spread of Nationalism,* rev. ed. (London: Verso, 1991), 199. My argument here is drawn from Anderson's treatment of Michelet, 194–99.

40. Anderson, *Imagined Communities,* 198.

41. Longmore, "Life of Randolph Bourne," 586.

42. Longmore, "Uncovering Hidden History," 355.

43. See Robert N. Proctor's *Racial Hygiene: Medicine under the Nazis* (Cambridge: Harvard University Press, 1988).

44. Hugh Gregory Gallagher, *FDR's Splendid Deception* (New York: Dodd Mead, 1985).

45. Bill Trzeciak located recordings of FDR, and the speech we chose to frame this scene made ironic comment, as we hear Roosevelt promise every man and woman in America a job.

46. Two preliminary workshop drafts of *P.H.*reaks* were performed in the Mark Taper Forum's rehearsal hall A (the first on October 8, 1991, and the second on January 27 and 28, 1992). There were approximately 125 audience members in attendance each night. The audience was composed of theater and disability community guests who provided feedback in open forums following the performances. A third draft of *P.H.*reaks* was selected for production in the 1993 Mark Taper Forum's New York Festival and presented at University of California–Los Angeles's Black Box for four performances, March 26–28, 1993.

47. Paul Steven Miller, letter to the author, June 27, 1993.

PART III Rehabilitating the Medical Model

Despite thirty years of activism that has fought to claim a minoritarian identity for people with disabilities, the dominant culture persists in considering disability in terms of the medical model. Unlike the social-construction and minority models of disability that emphasize group cultural identity, the medical model individualizes disabled people by considering them unique, unfortunate victims of pathologies, rather than a group of citizens deserving of civil rights.[1] The medical model casts people with disabilities as "patients," a role that is often infantalizing, pathologizing, and disempowering. Patients who cannot be cured or at least rehabilitated enough to "pass" are often segregated from the nondisabled mainstream, either forcibly through institutionalization or passively through lack of access to public and private spaces. The consequences of the medical model have been devastating for disabled people throughout history, resulting in denial of public education, incarceration in nursing homes, involuntary sterilization, and "mercy" killings. In contrast, the social-construction and minority models of disability accept impairments as natural, inevitable human differences that should be accommodated. Activists persuasively point out that medical advances have not eliminated impairments, but proliferated them. With each advance in medical science, more and more people survive premature birth, injury, and illness to live life with significant impairments.[2] Because they see the elimination of impairments as an unreachable goal, disability activists instead focus on eliminating restrictive attitudes, public policies, and environments to allow people with disabilities equal access to education, employment, and public spaces.

We do not wish to demonize doctors or other medical professionals here; on the contrary, these very professionals have given many people with disabilities extended, more comfortable lives. We are instead critiquing prevalent ideologies that delimit the lives of disabled people to the "patient" role. The medical model, as we have been describing it here, extends beyond individual medical practitioners' relationships with individual patients to include quotidian encounters between people with disabilities and the nondisabled. The tendency to scrutinize disabled bodies for aberrant symptoms is what Petra Kuppers (after Michel Foucault) has called the "diagnostic gaze."[3] The diagnostic gaze is, as Rosemarie Garland Thomson suggests, the unspoken question behind the stare, the question that inquires, "What happened to you?" This question seeks to affix a diagnosis to a disabled person, categorizing him or her as safely "other."

"What happened to you?" whether asked aloud or not, begs a response, spoken aloud or not. David Mitchell and Sharon Snyder explain that "one must narrate one's disability for others in sweeping strokes or hushed private tones. And this narration must inevitably show how we conquer our disabilities or how they eventually conquer us."[4] Visibly disabled people know that when out in public, they must respond to these questioning stares, and their response can be verbally articulated or performed through subtle, or not-so-subtle, body language and facial expression. The stage provides a platform for exposing the otherwise covert dynamics of the diagnostic gaze.

Disabled performing artists often expose these dynamics through the use of hyperbole and the theatricalization of the everyday. Consider how David Roche opens his one-man show *Church of 80% Sincerity* with an act of what Mitchell and Snyder would call "transgressive reappropriation," or the naming, claiming, and revising of disability stereotypes.[5] Roche first names the stereotype that defines him in public. Looking directing and sincerely at his audience, he says, "We who are facially disfigured are children of the dark. . . . You have read the fairy tales and seen the movies that invariably portray us as evil, subhuman monsters." He does not deny this stereotype, but inhabits it hyperbolically by adopting a menacing posture, facial expression, and tone. He quickly revises the stereotype's meaning: "My face is a gift, because my shadow side is on the outside where I have to learn to deal with it." Then, Roche theatricalizes the dynamics of the diagnostic gaze by instructing the audience to voice the usually silent question behind the stare. At the count of three, the audience asks in unison, "What happened to your face?" Roche thanks the audience for its candor, and then goes into a detailed clinical definition of his impairment. He juxtaposes this sterile definition with a bit of humor, "I don't always give that nice educational answer. . . . I have been tempted to tell a child who is pestering and obnoxious, '. . . Well, my face is like this because when I was a little boy like you, I touched my wee-wee.'"[6] Roche directly confronts the medical model in the first five minutes of his piece, deflecting its power by wittily satisfying the audience's curiosity, then moving on to what he really wants to say.

The contributors to this part analyze additional ways that performing artists with disabilities engage with the medical model. Johnson Cheu looks at the work of Neil Marcus and Jaehn Clare. In "Performing Disability, Problematizing Cure," Cheu suggests that the presence of disabled bodies onstage makes audiences aware of the tension between the performers' body as corporeal entity and the body as a representational system. This tension allows audiences to read competing cultural narratives of disability (i.e., impairment vs. minoritarian identity) on the performer's body. Cheu contends that these performances are central to the creation of disability culture and community.

In "Bodies, Hysteria, Pain: Staging the Invisible," Petra Kuppers considers the implications of historical regimens of the visual for contemporary practices. She argues that the history of ocularcentrism in its relation to the medical gaze has problematized visibility as a strategy for disability performance. Taking Charcot's public presentations of "hysterical" subjects in nineteenth-century Paris as a template for how mental disabilities are rendered visible, a template that remains in place today, Kuppers asserts that disability performance practices must find ways of turning ocularcentrism against itself by creating images that invite visual contemplation yet question and undermine the equation of visual evidence with truth. She goes on to discuss her own movement-based performance work with people in mental health contexts, work that uses video technology not to create sympathetic, accessible images of disability but to create complex, reflexive, implicitly self-critical representations of the body.

Issues surrounding both cure narratives and visibility politics play a significant role in Philip Auslander's analysis of Spalding Gray's ongoing series of autobiographical performances in "Performance as Therapy: Spalding Gray's Autopathographic Monologues." Unlike some of the other performers discussed here, Gray is not visibly disabled, nor does he claim a politicized disability identity. Nevertheless, Gray's performances recount his experiences with physically, emotionally, and psychologically impairing conditions. Auslander argues that while the written form of Gray's narratives appears to adhere to the traditional comic plot structure (which end happily or at least satisfactorily), they resist closure in performance. Audiences participate in an ongoing therapeutic process with Gray, rather than read a final literary product of a "recovered" individual.

The last three essays in this part explore how nondisabled artists rehabilitate the medical model from within its own contexts: the clinic and the nursing home. These nondisabled artists attempt to collaborate with disabled people as equal artistic partners as means of unsettling the artist-astherapist, disabled-person-as-client relationship. However, the differences between nondisabled and disabled artists in these contexts—economic, cultural, physical, and cognitive—present unique challenges to true collaboration.

In "The Facilitation of Learning-Disabled Arts: A Cultural Perspective," Giles Perring points out that while the United Kingdom's "arts and disability" movement is a project separate from "arts therapies," both involve nondisabled facilitators working with disabled participants in institutional environments, funded by government agencies that expect therapeutic outcomes. Despite this medicalized context, nondisabled facilitators report that both they and the disabled participants grow artistically from their collaborations. Perring tempers such optimism, though, with cautionary historical accounts of nondisabled artists' fascination with the disabled "exotic other."

Melissa C. Nash's essay "Beyond Therapy: 'Performance' Work with People Who Have Profound and Multiple Disabilities" examines the London dance company Entelechy. In workshop performances, Entelechy's nondisabled facilitators provide dance and movement workshops for cognitively and physically impaired participants. Entelechy considers these workshops "equal encounters" between two groups that have the potential to spawn new aesthetic languages. Nash troubles this ideal by asking whether disabled participants must consent to collaboration, or be conscious of performing, to be considered performers.

Anne Davis Basting's "Dementia and the Performance of the Self" provides a model for collaboration between disabled and nondisabled artists that moves from private workshop to public theatrical performance. Basting devised methods for representing the experiences of those who are literally unable to represent themselves on stage: institutionalized people with Alzheimer's and other forms of age-related dementia. Basting suggests that people with dementia are believed to have lost a sense of self because of their inability to construct coherent life narratives. Basting's multimedia project Time Slips advances alternative notions of selfhood that emphasize provisionality and interdependence instead of consistency and individuality.

Notes

1. See our introduction for an explanation of the medical model. Also see Paul Longmore, "The Second Phase: From Disability Rights to Disability Culture," in *Why I Burned My Book and Other Essays on Disability* (Philadelphia: Temple University Press, 2003), for an extended discussion of the medical model versus the minority model of disability.

2. See Joseph Shapiro, *No Pity: People with Disabilities Forging a New Civil Rights Movement* (New York: Times Books, Random House, 1993) for a discussion of how medical advances create more disabled people than they cure.

3. Petra Kuppers, "Towards the Unknown Body: Silence, Stillness, Space in Mental Health Settings," *Theatre Topics* 10, no. 2 (2000): 129–43.

4. David T. Mitchell and Sharon L. Snyder, *Narrative Prosthesis* (Ann Arbor: University of Michigan Press, 2000), xi.

5. Ibid., 35.

6. David Roche, *Church of 80% Sincerity*, 2–3, unpublished, quoted by permission of playwright.

Performing Disability, Problematizing Cure

JOHNSON CHEU

In her one-woman show *The Woman with Juice,* Cheryl Marie Wade sets forth a new political agenda for people with disabilities. She writes, "No longer the polite tin-cuppers, waiting for your generous inclusion, we are more and more, proud freedom fighters, taking to the stages, raising our speech-impaired voices in celebration of who we are." Disability activists, artists, and performers are throwing off age-old stereotypes of the pitiable freak, the charitable, helpless cripple, and the inspirational poster child in favor of a new understanding of the meaning of our disabilities. More people with disabilities are coming to an understanding of something called "disability culture" and adopting a new understanding of our bodies and lives

Recent scholarship in disability studies has both reflected and helped spur on this "new" understanding of the disabled body and disability experience, as something more than just a "defective" body. While *disability* is a term largely imbued with medicalized notions of an impaired body, scholars such as Mairian Corker, Carol Thomas, and Jenny Morris have articulated a distinction between the terms *impairment* and *disability.* In this new configuration, *impairment* generally refers to the physical and psychological medical conditions of the body, while *disability* encompasses a larger cultural understanding of disability experience—teasing, stigma, the history of institutionalization, literary and media representations of disability, and so forth.[1] In this way, the configuration of *impairment* refers to the body as a corporeal entity, while *disability* refers to a societal and cultural phenomenon, an identity.

While the work of the artists I examine—Neil Marcus's *Storm Reading* and Jaehn Clare's *Belle's on Wheels*—addresses many stereotypes about disability, I focus my analysis on the challenges these artists make to the need for medical cure. These artists see beyond bodily impairment (as something that can, or needs, to be cured), to disability as culture, as identity.

This shift is a marked difference from, for example, portrayals in mainstream Hollywood cinema, such as blind Al Pacino in *Scent of a Woman* lamenting his impairment. "I'm in the dark here! I have no life!" he wails. In *Rain Man,* though his brother Charlie accepts Raymond's autism, Raymond is unable to integrate successfully into mainstream society and boards the bus alone. He fulfills what Martin Norden has termed "the cinema of isolation." It is precisely Raymond's inability to be "cured" that leaves him no alternative but to be reinstitutionalized. Not all Hollywood representations of disability imply, as these do, that medical cure is desirable; however, medical cure of impairment is indeed not only scientific, but also cultural. As such, it is a cultural idea that many disability activists and artists actively resist. How others represent us, how others who are able-bodied write about and perform our disability experiences, is not always how we write about, define, and see ourselves. Of black female spectatorship in cinema, bell hooks writes, "Critical black female spectatorship emerges as a site of resistance only when individual black women actively resist the imposition of dominant ways of knowing and looking" (210). Like the black women to which hooks refers, in producing their own bodily performances, these disabled performance artists resist cure as a way of complicating bodily impairment and disability experience. Just as the critical black female spectator must resist dominant ways of knowing and seeing, so too must disabled people. These disabled performance artists are questioning the idea of the body as spectacle, beyond the corporeal, impaired body in need of cure on stage. In doing so, the audience is asked to understand the disabled body as a performative entity within a larger social and cultural context. This shift, however, requires a change in spectatorial understanding on the part of most viewers who must renegotiate a perspective on disability as simply bodily impairment. In this essay, I extend performance theorists Herbert Blau's and Peggy Phelan's notions of the "vanishing point" in performance to disability and to the concept of medical cure of an impaired body. I then describe a technique artists use to challenge medicalized notions of disability by creating a three-dimensional illusion, which mirrors the implicit meaning of Phelan's theory—that the vanishing point is both illusionary theatricality and a questioning of that illusion. I begin with the complexities of viewing the disabled body in performance.

Disabled Bodies at the Vanishing Point

A point of contention in performance studies is the transitory nature of performance itself. As Phelan notes in *Mourning Sex,* "Performance and theatre
are instances of enactments predicated on their own disappearance." The
"hole" she created after tearing out a pop-up image in a children's book
"was my first sense of the relationship between bodies and holes, and
between performance and the phantasmatical" (2). Clearly, there exists a
tension between the physicality of a performance, the presence and enactment of the corporeal body on stage, and the ethereal, transitory nature of
the performance (and the bodies therein) itself. Performance artist and
critic Jon Erickson articulates it thus:

> It is the "problem of other minds" which posits the "as if" of projection, but
> finds its identification always incomplete. On the other hand, it is a lack of dis-
> tance, a reflection of human vicissitudes, which makes the sign less than full
> for the spectator. The body can be seen, then, as both instrument *for* the sign
> and as something inexplicitly Other. (242)

What Erickson points to is how the author creates a metaphor by dehumanizing the subject, creating an object. In this way, we might begin to
understand how disability in performance might draw one's focus to the
corporeal body as the object of a spectator's gaze on stage, and as the site of
medical impairment.

The disabled performance artist, then, holds a double-edged sword. On
the one hand, the artist is exhibiting the body as corporeal object; on the
other, the body serves as metaphor, as representational system that denotes
a set of experiences, a way of being, as I term it, which revolves not around
impairment, but around cultural responses to that impairment.

Medical cure, then, becomes a problematic point between bodily impairment and constructed identity. Phelan's reading of performative bodies
existing at a "vanishing point" from a theatrical perspective underscores
this nexus between corporeality/impairment and disability as cultural representation.

> Put simply, the vanishing point was derived from a theory of optics based on
> the illusion that parallel lines converge at a point in the distance. The
> painter placed that convergence at the optical center of his or her composi-
> tion; that became known as the vanishing point. . . . Parallel lines do not
> meet, yet the vanishing point makes it look as if they do. The "as if," the illu-
> sionary indicative that theatre animates, allows for the construction of depth,
> for the invention of physical interiority and psychic subjectivity. (*Mourning
> Sex,* 23–24, 27)

Phelan uses the vanishing point to articulate spectatorial perspective of bodies in painting: "The vanishing point also underlines the hole in the viewer's body: it points to what painting, and corporeal vision itself, cannot show, cannot see" (33). The vanishing point in painting and performance presumes an illusionary point of convergence between viewer and performer, and thus allows a viewer to add "depth" at the vanishing point. In disability performance, I suggest, medical cure serves as the "vanishing point" because it is the proverbial convergence where medicine and the disabled body appear to intersect. Medical cure lies at the very heart of the tension between disability as medical impairment and disability as cultural identity. If disability is simply understood as a bodily impairment that is medically curable, then disability as culture is nonexistent. However, if disability exists as a culture, if the disabled body is to be seen as a representational system upon which experiences of disability in society are projected, then medical cure of the disabled body must be understood as a construction. In other words, medical cure, the possibility of a "normal" body, is a *perspective* that is assigned by the able-bodied viewer to the disabled body. From its hegemonic position, cure stands at the very center of the corporeal impaired body and the disabled body as identity.

Herbert Blau writes of the vanishing point that "the principle issue is perception" (*Take Up the Bodies*, 28). The perspective of the able-bodied spectator drives the ideas of normalcy and medical cure in disability performance.[2] I do not mean, however, to ignore the potential viewpoint of audience members with disabilities. Cultural studies itself, though, falters a bit here. Like film studies, which, until the rise of women's studies did not presume a gaze other than the dominant male gaze, the presence of a disabled gaze, as something distinct from what I term here the *normative gaze,* has not been theorized and deconstructed fully. As disability studies expands in ways similar to ethnicity, sexuality, and gender studies, which caused a reevaluation of whiteness and heterosexuality as dominant paradigms, we may begin to see more work on such ideas as a disabled gaze in film and a disability perspective in performance. Like feminist studies, disability studies should presume a perspective different from the dominant, in this case, able-bodied, perspective. It is, however, the able-bodied perspective on normalcy and cure as desirous that drives my reading of the vanishing point.

The disabled body is caught between, on one side, the impaired body and the life it lives, and, on the other side, the "normal" body and the life it may procure via the possibility of medical cure. Yet it is the able-bodied viewer who assigns desire for normalcy, achievable through medical cure, to the disabled body. Normalcy serves as the viewer-assigned "depth" and "psychological interiority" of the disabled body. However, neither the disabled body nor the viewer's able body can view "cure." Cure becomes the "hole" in the viewer's body, pointing to the limits of the viewer's corporeal vision. The body on stage, the one available to the viewer, is the corporeal impaired body. Taken more literally, the moment of medical cure becomes the point at which the disabled body, as corporeal entity and as performative signifier, supposedly vanishes to become reconstructed as whole, cured, normal, and so forth.

In theatrical terms, Phelan uses the vanishing point to articulate an idea of the fictionality of theatrical space and the creation of a viewing point in the audience member. The vanishing point, then, serves as a way for things to appear in dimensionality rather than a way for something to literally "disappear." It may seem, then, that my use of the vanishing point both as literal wordplay and as theoretical concept applied to medical cure is misapplied. However, I suggest that this is not the case. To the contrary, asking the viewer to see beyond the impaired corporeal body, asking the viewer to understand medical cure as a construction that can be resisted, does not cause the medical cure to disappear. Instead, medial cure, as a dimension of how disability is constructed and represented, becomes more visible and more solid to the audience.

Take the real-life example of the gay adoption case of Bert Lofton. Since he was nine weeks old, Bert, now ten years old, has lived with his foster parents, Steve Lofton and Roger Croteau, and his foster siblings, all of whom are HIV-positive. Because Bert no longer tests positive for HIV and is under fourteen years of age, he is now deemed "adoptable" by the state of Florida. Since gay adoption is not legal in that state, the state is actively looking for another home for Bert.[3] What this example shows is the cultural construction of cure as yet another dimension of the issues surrounding Bert's case, for only after Bert's HIV status changed did the state deem him adoptable. In addition, it speaks to the very issue of a viewing point by others. Bert's negative status, his "adoptability," lies not with how Bert sees himself, but how others see him and his body. Given the media coverage of his specific case, Bert may never lose his status as someone with AIDS, regardless of medical tests. Even though the medical impairment (the presence of HIV antibodies) may be gone, Bert's former social status as HIV-positive and the social implications of that status have become more evident, and he may never lose the stigma connected with what society has deemed an "incurable" disease.

To articulate, to perform a disabled body, thereby positing disability as cultural construction and as "a way of being in the world," the disability performance artist, then, must refute the need for medical cure and assert the right of the disabled body to exist. The vanishing point becomes the (able-bodied) spectatorial position against which the disabled performance artist produces his or her own bodily performance and thus, an insistence on the permanence of the disabled body. By seeing the impairment, the spectator necessarily sees the cultural responses to that impairment. Both Neil Marcus's *Storm Reading* and Jaehn Clare's *Belle's on Wheels* problematize the desire for medical cure through the performance of disability as both corporeal and cultural entity.

A performer might use several actions to challenge the viewer's assumption of the need for medical cure. Clare, for instance, incorporates her wheelchair, a marker of her impairment, as a natural extension of her body and space. Marcus places his impaired body into everyday interactions with able bodies. Such actions help viewers to see the permanence of the disabled body, while asking viewers to redefine able-bodied notions of what it means to be disabled. The viewer begins to understand disability as both corporeal entity (impairment) and as social construction.

Neil Marcus Storm Reading

Touring nationally for several years, Neil Marcus's *Storm Reading* (1997) is the best-known piece produced by the now defunct Access Theatre of Santa Barbara, California.[4] While the performance touches on many stereotypes, such as the body beautiful, media representations, and sexuality, I will focus on the monologues and vignettes in which medicine and cure are addressed most explicitly.[5]

Storm Reading consists of vignettes and monologues based on the author's experiences of disability. Marcus has dystonia musculoram deformans, which affects muscle control, movement, and, in Marcus's case, speech. Marcus uses his body, and its various contortions, to convey meaning and humor throughout the performance. The performance is a three-person affair, with an able-bodied actor, Matthew Ingersoll, who assumes the roles of Marcus's voice and various characters, and Kathryn Voice, an ASL interpreter.

In one sketch Neil is called upon to be the "disabled specimen" at a medical convention, with Ingersoll playing the medical expert. Ingersoll directs Marcus's bodily movements, treating him like a trained seal. When Ingersoll mentions "heavy breathing" as one of the symptoms of dystonia, he turns to Marcus and requests heavy breathing. Marcus groans, to which Ingersoll replies, "Good specimen." The tension between medicine's objectification of the disabled as little more than medical aberrations (positioning itself as both the bearer of the possibility of medical cure, and as testifier to the need for cure) is highlighted at the end of the sketch. Ingersoll offers his specimen a treat, holding it out in front of him, as though feeding a dog. Marcus's response is to bite his hand, while simultaneously his leg jerks, kicking the doctor in the behind. The audience sees the tension between the medicalized idea of an impaired body in need of cure, and Marcus's insistence that his disability is a part of his identity, signified in the resistant act of biting and kicking the doctor.

The assertion of the disabled body's right to exist as is can be seen clearly in the restaurant sketch. Ingersoll and Voice play patrons at the restaurant where Marcus is the waiter. Ingersoll has to write down the order himself, get the water, and the food. Marcus still waits on the couple, reporting to the chef and so forth, but certain physical tasks require Ingersoll's assistance. Ingersoll is angry, of course, and after the food arrives, complains to his wife. She responds, "But Honey, he couldn't do it. . . . Look at this wonderful meal that the three of us have prepared by working together." Voice's comments protest the need for an able body as the dominant. Disabled bodies can exist and serve a "useful" function as they are. By grouping all together as "the three of us," Voice subtly includes disabled bodies into the mix of humanity. The disabled body does not vanish; it becomes an accepted body in society. By performing a job, Marcus subtly shows the viewer the usefulness of his "impaired" body while showcasing a different, more inclusive response to his disability (that of Voice's), calling for the spectator to redefine his or her positioning and presumed response to impairment as something in need of medical cure.

Later in the performance, Marcus addresses the "healing" power of religion, often understood to be a means to cure. Ingersoll holding a candle, as if in church, becomes the voice of Marcus in the following monologue:

> Do I believe in God? I have nothing to say to him, if it is a him. I don't want to say there is a power greater than my power. My life represents a continual striving to be powerful. . . . I don't believe in sin. I don't want to give up control or responsibility. I want to believe in reality, my reality . . . just reality.
>
> I resent the possibility of religion healing me. I want to work with what is real to me. I believe in people. I believe in nature. I believe in life. God might be life. I might be God.

Marcus asserts his personhood, as a disabled individual, and also his right to exist as he is, challenging both the need and desire to be healed. While this is not a medical "cure" per se, the goal of the eradication of a disabled body is the same. *Storm Reading* continually asserts the disabled body as a point of contention and presence, not of absence through cure. Just as the vanishing point presumes a point of convergence between spectator and performer, in *Storm Reading* Marcus implicitly or explicitly asks spectators to "converge" at the point of medical cure, and, as he has done, to reassess the meaning of his body as the site of medical cure, on behalf of a more inclusive identity-based construction.

Jaehn Clare Belle's on Wheels

A clear-cut repudiation of the need or desire for medical cure of the disabled body occurs in Jaehn Clare's one-woman show *Belle's on Wheels*. The play revolves around the life of Clarity, a young woman in her early twenties. The play is set approximately three years after the accident that paralyzed her. It was originally written as "a celebration of survival" of the tenth anniversary of the author's own paralyzing accident (Clare, interview, April 8, 2000).

The play begins with young Clarity's falling off a tree, making disability the point of origin. It is, then, not a mourning of the past and a desire to return to that able body, to be cured; rather it becomes a play of birth and renewal, where disability serves not as the vanishing point, but as the beginning. Clare described her motivations in beginning the play with the accident:

> Clarity had fallen off trees before. She had had accidents, and fallen before. This was simply the worse one. . . . [The decision to begin the play there] was a conscious one. I wanted the play to be about the process of a reclamation of the self. Everyone already knows the tragedy story. Change is not loss; change is just change. I wanted people to understand that the "dis" in disability is someone else's "dis." (Clare, interview, September 7, 2000)

Yet knowledge and experience of that able body, of that way of being in the world, might make the desire for medical cure more pointed. Clare addresses the issue of cure specifically, presenting it as a "wish fulfillment" sequence with a fairy godmother in the section entitled "Program 9."[6] Clarity's fairy godmother, Faith, offers her a contract to "restore the complete and total function of your legs, feet, and toes." Cure is understood only in terms of bodily impairment, of a body's ability to "function" physically. The cultural implications of disability are not seen by the able-bodied, signified here by the fairy godmother and the contract. Further, all the experiences surrounding disability are rendered nonexistent by the medical cure of the impairment. The contract states:

> In exchange for the above-mentioned Blessing, the Beneficiary, as identified in Paragraph Two, shall relinquish to the Agent . . . those items acquired since

the onset of said disability, . . . including, but not limited to any and all knowledge, experience, wisdom, learning, understanding, advantages, parking privileges, and tidbits, ad infinitum. . . . In receipt of said infinites, the Beneficiary shall enjoy the benefits of said Blessing forevermore, until the end of Time, the Universe, or the existence of said Beneficiary's corporeal body—whichever comes first.[7]

Clarity, however, understands disability as culture beyond impairment. She responds, "So, basically, I give up everything—anything—I may have learned as the result of . . . becoming a gimp, and you do . . . whatever it is you do." The godmother, though, understands disability solely in terms of medical impairment and (restorative) functionality. Seeing Faith's lack of understanding of disability as a social experience, Clarity elaborates: "I survived . . . This—This . . . *This!* The accident, the surgery, the rehab, trauma, stress, incontinence, stares, loss, divorce, head-patters, pity, curiosity, celibacy, grief-anger-pain-fear-exhaustion-frustration-oppression . . . *This!*" She declines to sign the contract.

On the word *"This,"* Clarity pops a wheelie in her wheelchair and spins around in circles, including the wheelchair as part of her disability experience and claimed disability identity. Indeed, throughout much of the performance, Clarity's wheelchair is understood to be an extension of her body and her personal space. When she kicks her legs out as though swinging on the tree swing, she simultaneously lifts the wheelchair up; it acts as her imaginary swing seat, caught on an upswing. The wheelchair becomes a part of her body.

Clarity sharply rejects the godmother's idea that Clarity's body can and needs to be cured, claiming her disabled body and her disability experience in a brief monologue.

> No! *Clar-i-ty*. Like the knowledge and gift of unconditional love from my family and friends. An appreciation for the value and import of simple things; time well-used; eating chocolate. A deeper relationship with the force that keeps me going every day. The dignity of living in a body that challenges society's perception of beauty, and a greater appreciation for my body's sensuality. Understanding that I *choose* my priorities, my life. Awe at having survived.

We see not just a repudiation of medical cure, but also an embrace of the experience of disability. Disability becomes an empowering choice, rather than a reason for medical cure. "I *choose* my priorities, my life," Clarity says.

At the end of the scene, the fairy godmother tells Clarity to keep the magic wand. While this could be read as a desire to retain the possibility of cure, it could also symbolize the "magic" found in Clarity's disabled identity.

Clarity embraces her new life clearly in the epilogue, where the gift of bells signifies an acceptance of her body and a celebration of her life.

> *Faith:* Remember, my beautiful friend: All the people I pick have one thing in common—Life is burning a small candle inside them, and they are looking for oxygen to feed the flame. What brings us together, into the Circle of Life, is finding that little hole through which your breath can feed another's flame. Keep the faith, child.
>
> *Clarity: (Opens the gift, pulling out a string of nine bells. A grin of understanding steals across her face.)* Oooh! *(Tying the string of bells onto the frame of her wheelchair.)* With rings on her fingers and bells on her . . . wheels—She shall have music . . . *whenever* she feels. *(Popping a modest "wheelie," she jingles the bells slightly, then picks up the candle which still burns softly; lights fade to special as she quietly sings.)* "Out came the sun and dried up all the rain . . ." (Special fades to *blackout.*) ". . . And the itsy bitsy spider climbed up the spout *again.*"

The inclusion of her disability, of the wheelchair as part of her body and "the music" her life, is seen here as she wheels offstage, bells ringing to the sound of applause. By reconfiguring the disabled body beyond medical impairment, Clare's asks the viewer to reassess notions of a disabled body and the need of that body to undergo medical cure.

Conclusion

In *The Woman with Juice,* Cheryl Marie Wade and Amy Mulder caution the able-bodied viewer, "We are no longer waiting for your generous inclusion. . . . We are taking to the stages, raising our speech-impaired voices in celebration of who we are." Marcus and Clare are two such voices and bodies rising in celebration of their disabled bodies and shared disability culture and identity. Marvin Carlson describes minority and feminist performances that challenge dominant hegemonic notions of race and gender as "resistant performance." Similarly, the disability performance artist resists ableist notions of disability as a bodily impairment in need of medical cure. This shift in understanding of disability from impairment to culture necessitates changes in viewers' perspectives on the disabled body, that is, the vanishing point, and changes in understanding the experiences of that body as part of larger collective and cultural forces, that is, disability as identity.

I have attempted here to sketch a means of reading and viewing disability performance and the disabled body in performance. May we all, disabled and able-bodied viewers alike, find in these performers and performances, reasons to celebrate.

Notes

My gratitude to the Ohio State University Department of English for the Edward P. J. Corbett Grant for Dissertation Research, which allowed me to develop much of the primary research material for this essay. My thanks to the artists for their generosity.

1. For more on the impairment-disability distinction see such texts as Mairian Corker and Sally French, "Reclaiming Discourse in Disability Studies"; Jenny Morris, *Pride against Prejudice;* and Carol Thomas, "Theorizing Disability and Impairment."

2. The pair of terms *disabled/able-bodied* historically alludes to the idea of impairment. The terms *disabled/nondisabled* is gaining parlance in disability studies to signify cultural identity. By utilizing the term *the able-bodied,* I am referencing the historical use of the "disabled/abled" paradigm—i.e. impairment, the focus on bodily corporeality as a particular perspective.

3. For more on this case, see http://www.lethimstay.com, accessed June 28, 2004.

4. Though I saw a live performance in Berkeley, California, in 1991, my comments here are based on a videotaped version obtained through Access Theatre in 1996. The videotape contains scenes that were not in the live performance I viewed.

5. For more on the history of Access Theatre and the evolution of *Storm Reading,* see Cynthia Wisehart's *Storms and Illuminations.* She also discusses *Belle's on Wheels.*

6. As the stage notes point out, the Faith can be played by a live actor or presented as a voice-over. Hence, the use of the term *one-woman show.*

7. Quoted material is from a transcript provided by Clare. For clarity, boldface type used in the original transcript has been changed to normal type. Descriptions of staging rely on a videotaped version also provided by Clare.

Works Cited

Belle's on Wheels. Written, produced, performed by Jaehn Clare. Center Stage Theater. Santa Barbara: Access Theatre, 1995. (Videotape of performance courtesy of the author.)

Blau, Herbert. *Take Up the Bodies: Theater at the Vanishing Point.* Urbana: University of Illinois Press, 1982.

Carlson, Marvin. *Performance: A Critical Introduction.* New York: Routledge, 1996.

Clare, Jehan. Interview with author, Atlanta, April 8, 2000.

Corker, Mairian, and Sally French, eds. *Disability Discourse.* Buckingham: Open University Press, 1999.

Erickson, Jon. "The Body as Object in Modern Performance." *Journal of Dramatic Theory and Criticism* 5.1 (fall 1990): 231–43.

hooks, bell. "the oppositional gaze: black female spectators." In hooks, *Reel to Real: Race, Class, and Sex at the Movies,* 197–213. New York: Routledge, 1996.

Let Him Stay. ACLU Lesbian and Gay Rights Project. March 3, 2003. http://www.lethimstay.com.

Morris, Jenny. *Pride against Prejudice: Transforming Attitudes to Disability.* London: The Woman's Press, 1981.

Norden, Martin F. *The Cinema of Isolation: A History of Physical Disability in the Movies.* New Brunswick, N.J.: Rutgers University Press, 1994.

Phelan, Peggy. *Mourning Sex: Performing Public Memories.* New York: Routledge, 1997.

Storm Reading. By Neil and Roger Marcus, dir. Rod Lathim, perf. Neil Marcus, Matthew Ingersoll, Kathryn Voice. Santa Barbara, Access Theatre Productions, 1996. (Unreleased video, courtesy of Access Theatre Productions.)

Thomas, Carol. *Female Forms: Experiencing and Understanding Disability.* Buckingham: Open University Press, 1999.

Wisehart, Cynthia. *Storms and Illuminations: 18 Years of Access Theatre.* Santa Barbara: Emily Publications, 1997.

The Woman with Juice. Dev. and dist. Amy Mulder, written by Cheryl Marie Wade and Amy Mulder, perf. Cheryl Marie Wade and Amy Mulder. BRAVA: Ford and in the Arts, 1994. (Videotape performance courtesy of the author.)

Bodies, Hysteria, Pain
Staging the Invisible

PETRA KUPPERS

Disability can stand in interesting relations to medical science and performances of identity. This essay deals with signifying bodies, invisible impairments, and the historical stagings of meanings. It begins with theatrical discourses and historical practices surrounding hysteria, and charts resonances with two contemporary performance projects by people with invisible, "inner" impairments: *Traces,* an installation–performance project by people with mental health issues, and *Fight,* a project involving a performer with a pain-related impairment.

Whatever the internal effects of their specific conditions, all of the performers in these projects are aware of the social reading of their conditions. All have experienced discrimination and, sometimes, violence. They are aware that exposing themselves, making their differences visible, can be a dangerous choice with harsh consequences. At the same time, some are also aware of the fascination and the desire to know that accrues to differences between people. Whether visibly impaired (as I am when I am using my wheelchair) or in a problematic relationship to visibility (with mental health and pain issues), disabled people are often asked to describe their experiences, and to open up their personal histories to both the medical gaze and public curiosity.

Given these complexities surrounding disclosure and curiosity, how can we approach performance, value our experiences, and place our performing bodies in the public sphere? How can we move between the staring eyes, the abstraction of the brain scan, and the dangerous shores of "normalization," the elision of difference?

The trajectory of the performance projects discussed here is from knowing and fixing to unknowability and generative uncertainty. One of the answers we have found in our projects is the extension of performance to multimedia environments, which allow us to manipulate and work with presence in interesting ways. By structuring the visibility machine of performance, we intervene in the violations of the "medical stare" at different bodies.

In order to grasp the multiplicity and manipulation of meaning in the performances that will be discussed, I use the signifying concept of a technology of meaning. With it, the essay points to the historical manufacture of meaning and its stage apparatuses, the realist devices and visibility machinery of both medical discourse and political performance. In the multimedia performances engaged in by the medical practitioner Charcot, the aim was to fix a specific symptomatology, to make it visible and categorizable. In contrast, the two disability arts installations discussed in this essay undo these certainties, using multimedia performances as ways of breaking through the fixing of difference.

Visible Minds

Jean Martin Charcot (1825–1893) investigated and stage-managed hysteria from the 1870s onward in the Parisian Salpêtrière. Hysteria had been a named condition with a broad symptomatic catalog since roughly 1900 B.C. Medical writing

> generally emphasized the physical manifestations of the hysterical seizure: suffocation, vomiting, palpitations, convulsions, fainting, the voiding of large quantities of urine, and speech disturbances. (Beizer 1994, 4)

The late nineteenth century saw culturally important struggles over the bodies of people, still predominantly women, diagnosed with the condition. At stake was the liberation of the neurological apparatus from the gynecological one: the mind from the body.

Charcot was an influential figure in this fight.

> Charcot sought to construct a coherent, nosological narrative that would impose an order on what presented itself as utterly grotesque body and voice

articulations, in it systematization would subject to the laws of a regulated pathology an evasive, psychosomatic illness and the resilient unruliness of the patient's exhibiting it. (Bronfen 1998, 181)

His popular shows and photographs contributed to the romantic status of the hysteric in both realist and surrealist literature in turn-of-the century France and elsewhere. To the surrealists André Breton and Louis Aragon, hysteria was "the greatest discovery of the late-nineteenth century," a poetic liberation (Beizer 1994, 2). A raft of literature discusses the political impact of using women's physical paralysis as a metaphor for narrative liberation and refusal of discourse.[1] But it is in another aspect of the entry of the hysteric woman into the cultural limelight that this essay takes an interest: the staging of visible evidence of difference. An elaborate machinery was at work to bring the neurological, internal working of the hysteric condition into visibility, and to mark it on the body it "possessed." This machinery articulated in interesting ways issues of agency, visibility, and knowledge. Charcot's greatest achievement was to both take away and grant power to the women and men he diagnosed:

> Through careful observation, physical examination, and the use of hypnosis, Charcot was able to prove that hysterical symptoms, while produced by emotions rather than by physical injury, were genuine, and not under the conscious control of the patient. (Showalter 1987, 147)

By proving that these people were not consciously in control, Charcot established the legitimacy of psychological conditions and their effects on the physical body—a fight that echoes with contemporary struggles to validate Myalgic Encephalonyelitis (otherwise known as chronic fatigue syndrome) and many pain-related impairments as genuine medical conditions that warrant the extension of social welfare or insurance benefits. Charcot's pupil Freud would take up and extend this issue of the power of the mind over the body, extending the theater of readability by paying attention to the interpretable nature of the utterances made.

Theaters of Knowledge

In order to cement a particular form of knowledge about bodies in both medical and popular discourse, Charcot embarked with his patients on a theatrical and performative journey.[2] He staged fits, photographed archetypal images of hysterical women, and established himself as director and manager of bodies whose symptoms were made to speak loudly and clearly of invisible conditions. The "medical stare," intent on symptoms and lesions, opened its visibility machinery up to the public.

Axel Munthe, a doctor practicing in Paris, described Charcot's Tuesday lectures, attended by the *charcoterie* (Beizer 1994, 6):

> The huge amphitheatre was filled to the last place with a multicolored audience drawn from tout Paris, authors, journalists, leading actors and actresses, fashionable demimondaines. (Munthe 1930, 296)

The spectators were treated to various set pieces, with Charcot as master of ceremonies who hypnotized his subjects to show the power of the mind over the body. Charcot dismantled "natural" connections between mind, body, and environment in his demonstration, with examples of confusion of senses, disidentification with one's own body, and manipulation of emotions.

> Some of them smelt with delight a bottle of ammonia when told it was rose water, others would eat a piece of charcoal when presented to them as chocolate. Another would crawl on all fours on the floor, barking furiously when told she was a dog. (Munthe 1930, 302)

In these set pieces, the presence of the illness manifested itself when full control was taken from the subject and executed by the director. Charcot's lecture-spectacles often ended in a full hysteric fit. The famous painting by André Brouillet (1887), *Charcot Lecturing on Hysteria in the Salpêtrière,* shows the doctor, focus of the gaze of his disciples, with an unconscious woman in his arms, barely held upright by him. The woman's clothing is disturbed, and her bare shoulders and disarray stand in contrast to the tiered, regimented order of the onlookers. The gender dynamics of these images have been discussed widely,[3] but it is also interesting to note the staging that is taking place: the chairs are indeed arranged into an amphitheater, and behind the professor two stagehands are waiting to take the woman away as soon as the act is finished. The theater space is clearly delineated by a swath of light that cuts diagonally through the image from center front to a big window in the background, and it is in this swath that the doctor stands and holds forth. "Footlights" are provided by the white pinafores of the persons on both sides of Charcot, as well as by the white bosom of the unconscious woman. The iconography marks out his lit face with its deep eye sockets, much clearer lit than the poor woman's hanging head.

Apart from these written and painted documents of live theatrical practices,[4] Charcot's most famous contribution to the aesthetic of the hysteric— the woman unconsciously caught in her flesh—used another machinery, photography. A professional photographer worked at the Salpêtrière in his own studio, and the photos were published in the *Iconographie photographique de la Salpêtrière*. Showalter quotes Freud on Charcot's mode of gaining and fixing knowledges of the body:

> As Freud has explained, Charcot "had an artistically gifted temperament—as he said himself, he was a 'visuel,' a seer." Charcot's public lectures were among the first to use visual aids . . . as well as the presence of the patients as models. (1987, 150, quoting Freud 1948, 10–11)

This visual evidence that was to become the foundation of Charcot' s theory can again seen to be staged, and a result of theatrical labor.

Many of Charcot's images use the same model, Augustine, a fifteen-year-old girl at the time of her admittance into the Salpêtrière, who later disguised herself as a man and escaped (Showalter 1987, 154). Images of Augustine such as *Extase, Erotisme,* and *Supplication amoreuse* (all 1878) look like tableaux: held positions, rather than snapshots of a "fit." The subject is positioned in front of the spectator's gaze with full assurance. Nothing is incidental; everything seems planned (Augustine is displayed on a bed, with disarrayed, flowing hair, plunging neckline, frontally oriented to the camera) and captured in such a way as to coincide transparently with the caption.

To the contemporaneous scene, the images seem to have been fully accessible visual testimonies of symptoms of mental disarray. To us, issues of staging and theater present themselves, as do issues of gender and power. Charcot's attempt to regulate and stabilize hysteria as a clear symptomatology is questioned by the excess of performance.

> On a more submerged level, latent because it was not interpreted by her chroniclers, the urgency of Augustine's anguish remains as a trace, a foreign body whose voice we sense precisely because it marks the gap in knowledge in Charcot's grand representational design. (Bronfen 1998, 194)

The supposedly "neutral" medical gaze onto the patient is refigured, shows its own technology of knowledge, when performance enters the field. The medical stare with its attendant effects on power relations becomes visible in our historical reading of Charcot's work, and attunes us to the performative and rhetorical function of contemporary representations of "madness," or other invisible impairments. It is this suspicion of visibility machines that the performances I want to discuss below exploit—they widen the gap between seeing and knowing, they attempt to make visible the technologies of meaning that impart authority on medical knowledge.

Traces of a Charcot's intertwining of visibility, photography and psychiatry, visual and theatrical representation of mental illness are still highly prevalent. Indeed, the performance spectacle of Charcot's theater perpetuates itself in the many representations of mental illness in the cinema, on TV, and in other aspects of popular culture. Our everyday, popular knowledge about mental health is largely dominated by visual representation of twitching bodies, holding on to the traces of hysteria's catalog of symptoms. Examples include *Session 9* (2001, dir. Brad Anderson), a film in which ghosts revisit Danvers Hospital, where the practice of lobotomy was developed, and take over workmen, or Jack Nicholson's wild-eyed stare and automatic writing in *The Shining* (1980, dir. Stanley Kubrick). The "mind" is unconscious, outside of one's own control, manifested theatrically on one's body (or, in the case of *The Shining*, on paper through the translation of the body into the typewriter)—like Anna O.'s limp[5] or the erotic convulsions of the Salpêtrière women. This loss of control is made evident and iconic on the body's surface: the body becomes the readable symptom and loses its privacy. The machinery that captured Charcot's staged bodies, the medical theater and the photo apparatus, preserved this relationship between visibility and knowability.

Although the history of medical intervention into mental health issues has moved on from Charcot, as the cinematic examples above show, the contemporary situation of disabled people with invisible impairments can still echo this representational past. Visibility, performance, and knowledge are still points of navigation for artists dealing with disability. In the examples discussed in what follows, stable viewpoints and surveillance modes are questioned, and the spectator is put into a variety of positions of engagement and implication. Staging and theatricality impinge on all of these examples: "truth" is undermined through the mode of representation, and spaces for difference open up.

Mental Health & the Presence of the Body

If Charcot was intent on creating visible discourses for mental difference, contemporary disability artists struggle with the undoing of fixities and categorical differences. Their work is part of a larger political project, the challenge to, and dismantling of, the stigma of disability.

Part of my own performance work as artistic director of the Olimpias[6] has been in mental health settings, working with people who have been diagnosed with severe mental distress, who are on medication and many of whom are occasionally hospitalized (see also Kuppers 2003). The histories of hysteria, visibility, and medical performance shape the aesthetic and structure of our work. We explore how we can gain visibility—as an entry into the public realm, making ourselves present in our social environment—while denying the fixing of symptoms associated with the history of medical visualization of mental issues.

Some of the Olimpias' performers show symptoms reminiscent of the old definition of hysteria, now diagnosed as a range of conditions including schizophrenia and mania: partial limb paralysis, speech disturbances, feelings of suffocation, vomiting, and dissociation. My performers are aware of the social status of their specific physicality, and they do not wish to expose themselves to stressful situations that can induce and acerbate these "symptoms," including conventional live performances. Having been taught that these behaviors are unsightly, they do not wish to be seen in ways that allow their bodies to be read for "symptoms" of mental health issues.

In order to allow us to present our difference, but not cater to the stare trying to find symptoms of our difference, reading us for cues, we complicate the performance encounter.

In 1999, we used a translation device, a gallery video installation. This is an apparatus different from that used on the medical stage, but one that likewise addresses the audience theatrically.

We did not create "positive images" of disabled people—showing them to be "the same" as everyone else. We also did not create "new" images, full of pride in our differences—for this meant nailing down aspects of that difference in ways that we meant to avoid. Instead, we worked *with* images toward a *transcendence of imagery* that addressed the audience physically.

My own learning curve as a choreographer and director is important to the development of this strategy. Working on movement with the performers, I soon realized the connection between the physical and the representational, their deep mutual implication. Many of the performers' physical experiences mirrored their silencing in, and exclusion from, representation. Some find no space for themselves, their bodies, their movements in the social and physical environment. They are excluded from life alone, from getting an apartment; conformed to a timetable of contact with medical practitioners, or the even more rigorous timetable of pills and injection. Their bodies can be invaded, as the law allows them to be drugged against their will and involuntarily hospitalized. Their physical and mental privacy is often under threat.

At the start of our work together in 1996, I found that this lack of spaces in which to simply be, to be private, to be present, had undermined many people's confidence in their use of space. Thus, the representational and social aspects of "madness" had effects on the sense of embodiment of people diagnosed with mental health difficulties. *Traces* asked whether work with embodiment could affect in turn the representational categories of mental health and difference.

As every performance class knows, "centering exercises" can be difficult. They were doubly so for the Olimpias performers because of the representational and social exclusions discussed previously. Drug-induced spasticity and rigid body-tensions prevented the performers from literally claiming room, owning the portion of a room's space that is inhabited by their body. Some had difficulties asserting their physical space—standing still, breathing deeply, or allowing their voice to resonate. With this inability to take space, simple actions such as reaching and connecting became problematic.

As a result, validating our spatial experience became an important aspect of our work. We rethought spatial and temporal aspects of embodiment, politicizing them. We had to find ways to assert breathing and being as an intervention in the social sphere. By working with our sense of embodiment, we were at the same time working on the images and practices that limited the experience in the first place. In our work together, breathing exercises, creating an awareness of the body's inner space through visualization, feeling our muscles relax, reacting to the influx of breath, was not *preparation* but the core event. We were not tuning our bodies such that we could fully "be" in a movement, or explore the pre-expressive energy of intensity in order to channel it into a performance. Instead, these usually preparatory aspects of movement work became the focus of the session.

Out of the intensities and corporeal states of these sessions, we created our gallery video installation *Traces,* which we showed in community centers and theaters between 1999 and 2001. The installation was usually set up in a dark room. Spectators were invited to sit or lie down on comfortable cushions or position themselves with their wheelchairs.

The spectator had to find a space to "be" inside the arrangement of screens and monitors. In order to see the images, the spectators need to come into the center of the monitors and screens. The neutral position of the theatergoer, or the roving, noncommittal stance of the gallery visitor, was not available. Spectators had to decide where they wanted to be in the space, and how far they wanted to "participate." Their own bodies won three-dimensionality as they decided where to sit, how to negotiate the videobeams that made their silhouettes part of the visual experience.

On three screens were close-ups of the performers, lying on the floor, with their faces and bodies concentrated on a visually absent, inner experience. Videotapes of our bodies in states of relaxation cycled against each other, so that no arrangement was the same. The shots showed heads, upper bodies, hands, or traveled down a prone body. The images had been shot as part of a performance session, our weekly meetings, not in a studio, so traces of the photographer's body remained in the movement of the handheld camera and the rhythm of panning and cuts. On a soundtrack, a voice narrated a choreographed dream journey (working through different inner experiences), paced to allow the spectator to slip into the experience herself. The journey was "choreographed" in the sense that the dream imagery focused on spatial and movement experience: flying, rolling, drifting, circling, fast and slow, sustained, abrupt, etc. Much freedom was given: the scenes were not described in highly visual terms, no colors or specific shapes were mentioned. Likewise, no epiphany was called up: no opening doors or mirrors, which are used in more therapeutically focused guided imagery.

In a book left out for the purpose, some spectators commented on the challenge that their position as spectators-performers posed to them, and how this challenge focused on issues of self and other, embodied participation and visual representation. They were ready to go with the relaxation sequence, lie down and close their eyes, but that meant that they could not see the images. They had to make decisions and reflect on them.

Others commented on the differences that opened up for them in this attention to the minute, to the close-ups of living: one commentator wrote that concentration and "flowing" were interrupted by the twitching eyelid of one performer on screen—and found the attention and reaction to this "irritant" very interesting and thought-provoking.

The aesthetics of *Traces* relied on the interaction between the spectator's witnessing engagement and the potential of physical movement unfolding before her. The silence of the still bodies invited intense scrutiny. At the same time, this desire to see never delivered its object into the full purview of the spectator. Too much was unseen, unknown. The silent bodies on the screen were not the silenced hysterical women of Charcot's photographs, who are fully read through their physicality, wholly known through the display of their symptoms through their limbs. Rather, the multiple-screen event fostered the intense presence of the performer's bodies, while withholding "truth": the soundtrack and the spectator's own experience cued her into the fact that these people were experiencing something that she could not see. The use of multimedia in a performance context allowed us to work with our images—not so much by withholding our bodies, but by placing ourselves in a liminal space between presence and absence, framed mediation and full availability. Breaking open the arrangements of activity and passivity that pertained in Charcot's presentation made spectators aware, seductively, of their own position in the vision machine. Traces of

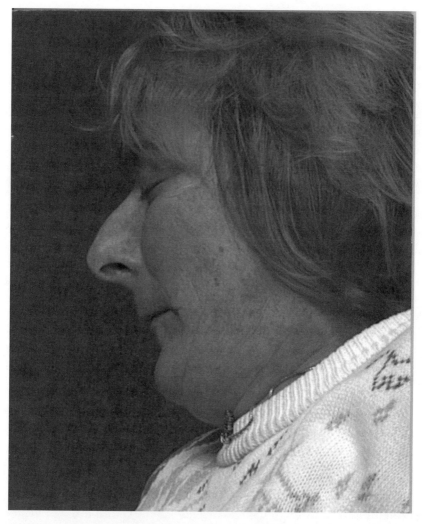

Video still from *Traces*. (© The Olimpias, 1999, photograph by Ju Gosling.)

difference remained (as in the "twitches" discussed by the spectator above), but they did not cohere into a still image, capturing a subject of a categorizing, intruding stare.

Moving & Touching

This engagement with knowing/unknowing and with the instability and mutability of difference in invisible impairments also fuels a different performance investigation. *Fight,* a performance installation by Ju Gosling, explores the echoes of bodies and movement across minimal spaces, in close-ups, caught by a camera that is physically presenced in the contact jams and dance improvisations. This work again used the video medium as a way to bring issues of identity much closer to the spectator, and to address the spectator in intimate ways. I came in contact with the creation of this work in 1999, as I was asked by disabled visual artist and webmistress Ju Gosling to workshop a dance sequence on her and a nondisabled performance artist, Helen Paris, as a preparation for the final gallery installation. Gosling has a pain-related impairment.

In the workshop, I asked the dancers to work with their eyes closed, and to rely on sound and touch as the initiators of movement. In warm-ups, I asked them to focus on somatic knowledges that differ from the outside view of the body; they worked with instructions to "move as if all skin, all muscles, etc." I attempted to get the dancers away from the outer, visual image of their bodies, disabled or nondisabled. As they struggled to explore their differences without visual input, that sense which most clearly divides them into different physicalities, I captured their touches and sways with a video camera. I attempted to get close and therefore had to move fast out of the way of feet or falling bodies. As the dancers became more comfortable with each other, and learned to thrust each other and the space in which they moved, I, as the camera person, had to engage with this trust. I had to feel kinesthetically where the dance would go, keeping close to gather the small exchanges and explorations. Watching the video afterwards, I could see the camera as a physical presence, not as the disembodied eye of classical cinema.

Challenged to move away from visual means of gathering knowledge, the dancers' movements went through strange phases. The close-up camera caught the traces of fights: the fight against fear, the fight against stereotypes, the fight against staying in secure places. Can I touch here? Will this induce pain? Where am I with the other's body? Who is leading? Who should lead? Is this safe?

Given the social differential between disabled and nondisabled people, these questions were fundamental to the choreography—they weren't there to be "overcome." Leading this workshop, I was not interested in "normalizing" the disabled body into the same space as the nondisabled body, but in trying to tease out implications of social categories, personal fears and their traces of bodies on the close, physical, noneveryday level of dance work. The fast, strange, distorted images of movement challenge the viewer to understand what she sees: the camera is too close to fully reveal the situation. This close-up, the intimacy of the camera and the video screen, cannot be achieved by the conventional stage situation. A dance performance in a very small circle, with dancers nearly touching the audi-ence, captures a similar engagement, but the strenuousness of the perfor-mance situation would have been dangerous to this disabled dancer.

Gosling went on to develop ideas from the workshop into a full chore-ography and filming process for the *Fight* gallery installation, which toured the United Kingdom in 2002 as part of the Adorn, Equip exhibition. The video shows her dancing with Layla Smith, a dancer and movement analyst, to music developed in composition and sound-engineering workshops at the Drake Music Project in South East London, which trains disabled peo-ple to use music technology. Another important visual aspect of the video is Gosling's decorated back brace (the costumes were by Andrew Logan). Adorn, Equip dealt specifically with design, and the aesthetic possibilities, of mobility aids, clothing, and adapted household products.

The specific meeting of performance and technology gives perfor-mance the chance to show us new constellations of bodies in movement.[7] The close-up of the camera allows us to break through stereotypes that we have of each other, of our bodies, and get nearer than the full, unified image would let us. The textures and hesitations of cloth, hands, swirling hair, and arching backs in contact with each other defy an easy political reading. No clear narrative is acted out by these bodies; we cannot see them as the disabled and the nondisabled artist, cautiously approaching each other in a metaphor for our political struggle. Instead, the fast-cut images and their kinesthetic charge, their dance across the video screen, merged these two dancers into a mélange of movement. The video mon-tage tried to re-create the experience of dancing, of moving wholly, focused on space, bodies, hesitations, encounters—too fast to step back into social categories. The spectators' access to these bodies is mediated, framed; we can see the traces of the live movements on the screen, but we are also aware that the viewpoint, the camera eye itself, is moving with the rhythm of the dancers. We are never outside the action, viewing it from a vantage point. Instead, we are in the dance itself, off-balance and impli-cated. The encounter between different physical experiences, different embodied lives, creates mysteries that are not resolved. You cannot get the bigger picture.

As the spectator is seduced by the camera in her act of viewing, we are dancing together. The spectator gives up her stable hold on seeing the dancers as others, staring at us as different bodies from her own. The spec-tator is no longer an audience member in a wooden lecture-theater, focused on imbibing the theatrical representation of difference. Instead, the spectator can choose to be taken up by the kinesthetic appeal of the moving camera joining the dance.

Installations such as *Traces* and *Fight*, with their implication of the active, corporeal viewer, are moving toward a space where difference is exciting and interesting, not swallowed up in the certainties of social meaning, with its distinction between normal and other. In *Fight,* the sensuous meeting of moving bodies, a caressing, dancing camera, and a spectator who has to experience in her own body the echoes of movement in order to see what is happening, can create this new performance space. In this space, the sensation of moving together becomes more important than the need to know what body is moving where, and what the movement signifies.

Instead of finding positive images for people with (partially) invisible impairments, the works discussed in these pages engage the un-knowing of difference as their horizon. They challenge the assumptions of visual symptomatology, clear photos, stages with delineated positions, and a choreographed theater of stares. Instead, they implicate the viewer in a physical engagement with the machinery of knowledges and encounters. Together, they move on.

Notes

1. The foundational texts for the study of hysteria as a narrative/physical disturbance are provided by Freud and Breuer (see Freud 1974). Hysteria has often been discussed as an individual strategy of absenting oneself from a patriarchal order. See, for example, Rosemary Betterton's discussion of hysteria imagery in the fight for women's suffrage (1996, 65–72). Luce Irigaray is the feminist writer most clearly associated with unanchoring the female body in serious play with language and materiality from its placement in male discursive practice, evoking it as a potentially powerful feminist languaging. Moira Gatens writes about the shift in gender relations that occurs when agency is redefined:

> At the same time as Irigaray's writings offer a challenge to traditional conceptions of women, [they introduce] the possibility of *dialogue* between men and women in place of the monological pronouncements made by men over the mute body of the (female) hysteric. (1992, 134)

Here, the refusal to "speak appropriately" becomes a positive act of inserting gendered difference on the limits of intelligibility. Another exciting avenue for research is the position hysteria maintains on the borders of soma and psyche. Like a number of other medical conditions, hysteria has been discussed as a moment where images stand in dialogue with morphology. Elizabeth Grosz discusses Lacan's perspective on hysteria:

> Lacan argues that instead of observing and following the neurological connections in organic paralyses, hysterical paralyses reproduce various naïve or everyday beliefs about the way the body functions. In an hysterical paralysis, it is more likely that limbs which are immobilised are unable to move from a joint, whereas in organic paralyses, the immobility extends further upwards

and encompasses many nerve and muscle connections not apparent to the lay observer. (1995, 190–91)

Grosz's understanding of the constructive nature of embodiment is not patronizing in relation to gender and class, a view that echoes Maurice Merleau-Ponty (1964) and Paul Schilder (1950) and their work on the plasticity of morphology:

> Like hysteria, hypochondria and sexuality itself, the phantom limb testifies to the pliability and fluidity of what is usually considered the inert, fixed, passive biological body. The biological body, if it exists at all, exists for the subject only through the mediation of an image or series of (social/cultural) images, of the body and its capacity for movement and action. (Grosz 1995, 191)

The issues of who is allowed to speak (or to remain silent), what is to move and where, and who can pronounce the "truth" of the body and fix its functioning are at the heart of debates in psychoanalysis, philosophy, and critical theory.

2. The relationship between somatic performance, knowledge, and psychology in late-nineteenth-century France is analyzed in Felicia McCarren's study of dance discourses (1998).

3. See, for example, Showalter 1987, 149ff.; Stephen Heath's discussion of hysteria's cultural transition from a disturbance in visuality to one cured by Freud's talking cure (1982, 33–49); Judith Mayne's discussion of the hysteric and the primitive (1990, 219–21); Barbara Creed's (1993) analysis of the womb, associated with the site of hysteria, as object of horror; Rebecca Schneider's discussion of performance artists such as Karen Finley who quote from women's history (1997, 115–16); and the account of visual fantasies of women in Victorian culture by Bram Dijkstra (1986), who discusses such topoi as the nymph with the broken back, the cult of invalidism, clinging vines, many of which are at work in the representations and cultural imagery of hysteria. Janet Beizer discusses "ventriloquized bodies," where the construction and maintenance of hysteria is a gendered struggle over the site of speech. She sees Charcot's engaged in the creation of a scenario where women's bodies signify through "inarticulate body language, which must be dubbed by a male narrator" (1994, 9).

4. Alan Read extends this discussion of theatrical hypnotism and psychoanalysis to Freud's consulting room, where a print of the Brouillet image hangs over the famous couch (2001, 156–58). In Charcot's lecture room, the Brouillet image together with two other representations of hysteria were installed over the actions and provided a pictorial script for appropriate actions (Bronfen 1998, 189; Gilman et al. 1993, 346).

5. Peggy Phelan reads the hysteric immobility in Freud's patient as staging ground for meanings, a case study of a proliferating production of resistance.

> The feminine body is, profoundly an auto-reproductive body, one that continues to reproduce symptoms and movement phrases that dance across the slippery stage of the paternal order. (1997, 68; also, in a different version, 1996, 101)

6. The Olimpias Performance Research Projects investigate participatory art, identity politics, and new media performance. Many Olimpias projects focus on disability culture, showing the richness and complexity of disabled people's lives and creativity. More information can be found at www.olimpias.net.

7. As Gosling continued to developed her piece in London, I created a video based on the aesthetics discussed here: *Touch* (2001) is a piece that focuses on two dancing backs: mine, the padded back of a woman of size, moving but mobility-impaired, and my collaborator, Raphaella Hill, who is a small-framed, mobile young woman. The resulting collaboration employed different senses—touch, smell, kinesthesia, etc.—to create the amalgamation of self and other discussed here. *Touch* was first exhibited as an installation consisting of lavender flowers, a small monitor with a looping video that viewers needed to hold, a silk meditation cushion and a Tibetan sound bowl, in Toronto as part of body/machines (2001), and was also screened at part of the Queer Disability conference in Oakland, California, in 2002.

Bibliography

Beizer, Janet. 1994. *Ventriloquized Bodies: Narratives of Hysteria in Nineteenth-Century France.* Ithaca: Cornell University Press.

Betterton, Rosemary. 1996. *An Intimate Distance: Women, Artists and the Body.* New York: Routledge.

Bronfen, Elisabeth. 1998. *The Knotted Subject: Hysteria and Its Discontents.* Princeton, N.J.: Princeton University Press.

Creed, Barbara. 1993. *The Monstrous-Feminine: Film, Feminism, Psychoanalysis.* London: Routledge.

Dijkstra, Bram. 1986. *Idols of Perversity: Fantasies of Feminine Evil in Fin-de-Siecle Culture.* New York: Oxford University Press.

Freud, Sigmund. [1948] 1974. *Collected Papers.* Vol. 2 of *The Standard Edition of the Complete Psychological Works of Sigmund Freud,* trans. J. Strachey. London: Hogarth.

Gatens, Moira. 1992. "Power, Bodies and Difference." In *Destabilizing Theory: Contemporary Feminist Debates,* ed. Michele Barrett and Anne Phillips, 120–37. Cambridge: Polity Press.

Gilman, Sander, et al. 1993. *Hysteria beyond Freud.* Berkeley: University of California Press.

Grosz, Elisabeth. 1995. "Psychoanalysis and the Imaginary Body." In *Feminist Subjects, Multi-Media: Cultural Methodologies,* ed. Penny Florence and Dee Reynolds, 183–96. Manchester: Manchester University Press.

Heath, Stephen. 1982. *The Sexual Fix.* London: Macmillan.

Kuppers, Petra. 2003. *Disability and Contemporary Performance: Bodies on Edge.* London: Routledge.

Mayne, Judith. 1990. *The Woman at the Keyhole: Feminism and Women's Cinema.* Bloomington: University of Indiana Press.

McCarren, Felicia. 1998. *Dance Pathologies: Performance, Poetics, Medicine.* Stanford, Calif.: Stanford University Press.

Merleau-Ponty, Maurice. 1964. *The Primacy of Perception.* Trans. James Edie. Evanston: Northwestern University Press.

Munthe, Alex. 1930. *The Story of San Michele*. London: John Murray.

Olimpias: www.olimpias.net.

Phelan, Peggy. 1996. "Dance and the History of Hysteria." In *Corporealities: Dance, Knowledge Culture and Power,* ed. Susan Leigh Foster, 90–105. London: Routledge.

Read, Alan. 2001. "The Placebo of Performance: Psychoanalysis in Its Place." In *Psychoanalysis and Performance,* ed. Patrick Campbell and Adrian Kear, 147–65. London: Routledge.

Schilder, Paul. [1935] 1950. *The Image and Appearance of the Human Body: Studies in the Constructive Energies of the Psyche.* New York: International University Press.

Schneider, Rebecca. 1997. *The Explicit Body in Performance*. London: Routledge.

Showalter, Elaine. 1987. *The Female Malady: Women, Madness and English Culture 830–1980.* London: Virago.

Performance as Therapy
Spalding Gray's Autopathographic Monologues

PHILIP AUSLANDER

G. Thomas Couser argues that one of the central characteristics of life writing (first-person, autobiographical writing) is the comic plot—the story that leads to a happy ending or, at least, to satisfactory closure. He points out, however, that one genre of life writing, autopathography (auto-biographical accounts of illness, injury, or disability), has a complex relationship to this convention. Although the mere existence of an autopathographic narrative suggests that the author was healthy and able enough to write it and thus implies a happy ending, the drive toward resolution that characterizes life writing is problematic "with regard to conditions that are chronic, systemic, or degenerative" and that may not lend themselves to being recounted using a convention that implies resolution.[1]

This question is even more exigent for *performed* autopathographies than written ones. While the written account stands as evidence that the author was in good enough shape to write it at the time of composition, it says nothing about the author's state at the time of reading—whether or not the narrative resolution was definitive or the author experienced a relapse, for instance. It may seem that *performing* autopathography resolves this question since the performer's presence before the audience provides a clear index to the performer's condition at the time of presentation. While this may be true for highly visible, physical conditions, less visible illnesses or disabilities—such as mental conditions—present a different problem since the act of performance may not provide direct insight into the performer's state.[2]

In this essay, I will explore the differences between written and performed autopathography in reference to Spalding Gray's autobiographical monologue performances. I will show that in Gray's case, the act of performance stands in a complex relationship to the pathologies he describes in his monologues. As written, Gray's autopathographic monologues partake of the comic plot structure. As performed, however, they function differently, in large part because performing is for Gray a form of therapy. I will discuss the relationship of certain basic dimensions of performance, including repetition and the presence of an audience, to the therapeutic uses Gray makes of performance. While the stories Gray tells resolve with versions of the comic plot's conventional happy ending, the act of performance does not lead to closure, and its therapeutic value to Gray does not reside in its ability to lead to a cure.

Gray, who turned sixty-two in 2003, has spent countless hours since 1979 carrying out the obsessive project of recounting his own existence in public. Sitting behind a desk and usually using only a microphone and a notebook as props, Gray regales his audiences with artfully constructed autobiographical stories that combine the ordinary with the extraordinary, fact with fancy. Ranging over time, Gray pursues themes and images back to his childhood and early life, then forward to his very recent past. By combining reminiscence with reportage, he juxtaposes long- and relatively short-term memories, experiences he has had time to consider and others that are still raw, to create associative patterns of experience rather than purely chronological narratives. Thanks to these autobiographical monologues, Gray has achieved considerable success—although he began by presenting them largely in avant-garde performance venues in New York City, he is now on the programs of many mainstream theaters around the world. Gray often presents himself as a writer; his monologues have been published in book form, and his performances have been adapted for film or television. His prominence as a monologist has also led to roles in mainstream theater, film, and television.

In his monologues, Gray sometimes focuses on instances of illness and disability, and it is to those narrative strands that I shall direct my attention here. I will discuss two of Gray's autopathographic narratives, one that deals primarily with a physical malady, the other with psychological distress.[3] The first is *Gray's Anatomy* (1993),[4] his account of developing an eye disease and seeking treatment for it. The second is Gray's recounting of the psychological discomfort caused by his identification with his mother, a Christian Scientist who committed suicide. The latter narrative has developed over the course of Gray's performing career and culminates in *It's a Slippery Slope* (1996). Gray refers to the years between ages fifty and fifty-three as "the Bermuda Triangle of health. Things start going wrong with you then, but if you make it through, then you live to be a ripe old age" (*Gray's Anatomy*, 53). It is significant, then, that the physical and psychological maladies he discusses in these two monologues occurred when Gray was between fifty and fifty-two. In addition to addressing specific problems Gray develops, these pieces reflect the anxiety intrinsic to the aging process: "HELP, I'M GROWING OLD! HELP, I'M GOING BALD! HELP, I'M GOING TO DIE!" (*Gray's Anatomy*, 77).

As literary works, both of these monologues conform quite closely to the generic conventions of autopathography. *Gray's Anatomy* follows most of the steps of a typical pathographic narrative: appearance of symptoms, medical diagnosis, assessment of treatment options, surgery, recovery and resolution.[5] In Gray's case, the symptom is an effect of disintegrating vision experienced during a storytelling workshop he's conducting. Afraid of finding out what actually may be wrong, Gray delays for four months before seeing an optometrist. The optometrist sends him immediately to an ophthalmologist, who diagnoses the illness and recommends a surgical procedure. Because he does not like the first ophthalmologist, he finds another but still delays the surgery to explore alternative treatments. After trying a variety of mostly New Age therapies, he agrees to the surgery. After recovering, Gray is pleased that his vision is partly restored. Gray acknowledges the conventionality of his story by comparing crucial moments to stereotyped media presentations of medical treatment. The optometrist's initial discovery of his condition is "like a scene from [the television soap opera] General Hospital"; Gray describes his first postsurgical visit to the hospital by saying, "I know this is supposed to be the dramatic part of the film: *Will the man see again or not?*" (*Gray's Anatomy*, 5, 73).

Arthur Frank points out that many stories of illness take the form of quest narratives: "Illness is the occasion for a journey that becomes a quest. What is quested for may never be wholly clear, but the quest is defined by the ill person's belief that something is to be gained through the experience."[6] Both *Gray's Anatomy* and *It's a Slippery Slope* are indeed quest narratives of this kind. In *Gray's Anatomy*, Gray quite literally embarks on a journey: his quest for alternative therapies takes him across the United States and then to the Philippines for psychic surgery. Ostensibly, he is testing out alternative cures; in reality, as he comes to realize, he is hoping that his illness will disappear magically. Gray embarks on his quest primarily to buy time. The surgery, when he finally undergoes it, is only partially successful, and he is left with very poor vision in his left eye, "like driving in a rainstorm without windshield wipers." What Gray gains through his quest is not what he expected; he is not fully cured. Rather, he gains a new emotional perspective: he cherishes his functioning right eye and no longer takes his vision for granted. And he concludes that "there's magic in the world. But there's also reality. And I have to begin to cope with the fact that I'm a little cockeyed" (*Gray's Anatomy*, 73–74). In other words, Gray has to overcome his initial panic at the prospect of losing his sight, accept that he will not be cured, and reconcile himself to the fact of being visually impaired. His play on the expression "cockeyed" is the punch line that brings the medical story to a happy ending.

Whereas *Gray's Anatomy* begins with a physical illness, *It's a Slippery Slope* takes mental dysfunction as its point of departure. As Gray approaches the age of fifty-two, he obsesses about his mother's suicide at that age and the possibility that he is destined to replicate her act. He describes himself as walking around Washington Square Park in New York City: "And I'm dwelling on the fact that I'm going to turn fifty-two years old, and I'm thinking about Mom, and how she committed suicide at fifty-two, and did that mean I was gonna do it, too?" Gray humorously indicates the strength of this identification moments later: "Now, I knew I wasn't my mother, or at least my friends told me I wasn't. I had to be reminded!" As his emotional crisis deepens, he finds himself replicating his mother's behavior during her breakdowns, behavior he had observed as a child: "As I got closer to fifty-two, [I began] to play it back or act it out in a kind of uncontrollable, obsessive reenactment of her. . . . I was acting out in public places, much the way Mom acted."[7]

It's a Slippery Slope is about many things: Gray's learning to ski, his betrayal of his wife, the birth of his son, and the death of his father. The issue of whether or not he must inevitably follow in his mother's footsteps and commit suicide is the central crisis, however, a crisis finally resolved during an epiphanic moment when Gray is skiing alone on a deserted mountain threatened by a storm. A childhood memory of wearing a snowsuit and being buried in snow provokes a suicidal impulse: "Why not let it all go and cuddle on down deep, deep into snow. . . . Not a bad way to go." But Gray does not surrender to the impulse; he presses on and catches sight of another skier, "a yellow figure that I immediately intuit to be a man" (104). The figure turns out to be an expert skier in his seventies, and Gray takes him on as a mentor by following him and skiing in his style. After they stop, the man asks Gray how he's doing. Gray responds: "To tell the truth, I don't know if I'm having a good time or trying to kill myself" and is told, "When you're in that place, you know you're alive." Gray takes comfort in this oracular rejoinder, concluding, "I have seen both a person and an apparition, the spirit of the future. That I, too, could be skiing at seventy, if I continued, if I took care of myself, skiing with my son if he wanted to ski" (105). Like his journey to the Philippines, Gray's quest on the ski slopes ends in insight and resolution.

Although the published texts of these monologues read very much like conventional examples of literary autopathography, they become something else when Gray performs them. Like all written autopathographies, Gray's monologues testify to the results of a course of treatment; performing them, however, is in itself therapeutic for him. To discuss this dimension of Gray's work, it is necessary to examine what he has said about performing. As a highly articulate and self-conscious performer, he has discussed his own work regularly in the monologues themselves, in other writings, and in interviews. Describing his transition from actor to autobiographical performer, Gray explains that he originally set out to be an actor in order to "live a passionate life onstage without consequences" (*Slippery Slope*, 5) but discovered that pretending to be someone else was not satisfying. He credits Richard Schechner, the director of the Performance Group, the experimental theater collective of which Gray was a member early in his career, with allowing him to "do what I wanted, be who I was," even while playing scripted roles, by permitting him to make "the role out of my immediate needs" rather than those of the character and thus to use the character as a vehicle for "personal actions."[8]

For Gray, the difference between conventional *acting* and *performing*, a crucial distinction in the lexicon of experimental theater and performance art, comes down to the difference between playing a character apart from oneself and playing oneself.[9] In Gray's view, the performer finally has no choice but to portray him- or herself: "Who else? Who else is there? How do you ever escape from yourself? Never."[10] This trajectory, from being an actor pretending to be someone else to playing himself through other characters, led Gray to the autobiographical monologue form. He became, as he puts it, "a kind of inverted Method actor. I was using myself to play myself . . . a kind of creative narcissism" (*Slippery Slope*, 6).

As early as 1977, Gray treated the self-examination in which he was engaged through performance as a form of therapy for his emotional and psychological difficulties. In the mid-1970s, the Wooster Group, a theater company that split off from the Performance Group, began a series of group performance pieces based on Gray's biography known collectively as the Rhode Island Trilogy (even though it ultimately had four parts).[11] One of those pieces, *Rumstick Road* (1977), grew in part out of Gray's fear "that I was identifying with my mother so much, that I had inherited the genetic quality of manic depressiveness" (quoted by Savran, *Breaking the Rules*, 74). For Gray, the making of *Rumstick Road* was a kind of therapy, as he notes in an essay published in 1979, around the time he started performing his autobiographical monologues: "At last I was able to put my fears of, and my identification with, my mother's madness into a theatrical structure. I was able to give it some therapeutic distance" ("About Three Places," 38–39).[12]

The therapeutic potential Gray attributes to performance distinguishes it from acting, which he sees as being "without consequences." In his 1979 statement on the subject, Gray describes the therapeutic distance that performance allows in terms that make it seem analogous to the autopathographic happy ending. Just as the comic plot allows the writer to contain a real event in a conventional narrative form that leads to an agreeable resolution, so the performer finds a way of expressing his psychic distress through a theatrical form and gains valuable, therapeutic distance from his own emotions by doing so. But when Gray has returned in later years to the question of how performance functions for him, he no longer suggests that therapeutic performance yields resolutions.

Brewster North, the protagonist of Gray's very thinly disguised autobiographical novel, *Impossible Vacation*,[13] published in 1992, explains that when he was a young actor, he wanted to play Konstantin Gavrilovich in a production of Chekhov's *Sea Gull*

> because of the way I often acted so tortured and hung up on Mom. That's exactly how Konstantin was: tortured, sensitive, and very much hung up on his mother. Also, and best of all, Konstantin gets to commit suicide at the end of the play—every night! over and over again!—and for some reason I thought that would be really neat, to be able to kill myself every night and come back to life the following evening to do it again.[14]

At one level, this passage may express what is at stake for Gray in negotiating his identification with his mother through performance: the appeal of committing suicide on stage without really dying derives from Brewster's feeling that because he is like his mother, he is destined also to commit suicide. Reappearing each night to kill himself anew is a way of both fulfilling and trumping her legacy. (It is worth noting in passing that the mode of performing Gray describes here draws on both acting and performance, as he defines them. Because the suicide is acted, it is without consequences. But because the performer is really playing out his own psychological trauma, not the character's, the performance can have a therapeutic effect.) In this case, the therapeutic effect derives not from the performer's using the stage as a means of re-creating aspects of his life but from the *difference* between the performer's lives on- and offstage: acting Konstantin would allow Brewster both to live out the consequences of his identification with his mother and to refuse that destiny. Offstage, he doubts that he has any control over what happens.

The element of *repetition* in this process is critically important. Brewster does not imagine that enacting suicide this way will enable him to resolve his troublesome identification with his mother and thus achieve the closure of a comic plot. Rather, he imagines his performance of suicide as something that would take place "every night! over and over again!" and in fact derives pleasure from the prospect of this endless opportunity to enact on stage the destiny he seeks to avoid in real life. In this passage from the novel, Gray points to an aspect of performance that many theorists take to be fundamental: that performative behavior is designed to be repeated. One of Schechner's basic definitions of performance is, in fact, "twice-behaved behavior"; such behavior creates the impression of never having occurred for a first time but of always having been caught up in an economy of repetition.[15]

What Brewster's anecdote and Schechner's definition both suggest is that performance complicates the autopathographic project because repetition of the same, rather than resolution and closure, are intrinsic to it. Although the plot of any given play or performance may reach an ending—happy or otherwise—that very plot is a pattern of action designed to be performed over and over again in a potentially infinite reiteration of the same. In other words, performance qua performance resists closure. This is not the case for a book, of course, and this is a key difference between literary autopathography and performed autopathography. For the literary version to function in the same way as a performance, the author would have to write the same text over and over again, more or less identically each time, for different audiences at different times.

In fact, Gray's ongoing autobiographical performance project thematically reflects the inability of his version of therapeutic performance to produce closure, for issues that might seem to have been resolved in one monologue reappear unresolved in later ones. I have already noted that Gray first addressed his damaging psychological identification with his mother in a performance piece of 1977, yet the emotional havoc wrought by that same complex is still at the heart of *It's a Slippery Slope* some nineteen years later. Likewise, the visual impairment to which Gray seems to have reconciled himself at the end of *Gray's Anatomy* reappears in *It's a Slippery Slope*. At one point in the later monologue, while skiing happily down a mountain, experiencing flow and enjoying the view, Gray reiterates the conclusion of *Gray's Anatomy* by expressing gratitude to his right eye for allowing him that enjoyment and "not behaving like my left eye." Later in the monologue, however, when he's skiing in a moment of growing crisis, he can no longer put a positive spin on his condition, but says only, "Can't see with my bad eye in this flat light" (*Slippery Slope*, 45, 96). The blunt description of his impaired eye as his bad eye, the telegraphic style of the sentence, and the staccato rhythm of single syllables all convey the depression that colors Gray's feelings about his physical condition and suggest that Gray has not really achieved the acceptance of his disability implied by the earlier monologue.

To the extent that Gray's individual monologues end happily, the agent of that resolution is often a man older than Gray himself. Gray's epiphany on the ski slope in *It's a Slippery Slope* results from an encounter with such a figure, the yellow-suited skier who serves as Gray's temporary Zen master. A similar, though surprising, figure appears in *Gray's Anatomy*. While waiting in his doctor's office, Gray sees someone he takes to be Richard Nixon; since Gray's eyes are dilated, he isn't sure of the identification, but the doctor confirms it, saying, "Nothing the matter with *him.*" For some unstated reason, this glimpse of Nixon allows Gray to agree to surgery after his quest for alternative cures: "It was seeing Richard Nixon come out of my doctor's office that gave me the faith and courage to have the operation" (71).

It is not clear just why seeing Nixon has this effect on Gray. But it is interesting that the epiphanic moments in both monologues, the events that allow Gray to address physical or psychological impairments, hinge on these chance encounters with healthy-seeming older men. Especially in the context of Gray's ruminations on his mother's suicide and the degree to which his own fate may be determined by hers, these moments suggest that Gray's ability to deal with both his eye disease and his psychological problems depends on his identifying with a father figure. His need for such a figure is perhaps indicated by his saying that he intuited that the figure he saw skiing was male before choosing to follow him. Both figures also seem to be surrogates for Gray himself—imagined older versions of himself who have come through trauma and appear to be in control of their own lives. In the monologues, Gray envisions himself achieving their apparent physical and mental health; to that end, he uses them as talismans or guides and as images of what his own future will be if he can surmount his current obstacles.

But these older male figures in the monologues function in another way, too. In addition to being surrogate father figures and stand-ins for Gray's imagined versions of his older self, they are surrogates for his audience. In a newspaper interview, Gray discusses a moment in the fall of 2002 when, suffering from the physical after-effects of a serious automobile accident and reeling from bouts of delusional behavior, he considered suicide on a bridge.

> I was contemplating jumping but what stopped me was this guy there. A foreign guy. A stranger. . . . He didn't speak much English. But I was kind of showing him that that's what I wanted to do. I was lifting my leg, and he was going, "No, no, no!" It probably was a cry for help, and I was certainly overmedicated. But I really don't know if I would have jumped if he weren't there.[16]

This real-life event clearly parallels those described in the monologues: Gray is rescued once again by a male figure whose presence dissuades Gray from engaging in self-destructive behavior. The older skier, Nixon, and the man on the bridge are all strangers to Gray and are all, in that sense, "foreign" (even Nixon, since Gray would have no reason to expect an encounter with him). Because they are strangers, Gray can project onto them whatever meanings he needs them to represent, and their appearances at traumatic moments seem to allow Gray to achieve therapeutic distance from his own impulses. It is not just that Gray needs someone to tell him what to do (or not do) or to serve as a model at such moments—it is also that he apparently needs to be in the presence of someone else. That presence, perhaps even more than the other person's ability to advise him, allows Gray to see himself through another's eyes and act accordingly. These older male figures are, in short, audiences, and their presence leads Gray away from the brink.

In a passage from *It's a Slippery Slope* in which he recounts his own increasingly erratic behavior, Gray recounts an anecdote that suggests the complex dynamic of performer and audience that makes performance therapeutic for him.

> I was beginning to act out. And I was acting out in public places, much the way Mom acted. I'd be muttering to myself and involuntarily shouting out, but no one really noticed that in New York City. I can remember screaming in the streets at night and hearing my scream picked up by other people who passed it down the street for blocks and blocks. What started out as real panic was turned into a performance by the people. (55)

Here, Gray refers again to the distinction between performance and real life that is central to his notion of therapeutic distance. Because his accidental audience perceives his behavior as a performance, it ceases to be "real panic." There is an interesting ambiguity in the way Gray tells this story—it is unclear whether his behavior becomes a performance because it is perceived as one by the others who replicate it or whether their replication of Gray's screams makes his own behavior into a performance for which he becomes the audience. Perhaps both things occur: New Yorkers on the street become the audience for Gray's behavior, which they perceive as a performance. Their response to that perceived performance, their replication of Gray's behavior, becomes a performance to which Gray serves as audience. He thus becomes a spectator to his own behavior filtered through performance. As in the circumstances he recounts in the monologues, the presence and reaction of an audience creates for Gray a different vantage point from which to perceive the symptoms of his mental illness.

In the very next passage of *It's a Slippery Slope*, Gray addresses his relationship to the theatrical audience for his monologues by observing that even when he was out of control in his offstage life, he could still perform effectively on stage: "In fact, I welcomed the isolated protection of the stage. Telling a life was so much easier than living one. Although there were times I'd be in the Mom Mode all the way up to the stage door, barking and twisting on my way to the theater" (55–56). Here, Gray treats the stage as a safe space, much as he does in the account of *Rumstick Road* cited earlier. But there is a crucial difference. At this point, the stage no longer provides Gray with therapeutic distance. Rather than being a safe place to enact and thus dispel his anxieties, the stage becomes the only place where Gray can behave *as if he were not in the grip of those anxieties.* Up to the moment at which he arrives at the stage door, Gray is fully possessed by his psychic demons; once he is out on stage, he is able to behave as if that were not the case by appearing to be in sufficient control to perform.

Gray's theatrical audiences do not necessarily function the way the older male figures in the monologues do—there is no reason to suppose that Gray sees in the audience models for his own behavior. It is not even clear that the audience in the theater serves Gray in the same way as the accidental audience on the street; it seems unlikely that the theater audience will allow Gray to see his own behavior differently by refracting it. But the theater audience's physical presence apparently does function like the presence of those older men in one important respect: it defines an occasion for Gray to present himself as someone who is in control of his actions. Like the presence of the older men in his stories, the presence of the audience allows Gray to retreat from his anxieties. This retreat is temporary—it is itself a performance that takes place only while Gray is in the other's presence. Perhaps this helps to explain why the prospect of simulating suicide nightly appealed to Brewster, Gray's alter ego. Onstage, Brewster can control his destiny by enacting suicide and survival, a desirable experience that he cannot replicate offstage.

Performance seems to serve Gray as therapy in two very different ways. His earlier formulation of therapeutic distance suggests that performance allowed him to achieve a more objective stance toward his own psychological problems by examining them through the mediation of theatrical production. More recently, however, Gray has suggested that it is not the opportunity to represent his own experience onstage that is therapeutic but the ability to use performance as a means of enacting himself in a controlled way of which he is not necessarily capable offstage. The presence of an audience before which he must appear as a performer capable of controlling his self-presentation rather than a man in the grips of psychological disorders that reduce such control seems crucial to this version of therapeutic performance. Whereas the earlier version depended on Gray's replicating his life onstage (at least metaphorically), the later one depends for its therapeutic effect on the differences between Gray's ability to control his own behavior onstage and offstage.

This latter form of therapeutic performance is bound up with performance's economy of repetition. If Gray experiences self-control onstage, he must perform in order to have that experience. The fact that Gray is able to perform does not imply that he has recovered from the psychological afflictions he describes in some of his monologues, even when those monologues reach narrative closure. Gray does not perform because he feels better—he feels better when he performs. Whereas we experience autopathographic writings as the end products of a process through which the writer recovered sufficiently to write, when we see Gray perform, we witness the process itself through which Gray seeks recovery rather than an artifact of his recovery, a repetitive process that offers no clear possibility of closure or resolution. John Moore, the journalist who wrote the newspaper profile of Gray from which I quoted earlier, clearly understood that Gray's version of therapeutic performance does not partake of the comic plot, for his article is entitled "No Happy Ending to Spalding Gray story."

Postscript

In January 2004, as this book was going to press, Spalding Gray was reported missing. His body was discovered two months later. His death apparently was the suicide he had threatened or attempted several times and that was a preoccupation of his monologues. He will be missed.

Notes

1. G. Thomas Couser, *Recovering Bodies: Illness, Disability, and Life Writing* (Madison: University of Wisconsin Press, 1997), 14; hereafter cited parenthetically.

2. Philosopher Stan Godlovitch, writing about musical performance, points out that "we certainly have no working theory of the inner mental side of artistic performance. . . . Performers at work may have their minds on any manner of things. In the spirit of professional entertainment, someone performing sensitively may simultaneously be bored to distraction" (*Musical Performance: A Philosophical Study* [London: Routledge, 1998], 127).

3. This distinction between physical and psychological maladies is artificial, of course, and Gray always represents the physiological as bound up with the psychological and vice versa. In *Gray's Anatomy,* when Gray is initially diagnosed with an eye ailment and his doctor asks him what he thinks caused it, Gray can think of only one possible physical cause, a woman's accidentally grazing his eye with her fingernail some fifteen years earlier. When that incident turns out to be implausible as a cause, he turns immediately to psychological causation, thinking at first that his eye problem resulted from his never having grieved properly for his deceased mother: "My left eye just cried, in a big way. It exploded into one big tear." He goes on to suppose that the macula pucker may have resulted from his Oedipus complex: "The unconscious part of me . . . is reaching up and scratching out one eye at a time" (*Gray's Anatomy* [New York: Vintage, 1994], 10–11; hereafter cited parenthetically). Here,

Gray suggests not just that his psychological state influences his perception of his physical condition, but that his psychological complexes may be the causes of his physical problems. Gray's analysis of the causal connection between the physical and the psychological may be part of Gray's inheritance from his mother, a Christian Scientist who impressed upon him that physical illness is caused by mental and spiritual "errors" (*Gray's Anatomy*, 14).

4. Parenthetical dates following titles of performances refer to when the piece was first performed, not to publication.

5. This list is adapted from Couser's list of the identifying features of breast cancer narratives (*Recovering Bodies*, 42). Because breast cancer narratives constitute the largest category of first-person accounts of illness, the subgenre provides a good model for autopathography in general.

6. Arthur W. Frank, *The Wounded Storyteller* (Chicago: University of Chicago Press, 1995), 115.

7. Spalding Gray, *It's a Slippery Slope* (New York: Noonday Press, 1997), 19, 21, 53, 55; hereafter cited parenthetically in the text.

8. Spalding Gray, *About Three Places in Rhode Island*, in *Drama Review* 23, no. 1 (1979): 33; hereafter cited parenthetically in the text.

9. Michael Kirby's 1972 essay "On Acting and Not-acting," an important early entry into the discourse that seeks to distinguish acting from other forms of performance, is available in *Performance: Critical Concepts*, vol. 1, ed. Philip Auslander (London: Routledge, 2003), 309–23.

10. Quoted by David Savran, *Breaking the Rules: The Wooster Group* (New York: Theatre Communications Group, 1988), 63; hereafter cited parenthetically in the text.

11. For a full account of the history of the Wooster Group and its relationship to the Performance Group, see Savran, *Breaking the Rules*.

12. Gray's is not the only formulation of performance as therapy, of course. For a brief overview of psychotherapeutic methods that draw on ideas of role-playing and performance, see Marvin Carlson, *Performance: A Critical Introduction* (London: Routledge, 1996), 45–48. In my essay "'Holy Theatre' and Catharsis," I discuss several modern theorists who see a therapeutic potential in theater itself (in *From Acting to Performance* [London: Routledge, 1997], 13–27). One of the most influential of current figures to bridge theater and psychotherapy is Augusto Boal; see Daniel Feldhendler, "Augusto Boal and Jacob L. Moreno: Theatre and Therapy," in *Playing Boal: Theatre, Therapy, Activism*, ed. Mady Schutzman and Jan Cohen-Cruz (London: Routledge, 1994), 87–109.

13. Gray worked on *Impossible Vacation* over a very long period of time. The highly problematic gestation of the novel is the subject of one of his monologues, *Monster in a Box* (New York: Vintage, 1992).

14. Spalding Gray, *Impossible Vacation* (New York: Alfred A. Knopf, 1992), 47.

15. Richard Schechner, *Between Theater and Anthropology* (Philadelphia: University of Pennsylvania Press, 1985), 36.

16. Quoted by John Moore, "No Happy Ending to Spalding Gray Story," *Denver Post*, February 28, 2003, FF1.

The Facilitation of Learning-Disabled Arts

A Cultural Perspective

GILES PERRING

> How we view people with disabilities'has less to do with what they are physiologically than who we are culturally.
> —Robert Bogdan, *Freak Show*

In a discussion of disability and performance, it is worth giving space to an exploration of the work of people with learning disabilities. This an area of arts practice that raises particular questions because of the frequent involvement of non-learning-disabled people in the production of the work. This may, at one level, involve "access providers," who render practical support, but it may also involve other nondisabled people who fund or plan the work at a strategic level. Finally, the work is often facilitated by nondisabled arts practitioners. Because of the frequently central role of these practitioners, their involvement in the creative process raises significant questions about the mediation of the learning-disabled artist's eventual work.

This essay will therefore discuss aspects of the relationship of nondisabled arts practitioners to the learning-disabled people with whom they work. It is drawn from research carried out between 1996 and 1999 that sought explanations and meanings for the active choices of nondisabled artists and arts practitioners to undertake creative project work with learning-disabled people. Because of the disparate and evolutionary nature of creative arts projects for people with learning disabilities, arts practitioners in the United Kingdom have often worked without the academic and methodological foundations or the intercommunication that are features of other disciplines such as the more recognized, and distinct, field of the arts therapies. My research, and with it this essay, is intended to raise what may be common themes and shared experiences that, in themselves, may contribute to a developing discussion of this subject.

Learning-Disabled People & the Arts

In recent years, the creative work and the performances of learning-disabled people have gained an increased profile in the United Kingdom. However, learning-disabled artists' preparation and exhibition of their works has invariably been achieved through collaboration with, and facilitation by, nondisabled people. In the United Kingdom, this is often achieved within the framework of an area of practice known as *arts and disability* projects. Historically, this term describes the bringing of the arts to people with disabilities, most frequently within and by a nondisabled host culture and often (in effect) as a reflection of the interests and values of that host culture. While it may share ingredients, and occasionally its practitioners, with the arts therapies, it remains a separate project. It aims to provide a means of accessing the arts while assuming little or no therapeutic agenda (although arts-and-disability projects may often be programmed by occupational therapists for whom some therapeutic outcomes may be an objective). Arts-and-disability work aims to ensure the integration and, more latterly, inclusion of disabled people in the arts.

In the United Kingdom, arts-and-disability projects grew out of the endeavors of organizations like Shape (later to become Shape London and form part of a national network of arts projects),[1] which was originally founded on a charitable model by a nondisabled dancer called Gina Levete. The arts-and-disability initiative in the United Kingdom has gradually encountered criticism from the similarly named, but politically and structurally different, disability arts movement. Organizations such as the United Kingdom's National Disability Arts Forum (NDAF) have looked to supplant the preponderance in arts and disability of nondisabled administrators, facilitators, and practitioners involved in both the artistic production of disabled people and the decisions about its funding, and to go on to promote a disability culture.[2] Indeed, Shape itself has gone on to recruit disabled people, both at a planning and production level and as artists and facilitators in order to see through this vision.

While the disability arts movement has carried its activity forward, much artistic work by people with learning disabilities continues to be facilitated by people without learning disabilities. The extent and nature of this involvement varies, and in many cases work continues in arts-and-disability projects run by arts practitioners and workers who are not disabled people. As a consequence, an interaction takes place that is not so apparent in the disability arts scene. Within a movement that looks to bring learning-disabled people into an arts discourse, the work of learning-disabled performers and artists is often mediated to audiences by nondisabled artists and facilitators. The nature of this interaction and the experiences of the nondisabled artists involved—their motivations, their goals, their artistic objectives, and their social and cultural intent—beckon questions.

In an arts-and-disability "industry" that is increasingly developing a trajectory founded on concepts of *inclusion,* it is vital to acknowledge and explore the interests of the nondisabled artist who often works with and facilitates the learning-disabled performer. Where such a reflexive approach is overlooked, the presentation of the learning-disabled "body" or subjectivity may be unconsciously determined and represented by a nondisabled cultural interest and perspective. However, if it is encouraged, it might offer the chance to work toward a creative collaboration that permits the full expression of individual subjectivity and experience for all involved.

In a recent small ethnographic study (Perring 1999), I conducted semistructured life history interviews with a self-selecting sample of nondisabled artists who were working across art forms with people with learning disabilities in London. The objective was to relate aspects of their experience to a cultural understanding of the arts and learning disability phenomenon. The findings raised a number of themes, which might inform a discussion and critique of the role of arts practitioners in the creative output of people with learning disabilities. For the purposes of this essay I shall introduce and summarize some of the main aspects of the research to date.

To understand the aesthetic, political, and cultural environment in which arts and disability takes place, it is valuable to contextualize the ideas at play. It is important to discuss the conceptual role of learning disability as a diagnostic tool, educational calibrator, and cultural construct. It may also be valuable to consider the historical interest of Euro-American artists in ideas and stimuli that spring from sources frequently collectively categorized as the Other—in particular, how they might regard and align themselves with alternative aesthetic approaches, altered states and an interest in alternative, *anti* or *non* technique. I shall cover some of these issues briefly below.

Learning Disability

In the United Kingdom, *learning disability* is a catchall terminology (used in conjunction with gradations with like *mild* or *moderate, severe,* and *profound*) that is employed by medical and social support agencies to categorize a wide range of "conditions." These include autism, Down's syndrome and impairments that were formally described, in lay and professional discourse, as *mental handicaps* and *mental disabilities.* In North American usage these categories might most closely translate as *intellectual* or *developmental disabilities* or its predecessor, *mental retardation.*

The modeling of disability is a well-rehearsed discourse that I shall not revisit at length here. However, I do not want to ignore key ideas that inform an understanding of the way that learning-disabled people *access* the arts. Within a "medical" model (Oliver 1999) of disability, the functional construction of "learning disability" (Perring 1999) as a deficit "condition" lies behind an institutional system that, as in many other areas of their lives, has limited learning-disabled people's opportunities to make informed artistic choices. The management of their lives through social (at both institutional and family levels) and medical care structures, combined with issues of access if they have physical impairments too, can limit the kind of heuristic exploration of the arts that a nondisabled person might take for granted. While the forces that lie behind such treatment are the focus of "social" modeling of disability, learning-disabled people's institutionalization, in addition to their marginalization, may, as we shall see, provide a measure of stimulus and motivation for the nondisabled artists who work with them.

Community Arts

The economic climate and employment legislation in Great Britain in the 1980s ensured that a number of arts practitioners enlisted with charitable and nongovernmental agencies to carry out work within community settings. This, in turn, brought them into contact, often for the first time, with people with disabilities (Perring 1999). The Thatcher government had responded to increasingly high unemployment by introducing a variety of temporary employment and training opportunities. Some of these schemes could pay for part-time workers on projects that were of a social or community outlook. This gave organizations like Shape and Community Music occasion to take on previously unemployed arts workers, so artists, actors, dancers, and musicians found themselves being offered a small wage to be trained and to work on arts projects in settings like hospitals, prisons, schools, and social services day centers. Although government schemes have come and gone, the arts-and-disability "industry" has become a means of offering practicing artists the opportunity to earn money away from the commodified arts market, and it has contributed to a "community arts" scene. However, significant artistic events and movements in the nineteenth and twentieth centuries may also have contributed to the readiness of later nondisabled artists to work with people with learning disabilities.

Art & the Other

The history of twentieth-century art points to the impact of the concept of "otherness" in the development of new aesthetic standpoints, and it has provided a means of finding new forms of expression and representational languages. It has enabled artists to position themselves (oppositionally) with respect to prevailing social and cultural mores. "The Other" and "Otherness" accommodate a number of notions that expand on the earlier *colonial* constructions of a non-European Other, and those ideas, promulgated among others by Prinzhorn, Dubuffet, Breton, and the surrealists, that dwelt on naïveté, primordiality, and the relationship of madness and genius. An artistic interest in the Other as a means of instigating debate and as countercultural metaphor, while it exploded with the surrealists and expressionists, has continued to develop in the "transgressive" work of writers, artists, and performers like Michel Foucault, Annie Sprinkle, Genesis P. Orridge, Boyd Rice, Kathy Acker, and Orlan.

In the context of this discussion, *the Other* describes a cultural manifestation of human characteristics or behaviors that effect a perception of the actor as different from mainstream constructions of a social person and societal member. It expresses the idea that difference, of many kinds, is a force in culture. It is at once recognition and assertion of someone's or something's right to be "different" and expresses it as a necessary counterweight to a notion of "normality." It is both a threat toward, and an incitement to challenge, established ideas of art and being.

Fascination with the *colonial* "Other" is evident in the valorization of non-Western artifacts and creation in primitivism and like movements (Rhodes 1994). However, with the unveiling, in 1922, of the Prinzhorn Collection of art, made in German-speaking psychiatric hospitals across Europe in the late nineteenth and early twentieth centuries, a new "Other" was seized upon by artists. On the one hand, the "insane" artist was an "endogenous primitive" (MacLagan 1991), on the other a transgressive. "Insane" art impacted heavily on the dadaists and surrealists who responded to the notion of an unleashing of the subconscious mind. So influential was this work that Max Ernst, for example, "borrowed" from work in the Prinzhorn Collection (MacGregor 1989). For expressionists like Paul Klee, "insane" art was primordial, *ursprunglich* (MacGregor 1989). Later on, Jean Dubuffet, through the Compagnie de l'Art Brut (Company of Raw Art) championed art by children, prisoners, and psychiatric patients in a body of work that actively sought to overthrow a dominant and "asphyxiating" aesthetic culture (Dubuffet 1988; Cardinal 1972).

In music too, interest in, and absorption of, the Other is a celebrated ingredient in classical, jazz, rock, and world musics. Recently, critical attention has been directed toward the impact of so-called world and ethnic musics on European and American composition and musical consumption (Born and Hesmondhalgh 2000). Rock music has drawn heavily on the Other in its absorption of African American music, but it has also felt the influence of Art school culture, and methodologies not solely located in musical technique and theory (Frith and Horne 1987). Meanwhile, the commodification of "madness" and "deviancy," through "wild men of rock" like Jim Morrison, Keith Moon, and Jimi Hendrix,[3] is an essential marketing tool in a countercultural package (Walser 1983) that is informed by earlier trends in art.

Like earlier figures in the history of art, musicians such as Frank Zappa have been able to act counterculturally through their espousal of "deviant" performers like Larry "Wild Man" Fischer. Zappa found Fischer singing on the street to people who "thought he was crazy"; Fischer's mother "had him committed to a mental institution several times" (Fischer 1968). The creative relationship between Zappa and Fischer provides food for thought in considering where the artistic gesture is situated in projects of this kind. Zappa cut what has become a cult album with Fischer, *An Evening with Wild Man Fischer;* far from making Fischer a big time name, it outraged the conservative record industry Zappa despised (Perring 1999; Watson 1995). This episode resonates, though less tragically, with Breton's relationship with the woman he called Nadja (Breton 1960), whose behavior, which ultimately led to her incarceration in a psychiatric hospital, Breton saw as the embodiment of a surrealist ideal and which he shaped into the material for a celebrated text (MacGregor 1989).

These latter examples are cautionary tales, but illustrate considerations in collaborations where power and access to an audience are vested unequally.

Alternative Aesthetics

While the example of Zappa points us toward political issues at play in the relationship of artists to the Other, his genuine regard for Fischer as a performer signals other influences and interests that need consideration in a contextual understanding of the potential motivations of artists and facilitators working with learning-disabled people. Apart from his fascination with the transgressive, Zappa, like others, valued intuitive performance and nonconventional technique and sonorities.

Across art forms, there is considerable historical, aesthetic, and intellectual investment in the concept of technique. In my own principal art form, music, other methodologies have permeated music education discourse and, as a consequence, that of music facilitation. Approaches that emerge both from improvisatory music such as free jazz (e.g., Alan Wilkinson and John Stevens) and nonmusical, non-Western philosophies such as the I-Ching (e.g., John Cage) challenge the orthodoxies that have flowed from the European classical tradition, for many years the dominant model in United Kingdom music education. They have been significant in the growth of a musical culture that has opened some practitioners up to musicality within people with learning difficulties that virtuosic traditions might overlook. Some musicians, such as John Stevens, and visual artists have explored what is possible at the *edge* of technique and what occurs with what might be described as *non-* or *anti*technique. Stevens's work with Community Music in London was the basis for the workshop practice of a number of musicians functioning in community arts settings from the mid-1980s onward. Equally, composers such as Cornelius Cardew and Karlheinz Stockhausen have developed creative processes in order to access intuitive, as opposed to preconceived or familiar, approaches to music making. Cardew, in such work as *The Great Learning* (composed in 1969), developed compositional strategies for a disciplined approach to a spontaneous performance that could involve a mixed ensemble (of trained and untrained players), while Stockhausen, for example, called for his performers to adopt particular strategies in order to prepare for a performance:

> live completely alone for 4 days
> without food
> in complete silence, without much movement
> sleep as little as necessary
> think as little as possible
> after 4 days, late at night,
> without conversation beforehand play single sounds
> without thinking which you are playing
> close your eyes
> just listen. (Stockhausen 1972, sleeve notes)

In both instances, the performer is expected, not to produce a virtuosic extravaganza, but to find a means of entering into an intuitive mode of playing.

John Cage, meanwhile, has influenced the way a contemporary musician listens to music and sound. This might include a musical appreciation of "the sound of a truck at fifty miles an hour" (1978a, 3). He also challenged the idea of the mistake: "A mistake is beside the point, for once something happens it authentically is" (1978b, 59).

While these musicians' works are not associated with learning-disabled people, their approach to music may directly or indirectly inform the musical interests of contemporary arts practitioners and may suggest modes of approaching musicality and performance that have a more open orientation toward aesthetic value.

The Study

In exploring the way in which nondisabled artists' involvement might affect arts-and-disability work, I adopted an ethnographic approach based in qualitative research methods such as grounded theory (Glaser and Strauss 1967). Unlike more positivist methodologies, which, for example, rely on the attempted *falsification* of a proposition in order to prove a hypothesis, grounded theory is based in the generation of hypotheses from themes that are grounded in the data and that progressively emerge as a research project unfolds. This organic approach to the identification and examination of questions resonates strongly with my own creative practice. This ethnographic approach to the subject material focused on what artists said about their work and lives rather than critiquing their artistic output. Through interviewing based on a *life history* approach, I obtained accounts that include descriptions of work and reflections on artistic goals and outcomes, but these are primarily examined in terms of what they say about the motivations and interests of nondisabled artists in working in this field. Life history interviewing offered a holistic approach to my exploration of the manner in which nondisabled arts workers come to be active in the arts-and-disability field.

The ten arts practitioners with whom I spoke came forward as a result of a letter that I circulated via three London arts-and-disability organizations. They came from areas of practice that included visual and plastic arts, dance, drama, and music, but their work often combined these art forms in a multidisciplinary way. Their backgrounds reflected training in the arts therapies, mainstream theater, fine art, community arts, and the often autodidactic training of rock music.

Arts Practitioners' Experiences & Personal Accounts

The respondents' first encounters with people with learning disabilities often resulted from placements at college or through government-funded employment with arts organizations in the 1980s, though some had experience of learning disability at home or in the family. In addition to formal arts-and-disability projects, some arts practitioners had found their way into the work through informal, community arts projects started in squatted premises, having bypassed more established routes to artistic practice and employment. In many instances, however, the artists described their first encounters with learning-disabled people as having been filled with apprehension, revealing the extent of segregation that occurs within Britain.

> *Caitlin:* When I think back from how I am now I was really scared. I'd never met learning disabled people. I didn't know how I'd react, how they would react to me. How would we communicate?
> *Q:* What formed those fears?
> *Caitlin:* Probably when I grew up . . . [T]here was a special school a mile away from us and I'd see them on the bus. I was scared [because] they were different, scared they might come and sit next to me and start talking. Now I'd think it was friendly but then I would have found it threatening, [because] I didn't know how to handle it. They were unpredictable, they don't stick to the same norms as us, and when I started placement I didn't know how to cope either. (Perring 1999, 87)

Fears like these did not often persist and were replaced by new constructions of people with learning disabilities. These positive reconstructions were often paired with an equally negative response to institutional environments in which respondents had to work. Many found the institutional environment oppressive and anticreative, and they saw the artistic work they facilitated as a means of showing what people could do when given the chance.

> The support staff make the person do something when you want it done through choice (shouting) "Go on then, do it!!" that kind of right and wrong atmosphere where people in the session might think you're looking for particular thing that is right and if someone doesn't do it they're wrong and they've failed, and my whole way of working is that you don't ever fail in the Arts.

> I think that for many people there's a low expectancy of what people with disabilities can produce, in terms of performance, and there's a lot of feeling of cotton wool around them. (Perring 1999, 93)

Respondents described an exciting and rewarding spontaneity in learning-disabled people.

> [There's] the whole aesthetic of how the [theatrical] ensemble works together as a really strong ensemble, there's the different quality they bring to performing that's informed by learning disability which I find really interesting—it works on a number of different levels, different layers.

> What I enjoy about watching people with learning difficulties perform—their aesthetic—is this sense of raw energy—Heart'n'Soul[4]—that kind of thing. You're using that spontaneity, energy and that interpretation of life and making it into a performance so you still feel it's owned by the people who are performing it and they've done it their own way. (Perring 1999, 100)

The interviews presented a wide range of experiences, uncovering themes that can only be mentioned briefly here.[5] Artists often came to their work with people with learning disabilities out of dissatisfaction with the mainstream arts. They were looking for something outside a milieu they felt to be at once competitive, conservative, and short on opportunity for self-expression. Drawing on this experience, in their workshop and project work they strove to create a different environment for participants.

Many respondents found that the experience of working in the arts had located them outside mainstream society, although work with people with learning disabilities had also offered them a meaningful social role.

> I get shocked by those who say "I don't want to talk about those people," you mention your work and they say "we don't need to talk about those people now." It's the sudden realisation that people have that perception. So it does integrate you into society in that you don't have a problem when you see someone in a wheelchair. (Perring 1999, 97)

A sense of learning-disabled people's marginalization, coupled with positive constructions of their creative potential and personhood, lay behind the desire on the part of some respondents to present their work to nondisabled audiences. One respondent described art as a "challenge to expectation," and the exhibition of work by learning-disabled people was an example of how it could function in this way. Such an approach was taken readily by practitioners who viewed themselves as artists. Those who had a therapeutic background, however, often did not regard what happened in their projects as art. Their work was part of a longer process of uncovering the means of achieving self-expression and understanding personal issues, not intended to generate work for public view. A respondent working as the director of a theater company, mounting productions performed by an entirely learning-disabled cast that toured the country, experienced a high level of artistic satisfaction; someone filling a slot at a social services day center, with few resources and little support from the institution's management, showed less confidence about working artistically.

Discussion

The approaches adopted by nondisabled artists and arts facilitators challenge the dominant institutional role of the learning-disabled person as "service user." Within artistic traditions that have valorized alternatives to the hegemony of technique in virtuosic and conservatory traditions, arts practitioners have found the basis for an affirmation of the personhood of learning-disabled people, a personhood fuller than the one constructed for them outside the arts project. This affirmation can occur through recognizing *intentionality* in learning-disabled creation that other constructions may disregard. In a sense, it is a question of taking what people do seriously. As more open aesthetic and performance methodologies are advanced and accepted, through practices like improvisation, project practice can foreground and valorize different skills, bodies, and subjectivities.

Intellectual bases of power such as medicine have developed a language to describe impairment as a function of nondisabled hegemony, and artists must approach their reconstruction of those with learning disabilities with caution. Arts practitioners may apply constructions of learning-disabled people as "creative" and "spontaneous"—new labels of "specialness"—and should take care lest an individual's construction of his or her self is undermined by labels that originate among the nondisabled.

The artists I interviewed presented a variety of approaches to their work, which reflected the different disciplines and art forms that they represented. However, the modes of practice they described may be categorized as three distinct artistic and methodological approaches.

> *Normalizing:* a methodological standpoint and aesthetic outlook that resonates with normalization theory and social role valorization (Ramon 1991). It focuses on bringing performers with learning disabilities into mainstream performance discourse, often through the application of mainstream production values and aesthetic criteria.
>
> *Post-therapeutic:* a methodological approach informed by therapeutic standpoints. Although it may be applied in nontherapeutic (i.e., creative) settings, it deals with the personal, perhaps emotional, "issues" presented by a person with learning disabilities. It affords an opportunity for these

issues to be expressed and explored. This approach often sets itself at odds with external or organizational imperatives for work to be exhibited or performed.

Countercultural: An objective that challenges mainstream cultural and aesthetic precepts and views about disability. It often flows from a perception of the value of transgressive and nonnormative qualities in learning-disabled people's creation and a concern with addressing their marginalization and institutionalization.

These categories are not intended to be discrete or exclusive, for in practice, ideas and influences overlap. However, they usefully summarize the perspectives of arts practitioners working in the field with whom I spoke.

The tacit application of these agendas in the creative and artistic creative collaboration of nondisabled and learning-disabled artists has implications for the meaning of arts-and-disability practice and its ability to foreground the subjectivities of people with learning disabilities. This question lies at the heart of learning-disabled performance. If art is made as a "challenge to expectation," then the nature, essence, and arena of this making must be deconstructed. If art can act as a means of constructing the self, then the subjectification, rather than objectification, of all the artists in an arts-and-disability project must be facilitated. Thus, arts practitioners must ask themselves if they are exploring their own artistic and cultural objectives through their work in arts and disability. If so, a reflexive approach to this issue needs to be supported. Work with artists with learning disabilities may offer creative rewards for nondisabled artists and facilitators, and therefore they may be able to open up their own aesthetic horizons, incorporating them as a positive feature of arts-and-disability work. Such work may offer nondisabled culture a means of reconstructing its own view of impairment—but not if "othering" is maintained, as learning-disabled artists are implicated in nondisabled artistic objectives of *challenge*. On the other hand, a practice that engages with the performance as a normative environment and presents difference in ways that do not challenge mainstream aesthetic discourse, perhaps in an attempt to minimize "otherness," does not necessarily make the *integrative* process an *inclusive* one. There are key differences between the normalizing and countercultural approaches that mirror the dialectic between integration and inclusion. One says: Bring people inside the existing margins! Another says: Move the margins out so that everyone is inside them! Finally, practice that follows therapeutic objectives may concentrate on process at the expense of getting work out in front of audiences and therefore into discourse. Such practice does not always see itself as "art" or accord the role of artist to participants.

These findings suggest that nondisabled arts practitioners need to

remain reflexive while fulfilling a role in the creative work of learning-disabled people. They apply to the arts companies where learning-disabled
performers and artists make choices about their careers, as well as to institutional settings where nondisabled practitioners perform the role of *ani-
mateur* for learning-disabled people who are offered activities within an educational model.

The arts-and-disability sector in the United Kingdom infrequently offers
workers the opportunity for formal reflection on their practice. Indeed,
such issues as the role and motives of the facilitator are overlooked in the
standard artist's report used to evaluate projects. These reports are usually
designed to satisfy funding bodies and focus on a project's *benefit*—educational, therapeutic or otherwise—for learning-disabled people, who are frequently cast in the role of "clients" or "service users." Supervision that can
expose other questions requires skills, time, and resources that are not
always available to organizations operating on a shoestring.

Conclusions

Art conceived and made by disabled artists reveals, reflects, and expresses
disabled subjectivity. In arts-and-disability projects, the manner in which
nondisabled people approach the task of facilitating or collaborating in
creative work by artists with learning disabilities has a crucial bearing on the
extent that learning-disabled experience and subjectivity is articulated.
Arts-and-disability projects, particularly if the work facilitated is by artists
without learning disabilities, must address this dichotomy of subjectivities.

My research shows that artists bring preoccupations, interests, and preconceptions to their work with learning-disabled people. Artists inevitably
bring to an artistic production their aesthetic and political preferences, as
well as their attitudes toward disability and society. These views are bound
up in their involvement in the work they do with learning-disabled performers and artists. To see the possibilities that lie ahead, we may need to
look at the work of a project like Heart'n'Soul. There we may see how non-
learning-disabled artists have developed work wherein learning-disabled
artists and performers can overcome the lack of self-determination that is a
function of the institutional construction of learning disability. While many
learning-disabled people will have come into contact with arts access projects through the efforts of nondisabled people, in more projects such as
Heart'n'Soul they may eventually be in a position to choose how they work.
They can place themselves at the center of creating the aesthetic and cultural message that they put across in their performances.

The choice made by nondisabled artists to work collaboratively with people with learning disabilities signals a construction of learning disability. I have discussed the difficulties in the notions of learning-disabled people as unusually "creative" and "spontaneous." However, these notions should be understood as part of a cultural practice that suggests the cultural significance, potential, and autonomy of learning-disabled people.

Notes

1. The Shape Network disbanded in 1999.

2. The terms *Arts and Disability* and *Disability Arts* suggest differing relationships to dependency and institutional culture. In political terms, David Hevey argues that disabled people need to "reclaim" that a cultural shift is necessary, which moves the disabled experience of the Arts "from Arts and Disability to Disability Arts" (Hevey 1991, 28).

3. Vincent (1995) argues that it was a white, colonial response to Hendrix's blackness that constructed him as a rock performer, marketed to white audiences by a white music industry, while overlooking and dissimulating his black R'n'B roots and later experimentations with the black line-up of The Band Of Gypsies. His blackness provided an exotic means of selling him as a "wild man of rock" that resonates with the response to blackness as mental illness that sees such a vast imbalance in the numbers of black patients in the U.K. psychiatric system.

4. This London-based music theater company performs its own work all over Europe, using an inclusive band with a singing cast that is entirely learning disabled. They have developed a club night, "The Beautiful Octopus," that is run, DJ'd, and produced by people with learning disabilities, which now franchises to learning-disabled communities across London and the rest of the United Kingdom.

5. The respondents' experiences are discussed much more fully in Perring 1999.

Bibliography

Bogdan, R. 1997. *Freak Show: Presenting Human Oddities for Amusement and Profit.* Chicago: University of Chicago Press.

Born, G., and D. Hesmondhalgh, eds. 2000. *Western Music and Its Others: Difference, Representation and Appropriation in Music.* Berkeley: University of California Press.

Bréton, A. 1960. *Nadja.* New York: Grove Press.

Cage, J. [1937] 1978. "The Future of Music: Credo." In Cage, *Silence—Lectures and Writings.* London: Marion Boyars.

———. [1959] 1978. "To Describe the Process of Composition Used in 'Music of Changes and Imaginary Landscape No. 4.'" In Cage, *Silence—Lectures and Writings.* London: Marion Boyars.

Cardinal, R. 1972. *Outsider Art.* London: Studio Vista.

Dubuffet, J. 1988. *Asphyxiante Culture* (English). New York: Four Walls Eight Windows.

Fischer, Wild Man. 1968. *An Evening with Wild Man Fischer* (vinyl record). Bizarre Records, RSLP 6332.

Frith, S., and H. Horne. 1987. *Art into Pop*. London: Methuen.

Glaser, B., and A. Strauss. 1967. *The Discovery of Grounded Theory: Strategies for Qualitative Research*. New York: Aldine de Gruyter.

Hevey, D. 1991. "From Self-Love to the Picket Line: Strategies for Change in Disability Representation." In *Disability Arts and Culture Papers: Transcripts of a Disability Arts and Culture Seminar, November 20th 1991*, ed. S. Lees, 23–30. London: Shape London.

MacGregor, John M. 1989. *The Discovery of the Art of the Insane*. Princeton, N.J.: Princeton University Press.

MacLagan, D. 1991. "Outsider or Insiders." In *The Myth of Primitivism—Perspectives on Art*, ed. S. Hiller, 32–49. London: Routledge.

Oliver, M. 1999. *The Politics of Disablement*. Basingstoke: Macmillan.

Perring, G. 1999. "Making a Difference: A Cultural Exploration of the Relationship of Non-disabled Artists to Learning Disability." M.A. thesis, University of East London. Available at http://homepages.uel.ac.uk/G.Perring/start.htm.

Ramon, S., ed. 1991. *Beyond Community Care: Normalisation and Integration Work*. Basingstoke: Mind/Macmillan Education.

Rhodes, C. 1994. *Primitivism and Modern Art*. London: Thames and Hudson.

Stockhausen, K. 1972. "Goldstaub" (vinyl record). Vol. 7 of *Aus den Sieben Tagen*. Deutsche Gramophon, 2561301.

Vincent, R. 1995. *Funk—The MUSIC, the PEOPLE, and the RHYTHM of the ONE*. New York: St. Martin's/Griffin.

Walser, R. 1993. *Running with the Devil: Power, Gender, and Madness in Heavy Metal Music*. Hanover, N.H.: University Press of New England.

Watson, B. 1995. *Frank Zappa: The Negative Dialectics of Poodle Play*. London: Quartet.

Beyond Therapy
"Performance" Work with People Who Have Profound & Multiple Disabilities

MELISSA C. NASH

This essay focuses on the possibilities of involving a very marginalized group—people who have profound and multiple disabilities—in aesthetic activity, moving beyond purely therapeutic paradigms. I carried out qualitative research, looking at the activities of the London-based arts company Entelechy, in the late 1990s.[1] Entelechy took upon itself the task of addressing the social and cultural needs of this group of people in South East London, many of whom had spent years in asylums.

Entelechy produced workshops and performance events involving a wide spectrum of people with differing abilities. The company is comprised of a mixture of people, some of whom have learning disabilities or profound and multiple disabilities. The work of Entelechy is "facilitated" by a small caucus of arts practitioners who do not have disabilities, and who see themselves in the role of "enablers," stimulating creative activity. Entelechy is funded from a number of sources, including the Department of Health and grants from local authorities.

Entelechy uses the mediums of dance, movement, and music to create communication channels. As some of Entelechy's artists-facilitators have pointed out, "movement," whether for therapeutic or creative purposes, "is often one of the strongest forms of communication, as well as a means of contact with other people and the outside world for people with a sensory impairment" (de Wit and Swift 1995, 6). Entelechy's facilitators were keen to assert that interactions took place on a creative level as an equal exchange: "Beyond the assumptions of 'difference' which dominate social and artistic policy and actions there exists the possibility of a new aesthetic language. A creative dialogue can take place between dancers with and without disabilities. Those who are sensory skilled through necessity and those who are sensory skilled as performing artists" (Entelechy document 1997).[2]

A central issue in the lives of many people with profound disabilities, vocalized by some care workers at Entelechy's workshops, was that there is very little time for social interactions in the day-to-day running of their care homes. This restriction reinforces social and cultural incompetence, through lack of stimulation. Many of Entelechy's groups were set up partially to compensate for this lack of meaningful interaction.

A rather simple observation, that the more people communicate, the better they are at it, has potentially drastic implications if applied throughout care services. Input from voluntary agencies such as Entelechy can enhance the "quality of life" of profoundly disabled people, but often causes resentment on the part of carers. This is partly because of the perception that carers carry out the "hard labor," whereas artists just "play" with the disabled. As James (1992) has pointed out, care workers distinguish between physical labor and emotional labor, with the former often regarded as the more legitimate form of paid work.

Throughout this essay, *performance* is taken to mean creative encounters between various groups and individuals, in a meeting of identities or "communitas" (Turner 1994). Entelechy's work did not subscribe to any psychotherapeutic school of thought, and cannot be seen as "art therapy." Aesthetic products (such as paintings) were not interpreted or imbued with specific meanings, or seen as representative of some inner conflict; instead they were regarded as acts of communication. However, Entelechy does share with art therapy an interest in exploring consciousness through aesthetic means, and valuing nonverbal communication in the form of paintings, dance, and movement. Entelechy sometimes expressed the outcomes of their work in what could be interpreted as "therapeutic" terms, but they were more interested in a holistic approach to creative activity. It is my contention that although Entelechy's artists-facilitators did not profess to be therapists in the Western psychotherapeutic usage of the term, they did aim to be "healers," using the arts, and specifically performance, as a transformative medium to inculcate changes at individual, cultural, and societal levels.

Issues in "Performance" & the Profoundly Disabled

People who have been classed as having "learning disabilities" hold an ambiguous status in the West. Throughout Western history their humanity has been the subject of continuous debate, their "personhood" in question. Cultures have compared them to animals or other entities beyond the human realm; that is, they are outside of "culture." In the case of people with severe learning disabilities, many are "unable to comprehend or follow most of their culture's rules, from implicit conventions to moral and super-natural rules. As a result, these persons require"—and sometimes receive—"almost total exemption from responsibility" (Edgerton 1985, 81–82).

The ambiguous personhood of people who have learning disabilities has a bearing on how they are perceived as "performers." Family and carers often project personal attributes onto them. Because they are often dependent on others for their care, it very difficult for the general population to see such people as "actors," capable of performing in their own right. If profoundly disabled people participate in a performance, can it really be called a performance when the performers often aren't aware that they are performing? Richard Schechner asserts that it is important to discern whether "a performance generates its own frame, that is, is reflexive . . . or whether the frame is imposed from the outside, as when TV crews arrive at the scene of a 'tragedy'" (1990, 28). Schechner includes in the category of "framed as" performances like the one by Richard Wilson and Christopher Knowles in the 1970s, called *Dialog Curious George*. Christopher Knowles had a learning disability and "performed" on stage with Wilson, by just "being himself":

> Wilson contexted his interactions with Knowles as a performance for the public who paid fancy prices to witness and admire it. Sometimes Knowles' responses . . . were very funny, wise, ironic, appropriate: one of those Simpleton Saints. Saint or not, Knowles was an elephant bowing at the circus—whatever his remarks meant to members of the audience they meant, or were, something else to Knowles. Because Knowles couldn't lie, he couldn't be an actor—he could only be *situated and displayed as if he were an actor* inside Wilson's show. (Schechner 1990, 38)

This position could be taken to imply that most performance work involving people with learning disabilities is a kind of voyeurism. In *Dialog Curious George* there was a traditional divide between audience and performer, with connotations of a freak show: the disabled person was on display. The work of Entelechy differs in that they attempt to make the traditional performance aesthetic more inclusive. Entelechy's groups took place most often in workshops, events, and "happenings" where there was no clear divide between audience and performer, and they explored senses other than the visual.

Expanding the Aesthetic Exploring Tactility
through Contact Improvisation

The anthropologist David Howes has pointed out that "the contemporary Western aesthetic is almost exclusively visual" (1991, 6). This, he asserts, results in a dissociation of the senses. The dominant aesthetics within Western culture preclude people with profound and multiple disabilities precisely because of this focus on the visual. If, instead, other sensory experiences are introduced into performance, different levels of communication and understanding can be reached, specifically through the medium of tactility.

One way in which Entelechy tried to communicate with and access the lived experience of people with profound and multiple disabilities was through the use of a kinesthetic technique, *contact improvisation*. This technique was originally devised by able-bodied dancers but has also been used by disabled dancers. The general ideas behind contact improvisation is

> a form of duet in which the movement is invented by the dancers as they go along, the only rule being that the participants have to keep in close contact with the other's body. Any part of the body can be used to lean against, hang on to or balance on, and the movements can range from rolling over each other, to pushing, pulling, throwing and catching . . . it is something in which both trained and untrained dancers can participate. (Mackrell 1992, 145)

Contact improvisation differs from other dance forms such as ballet or modern dance in that formal movements are much less prescribed, and it is inherently improvisational. The dance form can accommodate "deviant" bodies because it "does not rely on muscular strength . . . because each dancer is supposed to do only what he or she is able, people of radically different sizes and weights can dance quite well together; the key to being a good partner rests on one's movement awareness within the parameters of the form" (Novack 1990, 151). This seems to imply that physically disabled people can "perform" as well as able-bodied people, if the performers have an awareness of what they can do with their bodies. It is very difficult to know how people with profound and multiple disabilities experience their bodies. However, touch is a form of communication to which they have access, and, as Montagu has pointed out, "Awareness of self is largely a matter of tactile experience" (1986, 390).

Ambient Jam

One of Entelechy's workshops, Ambient Jam, was held in a local arts center on a weekly basis, attended by about eight people who had profound and multiple disabilities, their care workers, dancers, musicians, and volunteers. In addition, a couple of people with "mild to moderate" learning disabilities attended the group, working alongside Charles Hayward, the facilitating musician, as part of his Extraordinary Orkestra. The Orkestra accompanied the dancers, playing on drums and keyboards, as well as singing.

The workshop occurred in a fairly simple environment with mats and cushions laid out on a bare wooden floor. The facilitating dancers usually initially worked with one person at a time, although sometimes more, introducing themselves through touch to the disabled people, and doing gentle physical warm-ups with them, in a way reminiscent of physiotherapy, manipulating legs and arms to warm up the muscles. People with disabilities and the nondisabled dancers had a series of interactions and encounters, leading up to a contact improvisation jam. This included a variety of tactile exchanges, such as weight bearing, balancing, leaning, pushing, massage, mirroring movements, or just lying next to each other, "tuning in" to each other's body. There was very little spoken language apart from accidental and incidental words and phrases, for example, greeting someone or gently talking. Hayward played music that was a collage of sounds. Two or three people with learning disabilities played on the drums and keyboards; electronic samplers were often placed under people lying on the mats, which would record sounds and repeat them. Fragmented noises and drumming filled the room. Sounds echoed back and forth between the disabled people lying on the mats and the musicians, such as groans and screams.

I entered into contact improvisations, one of which I describe here between myself and Michelle,[3] a thirty-five-year-old woman who was blind and had profound learning disabilities. She did not talk, but was able to hear, and sometimes hummed in a rhythmical way. She was very vocal, however, and made a variety of noises according to her mood from high-pitched whoops of joy to hollering sounds when she was distressed. Michelle was described by her carers as having "challenging behavior," in that she harmed herself by hitting herself on the head and bit herself. In this excerpt from contemporaneous notes, I describe one particular interaction with her:

> She thrust her feet towards me, and placed my hands on them. For a while she lay against me, resting her back on my stomach, while she had her feet in the air, legs folded up against her body, wanting me to massage her feet. She then spun around and thrust her feet towards me. She did this several times.

Michelle's incidents of self-harm and violent outbursts decreased significantly during my fieldwork. Entelechy would argue that this was because her involvement in the group gave her a creative outlet through which to express herself, and also provided a space where behavioral boundaries were more flexible than in other areas of her life. This utilization of aesthetics to express "emotion" outside therapeutic paradigms is one of Entelechy's major agendas in their work with the profoundly disabled. Additionally, it seemed to be the case that Michelle responded in a positive way toward tactile and aural stimulation provided by the group, through contact improvisation and a form of music that was able to incorporate and reflect her own vocalizations.

Edward, a twenty-four-year-old man who had cerebral palsy and was described by his carers as an "elective mute" (i.e., he chose not to speak), also appeared to enjoy the groups. Initially, Edward was very much a loner and evidently did not like to be touched. He was very aware of other people in the room and from a distance reacted to what they did. When he was very relaxed, he sometimes sat up and clapped his hands in time to the music. The musicians sometimes tried to pick up his rhythms and shape the sounds around him. When he was distressed, he banged his fists against his head. The facilitators tried to calm him when he did this, using both music and touch, if he would allow it. During the period in which I observed the sessions, Edward's behavior clearly changed from avoiding touch, sitting on the edge of the mats, away from other people, to being in the center of the room, allowing limited communication through touch. It was suggested that he liked being ambiguously placed between performing and watching: "I'm in it, but I'm not in it," as one of the artist-facilitators put it.

In both the music and movement in Ambient Jam, communication often took the form of nondisabled dancer or musician mirroring the disabled person. The dancers struck up nonverbal dialogue through copying what the other person was communicating, perhaps a variation on it, and built up nonverbal "conversations" through small, often barely perceptible movements, such as the rolling of eyes, or the flicking of hands. Video cameras and monitors were introduced into the group, so that the disabled people could see themselves moving, and in many cases, interacted with their own video image, "performing" to themselves, in a self-reflexive way.

There was no clear-cut distinction between audience and performer in these workshops. When there was an audience, it was largely a "safe" one, composed of support workers or arts practitioners who are already attuned to the needs of people with learning disabilities. Support staff who stayed in the room were usually asked to join in, as Entelechy practitioners felt uneasy if they just watched (although this frequently happened). The "audience" and "performers" were therefore interchangeable, on some occasions at least. Sometimes people with learning disabilities chose to watch from the side. If support staff stayed in the room, they were requested to sit on the floor in order to be the same level as the people on the mats, thus blurring the distinction between audience and performer. The constriction or even elimination of the audience function served, I suggest, to refocus mainstream aesthetic views, particularly on "competency" in performance. In effect, the audience/performer divide was displaced physically onto the actual performance area (the mats), making the relationship between participants less prescribed, and allowing for a much greater flexibility of roles.

Cynthia Novack, a dance theorist, asserts that contact improvisation is appropriate in the context of negotiating identities and suggests that it has "constituted a social experiment, an attempt to place dance in a liminal social context which fitted neither the category of theater dance nor the category of social dance" (1990, 16). What Entelechy was attempting to do can be likened to a social experiment, using a "liminal" dance form to try to connect "liminal" marginalized people to the "cultural life" of their *community*. This was partly achieved through the restructuring of traditional modes of workshops and performance, so that there was no clear divide between audience and performers, and no one person directed the action. However, when the workshops became too chaotic, facilitators steered the action back to a more manageable aesthetic. Rebecca Swift, Entelechy's combined-arts coordinator, explained that she believed it was important to create spaces for "performance" between two people, which the rest of the group could observe, while participating in the group at the same time.

Reorienting the senses away from the visual mode dominant in Western art, Entelechy sought to shift "performance" from something viewed to something participated in. Because of the dominance of the distance senses in Western art, when proximity senses are involved, the experience is often framed as "therapy," perhaps because it attempts to tangibly "do" something to those involved. Therapy was not bad per se, but to frame the practices as such contradicts Entelechy's intention to move away from control by any one person. "Healing" and other beneficial effects were a by-product of creative expression, not the purpose of the activity. The potential of performance for "transformation," therefore, needs to be embedded within a multisensory, not monovisual, aesthetic.

Entelechy has sought to reembody the perceptual experience of all those involved in the performance events. The profoundly disabled person's embodied consciousness was, through touch, accessed by the able-bodied facilitator (but still in an embodied and nonlinguistic state). Meaning (whether imagined or experienced as "real") was then attributed to the profoundly disabled person's actions by his or her partner, and sometimes by an empathetic audience. The feeling of intercorporeality may exist only as an object of intention in the consciousness of the able-bodied. As cultural arbiters, Entelechy attempted to prevent the disabled from dying a social death. They emphasized development of person-to-person relationships, rather than on mind-to-self relationships. This was partly because of the qualities inherent in contact improvisation, but was also because of the fluid concept of performer and audience, leading to a questioning of all roles, such as "carer" and "cared for." This became especially apparent when care workers—many of them initially uncomfortable with physically intimate contact outside the carer/client relationship—joined in the "jam." Whether this approach positively incorporated the profoundly disabled within a "new" performance aesthetic is difficult to say.

Much of Entelechy's work contrived a meeting ground between verbal and nonverbal worlds. Some members described the creation of such a meeting place in terms of a state called "the drone." Charles Hayward described the "drone" as a kind of trance or meditative state where thought patterns were released: "Sounds such as a dijereedoo or a drum free people right up . . . [L]ike finding a home, a bedrock, or a womb, they feel carried and held by that drone note. Everything is in relation to that drone note." The drone state was reached when the artist-facilitators and musicians had been working with the participants for some time. The dancers improvised movements and musicians vocalized sounds that seemed appropriate for the moment. The people with learning disabilities echoed these sounds, with obvious variations, which in turn were taken up by the artist-facilitators. Eventually a continuous, uninterrupted drone was produced and held by everyone present, until a trancelike state was reached, and a shared feeling that all those present were one. This drone state could not be produced at will but was the result of a successful workshop. If an intercorporeal-intersubjective state of the drone was entered into, then, in theory, it was reached by all participants, both able and disabled, and potentially led to a recognition of everyone's dependency on others for his or her own recognition of self.

The hidden "skill" of improvisational performance is to make actions "unconsciously," without thinking. For someone with severe physical and learning disabilities, this skill may be difficult, if not impossible, to master. In these workshops, performers were trying to reach a state where skill was no longer an issue. Artist-facilitators emphasized that entering into the drone with a profoundly disabled person often meant moments of stillness and boredom, or "nothingness," which should be seen as important to moments of action. This suggests that people with profound and multiple disabilities in "integrated" performance can act to represent an inner consciousness, which can be unleashed in moments of spontaneous creative activity, allowing the able-bodied artist-facilitators to glimpse this "primal" instinct in themselves. Different states of consciousness evidently produce different forms of art. If people with learning disabilities are viewed as exhibiting a more "primal" self in aesthetic activity framed as "performance," dilemmas of "choice," "intent," and "exploitation" are raised.

Partly due to the influence of psychology and psychoanalysis upon Western culture in the twentieth century, academic and public debate has moved away from whether certain groups of people, such as those who have multiple disabilities, have a "soul." There is, instead, a desire to understand the inner subjectivity of another, to connect with another's "consciousness." When this connection is unusually difficult, for example, in the case of those who are deaf and blind from birth, those who can talk and see commonly react with frustration. Pity often overrides attempts at comprehension. According to Varela (1995), Cartesianism, which permeates how minds and bodies are conceptualized in the West, assumes that humans think rationally and linguistically. This suggests that linguistically produced thought controls movement, and that nonlinguistic communication is nonrational. Nonlinguistic opportunities for producing "meaning" in any shared cultural sense, are, by implication, extremely limited. This would suggest, therefore, that there is no meaning in motion. This is evidently not true, as Varela (1995), and others have demonstrated.[4] Rebecca Swift asserted that the Entelechy artist-facilitators, as trained dancers and theater practitioners, were accustomed to communicate "on a 'deeper' level within a public context. We are taught, I hope, to relate to and tap into the undercurrents of communication that are emotional, physical and non-verbal, as well as atmospheres and the invisible energies that transfer between audience and performer" (Entelechy document). The emphasis in such encounters, for Entelechy, was on physical and emotional "intelligence."

"Art" & "Life"

Arts companies such as Entelechy aim to challenge the boundary between performance and everyday life. The extent to which people with profound disabilities are "integrated" in the local community through participation in such groups is debatable. In the behavior of the profoundly disabled subtle changes can take place that, to the casual observer, may appear inconsequential. No great athletic dance event is taking place, but small-scale encounters between people with very limited communication and able-bodied artists. Care workers have attested that small but significant steps toward social experience and communication are made by the profoundly disabled participants in dance and movement workshops with Entelechy. Involvement in the group has also had the effect of enhancing the status of people with profound disabilities in the eyes of their care workers, who noticed abilities hitherto unknown. Increased respect from care workers can lead to changes in quality of life for their "clients," often in direct response to choices and preferences indicated through the projects by the profoundly disabled person.

Entelechy created situations of "antistructure" where people who deviate from mainstream norms could interact with professionals and their nondisabled peers, creating new platforms for social engagements that would not be part of everyday activities:

> In liminality, communitas tends to characterize relationships between those jointly undergoing ritual transition. The bonds of communitas are anti-structural in the sense that they are undifferentiated, equalitarian, direct, extant, nonrational, existential, I-Thou (in Feuerbach's and Buber's sense) relationships. . . . Communitas . . . tends to ignore, reverse, cut across, or occur outside of structural relationships. (Turner 1994, 274)

Turner (1969) distinguishes between the "liminal" and "liminoid," liminal activity having the ability to invert but not subvert the established order, whereas liminoid situations are more playful, contingent, and subversive. Entelechy utilized liminoid spaces to experiment with new forms of communication between disabled and nondisabled people, which can then be used to influence interactions and engagements in wider society. The phenomenological space in traditional theater between the spectator and the performer is renegotiated in much of Entelechy's work so as to create interchangeable parties, rearranging the categories of disabled versus nondisabled bodies.

Entelechy moves away from therapeutic paradigms, which they regard as constraining, toward cultural and creative expression, shifting the aesthetics of performance toward unpredictability, chance, chaos, and, perhaps, the oxymoron of "controlled anarchy."[5] This type of work has taken place in other areas of avant-garde performance for most of the twentieth century, for example in the work of Artaud, Growtowski, the Living Theater (United States) and the People Show (United Kingdom). The transposition of this thinking to the area of learning disability arts, where the intent of the performers is often unknown, is indeed radical but raises difficult questions. For example, by interpreting such activity as "art," is the experience devalued or even parodied? Is "power" (however understood) neutralized when activities are "framed as" performance? These questions remain to be answered. However, much of the lives of people with profound and multiple disabilities is passive. Involvement in the avant-garde may be a way out of such passivity, allowing them to be at the forefront of new performance aesthetics and ways of communicating lived experience, and bringing to light the fact that we all experience the world as intersubjective and intercorporeal beings.

Conclusion

In many respects, Entelechy's work is a kind of postmodern ritual, involving pastiche and mimesis in an attempt to create a meeting ground for people of greatly differing cognitive and physical abilities. In such work no necessary transformation is incurred, only the showing of possibilities. In their workshop-performances, I suggest, Entelechy creates situations of "anti-structure" (Turner 1994). The renegotiation of roles in Entelechy's work sets up provocative dialectics between the perception of "normality" and "abnormality." However, the impact of the activity is limited due to the relatively small number of people taking part, and the various social and material obstacles in place. In its most radical and experimental forms, the work of Entelechy has political potential, at the same time heightening the awareness of cultural differences and focusing on the body as "social text." Entelechy's experimental work, the outcomes of which were not easily predictable, can be seen as an "emergent" cultural work (Williams 1977). It supports Fulcher's suggestion: "In part . . . the possibility of new social orders lies in reading the struggle between the dominant ever-present normalising tendencies and properly emergent cultural elements" (1996, 185).

Notes

I wish to acknowledge the financial support of the Economic and Social Research Council, which provided me with a studentship to carry out this research. I would also like to acknowledge the input of my informants, who have shared with me the experiences related in this essay. I would like to show my appreciation of the help and support offered to me by Entelechy, in particular David Slater, Mara de Wit, Rebecca Swift, and Pam Martin. The views expressed in this essay are those of the author and do not necessarily reflect the views of the funding body or research participants.
   1. See Entelechy's website for current work and programs: www.entelechyarts .com.
   2. The Entelechy document referred to here was an internally produced progress report that was available to funders and the general public on request.
   3. Because of the difficulties in obtaining informed consent, I have used pseudonyms for informants who have learning disabilities.
   4. See, for example, *Meaning in Motion*, edited by Jane C. Desmond (1997).
   5. In the sense that certain "deviant" acts were prohibited in the workshops, such as violence toward self or others.

Bibliography

de Wit, Mara, and Rebecca Swift. *Moving Visions in Community Dance: New Moves Entelechy 1989–1995*. London: Entelechy, 1995.

Edgerton, Robert B. *Rules, Exceptions, and Social Order.* Berkeley: U of California P, 1985.

Fulcher, Gillian. "Beyond Normalisation but Not Utopia." In *Disability and Society: Emerging Issues and Insights,* ed. L. Barton, 167–90. Harlow, Eng.: Addison Wesley Longman, 1996.

Howes, David, ed. *The Varieties of Sensory Experience: A Sourcebook in the Anthropology of the Senses.* Toronto: U of Toronto P, 1991.

Hughes, B. "Medicine and the Aesthetic Invalidation of Disabled People." *Disability and Society* 15, no. 4 (2000): 555–68.

James, N. "Care = Organisation + Physical Labour + Emotional Labour." *Sociology of Health and Illness* 14, no. 4 (1992): 488–509.

Mackrell, Judith. *Out of Line: The Story of British New Dance.* London: Dance Books, 1992.

Montagu, Ashley. *Touching: The Human Significance of the Skin.* New York: Harper and Row, 1986.

Novack, Cynthia J. *Sharing the Dance Contact: Improvisation and American Culture.* Madison: U of Wisconsin P, 1990.

Schechner, Richard. "Magnitudes of Performance." In *By Means of Performance: Intercultural Studies of Theatre and Ritual,* ed. R. Schechner and W. Appel, 19–49. Cambridge: Cambridge UP, 1990.

Turner, Victor W. *Dramas, Fields and Metaphors.* Ithaca: Cornell UP, 1994.

———. *The Ritual Process: Structure and Anti-Structure.* London: Routledge & Kegan Paul, 1969.

Varela, C. R. "Cartesianism Revisited: The Ghost in the Moving Machine or the Lived Body." In *Human Action Signs in Cultural Context,* ed. B. Farnell. Metuchen, N.J.: Scarecrow, 1995.

Williams, Raymond. *Drama in Performance.* Buckingham: Open UP, 1991.

———. *Marxism and Literature.* Oxford: Oxford UP, 1977.

Dementia & the Performance of Self

ANNE DAVIS BASTING

Scholars and activists within fields of disability and age studies have fought hard to have disabled people of all ages recognized as *people* with disabilities, rather than a class of the *disabled* or the *old*. These broad categories are peopled with individuals with life experiences and opinions, not just needs demanding attention. To better understand the experience of disability, scholars and activists call for the voices of the disabled, for their stories to be told and heard. But such a call also presents several challenges. *How* can the voices of *all* disabled people be heard? Particularly the voices of people with cognitive impairments or severe physical impairments? In what forms can and do their voices have meaning? Might certain forms of narrative actually support ideals of independence and selfhood that fuel fears of disability in the first place? What can the stories of the disabled tell us about the very meaning of the "self"?

To address these questions, this essay follows Time Slips, a creative story-telling project with people with Alzheimer's disease and related dementia (ADRD)[1] that began in 1998 in both Milwaukee and New York. As director of the project, I organized eighteen weeks of storytelling workshops in Milwaukee and nine weeks in New York. In the second phase of the project, we translated a handful of the nearly one hundred stories into a professional play production, a website, and an art installation in order to deepen public awareness of the creative potential and the humanity of people with dementia.

Interviews with staff and family caregivers, student facilitators, and the storytellers themselves reveal that the storytelling was a surprisingly moving process. Certainly none of the students expected to be so invigorated by an hour of storytelling with people with Alzheimer's disease. How and why it worked are the questions that fuel the first part of this essay. In the second, I look to the production of the Time Slips play in Milwaukee in May 2000, and to responses in postshow discussions that revealed common fears and understandings of the self.

.

Between You & Me

> [The] self itself does not derive from its possessor, but from the whole scene of his action.
>
> —Erving Goffman

At the root of the Time Slips project was an effort to encourage creative expression among people diagnosed with Alzheimer's in a form that could capture the complexity of their experiences. The people with whom we worked were either living at home with family or in long-term care. All had twenty-four-hour care, and nearly all had symptoms consistent with middle-stage Alzheimer's disease. People with ADRD lose the ability to comprehend chronological time systems that orient and unite so much of global culture that it is nearly impossible for them to function without someone who can translate that world to them. Severe short-term memory loss can bring disorientation and paranoia—who is this person coming in my room? What is this room? Gradually the forgetting of details grows into the loss of concepts. One does not just forget where one put the keys. One cannot comprehend the *meaning* of a key. People with ADRD become "disabled," then, because they cannot negotiate time or memory in the ways that have come to be seen as necessary components of selfhood. People with ADRD are an extreme example of a "self" that is relational, formed through interaction with others. A person with dementia must often rely on others to accomplish simple daily tasks. Family, friends, and care providers must supply memories of the long-term and immediate past. At the end of the spectrum opposite from the person with ADRD, however, is not an "independent" self, but simply a less dependent person. For example, I am able to perform my daily activities largely by myself: cooking, cleaning, walking, and generally tending to my needs. But as Erving Goffman and George Herbert Mead both suggest, that independence is an illusion: my selfhood is still a pastiche woven out my relationships to other people and institutions. All selves are relational. But what forms of representation can capture the wide-ranging experiences of relational selfhood? How can we represent these two extremes—of people whose self appears independent, and of people whose sense of self appears nearly completely dependent on their care providers? What forms are available for their stories?

If a person with ADRD writes a linear autobiography, in which the consistent voice of an "I" goes on a journey, she will almost certainly have to mask the intensity of her caregiving relationships.[2] The writer with ADRD might borrow such a form to strengthen a sense of self, but in the process overlook or misrepresent the relational quality of her selfhood. Paul Eakin suggests that relational identities can be found in autobiographies whose writers emphasize the relationships in their lives, but this does not eliminate a larger problem. As Lennard Davis points out, "By narrativizing an impairment, one tends to sentimentalize it, and link it to the bourgeois sensibility of individualism and the drama of the individual story" (11). In general, I find that the history and context of the linear autobiographies, in which a consistent "I" tells a chronological tale of selfhood that is then defined by its control of memory, make it inhospitable to representations of the extremes of relational identity.

With the Time Slips project, we set out to encourage creative expression not reliant on memory, to emphasize the relational quality of the self, and to enhance the social identity of people with dementia by giving them a role to play in their institutional settings. By releasing the pressure to remember the past, the creative storytelling workshops invited storytellers to practice any and all forms of communication without risk of being stigmatized as evidence of the "disease." By creating a role for people with Alzheimer's (that of storyteller), caregiving staff could engage with them as people rather than simply bodies in need.[3]

The Method

Time Slips storytelling workshops make a clear and simple distinction: rather than focus on who people with Alzheimer's disease *were,* we are interested in who they *are,* complete with missing words, repeated sounds, and hazy memories. We stretched the boundaries of traditional reminiscence activities, common and effective tools for exercising memory, by telling participants that we were not interested in memory. Together our storytelling groups were going to make up *new* stories.

We held the storytelling sessions for one hour, once a week at four adult day centers. To unify the storytelling process, we created a five-phase ritual that we repeated each week at each center: the greeting, the story from last week, this week's story, the final retelling, and the farewell.

We began sessions by inviting participants to sit in a circle of chairs away from other activities that might be happening at the same time. We welcomed the storytellers into the circle and greeted them by name. To eliminate confusion or guesswork on the part of the storytellers, facilitators wore name tags and introduced themselves each week.

After the greeting phase, a facilitator read back one of the stories from the previous week. The retelling reminded the group that the stories were creative tales with no right or wrong answers. Before telling a new story, student facilitators asked storytellers to help them pick out an image for the week. The images we used shared two qualities. They were large enough to see without straining, and they suggested a fantastical story. If images appeared too realistic, participants assumed there was a "real" story that they had forgotten, and they were reluctant to make up new stories. But staged, somewhat surreal images invited creative expression.

The storytelling itself began with students distributing the image around the circle. One student served as "the writer," and sat in the center of the circle with the large sketch pad and a box of brightly colored markers. Other students posed questions, for example, "What should we call her?" "Where should we say they are?" Questions focused on the sensory ("What does the farm smell like?") and included the world outside the picture as well ("Does the woman riding the ostrich have a family?"). The storytelling became improvisational at this point. Storytellers' answers carried the facilitators' questions in new directions, and in turn our questions carried the storytellers deeper into the world of the story.

The workshops quickly developed their own momentum. All answers were folded into the story. One storyteller, whose language was limited to sounds, offered "Babababababa." It became part of nearly every story we told. If more than one name was provided, the character's name was hyphenated. Often the storytellers themselves interpreted each other's answers ("He meant this . . .") or countered a certain direction of the story they did not like ("She isn't jumping off the building, she's jumping to the next building to see her friend").

If storytellers got lost in the story, student and staff facilitators would call for a "retell," and the "writer" would read back all the answers up to that point. Retelling the story, interpreting a random list of sensical and nonsensical answers into a "story," demanded a certain theatrical flair. It also demanded that staff and student facilitators let go of their own reliance on linear narrative. Once they released the desire to guide the story in a particular direction, facilitators were able to elicit more responses from people who did not usually speak and to fold all the answers into the open narrative with greater ease.

One story could last nearly an hour. At the end of the session, the writer would do one last retelling of the story. Finally, the students said good-bye to each member of the group, individually thanking them for sharing in the storytelling process. For men and women with Alzheimer's, to leap into creative verbal expression is to risk revealing the stigma of the disease. Their efforts were no small gift, and the weekly "thank you" was much more than a token ending to the sessions.

From week to week the storytellers forgot our names. But the ritual greeting, the circle, and the story images became familiar to them, and with it they quickly associated trust, play, and the freedom to speak. For the staff, the ritual created a separate space in which they could, at least partially, let go of their authoritative roles. With no right or wrong answers, staff began to release into the stories, to laugh and sing along with the group.

Certainly lines of power and authority still encircled the storytelling. If anyone became aggressive or "inappropriate," they would have been removed from the group. But the lines were also blurred by the fact that we were no longer looking for symptoms of the disease in the spoken word. Language was free to carry emotional, rather than literal meaning. Staff, volunteers, and storytellers were under the spell of the present moment and our ability to communicate in it, occasionally in what seemed complete verbal nonsense. The storytellers clearly felt they played a special role in the day center, and we acknowledged the feeling by inviting family members and staff to a final celebration in which we presented each family with a book of the groups' stories and the images that prompted them.

The Stories

Filling In as She Goes Along
(In response to an image of an eighty-year-old pilot sitting in the cockpit of an old plane)
Ethel Rebecca may be old, but she's full of vim and vigor.
She knows how to fly, and flying makes her happy.
She's flying over Chicago on her way to work.
Ethel's got a perfect record—no crashes—because she's a very determined pilot.
She's not flying alone—Dizzy Gillespie is in the back seat playing the clarinet.
After Chicago, they'll fly to Seattle to visit her granddaughter Dorothy.
Ethel has three children, Hilda, ABCDEFG, and Grizelda Mary.
She has a husband—she better!—named James who drives a bus.
He's only seventy . . . Ethel's a bit of a cradle robber!
People tell her to keep good sense and keep her feet on the ground.
Her family worries themselves sick about her.
But Ethel flies because it makes her feel free, and because her family doesn't pay her enough attention.
One day, when Dorothy reaches the flying age of sixteen, Ethel will teach her granddaughter how to fly too.

All the way to Seattle, the weather is clear, Dizzy plays his clarinet, Ethel sings
an Italian song ("Cera Luna Mezza Mara, Mama Mia, Ma Mari Dari"), and
she remembers the farm her father Lee Hugh built up and his big red
horse.
But that's all gone now. (Milwaukee, 1998)

Unconsciously Making Things Too Small
(In response to an image of an elephant and a little girl)
This is a story about Anna.
Anna is friendly with everybody.
It's medium outside, a medium summertime day.
Anna's friend is an animal, an elephant, to be specific.
God knows where they met.
Together they have a home, but we're not sure where.
It's their own business what they do.
There are too many answers—everybody has different answers.
There's a chicken and a little tree in the background.
The story is much bigger than the elephant.
It's so big, you can't go oversimplifying it.
You cannot put things like that.
Unconsciously we try to make things too small.
Every person has a story.
There's not a human being that doesn't have a story.
But making it mish mosh [*sic*] is bad.
It's like a bomb.
This is a story about Anna.
Anna is sitting on a pail.
Anna is friendly with everybody.
Anna's friend is an elephant.
Leave Anna alone!
It's too much of a story to be a story.
Writing has its limits.
It can't be blown up like a balloon.
Anna is listening to the elephant's heartbeat.
Her hand looks like a chicken's foot.
Anna and the elephant are waiting for a ride.
But it's stupid to have a car in the background.
They are not iron and nails!
Anna and the elephant are singing a song. We knew the song, but we sold it.
There are prettier things to look at than an animal's whatchamacallit.
You can't go making things—leave Anna alone.
They are a family.
They've got the whole world in their hands. (New York, 1999)

The first story is typical of most stories that emerged in the workshops. As
trust grew, the storytellers played with each other as well as with facilitators.
Answers were designed to provoke or please tellers and facilitators alike.

The stories share common themes that are also reflected in this sample. They tell of longings for freedom, acceptance, and intimacy with family or lovers. These themes appear in nearly every story, and understandably so. The storytellers are under the watchful eyes of twenty-four-hour caregivers: some family members, some paid attendants. Some storytellers are removed from their families or cannot remember them. They know they had intimacy in their lives (and continue to long for it), but often cannot remember with whom. For those who feel simultaneously isolated and fully dependent, dreams of freedom and intimacy are not surprising.

"Filling In as She Goes Along" contains only one nonsensical answer—which were more common than this sampling suggests. Nonsensical answers fell into two camps: answers that challenge the process and answers from illness. "ABCDEFG" was a challenge answer. When we asked a storyteller what we should call Ethel Rebecca's daughters, her reply was (very typically) "I don't know." The facilitator reassured her with, "You can say anything you like." As if to say, "Oh yeah?" the storyteller smugly responded, "ABCDEFG." Recording challenge answers was a vital part of the process. Weaving challenge answers into the story assured storytellers that our promise to accept any answer was true. For those with deep rifts in their ability to speak and formulate thoughts, this proved deeply comforting.

The second story is unique. It sprang from one of the most difficult of storytelling days. A very poetic storyteller was overstimulated by the storytelling that day. The group as a whole was excited by the image and eager to weave together a story. But this participant stood up and emphatically insisted that our story was pointless, if not damaging. For a long time, I wrestled with how to shape the story. Should I honor her dissent and stop the process? Day center staff continued to assist in the storytelling, and I followed their lead. I included her dissent as another contribution to the story, and now I find the story to be, of all the Time Slips stories, the most powerful example of the strength of character of people with Alzheimer's disease. It serves as a valuable reminder that some experiences of dementia are beyond words.

For those of us without cognitive disorders, the stories provide a rare window into the world of dementia. They gave the storytellers' families a way to interact with each other, to acknowledge the loss the disease incurs, yet also recognize the creativity and humanity of their loved ones. Several family caregivers told us that they copied the final book of stories and sent it to relatives, or read the stories to grandchildren. The open, poetic quality of the stories enabled families to connect, at least psychologically, with each other and with the storytellers.

The storytellers had lost the ability to weave a narrative of selfhood from memory, but they retained (and sharpened) their abilities to respond as a group, to shape a story with fragments of memory, answers born of illness, and answers born of creativity. The stories are composites of the voices of all participants, the facilitators and the storytellers. The stories do not tell the narrative of one independent self, but of relational selves. They help us hear the experience of dementia without mistakenly falling back on a mythic sense of the independent self.

The Arts Events

As the storytelling workshops were taking shape, I assembled a team of artists to collaborate with storytellers and each other to translate the stories into a series of public arts events. Our aim was to captivate Milwaukee audiences with the creative potential of people with Alzheimer's disease. We also aimed to echo the relational quality of selfhood in the workshops with a collaborative process of artistic creation as well as the artistic products themselves.

The artistic team, which met once a month over the course of a year to design the arts events, included a photographer (Dick Blau), a videographer (Xavier LePlae), web designers (Chad Anderson and Ellis Neder), a book designer (Beth Thielen), a playwright (me), a coproducer (Karen Stobbe), and my project assistant (Nichole Griffiths). After the launch of our website in April 1999, the collaborative efforts shifted to the advisory board, made up of local and regional specialists in education, dementia care, dementia research, and the arts, who crafted an outreach plan for the arts events.

The collaborative model was also taken up by the team of artists creating the Time Slips play, inspired by six of the stories told in Milwaukee and performed in May 2000 by a largely professional, intergenerational cast.[4] Performed on the University of Wisconsin, Milwaukee's large thrust stage, the Time Slips play combined the stories and characters with the plot of the disease. In the first scene, all nine characters are introduced and define their unique vocabularies of movement, text, projected images, props, sound, and song. The characters are clearly outrageous. Ethel Rebecca and Grandfather the Elephant were both featured in the play. Ethel "flies" into the thrust stage by running up a steep ramp, wearing an old-fashioned aviator jacket and hat, singing "Cera Luna Mezza Mara," and holding a small, battery-controlled fan as a propeller. Grandfather the Elephant lurches on stage played by a middle-aged man in an enormous gray suit, waving a small American flag. He lifts a foot as if doing a circus trick. Gisacho Gusto lives underwater in a pond where his father lived as well. Tormented by fish who nibble at him all day, he dreams of returning to Ondiamo, a woman he left on the surface. Two nuns move from fishing hole to fishing hole, patiently waiting for a prize-winning walleye. An artist named Hanover paints his model Ericka, who harbors dreams of fame. Running/Jumping Woman is addicted to the feeling of falling. Throughout the play, she rushes on stage, finds precipices small and large, and leaps off them in an extended, dancerly fall.

After these characters are defined in the first scene, the entire scene repeats almost exactly. Slowly, as the second scene progresses, several props and costume pieces begin to circulate from one character to another. The characters do not acknowledge the change, but the audience now reads two layers of meaning for the objects that have transformed. In the third scene, the initial scene repeats again, but this time props and costume pieces are now circulating rapidly, characters are losing language, and slide projections of sentences have fragmented into single words or letters. The characters react with a growing sense of frustration, but not confusion. Their actions are still clear to them. It is their surroundings that seem to betray them.

In the fourth and final scene, characters have very limited means of expression. Simple gestures are arduous and language is fragmented at best, garbled at worst. The characters turn to each other to evolve their stories. Running/Jumping Woman helps the grounded pilot climb a wall for a final flight. Grandfather the Elephant sings "Abide with Me" with a choir made up of the voices of his fellow characters. Gisacho Gusto finally goes above water, only to find Ericka (the artist's model) in the place of his beloved Ondiamo. Ericka had hopes of becoming famous, but accepts the warmth of Gisacho's embrace instead. The nuns finally reel in their prize catch in spite of the fact that one of the sisters has lost language entirely. Hanover began painting a small canvas, but ends using his arm as a brush as his painting appears, animated, on the large back wall of the set.

Each character evolves through creative and communal effort. There is a clear and deliberate parallel here to the storytelling workshops themselves, where people with ADRD face broken language and disorientation and construct a sense of selfhood through communal creative expression.

The play ran for five performances. Our outreach efforts targeted schools, the arts community, health care workers, and those concerned with Alzheimer's and dementia from churches to support groups. As a result, audiences were largely a blend of these populations. Extensive local media coverage resulted in nearly everyone in the audience knowing a bit about how the play evolved, but some audience members came with no knowledge of the storytelling project at all.

Postshow discussions (which followed each of the seventy-minute performances) revealed some confusion over whether the actors were portraying imaginary characters or people with Alzheimer's disease. Certainly there

New York production of *Time Slips*, 2001; John Freimann as Bookman. (Photograph by Tim Atkinson.)

New York production of *Time Slips*, 2001; Sheridan Thomas as Holding On. (Photograph by Tim Atkinson.)

was a deliberate attempt on our part to overlap the characters and the storytellers. We had put the characters into the plot of the disease—they appeared to be suffering it themselves. The characters successfully drew the audience into the experience of repetition, disorientation, and the unreliability of objects, language, and memory. But too much confusion meant that audiences missed the most important point of the play—that these tales of loss and transcendence had been forged in collaboration between facilitators and people with Alzheimer's disease themselves.[5]

Assessing audience reaction is always a slippery endeavor. But after reviewing notes from postshow discussions, I believe the audience reactions point to two things. First, the structure of the play and preshow materials did cloud the distinction between the characters in the creative stories and the storytellers with Alzheimer's disease. As playwright and project director, I had been concerned that too much information about the origin of the play would repel potential audience members. Promotional materials emphasized that the play was an original, multimedia, poetic journey in one-act, and only secondarily mentioned that it was inspired by creative stories told by people with ADRD. The program materials alluded to the storytelling workshops, but included no more than a paragraph on them. The loose description of the storytelling process in promotional materials provided holes large enough for people longing to find meaning in the disease to attach to the characters as everyday people experiencing Alzheimer's.

My other reading of the audience reaction to the Milwaukee Time Slips production is fairly simple. ADRD can be a horrifying experience for those who suffer it directly, as well as for those who watch the memory (and some believe the personality) of their loved-one evaporate. Caring for people with ADRD can be an exceedingly challenging task, particularly in a culture that views them as less than a whole self due to their memory loss Caregivers, personal and professional, often feel that there is little hope for people embroiled in the world of the disease, little hope for the restoration of memory, for medical solutions, for economic relief, or for cultural understanding. In a country that declared its "independence" and that prides itself on its bootstrap success stories and rugged individualism, Alzheimer's disease is seen as the ultimate nightmare. We long to find reasons for it, to make sense of a disease that seems to strike regardless of gender, class, race, or education. With both eyes fixed on the losses suffered by those who have Alzheimer's and by their loved ones, people directly engaged with the disease may have difficulty finding hope and meaning in the creative expression of people with Alzheimer's disease.

Yet the majority of audience members that spoke at postshow discussions clearly "got it." Seeing the humor and power in the stories can only come when people are ready—when fear and anger and grief subside enough (perhaps only momentarily) to allow room for humor, for the voices of people with Alzheimer's themselves.

Notes

Thank you to the students, members of the Time Slips artistic team, the storytellers, and their caregivers (family and staff) for making this project possible. The Time Slips Project Milwaukee received generous support from the Helen Bader Foundation, Inc., the Brookdale Foundation, Alterra Healthcare Corp., the Extendicare Foundation, and Blue Cross and Blue Shield, and most importantly, the Center for Twentieth Century Studies at the University of Wisconsin, Milwaukee. The Time Slips Project New York arts events are being hosted by the Brookdale Center on Aging at Hunter College. For more information, visit www.timeslips.org.

1. Alzheimer's disease is the most common form of dementia. *Dementia* is an umbrella term for a variety of conditions marked by cognitive disorders including memory loss and difficulty with reasoning, anxiety, and disorientation.

2. There are several autobiographies written by people with ADRD, including Diana Friel McGowin's *Living in the Labyrinth*, Robert Davis's *My Journey into Alzheimer's Disease*, and Cary Henderson's *Partial View*.

3. Golander and Raz's study (1996) suggests that caregivers work best with people who have an identity—whether fictitious or "real."

4. The play followed an art installation at Milwaukee's Charles Allis Museum in March 2000, featuring ten larger-than-life portraits of storytellers, two handmade pop-up books that capture the storytelling process, a computer displaying the project's website, and two of the stories.

5. The Time Slips Project New York will feature a play inspired by stories that emerged in New York workshops. The structure of the play will include the storytelling workshops, and audiences will witness the characters emerge from the storytellers themselves.

Works Cited

Davis, Lennard. 1995. *Enforcing Normalcy: Disability, Deafness, and the Body.* London: Verso.
Davis, Robert. 1989. *My Journey into Alzheimer's Disease.* Wheaton, Ill.: Tyndale House.
Eakin, Paul John. 1999. *How Our Lives Become Stories: Making Selves.* Ithaca: Cornell University Press.
Goffman, Erving. 1959. *The Presentation of Self in Everyday Life.* New York: Doubleday.
Golander, Hava, and Aviad Raz. 1996. "The Mask of Dementia: Images of 'Demented Residents' in a Nursing Ward." *Ageing and Society* 16:269–85.
Henderson, Cary. 1998. *Partial View.* Dallas: Southern Methodist University Press.
Holstein, James A., and Jaber F. Gubrium. 2000. *The Self We Live By: Narrative Identity in a Postmodern World.* New York: Oxford.
McGowin, Diana Friel. 1993. *Living in the Labyrinth.* New York: Delacorte.
Mead, George Herbert. 1934. *Mind, Self and Society.* Chicago: University of Chicago Press.
Mitchell, David, and Sharon Snyder, eds. 1997. *The Body and Physical Difference: Discourses of Disability.* Ann Arbor: University of Michigan Press.

PART IV Performing Disability in Daily Life

Part of sociology's legacy to performance studies is the idea that we do not just live our "real life" identities, we *perform* them. An early touchstone text that employs a theatrical metaphor to describe interactions among people is Erving Goffman's *The Presentation of Self of Everyday Life* (1959). Goffman, who takes a functionalist approach, argues that who we are socially is bound up with who we are perceived to be by those around us (our audience) and that we behave as actors in order to control the impressions we make on others. This understanding of everyday behavior emphasizes that identity does not simply reside in individuals but is the product of social interactions among individuals. This perspective is congruent with the view of disability as something that is not an intrinsic characteristic of certain bodies but a construct produced through the interaction of those bodies with socially based norms that frame the way those bodies are generally perceived.

The essays in this part address the performance of disability in several contexts that lie outside of overtly aesthetic frames. It is noteworthy that two of the essays, Maureen Connolly and Tom Craig's and Carrie Sandahl's, discuss the ways in which educational institutions implicitly enforce corporeal norms: Craig and Connolly point out that notions of productivity underlie the regimentation and physical settings of schools, while Sandahl reveals that a related concept of the productive body underpins the acting pedagogy of theater programs in the United States. Schools not only implicitly instruct us in social norms—they also enforce those norms by demanding that students perform themselves and their physical relationships to their environment in particular ways.

Two of the essays here describe performative experiments that served as heuristics for uncovering social and cultural assumptions about disability and how it is performed. In "Looking Blind: A Revelation of Culture's Eye," Tanya Titchkosky describes her provocative decision to masquerade as blind as a means of getting a better look at the assumptions to which sightless people are subjected. By showing that people who conform to the socially defined image of blindness are considered to be blind and treated as if they were (even when they are known to be sighted), Titchkosky shows how this identity category is constructed through interaction. On the basis of her experience, Titchkosky develops a concept of disability as an "in-between state" that both conforms to and troubles the sociological concepts of master status and liminality.

In "Disrupting a Disembodied Status Quo: Invisible Theater as Subversive Pedagogy," Maureen Connolly and Tom Craig describe an intervention similar to, but more formally structured than, Titchkosky's, in which Craig's performance of physical disability in front of a class, accompanied by staged reactions from some members, led to spontaneous responses. Whereas Titchkosky herself was the ultimate audience for her performance of blindness, Craig and Connolly sought to use the technique of "invisible theater" to foreground the presence of disabled people and the reactions they elicit as part of a pedagogical effort to get the class to think and talk about disability issues. In both cases, an invisible, fictional performance revealed the social underpinnings of everyday performances.

If Craig and Connolly underline the value of performative pedagogical techniques for making people more aware of the social roles they play with respect to disability, Carrie Sandahl points to ways that performance pedagogy can be oppressive to the disabled. In "The Tyranny of Neutral: Disability and Actor Training," Sandahl shows that the approach to training young actors that is standard in the American academy today is based on a concept of the "neutral" body that derives from both modern European performance theory and concepts of industrial productivity, such as Taylorism. Sandahl demonstrates that young actors are told that their productivity as performers depends on their ability to achieve an affectless physical state from which to build characterizations and shows that this approach marginalizes and humiliates disabled actors whose bodies cannot conform to this standard.

Although many of the essays in this collection stress the multiple counternormative ways in which disability can be performed, an important part of the sociologically informed discourse on everyday life performance stresses that most people perform their identities in ways that conform to social norms most of the time. This is the issue Lenore Manderson and Susan Peake examine in "Men in Motion: Disability and the Performance of

Masculinity." As Manderson and Peake demonstrate through their report on an ethnographic survey of Australian male amputees, these men come to see themselves as feminized and incapable of fulfilling a conventional male role. Their response, the normative response, is not to redefine masculinity but to find ways of performing conventional masculinity with their redefined bodies, particularly through hypermasculine display and participation in disability sports.

→ this is also
what M-E does!

interesting b/c
M-E feels she
cannot be fem!

Looking Blind
A Revelation of Culture's Eye

TANYA TITCHKOSKY

I am not blind. I have, however, acted as though I were. I have performed the role of blindness, not in the theater, but on the stage of everyday life.

Sociologists refer to a non-normative person's performance of normalcy as "passing." I have passed as blind by using a guide dog and wearing sunglasses, and thus being seen and treated as blind. Although I caused others to regard me as blind, I did not simulate blindness for myself: I acted blind while seeing. This essay uses the experience to disrupt conventional notions of disability and theorize the tie between oppressive cultural assumptions and the meaning of embodiment—even though we are able, through our bodies, to perform, or insert into the world, new meanings of ourselves as bodied beings.

Interactions between blind and sighted, including sighted persons' performances of blindness, reveal cultural assumptions regarding the meaning of both identities. My performances of blindness were accomplished through wearing dark glasses and handling a guide dog. These two cultural representations meet the eye of sighted others and are enveloped by cultural assumptions regarding blindness. To be seen and treated as blind is to be subject to cultural conceptions. In this way, a performance of blindness takes place upon a stage where cultural conceptions of blind or sighted embodiment play themselves out.

While by convention disability is simply lack or limitation, consideration of blindness as performance reveals that disability is an achieved social status. It appears to others through social conceptions of embodiment, and thus any appearance of disability is a status constituted by and between people. Disability theorists and activists have shown that cultural conceptions of, and responses to, impairment can teach us about the social significance of disability.[1] In order to take a closer "look" at disability as an achieved social status, I consider how it is seen and treated by other persons, and how such reactions represent conceptions of disability performed by nondisabled others. I invite the reader to imagine the backdrop of my lived experience of my performance of blindness. By revealing the meanings constituting disability on the stage of everyday life, I problematize the dichotomy between ability and disability and highlight the complex relation between these categories of interpretation of our embodied existence. I focus specifically on experiences in which disability confounds conventional modes of thought, showing the permeable boundaries between the body and society.[2]

Insofar as a person passing as blind experiences collective assumptions regarding what blindness looks like, even the most ordinary experience can reveal extraordinary cultural values as they constitute the meaning of persons. I avoid quantification of my experience since the methodology derives from the understanding that any "slice of life," a text, a sentence, an action, can reveal the meaning of the social space within which lives are given shape. First let me set the stage of my passing by providing an account of why I did so.

Seeing Blindness

The first occasion on which I passed as blind occurred quite innocently. Some years ago my partner and fellow sociologist, Rod Michalko, was teaching in downtown Toronto on a hot and humid summer day. His workday extended into the evening, and Rod (a real blind person) became concerned that his guide dog, Smokie, was getting hot and tired. He asked if I would come downtown and take Smokie home on the subway.

Smokie was a big, strong dog who liked to be in charge. I left his harness on so that I could give commands and follow his decisions about moving through the crowds. We got within thirty or forty feet of the stairs down to subway, I gave Smokie the command "Left, find the stairs." To my surprise, he went right, toward a patch of grass. Just as I realized what Smokie was doing, a man grabbed me by the arm and said, "I'll take you to the subway." Down the stairs we went, the man tugging me all the way to the ticket booth.

On the way, I did protest. I said, "I can do it. I'm fine. He just wanted to have a pee. I can do it!" Curiously enough, I did not say, "I can see." In fact, I did not even look the man in the face. I had just been grabbed and pulled in public by a stranger, and yet I felt ashamed to say that I was sighted. I did not reclaim my sighted identity because moving between blindness and sightedness is not a normal move and would reveal that I had violated a taken-for-granted norm of public life, namely, that you *are* who you *appear* to be.[3] To the man who assisted me, I appeared as blind, a status pressed upon me not just by his grip, but also by our shared understanding that "looked" blind.

Having failed to look the man in the face, I sat on a bench, not knowing whether he was still watching me. I kept my eyes to myself. I thought about being sighted because a man had treated me as blind and had imposed his conception of blindness on me. Despite this stranger's impositional power, performed through his own status as a "helpful sighted person," he failed to see that I was sighted. Still more, he failed to imagine a connection between "blind woman" and "competent, independent user of a guide dog." The taken-for-granted power of sight, which allows us to ignore the conceptions that organize seeing, disempowered not just me and Smokie, but the man's imagination.

Notice though that in my account, the unspoken words "I can see" are treated as if they would have been magic. I assume they would have released me from the man's bodily control. I, like the man, have a taken-for-granted sense that sight *is* might. Of course, living with Rod and Smokie, an obvious marker of blindness, had previously brought me face-to-face with collective assumptions regarding the magical power of sight, its ubiquitous control, and its recognition as primary, good, right, mighty, and, even natural. While I innocently fell into my first act of passing, these obvious dichotomies of power provoked me to take up the performance of blindness on other occasions.

I acted as though I were blind on an airplane flight. I traveled with Rod, Smokie, and Cassis, a small black Labrador retriever with whom I had learned guide dog training. Cassis was in her harness for this trip, and I was wearing dark glasses. Passing was partly motivated by our concern for Cassis; Rod and I did not want her to travel in the baggage compartment. In harness, guiding a "blind person," Cassis would travel in the cabin. With the collaboration of Rod, Smokie, and Cassis, I "accomplished"[4] blindness and was treated as I appeared. As we discovered, this passing had the serendipitous effect of allowing us to collect ethnographic data on cultural representations of blind-sighted interaction. Blind as I "looked," I could also see such interactions.[5] In what follows, this trip is the background for the figure of the meaning of embodiment as it becomes available to people through interactions and environments where conceptions of disability make an appearance.

On the Way with Blindness

Sociologists have called the marking of our identity by one aspect of our appearance *master status*. It contrasts with the general concept of status, that is, a person's cumulative position within society. The concept of status is used to represent the sum total of the rights and responsibilities understood to belong to a position.[6] "Woman," "partner," "friend" are all positions delineated by my society, and their sum total is supposed to represent the minimal set of rights and responsibilities expected of me. Add blindness, and the sum total changes, as do the expectations: I am now blind woman, blind partner, blind hotel-patron, blind friend.

A master status refers to the process of constituting the minimal sense of social rights and responsibilities from one status position, not the sum of all. In some circumstances, all statuses other than the master status do not amount to much—they are at best qualifiers of one main status. However, my experiences between blindness and sightedness suggest a "second look" at the concept of master status. For example, prior to our airplane flight, our friends, Jason and Maggie, drove us to a hotel. Rod and I harnessed our respective guide dogs, gave the command "Follow," and, following Jason, entered the hotel. After checking in, we proceeded to our room. The room was hot; Rod got water for our dogs while the rest of us searched out the mechanism for the air conditioner. Maggie began tapping a wall saying, "Tanya, it's here. Tanya, it's here on the wall next to the door." I could, of course, see the control. Still she tapped. I had preformed the check-in procedures with my dark glasses and guide dog, and this performance influenced Maggie's treatment of me, even though she knows that I am not blind.

My being treated as blind by someone who knows that I am sighted has happened before, not only with other friends, but also with Rod. Often Rod will describe the exact location where he put a chair, cup, or my books, even when I am in close proximity to the objects. He will say, "Oh yeah, I am treating you as if you are blind." As with Maggie's tapping of the wall, Rod's actions seem to be inadequately addressed by the concept of master status. When Maggie treated me as blind, I felt humorously startled. When Rod does so, I feel a pleasurable sense of relief, glad that someone else, not just I, ignores the other's perspective. This pleasure quickly dissipates as I realize that the consequence of my ignoring Rod's perspective is radically different. My "inarticulate preliminary understanding"[7] is that while Rod and others are engaged in the same behavior of forgetting my sightedness, the social significance is not the same and is not adequately conceptualized through the concept of master status.

Using a guide dog, that is, "doing" blindness, in public around my sighted friends, I am bringing myself and others face-to-face with the always present, but often hidden, interrelation between sightedness and blindness. I make their interrelation obvious, yet I do so in such a way that my behavior cannot be made to fit neatly into either sightedness or blindness. There is no easy way to make sense of what I am doing: am I a person taking advantage of blindness or of sightedness, both, neither? Am I being unethical or helpful, a faker or someone trying to establish a close tie to blindness? Am I taking advantage of Rod or of others? Is he taking advantage of me? And, if either of us is seeking an advantage, what would provoke us to choose such an difficult way of doing so?

Noticing that only sight *or* blindness does not mean that one or the other is "mastering" my status. Instead, a status steeped in ambiguity calls forth a need for mastery, the imposition of a definitive clarity, a judgment that a person is one or the other but not both. What needs to be mastered are the "leaky boundaries"[8] between the supposedly dichotomous status positions of sightedness and blindness. Acting blind among those who know that I am not introduces these boundaries and inserts ambiguity into the interaction. Moreover, given that *any* appearance of blindness is always achieved between people, this appearance is always an occasion to think about the embodied partnerships between blindness and sightedness, disability and nondisability. The conventional desire to master ambiguity and to make identity certain often results in "compulsory able-bodiedness,"[9] enforcing the cultural assumption that sight is good and blind people should do their utmost to get as close as possible to it. True enough, but there is more; for example, blind travelers are a disruptive sight to sighted others. Through our bodies, as Jim Swan reminds us, we have the "capacity to slip past the categories and codes of social discourse or to infiltrate and transform them."[10] Conventionally, "blind" is a category that marks with "lack" all other statuses a person holds, yet in doing blindness, sight's inability to deal with blurry demarcations or leaky boundary crossings is made apparent. This is part of the radical critical power that *lies between* the differences of disability and nondisability and makes cross-disability experiences potential spaces for critical inquiry into ableist culture.

Perhaps it is just such ambiguity that the concept of master status implicitly responds to or aims to manage. Referring to a person as a blind woman, blind traveler, or a blind friend does more than simply suggest the power of an attribute, such as blindness, to "master" all other status positions. It would be rare, indeed, to refer to someone as a sighted woman or a sighted traveler, even though, like blindness, sight is a powerful attribute. We expect people to be sighted, and we organize the environment and social statuses accordingly. Categories such as traveler or professor are often treated as clear and certain, but add the adjective *blind* to any of these categories and the clarity melds into ambiguity. The rights and responsibilities assumed to belong to the status "traveler," or "professor," and those to "blind," may be contradictory.

Such categorical ambiguity is often quickly clarified. Person-first ideology[11] is one way to do so. Claiming that disabled people are "persons first" manages ambiguity by de-mastering disability, placing it somewhere other than the person, or forgetting about disability all together. Focusing solely on a person's "impaired" character, as in the case of stereotyping and discrimination, is another way to attempt to clarify the ambiguity that disabled bodies represent. In the first case, disability is cast out from some (abstract/disembodied) concept of personhood, while in the second, the disabled person as a whole is cast out. In both cases, the experience of ambiguity is all but annihilated.

Still, there are no conventions that tell us how to relate to people who are between the major status categories that constitute a discernable identity. People, for example, who are between male and female are typically pathologized and "remedied" by moving them into one category or the other.[12] Being *between* is a problematic of both the identity and the difference of disability. However, when Rod treats me as blind, I assume that my between-ness is not being denied and is, instead, being acknowledged. Given the ubiquity of the taken-for-granted notion that sight is might, every day something happens that puts me fully in the realm of sightedness and Rod fully in the realm of blindness, as if there is no relation between the two. Forgetting my sightedness, Rod performs an absolution and allows for the possibility of a between-ness to begin again where, if only for a moment, the convention of compulsory able-bodiedness is disrupted, not enforced.

The Ambiguous Meaning of Disability

Every person, disabled or not, confronts a complex milieu of interpretation, especially at the level of *who or what* they are—are you rich or poor, woman or man, black or white? People are "usually" and "normally" put into either one or the other of these sets of dichotomies.[13] Indeed, being "normal" usually means enabling others to place one's self into one slot or the other of any dichotomized category used to constitute identity. What disabled people bring to the fore is a vivid and complex stream of interpretation, not simply at the level of who a disabled person is, but also, at how a disabled person's embodied presence is organized as ambiguity incarnate.[14] Economic, physical, and administrative forces impinge upon all people, and thereby exclusion and control are enacted. But the matter is different with disabled people since disabled people mediate or symbolize an important aspect of this process.

The presence of disability throws into question the meaning of being in or out, marginalized or mainstreamed, controlled or empowered. When the man grabbed me as I was getting close to the subway stairs, the appearance of blindness seemingly empowered him even as it disrupted my taken-for-granted relation to sight. Is not the meaning of disability tied to ambiguity, given that my friends "know" that I am sighted and yet are influenced by the "sights of blindness" to treat me otherwise? My experiences of passing demonstrate that disability raises the question of being "in-between."[15] According to Thomson, "Within this liminal space the disabled person must constitute something akin to identity."[16]

Liminal is a term developed by anthropologists to describe events such as initiation rituals of, for example, birth, death, or harvest. It refers to that space within collective life where people are, in the politically charged words of Hannah Arendt, "no longer and not yet."[17] As an individual moves from the identity of girl to woman, a community may make use of segregation, symbolism, and ceremony, providing a ritual-filled marker of her time as neither. Liminality, according to Victor Turner,[18] is a dangerous or uncertain phenomenon that communities traditionally both mark off and transform. In Western(ized) cultures, the tradition of medicine envelops most newly disabled people, for example, moving one back into the position of able-bodiedness through medical, remedial, or rehabilitative practices or by confirming one's identity *as* disabled. But once disabled . . . limbo. Interestingly enough, this liminality does not only envelop disabled participants. Interaction with disability can place everyone in limbo between the expectations of normality and the *necessity of alterity.*

Some hold that disability is essentially a socially constructed category built from the actions of nondisabled others—a kind of derogatory and devalued master-status. But surely there is more. Is there not something about disability, as it is lived and performed in the midst of others, within exclusionary and oppressive environments, that adds to or acts upon mainstream life and "normal" identity?

This possibility of something more was brought home to me during the return flight home. Our seats were in the middle row. I sat at the outer edge, and Cassis and Smokie, very tired now, were tucked in safely within the confines of the small bulkhead seating area. Part way through the flight, the woman seated across the aisle from me got my attention and said, "I am going blind. When did you go blind?"

Hoping that the flight crew would not hear me, I replied, "I am not blind. I'm just training this dog." Disappointment was writ large on the woman's face, and I quickly introduced her to Rod as a "real blind person." They attempted a conversation over the hum of the plane and the space of the aisle. Before this moment, passing signified two main sets of relations: a kind of private intimacy with Rod and an ironic distance from sighted culture that allowed for critical inquiry. Passing as blind was a way to resist compulsory able-bodiedness and forge an alliance with Rod and other disabled people. The woman's question made me realize that the ambiguity expressed within my passing project was loaded with more meaning and contradiction than I had wanted to see. It is offering up the matter of disability for other kinds of meaningful engagement between disabled and nondisabled people. Passing is not just blank material upon which culture inscribes its conventions regarding embodiment. Passing, like any instance of the appearance of disability in a culture, is filled with the potential of remaking or confounding our collective conventional assumptions of bodies. Passing, unlike many other instances of the appearance of disability, seems much more committed to *receiving* the meanings that others give to disability and is not so interested in performing the insertion of *new* meanings of disability. Passing is not very interested in radical new takes on disability, or new meanings, as this would put the passer at risk of being exposed as a mere imitation of disability.

The realization that passing is something more than catching the reflections of cultural attitudes toward blindness eliminated my desire to ever do it again.

Concluding Remarks

The body can be explained, says Alan Radley, as the "object of the actions and interests of others." But, Radley insists that there is more: "the body is a key expressive medium and, in its material aspect, the basis upon which we symbolize our relationship to the world of which we are a part."[19] The disabled body brings this expressivity to the fore. While signs of empowerment and control are not clear, Rod and I with guide dogs in hand did express alternative relationships to the world of which we are a part. The meaning of our comings and goings will never be clear and certain, but we certainly *expressed and performed* such ambiguity, and we did so in many different ways in all our ordinary activities of our trip as the not-so-ordinary blind travelers.

Radley refers to the expressiveness of the body as the "body-subject"; this is the body that is always more than what others make of it. The body-subject, he says, plays "a special role in the configuration of meaning, a meaning whose significance is bound up with its . . . elusory nature."[20] This elusory nature is tied to the fact that disability embodies "illegitimate fusion[s] of cultural categories."[21] Through engagement with the stuff of culture (interpretive categories) and through the process of illegitimate fusions, disabled people constitute something akin to identity. Disability as "violated wholeness, unbounded incompleteness, unregulated particularity, dependent subjugation, disordered intractability" symbolizes the ambiguous mixing of a not-me and me, of normal and abnormal, of uniqueness and uniformity, of known and unknown.[22] Disability thus always represents the possible insertion of alterity into the assumed world of normalcy.

Disability is not simply a sign of deviation from the majority that attempts to control it. To claim such a simple limit would render the body "so docile, so pliable as to be nothing more than a passive mirror in which to catch the reflections of social action."[23] Understanding the body as object requires we take account of what the disabled body as subject inserts into the world here and now. Seeking just such an understanding of the body can allow us to conceive of it as infusing new significance, disturbing the picture of the everyday reality of the "majority," and as a comment upon, even a conversation with, cultural assumptions regarding embodiment in environments not of our own choosing. Disability is always more than stigmatized deviation and oppressive minoritization. It is an alternative way of being steeped in between-ness; the disabled body is situated *between* all the stuff a culture gives to its people. In this between-ness, disability can permit us to rethink the meaning of identity formed through assumptions regarding embodiment and subjectivity. It is by taking disability as a subjectively problematic stance for inquiry that sociological conceptions of "passing," "master status," and "stigmatized attribute" have been rethought in this essay.

Notes

A longer version of this essay can be found in my *Disability, Self, and Society* (Toronto: University of Toronto Press, 2003), chap. 6.

1. See, for example, Michael Oliver, *The Politics of Disablement* (London: Macmillan, 1990); Irving Kenneth Zola, *Missing Pieces: A Chronicle of Living with a Disability* (Philadelphia: Temple University Press, 1982); Tom Shakespeare, ed., *The Disability Reader: Social Science Perspectives* (London: Cassell Academic, 1998).

2. See, for example, Margrit Shildrick and Janet Price, "Breaking the Boundaries of the Broken Body," *Body and Society* 2, no. 4 (1996): 93–113; Elizabeth Ettorre, "Re-shaping the Space between Bodies and Culture," *Sociology of Health and Illness* 20, no. 4 (1998): 458–555; Ray McDermott and Hervé Varene, "Culture as Disability," *Anthropology and Education Quarterly* 26, no. 3 (1995): 324–48; David T. Mitchell and Sharon L. Snyder, "Disability Studies and the Double Bind of Representation," in *The Body and Physical Difference: Discourses of Disability* (Ann Arbor: Uni-

versity of Michigan Press, 1997), 1–31; Rosemarie Garland Thomson, *Extraordinary Bodies: Figuring Physical Disability in American Culture and Literature* (New York: Columbia University Press, 1997); Tanya Titchkosky, "Disability Studies: The Old and the New?" *Canadian Journal of Sociology and Anthropology* 25, no. 2 (2000): 197–224; Rod Michalko, *The Difference That Disability Makes* (Philadelphia: Temple University Press, 2003), *The Two-in-One: Walking with Smokie, Walking with Blindness* (Philadelphia: Temple University Press, 1999), and *The Mystery of the Eye and the Shadow of Blindness* (Toronto: University of Toronto Press, 1998); Mairian Corker, "New Disability Discourse: The Principle of Optimization and Social Change," in *Disability Discourse*, ed. Mairian Corker and Sally French (Buckingham: Open University Press, 1999), 192–209.

3. Erving Goffman, *The Presentation of Self in Everyday Life* (New York: Doubleday Anchor, 1959).

4. Harold Garfinkel, *Studies in Ethnomethodology* (Englewood Cliffs, N.J.: Prentice Hall, 1967).

5. It is illegal to pass as blind. Whether it is unethical is a different question. The conception of disability should be examined together with the ethics of passing. For a discussion of the law as a formulation of identity, see James Vernon, "'For Some Queer Reason': The Trials and Tribulations of Colonel Barker's Masquerade in Interwar Britain," *Signs* 26, no. 1 (2000): 37–62, esp. 39–46. It is expected, particularly in the rehabilitation realm, that blind people pass as close as possible to sighted standards and practices. See Robert McRuer, "Compulsory Able-Bodiedness and Queer/Disabled Existence," in *Disability Studies: Enabling the Humanities*, ed. Sharon L. Snyder, Brenda Jo Brueggemann, and Rosemarie Garland Thomson (New York: Modern Language Association of America, 2002), 88–99.

6. Ralph Linton, "On Status and Role," in *Sociology: The Classic Statements*, ed. Marcello Truzzi (New York: Random House, 1971), 90–97.

7. Hannah Arendt, *Essays in Understanding: 1930–1954* (New York: Harcourt Brace, 1994).

8. Ettorre, "Re-Shaping the Space"; Titchkosky, *Disability, Self, and Society*, esp. chaps. 6 and 7.

9. McRuer, "Compulsory Able-Bodiedness."

10. Jim Swan, "Disability, Bodies, Voices," in Snyder, Brueggemann, and Thomson, *Disability Studies*, 286.

11. James Overboe, "'Difference in Itself': Validating Disabled People's Lived Experience," *Body and Society* 5, no. 4 (1999): 17–29; Tanya Titchkosky, "Disability—a Rose by Any Other Name? People-First Language in Canadian Society," *Canadian Review of Sociology and Anthropology* 38, no. 2 (2001): 125–40.

12. Judith Butler, *Bodies That Matter* (New York: Routledge, 1993); Sander Gilman, *Difference and Pathology* (Ithaca, N.Y.: Cornell University Press, 1985); Elizabeth Grosz, "Intolerable Ambiguity: Freaks as/at the Limits," in *Freakery: Cultural Spectacles of Extraordinary Bodies*, ed. Rosemarie Garland Thomson (New York: New York University Press, 1996), 55–66.

13. Joan Scott, "Deconstructing Equality-versus-Difference; or, The Uses of Postcolonial Structuralist Theory for Feminism," *Feminist Studies* 14, no. 1 (1998): 32–55, and "Multiculturalism and the Politics of Identity," in *Identity in Question*, ed. John Rajchman (New York: Routledge, 1995), 3–12.

14. Rod Michalko and Tanya Titchkosky, "Putting Disability in Its Place: It's Not a Joking Matter," in *Embodied Rhetorics: Disability in Language and Culture,* ed. James Wilson and Cynthia Lewicki-Wilson (Carbondale: University of Southern Illinois Press, 2001), 200–228.

15. F. G. Asenjo, *In-between: An Essay on Categories* (Lanham, Md.: Center for Advanced Research in Phenomenology, and University Press of America, 1988); Mairian Corker and Sally French, "Reclaiming Discourse in Disability Studies," in Corker and French, *Disability Discourse,* 1–11, esp. 2–6; Mitchell and Snyder, *Body and Physical Difference;* Tanya Titchkosky, "Cultural Maps: Which Way to Disability?" in *Disability and Postmodernity: Embodying Disability Theory,* ed. Marian Corker and Tom Shakespeare (London: Continuum, 2002), 145–60.

16. Thomson, *Extraordinary Bodies,* 114.

17. Hannah Arendt, *Men in Dark Times* (New York: Harcourt Brace Jovanovich, 1955), 3–15.

18. Victor Turner, *On the Edge of the Bush: Anthropology as Experience* (Tucson: University of Arizona Press,1985), 151–73.

19. Alan Radley, "The Elusory Body and Social Constructionist Theory," *Body and Society* 1, no. 2 (1995): 3, 4.

20. Radley, "The Elusory Body," 7.

21. Thomson, *Extraordinary Bodies,* 114.

22. Thomson, *Extraordinary Bodies,* 44, 41, 114, 112.

23. Radley, "The Elusory Body," 7.

Men in Motion

Disability & the Performance of Masculinity

LENORE MANDERSON AND SUSAN PEAKE

I was very fit when the accident happened. And now I am stuck in a bloody wheelchair. I want to play sport—I want to play basketball. I want to play wheelchair athletics. They reckon you do your own practice in the wheelchair. [Playing basketball] makes me feel whole again. Like I'm a whole person. You can actually *do* something—you are not just stuck in the house. You can *do* something. I have to learn how to do everything for myself. I am a paraplegic. I am a paraplegic, but I have to be one of the best paraplegics going. I'm a paraplegic, but I am going to be a good paraplegic. People remember you as you were, but now I am different. I may be paralyzed, but I'll be playing basketball soon. It just makes you feel like a person again. You are your own person again. You actually do something. You do a sport. Basketball through wheels. My life has changed, but I just have to make the best of it. I am in a wheelchair. All right, so I am in a wheelchair. I am stuck in a wheelchair. But I am going to make the *best* way of life I can.

This extract is from an interview with a young man whose paraplegia derives from a spinal injury from a workplace accident two years earlier. His account of his social rehabilitation through sport, with its implicit notions of masculinity, is characteristic of the Australian men whose experiences of disability are discussed in this essay.

Australia is not alone in its promotion of "perfect" bodies through diet and drugs, health and exercise programs, cosmetic surgery, and sport, resulting in the presumed nexus of physical appearance and ability, life chances and personal worth. Individuals whose bodies function and/or look different from most have to decouple physicality and social membership in face of often highly discriminatory attitudes. In this essay, we explore how men effect their social rehabilitation by drawing on a conventional and conservative discourse of masculinity and normality, as practiced through competitive sport. Men seek to reestablish what they understand to be their former relationships with their bodies, while also distinguishing their bodies from other sexless, feminine bodies.

The body is both a vehicle and canvas, able to be inscribed, read, and used to cultural ends, either embodying the conventions of a given society or challenging and resisting such conventions. People whose bodies do not fit comfortably with ideals of embodiment must therefore counter the presumptions of their capability based on others' prejudgments. Hence people claim that they are "normal" despite bodily change and disability, resisting how others regard bodies as a superficial guide to individual character and capacity and as a way of resisting the consequent stigma (L. Davis 1995; Terry and Urla 1995; Mitchell and Snyder 1997).

In the following discussion, we use the term *performance* broadly to refer to the processes of self-presentation, impression management, and the theatricalities of everyday life (Goffman 1959; Scheibe 2000). The idea of performance has additional relevance, however, since competitive sport is performed before a public, each sports player an actor. In this text, we explore how men resist the stigma of disability acquired by accident or illness. As we illustrate, although there is the potential for resistance to the conventions of masculinity as well as disability, the men with whom we worked resisted social constructions of disability by embracing conventional representations of masculinity.

Methods

In this essay, we draw on our research conducted individually and collaboratively on injury, illness, and embodiment. The study involved some 120 participants recruited through voluntary organizations, personal introductions, and social network sampling; it included people who had had amputations from accident or serious illness, people who had stoma surgery from Crohn's disease, ulcerative colitis or colorectal cancer, women who had had mastectomies, and people who had had kidney transplants (Manderson 1999). Unstructured interviews were conducted at the venue of choice of interviewees, generally their own homes, where we invited them to talk about their experiences: how bodily changes affect self-image, and how this

232 Bodies in Commotion

affected interactions with family, friends, work mates, and participation in wider society. Interview data were supplemented by letters, questionnaire returns, newsletters produced by consumer groups, and participant observation. Here, we draw particularly on interviews with men who had amputations following vehicular or workplace accident or disease, and their accounts of individual embodiment, exercise of agency, ideas of personhood, and performance of gender. For descriptive purposes, we focus on the accounts of eight professional sportsmen, most in their late twenties or early thirties, but their experiences and views are consistent with those of the majority. In accrediting the opinions of men with disabilities, we use the pseudonyms men chose themselves.

Theorizing the Body

The focus on perfect bodies draws attention to the need to understand how body image of individuals affects the adjustment of individuals to major surgery and bodily change. Considerable work has been undertaken on the problematic nature of changes to the body when they affect individuals in ways that are discordant with social ideals of beauty, youth, slimness, and fitness (K. Davis 1995; Becker 1997; Gilman 1999). Although scholarly interest in bodies and body image has concentrated on young women, older women and men are vulnerable to these same ideals. Our research (Manderson 1999; Peake and Manderson 1999, 2003) illustrates how individuals draw on a discourse of normality, reflecting their negotiation of sense of self in reaction to the changes to their bodies.

The injured or diseased body is a body out of control, often at both the cellular and the systemic level, in terms of stability, mobility, and bodily functions. Most immediately, people loose their autonomy and hence adulthood with insults to the physical body. Changes to bodily functions, for instance, place the individual in a position analogous to childhood; needing assistance with feeding, bathing, toileting, and dressing, the individual inhabits a social location that is presexual and, to an extent, preengendered. While technologies such as a wheelchair are signs simply of physical incapacity, they are read also as signs of intellectual and mental (in)capacity. While disease and injury can create situations whereby individuals lose control, social membership demands autonomy and control of the physical body.

As they articulated in interview narratives, individuals need to adapt to their losses and develop new ways of performance to give life new, or to recover old, meanings. Gender and sexuality are open to renegotiation, usually, despite the potential for resistance, by appropriating and reconstructing conservative performances (Butler 1990). Women who have had a mastectomy must redefine themselves as female gendered and (hetero)sexual in the absence of a breast, and so "perform" gender in new ways; men who having lost erectile function, or have lost a testicle, must redefine and reenact their masculinity and sexuality. As we discuss, men who have lost mobility learn new ways to present themselves through every-day actions and activities. Given the importance of the corporeal body to gender and sexual identity, the recovery and reenactment of gender in rela-tion to the (re)construction of identity is particularly interesting. As Sey-mour (1998) has already observed with respect to various conditions, men reconcile gender and disablement by embracing conservative masculinity through participation in sport. We want to start with a case study of a young man, who at sixteen years of age lost a leg in a motorbike accident. His story enabled us to formulate the mechanisms involved in his loss and recreation of masculine identity. Particularly through his involvement in sport, he gained a felt sense of masculinity and with it, newfound bodily agency and sociality. The physical status of the body influences perceptions of gender and sexuality, and this is illustrated by exploring how the active male body undergoes a switch in prominence from the hard, contained, set-aside body of "mind" to the "real body." From the standpoint of this informant, a man may go from an "active, fit, healthy rugby player" to a "pathetic, lame, disfigured, scarred, ugly individual" who is situationally and metaphorically placed by his changed body image "to sit on the outers with the girls, watch-ing the boys play."

On Oxymorons

Shakespeare (1999) describes how recent social movements of disabled people have explored disability as a social construct, like gender. Recent disability theory—and increasingly, biomedicine—acknowledges that peo-ple with a disability are impaired by society and not by their bodies. One aspect of the construction of disability is to describe disabled people as sex-ually ambiguous, asexual, or as a "third gender," as emphasized in the struc-ture of social arrangements for elimination—men's, women's, and disabled (Shakespeare 1999, 55).

Since masculinity is defined as able-bodied and active, the disabled man is an oxymoron. Becoming disabled for a man means to "cross the fence" and take on the stigmatizing constructs of the masculine body made femi-nine and soft. In contrast, being feminine and disabled are consistent and synergistic; the traditional notions of woman and disability converge, reflected in the ascription of characteristics such as innocence, vulnerability, sexually passivity or asexuality, dependency, and objectification. For many, disability may include incontinence, placing disabled men even closer to the feminine, leaking body with its indeterminate borders (Peake and Manderson 1999). While femininity and disability reinforce each other, disabled masculinity rests on the notion of contradiction. Shakespeare's argument is directed toward denouncing cultural representations of disability in popular cultural media, in which the disabled man is typically construed as coming to terms with loss of masculinity through impairment, crystallized in the context of impotency or sexual incapacity, as suggested in various films of the Vietnam War (e.g., *Coming Home,* dir. Hal Ashby, 1978; *Born on the Fourth of July,* dir. Oliver Stone, 1989). In such representations, both male sexuality and disabled people's dependency are stereotyped. Cultural constructions of masculinity and femininity are reinforced by changes in physicality: male disabled bodies are seen to lose hardness, containment, and control, becoming leaky (with explicit connections with infants and women), indeterminate, liminal and soft, vulnerable to the stares of others. In contrast, women are seen as living through their bodies, and thus are accustomed to being the subject of the gaze and to practicing self-surveillance. Awareness of the gaze, the practice of self-surveillance, and the experience of the body as a prime signifier are new experiences for most men.

Men's accommodations to amputation reflect their need to normalize and to conform to a dominant view of (masculine) individuality, somatically and ideologically, to avoid marginalization (Shakespeare 1994, 328; 1999). Foucault (1977, 1978) stresses that society tries to normalize all that is abnormal by supervision and examination. Men we interviewed emphasized their own masculine conformity:

> I'm lucky that I'm big, as in physical-type big, and that helps. I mean, I've been patted on the head and all this, but I'm quite big and that helps. If I was a smaller physical stature, that would make it harder. . . . I mean, you go to the casino, and people will say, "Great to see you out here, mate." . . . You're normally so stunned when you get that sort of stuff.

Joining a disabled sporting group enables many men to effect normalization, to escape placement as the socially positioned "other" and instead, immerse in the trappings of masculinity with a community of like-minded and like-bodied persons. In Butler's terms (1990), this is a performance of masculinity: gender is "constituted through discursively constrained performative acts that produce the body through and within categories of sex. Gender must be understood as a 'doing,' a performance that constitutes the identity it purports to be" (24). Sport allows disabled men to experi-

Still from the film *Born on the Fourth of July*. (Courtesy of Photofest/Universal.)

ence their bodies as bodies of agency, movement, and control: "It makes you feel whole again. Like I am a whole person. You can actually do something; you are not just stuck in the house. You can *do* something" (Jonas). For some men, too, participation in disabled sports allows for new social mobility and status. Seymour (1998, 3) has reflected on the use of the trope of "second chance" by people to refer to how changes in physical ability can present new directions and opportunities, and for men, this is reflecting in relation to sport (Seymour 1998, chap. 4). As John commented, "If I were not an amputee, I wouldn't be at the level I am in the sport that I'm in, if you know what I mean." Connell (1995) argues further that involvement in sport allows its participants the pleasure of sociability through shared bodily performance, an "electrification" that can occur where senses are called into play, leading to new social relations. Connell calls this "body-reflexive practice," described by one of our respondents as follows:

When you do lose your leg, you become immobile, and you do lose that mobility and that physical activity that you are so used to. You notice all those smells and everything when you first rock up, but to me that is just my sport. Now, I don't even notice the burning rubber any more, physical sweat, bodies pounding in chairs. That is just what I get out and do now. (Mick)

This respondent expresses the combination of both agency and community when he speaks of "one body and one mind, all concentrating on the Olympics."

Sport also provides an avenue for culturally normative competition, allowing many men to create new, hypermasculinized personae built on the contradictions of their physical impairment. Jock, introduced in the epigraph to this essay, commented, "Okay, so I am a paraplegic now. I am a paraplegic but I have to be one of the best paraplegics going." Indeed, Seymour (1998, 93) maintains that men's participation in disability sport as part of their formal rehabilitation serves dominant interests by supporting male bodily skills and sanctioning aggression, force, and violence as expressions of maleness. In interviews, men coupled competitiveness, masculinity, and success, with the ultimate goal, for many, to "make it" internationally. Interviews with Paralympians and other elite sportsmen are particularly enlightening in this respect, but other men, too, allude to competitive successes as well as success in reclaiming more broadly gender and sexual identity through their performance of everyday tasks.

Sexuality & Disability

To be obviously disabled is to be positioned as object and other, both from the perspective of the able-bodied and from how the individual himself (or herself). Luke in *Coming Home* comments, "People look at me and they see something else . . . they don't see who I am." Terry and Urla (1995, 6) similarly comment on how people read the "contours, anatomical features, processes, movements, and expressions" as accurate indications of an individual's essence and character. Blue Boy, to whom we return below, spoke of how he disguised his amputation to avoid putting "the fact of the missing leg in the public's face." He commented in particular on the difficulty he had interacting with women: "I was shattered—wouldn't let them go near me. I was totally withdrawn sexually." While women, too, are self-conscious of their bodies and new disabilities, they are used to being objectified; it is through her body that a woman experiences herself. As Berger suggests, she "must continually watch herself. She is almost always accompanied by her own image of herself. . . . And so she comes to consider the surveyor and the surveyed within her as the two constituent yet always distinct elements of her identity as a woman" (1972, 46–47).

In contrast, men are conventionally actors rather than objects, and men in this study frequently raised the issue of sexual function from this perspective. While a few were initially self-conscious, social rehabilitation involved adjustment to their physical disability, with sport providing a vehicle for such adjustment through display. One man spoke at length of his difficulties in performing sexually, but not his ability to attract:

> It is frustrating to me to be able to use only one hand to touch. I'm a very tactile person. To be able to touch with only one hand, yes, it is a problem—you need two hands to be able to support yourself—so that eliminates a number of sexual positions. Yes, there have been a lot of problems. The problem as far as the arm is concerned I would class as being minor, the erectile problems caused most of the problems. I didn't fear rejection (from the partner)—*that never entered my head*—but I guess I knew I was going to have extreme difficulty in being able to perform the sex act myself.

Other men offered similar perspectives. Allan lost both legs from an auto accident; his nervousness in reestablishing sexual relationships with his wife related not to fear of rejection, but concern about gaining and sustaining an erection. Other men were more confident about their body changes and used their own bodies and prosthesis to destabilize constructs of normality. John used to remove his prosthetic leg as a party trick, and let his young son take it to school for show-and-tell. Leslie joined Sporting Wheelies and participated in competitive weight lifting, and was also flamboyant, for example, taking off his leg and resting the stump on another chair at work. He thinks amputation gave him a chance to "make it with the ladies." Other men talked of their ability "to give women satisfaction" and "help a woman out," of being able to pick up women of all ages or from any background. Consistently, therefore, masculine sexuality and masculinity are defined conservatively and phallocentrically. Being visibly disabled (e.g., in a wheelchair) encourages men to be extroverted: "You can't be a shrinking violet in a wheelchair" (Alex).

Blue Boy's Story

In the past, Blue Boy saw himself as a "mocker of the disabled." He was a tough, masculine rugby player. After an accident and amputation, he withdrew from school. He feared being looked at, being vulnerable to the whispers and uninhibited gaze of others; he saw himself as "pathetic, lame, disfigured, scarred, ugly." He talked of the friends he had to leave behind as he "jumped to the other side of the fence": "I used to associate with the boys. I did rugby and was very sports-oriented. After the accident I felt very insecure. I didn't want to go out in public with a leg missing. I wanted to hide it. I did not want anyone to know and wouldn't wear shorts. . . . I can't go back to being one of the boys." He put up with excessive amounts of pain to mask his use of a prosthetic limb. He also was careful to avoid situations where he might be "unmasked" as disabled.

In his late teens, his family moved from a temperate to a tropical environment, and he was forced to swap his enveloping long pants for a pair of shorts. He was worried about people's reaction, in case he "scared the heck out of them, looking at your stump. In my mind, I was a freak in a show." However, "although everybody was always looking at me," he found that the reaction was mostly one of curiosity rather than horror. Being looked at, as women are, became for him "like a sex change."

Wearing shorts forced him to confront his disability. When he joined a disabled sporting group and started to receive compliments from group members, for example, on how well he walked, he graduated to showing his body to the public, removing his leg, and swimming competitively. This was a turning point. He realized "how lucky I was." His disability was "like stubbing my toes," "nothing" compared to the disabilities of some others, such as those with cerebral palsy. Others' positive responses and acceptance helped him to concentrate on his abilities and not his disabilities, and started to see things differently: his teammates "brought [him] back into the paddock [field]." He was now part of a team and as a leader: "I perceive myself to be back up the top end of the scale—one of the leaders amongst my peers. Who do I identify myself with? I see myself as being normal again. I associate with these people. I am just one of the crowd." Yet he stands out from the crowd ("the top end of the scale"), and therefore adapts to his disability through extroversion; that is, his disability was performed, his stump a prop. Others too are able to perform disability, including through their choice of equipment. A lightweight racing wheelchair, for instance, or a flamboyantly artificial prosthesis, rather than a prosthetic limb that is "life-like" in appearance and feel, suggests that some people are aware of the potential for disruption and resistance even while embracing other conservative practices.

Connell (1995, 54) suggests that "the constitution of masculinity through bodily performance means that gender is vulnerable when the performance cannot be sustained," as occurs with physical disability. We argue, contrarily, that sport is a performative mode that enables men to "jump back over the fence," to reposition themselves and escape the excessive category of the "other." Sport enables disabled men to join a community of

Athlete in a wheelchair. (Photograph by Sandy Scheltema, Courtesy of The Age.)

men and to experience their bodies as bodies of agency, movement, and control (see also Seymour 1998). For many wheelchair athletes, the chair becomes the vehicle for enhancing performance and virility (as illustrated by the Paralympic basketballers in action). In competitive sport, men are able to overcome the feminizing encroachments of disabled masculinity. Sport not only bridges the gap between the disabled and able-bodied world, but it can also offer a radical critique of the apparent limits of the disabled body and a disruptive break with normative identities. But for Blue Boy, being without his prosthetics was the key to agency: "Without prosthetics I feel whole. More pure and whole. I am just myself—no outside engineering put in. One, complete, whole."

The popularity of the Paralympic Games exemplifies the successful "sportsperson" rather than "cripple" as an identity signifier for participants, reinforced by magazine articles and books about and by disabled sporting heroes (Blythe 2000), television shows on disability and heroism, and the contemporaneous use of sportsman Sandy Blythe to advertise occupational safety. Print and television news headlines at the time of the 2000 Paralympic Games, such as "True Grit: And a Heart of Gold" (*Sixty Minutes,* Channel 9, September 3, 2000), capture precisely the mixture of personal attributes linked to such athletes (and see fig. 2).

For some players, the long identification with the normative standards of the disabled sporting group has a closed and reifying effect on body boundaries. Shildrick and Price (1996, 94) argue that able/disabled categories are constructed and maintained through the "constant reiteration of a set of norms," and that performance acts of disability, corporeal signs, gestures, and movements play a major role in the reinscription of the body and the reformation of identity. But, in a reversal of the usual argument, Shildrick and Price (1996) suggest that the seemingly stable categories of disability can shore up the ontological boundaries of the "broken body." Alex describes for us both the positive and negative aspects of identifying with and belonging to a sports group. On the one hand, sport for paraplegics "helps your skill set, makes you stronger, helps your wheelchair skills, helps you transfer off the floor, introduces you to other people who are doing well or someone who's got a girlfriend—or just shows you the way."

For Alex, overreliance on membership in a disabled group eventually becomes a limitation to self-renewal, and he must seek the wider arena for normalizing sameness and difference. It is not enough to be a "battler," he argues, as this eventually works against survival in the wider nondisabled world:

> There's one guy in the basketball team who will turn up . . . with a work ethic that is just deplorable. But he'll get there because he's unique, he's this and he's that, but if he was in the able-bodied world, there'd be 412,000 people trying to get his spot. Yeah, I mean, over the years I've seen people make pricks of themselves round wheelchair basketball that would never be tolerated, never be tolerated in an able-bodied environment, but it is. You know, if you can't cut it in the real world, it's a softer world in the disability world. . . . Look, I think we get too focused on disability. I think, you know, everyone's got abilities and everyone's got disabilities. It's stereotypical and it's pigeonholed. . . . There are going to be people that are looking for the soft option, and there are going to be people who will continue. It's one of my real bitches in life, in basketball or whatever—it's always an excuse. "I missed the shot because you hit me. I fumbled the ball because you threw it to me badly. I fell out of my chair because I'm a paraplegic and my balance is no good." You'll either be an excuse maker, or you earn it.

Conclusion Heroes on Wheels

The solution against shoring up the boundaries of the broken body for Shildrick and Price (1996) is to look for "the other within." For study participants who need wheelchairs for mobility, self-change involves both resistance and performance by "going out on a limb," accepting the visibility of their disability because, as Alex has explained, "you can't be a shrinking violet in a wheelchair." People with disability have no option but to stand out, and hence opt for excellence as a vehicle to social inclusion.

In numerous Australian legends and film, the heroes are social misfits, resisting the values of those with power. National icons include swagmen (tramps, e.g., *Waltzing Matilda*), bushrangers *(Ned Kelly)*, itinerant workers (shearers and drovers), and failed soldiers *(Gallipoli)*, but also others who rise "against the odds" of class, race, age, or disability. Douglas Bader, the double lower-limb amputee who was a hero of the Battle of Britain, is one example (Jackson 1983). Roden Cutler, former governor of New South Wales, is another (McCullough 1999). And while Australian cinema appears to have a narrative fascination with defeat, it also focuses on heroism following defeat. Heroism in national iconography and cinematic narratives is "predicated upon the failed attempt, the inordinately stacked odds, and a preponderance of bad luck" (Biber 1999, 27). For disabled Australian men, the link with iconic masculinity and nationalism is their hypermasculinity, either as a result of (noble) war efforts (as represented by Bader and in any film footage of Anzac Day parades, for any year and any state), or as a result of vehicle accidents or sporting injuries. However, men who must live with disability need to reestablish their own (hyper)masculinity. While the disabled male body, with its deviance from the normative male body "palpable and visible" (Terry and Urla 1995, 6), is in theory a site of resistance, it is important to acknowledge the impact of disability for those who acquire and must now live within "deviant" bodies and the effect on them of the construction of disability, and to see in their resistance to one construct (disability) the reasons for embracing the other, dominant construct (masculinity). Hence disabled men contest the negative associations of their corporeality and agency through sporting prowess, by moving from the feminized body to hypermasculinity, claiming symbolic power in the process.

Bibliography

Becker, G. 1997. *Disrupted Lives: How People Create Meaning in a Chaotic World*. San Francisco: University of California Press.
Berger, J. 1972. *Ways of Seeing*. Harmondsworth: Penguin.
Biber, K. 1999. "'Turned Out Real Nice after All': Death and Masculinity in Australian Cinema." In *Playing the Man: New Approaches to Masculinity*, ed. K. Biber, T. Sear, and D. Trudinger, 27–38. Annandale: Pluto Press Australia.
Blythe, S. 2000. *Blythe Spirit*. Sydney: Pan Macmillan.
Butler, J. 1990. *Gender Trouble: Feminism and the Subversion of Identity*. New York: Routledge.
Canguilhem, G. 1991. *The Normal and the Pathological*. New York: Zone Books.
Chapkis, W. 1986. *Beauty Secrets: Women and the Politics of Appearance*. London: Women's Press.
Connell, R. 1995. *Masculinities*. Sydney: Allen and Unwin.

Davis, K. 1995. *Reshaping the Female Body: The Dilemma of Cosmetic Surgery.* New York: Routledge.

Davis, L. 1995. *Enforcing Normalcy: Disability, Deafness, and the Body.* London: Verso.

Foucault, M. 1977. *Discipline and Punish: The Birth of the Prison.* London: Allen Lane.

———. 1978. *The History of Sexuality.* New York: Pantheon.

Gilman, S. L. 1999. *Making the Body Beautiful: A Cultural History of Aesthetic Surgery.* Princeton, N.J.: Princeton University Press.

Goffman, E. 1959. *The Presentation of Self in Everyday Life.* New York: Doubleday Anchor.

Grosz, E. 1994. *Volatile Bodies: Towards a Corporeal Feminism.* Bloomington: Indiana University Press.

Jackson, R. 1983. *Douglas Bader: A Biography.* London: A. Barker.

Manderson, L. 1999. "Gender, Normality and the Post-Surgical Body." *Anthropology and Medicine* 6 (3): 381–94.

McCullough, C. 1999. *The Courage and the Will: The Life of Roden Cutler V.C.* London: Weidenfeld and Nicolson.

Mitchell, D. T., and S. L. Snyder, eds. 1997. *The Body and Physical Difference: Discourses of Disability.* Ann Arbor: University of Michigan Press.

Peake, S., and L. Manderson. 2003. "The Constraints of a Normal Life: The Management of Urinary Incontinence by Middle Aged Women." *Women and Health* 37 (2): 37–51.

Peake, S., L. Manderson, and H. Potts. 1999. "'Part and Parcel of Being a Woman': Female Urinary Incontinence and Constructions of Control." *Medical Anthropology Quarterly* 13 (3): 1–19.

Scheibe, K. 2000. *The Drama of Everyday Life.* Cambridge, Mass.: Harvard University Press.

Seymour, W. 1998. *Remaking the Body: Rehabilitation and Change.* Sydney: Allen and Unwin.

Shakespeare, T. 1994. "Cultural Representation of Disabled People—Dustbins for Disavowal." *Disability and Society* 9 (3): 283–99.

———. 1999. "The Sexual Politics of Disabled Masculinity." *Sexuality and Disability* 17 (1): 53–64.

Shildrick, M., and J. Price. 1996. "Breaking the Boundaries of the Broken Body." *Body and Society* 2 (4): 93–113.

Terry, J., and J. Urla, eds. 1995. *Deviant Bodies: Critical Perspectives on Difference in Science and Popular Culture.* Bloomington: Indiana University Press.

Disrupting a Disembodied Status Quo
Invisible Theater as Subversive Pedagogy

MAUREEN CONNOLLY & TOM CRAIG

Invisible theater is a sociopolitical, dramaturgical, and pedagogic intervention formulated by critical educator and performing artist Augusto
Boal. It is usually enacted in drama, theater, or performing arts programs,
but is adaptable to almost any subject matter. A group chooses and
researches an issue and the context in which it plans to make its intervention. The group creates, choreographs, scripts, and rehearses the "everyday
event" it will perform, plans for members to observe the event, and
arranges safe exits (should the staged nature of the event become "visible"
or the participants find themselves in danger). Intervention works best if no
one realizes that it is staged, that is, if the people for whom it is intended
believe they are witnessing an unscripted event, not an educational intervention designed to create rupture and awaken dormant sensibilities.
Hence the name *invisible* theater.

As an intervention in disability, this pedagogy causes commotion. It
unsettles the passive landscape of academic learning as separate from daily
life. Indeed, it makes subversive demands that learners be intensely and
thoughtfully immersed in everyday life, and it establishes the mundane
world as a fruitful site for the construction of theory. Students in this par-
ticipant-observer project must go beyond superficial preparation and take
learning into their bodies in rigorous processes of social observation, dis-

ability etiological research, and social, political, and financial research as it pertains to living in the world with disability. The eventual performed events do not directly involve spectators, nor are they parodies of human experience. Rather—students come to discover—they are embodied constructions of disability experience informed by a disability studies orientation designed to disclose the cultural boundaries of "abnormal" behavior.

One of the authors teaches a core introductory course in disability studies within a physical education and kinesiology degree program. In 1998, we introduced invisible theater as an assignment option in that course, and in other courses in the disability studies stream. We introduced invisible theater as a way to help students encounter the lived experience of "heterogeneous bodies," that is, bodies that bring contingency, texture, complexity, contradictions, overlapping intersections, and, ultimately, the kind of difference that does not blend well into the landscape of a normally disembodied status quo. Our goal is to introduce students to the severely ableist culture we live in, a production-oriented culture in which persons with disabilities represents an unacceptable rupture in the expectation of fast-paced efficiency, conformity, and the visible signs of financial productivity and capitalist success. Making visible the insidious cultural codes of production-oriented pace, we then describe the heterogeneity of all human bodies.

Having included this assignment in the course, we also decided that the best way to explain it would be to model it in class, then unpack it as a group. We assembled a team that included students in the class, the teaching assistant, an instructor unknown to the students (one of the authors of this paper), and the course instructor (the other author of this paper). Together we designed our own invisible theater that we staged in class—students being unaware that anything other than a regular lecture was unfolding.

In this essay we describe and analyze this textured, bodily experience, including the planning process, the actual intervention in class, students' responses, and their experiences with their own invisible theater productions. We will foreground our description and analysis with a discussion of the theorists and theories that have influenced our project and animate our work.

Theoretical Influences Freire, Lather, Kristeva, Lanigan

In his "Letter to North American Teachers," Paulo Freire (1987) insists that since education is by nature social, historical, and political, the role of the teacher must not be discussed in terms of an imaginary, detached position. Freire argues that "a teacher must be fully cognizant of the political nature of his or her practice, and assume responsibility for this rather than denying it" (211). From this critical perspective, the educator is an agent of change within a contested site of heterogeneity wherein "the political nature of education requires that the teacher either serve whoever is in power or present options to those in power" (212).

Freire also insists that the "one dimension of every teacher's role that is independent of political choice . . . is the act of teaching subject matter or content" (212). A progressive, politicized, sensitized teacher does not neglect course content simply to politicize students. Nor does understanding of content by itself liberate. Political clarity and learning are crucial, but neither alone is enough. Freire suggests that teaching how to learn is valid only when learners absorb the textures and complexities of a subject as they develop an intimate relationship with the subject matter (213).

Freire is advocating the whole-bodied investment in a context that implicates teachers and learners as *heterogeneous subjects* engaged in a process of self- and social transformation. The subject matter as ground must be made personally and politically relevant, and the teachers and learners must engage in ongoing self-reflexivity; that is, their critique also must implicate their own ideology and its assumptions, habits, and codes. Subject matter is a living entity to be explored as a site of ongoing destruction and regeneration, and embodied subjects take the risks of investing in personal and political relation with the subject matter and other embodied subjects.

Patti Lather (1991) argues for research and teaching approaches openly committed to a more just social order. She claims that an emancipatory social science allows not only an understanding of the maldistribution of power and resources underlying our society but also the possibility for change in ways that help create a more equal (we would say, equitable) world (50). Lather also calls for reciprocal educative and sustainable postinterventive processes.

The basic ingredients of such approaches include the "informants" as active agents in the construction and validation of meaning out of their own experiences, the questioning of the "given" or "natural" in a dialogic enterprise, and a focus on fundamental contradictions. Invisible theater is just such a methodology. Theoretically grounded in semiotic phenomenology, it compels teachers, students, and recipients to be aware of the undeniably political presence of the lived body of disability and chronicity. Invisible theater is a powerful embodied response to cultural norms that keep unpredictable bodies invisible.

Lather's model of critical, emancipatory human science research resonates with Julia Kristeva's (1986) proposition for semiotic research (or semanalysis). Kristeva makes a call to move beyond "detached" descriptive practice and to be aware of the pitfalls of assuming that it is possible to be "outside looking in" when one is a practitioner of research.

As soon as we embrace heterogeneity as an always possible feature of an embodied speaking subject, we must be prepared for the political consequences. According to Kristeva (1986), heterogeneity fractures the symbolic code and risks being assimilated (30). This means that people and events formerly seen as "unfamiliar" or insignificant can be all too easily absorbed into familiar social habits and rituals, thereby negating their original "heterogeneous" impact. Hence, Kristeva's insistence on alterity, continuously placing subjects on trial.

Richard Lanigan's semiotic phenomenology provides a helpful theoretical frame for experiencing embodied contingency by combining phenomenological explication of the *freedom* of individual expression with semiotic analysis of the *field* of culturally sedimented perception, that is, what Bowers (1984) presents as a dialectic between *(a)* people's self-understandings and efforts to create an enabling context to question taken-for-granted beliefs and *(b)* the authority culture has over us. In educational settings we need to discover the necessary conditions that free people to engage in critique given the often unconscious hold of illusion or habit. The advantage of working through a semiotic phenomenology of "the experience of the body coupled with the consciousness of choice" (Lanigan 1988, 105) is that it provides a critical theoretical frame to balance the normative logics and inscriptions, the phenomena of the lived body as sign of political discourse, and the sign systems that hold them together (Lanigan 1988, 105; Craig 1997, 52, 54). What this means, practically, is that once we become conscious of ourselves as agents who choose, we no longer can pretend that we make choices in an unconscious, politically unaware, fashion.

Lanigan's (1988) work in semiotic phenomenology allows us to examine the relationships between culture and embodied consciousness as expressed in the lived body's engagement with, and interrogation of, discourses, norms, and inscriptions.

Describing & Analyzing Subversive Political Pedagogy

How might we, as teachers, create environments that draw subjects out from inside a protective shell to take the risks of a heterogeneous subject on trial? How might this lead to engagement with personal and sociopolitical transformation?

Here we describe the invisible theater intervention, and analyze it through a semiotic phenomenology of "the experience of the body coupled with the consciousness of choice" (Lanigan 1988; Craig 1998).

By walking readers through the process of our in-class intervention, we provide real-world examples of the experience of the body—the bodies of our students, the bodies of teacher and teaching assistant, and the body of the person with a disability. We also provide the consequences that unfold when these aforementioned bodies are coupled with the consciousness of choice; that is, we demonstrate how bodies—whether they be perceived as "able," stable, and financially productive, or living with disabilities in contexts of chronic cultural disregard—are implicated when one is aware that one chooses *how* to be in the world. In this way, embodied speaking subjects can develop political critique in their awareness of normative logics and inscriptions, the lived body as sign, and the sign systems that hold them together.

In-Class Intervention

Andy, Debra, and Valerie were the students involved; Scott was the TA, and Tom was the instructor unknown to the students in the class. Tom, who actually does live with a chronic pain disability, took the role of a mature student in class with a mobility impairment and other dysfunctions such as visual impairment and balance challenges.

Scott and Maureen are at the front of the lecture hall awaiting the students. There are approximately 125 students in the class, and they are moving into seats and getting out notebooks. Andy, Debra, and Valerie wander in and take their places, Andy near the back of the room, Valerie slightly in front of him, and Debra near the middle. About one minute into the lecture, Tom arrives and begins his agonizing walk down the steps to the seat near Debra. He is dressed in a bulky winter coat, is carrying a backpack filled with books, notepaper, and other supplies, and is walking with a noticeable limp and using a cane. The lecture hall is sloped downward, so he is moving carefully. He looks tired, confused, and awkward. The students in the class are noticing him—he is not one of their peers, so they are not sure what he is doing here. Tom shuffles across the row in front of Debra so she has to lean back; then he sits down and begins arranging books, cane, and backpack in the small seat.

Maureen is at the front of the room by the overhead projector, talking the class through some points on the overhead. Tom puts up his hand and asks if there is any way she can magnify the overhead—he cannot read it. Maureen apologizes for the size of the type and her inability to make it any bigger, and suggests that he move closer. Tom gets up, collects his things, and laboriously moves out of the row of desks, once again pushing Debra back. There is a murmur going through the room; Maureen is not sure what students are talking about. As Tom makes his way—still carefully—down the steps, to find a seat closer to the front, he drops his papers. He makes a motion to get a sense of where they are, his backpack falls off his shoulder; he puts his cane on top of his papers to keep them from getting any farther. Valerie is trying to get out of her seat to help, and Scott is moving toward Tom from the front of the room; meanwhile Margaret, a very quiet student in the class, and Chris, a large, muscular young man in the class, both move to pick up Tom's papers. Margaret defers to Chris, who hands the papers to Tom. While the paper dropping and recovery is unfolding, there is a commotion in the back of the room, around Andy's seat. Apparently he has made his preplanned derogatory remark about Tom ("Who is this clown? Why can't he get out of the way?"), and it has gotten a vehement response from those around him. Tom finds a seat near the front and sits down. Maureen waits for a few moments, then tells the class they have been the recipients of an invisible theater intervention and that we will now talk about it.

Class Response

Tom, Scott, Andy, Debra, Valerie, and Maureen explain what invisible theater is, and how we scripted and choreographed the one they had just witnessed. We described what we had planned, what we thought might happen, what went well, what unraveled. Tom gave his description of what he was trying to portray. The class responded with comments like the following.

> I felt sorry for you; you looked so pathetic.
> Maureen was so mean asking you to move up—I couldn't believe she would do something like that.
> I didn't know where to look or what to do.

Tom went on to say that he was going to resist Chris's help and try to get his papers himself, but then he decided that he did not want to argue with a big guy like Chris. The class laughed. Chris said that he just picked up papers for someone who dropped them and seemed to need help. Chris had not even seen Tom's entry into the room; he was simply responding in the moment. Valerie spoke of her frustration at not being able to get to her role as overeager helper, but she had to sit with her friends, or they would have gotten suspicious. Debra spoke of several people making eye contact with her and sympathizing as Tom moved past her and placed her in an uncomfortable position. Andy talked about the immediacy and vehemence of the responses he evoked. People around him called him "a jerk," "insensitive," and said, "I can't believe you said that"; some moved away from him. Andy had forewarned his girlfriend, Stephanie, that he was participating in a demonstration "for Maureen" and that he would be behaving in a way that was out of character.

Maureen was somewhat disappointed. She thought the episode had been too short, not enough students were engaged in the drama, and she did not really get a sense of the impact of Andy's words. However, as we unpacked the scene, she realized how effective the intervention had been, both as a modeling of invisible theater and as an invisible theater intervention. People were outraged and responded to what they saw as cruel and insensitive treatment. The class continued to speak about the event and its unpacking as a critical incident in their year. The intervention was spoken about in the Physical Education complex, among students, faculty and staff, for weeks after.

We debriefed as a performing group, Maureen thanked everyone, and we spoke about our insights arising out of the experience. It seems that it was a positive experience for the performing group and the class. It also laid the foundation for the pedagogic value of the invisible theater assignment, as well as introducing the student to the theoretical discourse on "alterity."

Normative Logics & Inscriptions

Invisible theater works as a pedagogic and political intervention because there *are* normative logics and inscriptions. In our example we have the norms of group homogeneity (age, appearance, attire, degree program); an expected place to sit in class; classes that start at a particular time; and the expectation of people being there on time; expected unobtrusiveness of late arrivers (i.e., find a convenient seat, not one where you push past others); once you find a place, stay put; make your difficulty and distress invisible (do not walk down the center of the room slowly and carefully— minimize your discomfort and awkwardness); accept the help that is offered; do not make insensitive comments (even if you are thinking them)—and if you do make them, make them in the appropriate context (i.e., more private).

Other inscriptions are less apparent—relational expectations and power dynamics among teachers, learners, and TAs, for example. As teacher, Maureen was supposed to have the magic solution to make everyone feel less awkward. As a performer in a staged intervention, Andy had to let Stephanie know that his behavior would be out of character: his relationship would be jeopardized, or there would be serious consequences if he actually were that cruel and insensitive. The outrage at Maureen's and Andy's insensitivity demonstrates that students believe they know them and could not believe they would behave thus . . . yet what is the basis of their knowing? What of Maureen's power as teacher? These students and the TA were willing to engage in this risky business simply because she asked them. Of course, she chose students who she believed were politically sensitized, but they could have refused. They did not. Would they have done this for another teacher? Was it simply Maureen's position of power that compelled them, or do they resonate with what she brings to her work as a teacher? How does that contradict their notions of hierarchy? How do we maintain respect and boundary through our reciprocity?

And what of Tom's participation—a vulnerable outsider in every sense; what risks are worth taking for political and pedagogic intervention? What embodied principles inform such risk taking? In *Teaching to Transgress*, bell hooks (1994) insists that teachers working for political and social justice cannot expect their students to take risks that they, the teachers, are not willing to take. In invisible theater—despite its connotations of wild, "guerrilla" theater—it is imperative that the dignity of the audience engaged in the performance not be compromised. In order for an invisible theater project to unfold, the group must be committed to profound investment in research, practice, unsparing self-reflection, and focus. We cannot ask students to undertake this assignment if we do not experience it—and perform it—ourselves. The debriefing that followed our in-class experience allowed us to deal with issues of dignity as well as the intense planning process that was necessary. Here, although we broke with Boal's commitment to maintaining invisibility, we believe it was consistent with Freire's commitment to teachers and learners engaged in a relationship with course content, and not using political activism as an excuse to avoid content.

> Just as it is impossible to teach someone how to learn without teaching some content, it is also impossible to teach intellectual discipline except through a practice of knowing that enables learners to become active and critical subjects, constantly increasing (and questioning) their critical abilities. (213)

The Phenomena of the Lived Body as Sign (of Political Discourse)

Tom lives with a chronic pain disability that is an affront to the productivist norms of most institutions—including educational institutions. His slowness, his taking up space, his use of a cane all point to the inconvenience, messiness, and uncontrollable character of disability. Students in the class felt self-conscious for him; naming his inconvenience as real was a breach of social agreement—not the insensitivity alone, but the speaking of what ought to remain unspoken. This kind of deceit often accompanies encounters with disability. Most people prefer the refuge of enlightened social policy to the face-to-face encounter with that which calls their conduct into question.

However, we need not take up the threat of bodily contingency to examine the institutional apathy concerning the actual body. How is it pedagogically and healthfully defensible to put over a hundred students in a downward-sloping lecture hall with seats that are too small, with no windows, and with no ventilation? What are the physical risks of class changeover when rooms of one hundred students pour into corridors already filled with the next one hundred waiting to get in? What are students learning about the respectful sharing of space, or do they even have the opportunity to consider it? What habits of body are being formed in these contexts of time efficiency and bodily disregard?

Students in the disabilities studies class experienced an unsettling raising of consciousness. They became aware that disability and chronicity do indeed cause commotion: they point to the inadequacy of institutional norms of some disembodied status quo (for *any* living body!), and they point to the inequity of institutional habits of pace, productivity, and unquestioned uniformity (that is, the assumption of homogeneous, docile bodies) for persons with disabilities or chronic conditions, whether they be students, staff, or faculty. These are the same habits they will question in their own invisible theater interventions.

The Sign Systems

Julia Kristeva (1984) posits that Western capitalistic culture is governed by semiotic codes of maternal and paternal functions. Maternal functions are seen as bodily based, in the unconscious and in the drives, uncontrollable, unpredictable; paternal functions are seen as rational, based in the modes of production, necessarily controllable and predictable. The institutional values of efficiency, manageable bodies, and cosmetic civility certainly fall within the paternal function. And while it seems clichéd to point to the roots and systematicity of patriarchy as an unacknowledged arbiter of behavior, it is the case that patriarchal, productivist, capitalist values are pervasive in educational institutions, and sanction these institutions as sites of profoundly degrading habits and treatments of bodies.

In the invisible theater we modeled, Tom—late, obtrusive, moving slowly and inefficiently, his body's unmanageability demanding a response—represents the maternal function, paradoxically embodied in a fit and healthy-

looking male body; the system he threatens—linear time, efficient movement, appropriate unobtrusive behavior, manageable and controllable
body—is governed by the paternal function. Andy's derogatory remarks
make visible the publicly unacknowledged yet already given superiority of
the paternal, and the responses of the students illustrate the swiftness with
which inappropriateness must be met—whatever the ostensive intentions.

Mind-body dualism is another sign system, closely allied with patriarchal
and capitalist values, and the maternal and paternal functions. We see
mind-body dualism as an emphasis in itself, given the low status of embodied scholarship in the academy, the suspicion and disdain awarded to work
that is applied or of a personal or political nature, and the unquestioned
legitimacy of work that presents itself as theoretical (and usually abstract).
We are not advocating these scholarly dichotomies; we are simply describing them, and trying to survive them. It is time to deconstruct the false status awarded to disembodied practices; such deconstruction must be translated into academic policies and scholarly and pedagogic conduct. It also
must be translated into assignments that have institutional as well as political value. Otherwise students can continue to reproduce ableist norms in
unreflective ignorance.

Concluding Comments

It is unconscionable, given what we know about ergonomics, the relationship between environment and disease, and the neurophysiological basis of
cognition, that educational institutions continue to design structures,
schedules, and curricula as if the actual body did not exist. The separation
of knowledge and action has reached new lows in the present-day academy,
and the choices that allow this separation are made by people most likely
with vested interests of which they may not even be aware.

As has been mentioned earlier, the students in the disability studies class
were compelled to recognize harsh political realities. They realized that
institutional practices are not accidents or oversights, but are choices, and
that these choices are informed (consciously or preconsciously) by larger
sign systems. Furthermore, they realized that *their own choices* may also be
informed by these same sign systems. Coming to terms with the lived body
as sign, however, has created ruptures in business as usual for a disembodied status quo, and their insights arising out of their embodied awareness
compel them to confront a consciousness of their choices.

Maurice Merleau-Ponty critiques rationality as unable to go beyond
itself, by virtue of having to use internal criteria to validate its own concor-
dances (1962, 408). According to his self-reflexive and critical orientation,

all that one has to do to get out of this loop is to "recognize these phenomena which are the ground of all our certainties. The belief in an absolute mind, or in a world in itself detached from us is no more than a rationalization of this primordial faith" (1962, 409).

> If the subject *is* in a situation, even if he is no more than a possibility of situations, this is because he forces his ipseity into reality only by actually being a body, and entering the world through the body. . . . the subject that I am, when taken concretely, is inseparable from this body and this world. The ontological world and body which we find at the core of the subject are not the world or body as idea, but on the one hand, the world itself, contracted into a comprehensive grasp, and on the other hand, the body itself as a knowing body. (408)

Maureen's students went on to design, script, choreograph, perform, unpack, and describe invisible theater projects of their own as part of their course requirements. Their reports at the conclusion of the semester indicate that the in-class experience and their own subsequent experiences with invisible theater have left lasting transformations in their "knowing bodies," their consciousness and conduct. Their knowledge of particular disabilities and of local and national policies on disability improved exponentially (as was evidenced in their final grades); their observation, cooperative, decision-making, and leadership skills also improved. More than half of the class has gone on to a career or graduate work in fields related to disability, and most of the class participated in volunteer disability advocacy for the remainder of their undergraduate programs.

Maureen made this an assignment because she believes it compels a phenomenological sensibility: students have to dwell in a moment long enough to become aware of what is being revealed to consciousness, and how. They have to examine the givens of the natural attitude and use them to crack open that self-same natural attitude. Our modeling intervention offered them a taste of the transformative potential of being put on trial; the shared ground of our subject matter—disability—implicated their bodies in a questioning of structures that survive by keeping bodies silent, invisible, and expendable. Such a project is theoretically defensible through a semiotic phenomenology of the experience of the body coupled with a consciousness of choice, and is experientially constituted by a phenomenological and semiotic sensibility grounded in the actual bodies we live.

It is pedagogically defensible as a project of shared risk that develops the literal, interpretive, and critical skills of the learners without compromising the course content or the dignity of participants. Teaching in a way that engenders embodied political commotion is more time consuming and certainly more risky for the teacher. However, the outcomes are profound, both professionally, in the learning of subject matter, and personally, in development of individual integrity. It is our hope that both students and teachers will make the journey to a consciousness of choice and continue to the joyful, ongoing task of dwelling in the heterogeneous body with unsparing self-reflexivity and attentive wonder.

Works Cited

Bowers, C. A. 1984. *The Promise of Theory: Education and the Politics of Cultural Change.* New York: Longman.

Craig, T. 1997. "Disrupting the Disembodied Status Quo: Existential Communication and Chronic Disabling Conditions." Ph.D. diss., Southern Illinois University.

————. 1998. "Liminal Bodies, Medical Codes." In *Semiotics, 1997: Proceedings of the 22nd Annual Meeting of the Semiotics Society of America,* 223–24. New York: Peter Lang.

Freire, P. 1987. "Letter to North-American Teachers." In *Freire for the Classroom: A Sourcebook for Liberatory Teaching,* ed. Ira Shor, 211–14. Portsmouth, N.H.: Boynton/Cook.

hooks, b. 1994. *Teaching to Transgress.* New York: Routledge.

Kristeva, J. 1984. *Revolution in Poetic Language.* Trans. Margaret Waller. New York: Columbia University Press.

————. 1986. "The System and the Speaking Subject." In *The Kristeva Reader,* ed. Toril Moi, 24–33. New York: Columbia University Press.

Lanigan, R. 1988. *Phenomenology of Communication.* Pittsburgh: Duquesne University Press.

Lather, P. 1991. *Getting Smart: Feminist Research and Pedagogy with/in the Postmodern.* New York: Routledge.

Merleau-Ponty, M. 1962. *The Phenomenology of Perception.* Trans. Colin Smith. Atlantic Highlands, N.J.: Humanities Press.

The Tyranny of Neutral
Disability & Actor Training

CARRIE SANDAHL

The size, shape, and carriage of an actor's body on stage convey much more than a character's physical dimensions. In Western dramatic and performance traditions, outward physicality is most often used as shorthand for the character's inner psychological or emotional state. Consider Oedipus's self-inflicted blindness, a bloody wound that signifies his denial of truth; Richard III's hunchback, a beacon of evil, justifying his antisocial behavior; or Laura Wingfield's limp, a mark of shame, explaining her depression and unrealized cravings for male companionship. Disability in the dramatic canon always signifies, serving most often as a work's central image, what literary critics David Mitchell and Sharon Snyder have called "narrative prosthesis."[1]

Despite the ubiquity of disabled characters in the dramatic canon, there is a paucity of professionally trained disabled actors to perform them. And because disability always signifies in representation, the trained disabled actor is rarely given the opportunity to play nondisabled characters. Disabled actors are told that their impairments would detract from the playwright's or director's intent for a nondisabled character. Disabled people who want to be actors learn this tenet early on and are dissuaded from pursuing training. Other barriers to training include inaccessible classroom and theater spaces and demeaning, stereotypical roles.

Training programs, though, are no longer able to deny otherwise qualified disabled students access to their programs based on these barriers and attitudes. Because of civil rights laws such as Section 504 of the Vocational Rehabilitation Act of 1973 and the Americans with Disabilities Act of 1990, training programs are required to provide access to their curriculum. As a result of such laws, disabled people in general are becoming visible in U.S. culture, making themselves more and more a part of mainstream life. Some theater artists have begun to take note of the emergent, vibrant disability arts and culture scene and are willing to incorporate disabled people in their programs.

Good laws and good intentions, unfortunately, will not significantly improve training opportunities for the disabled actor. While obvious barriers such as the lack of meaningful roles and inaccessible spaces are being addressed by nontraditional casting practices, new plays by and about disabled people, and the alteration of physical space, less obvious barriers remain that require scrutiny if training programs are to become more accessible. This essay addresses one of these less obvious barriers: acting curriculum. I confronted these barriers myself as a physically disabled student in undergraduate and graduate acting classes where, despite the good intentions of my teachers, I earned credits despite the curriculum rather than because of it.

Here, I focus on how conventional associations between outward physicality and inner psychological states are embedded in the disciplinary practices of many actor-training programs. This correlation between body type and inner life suggests which bodies are capable of portraying which inner states and even which bodies are capable of representation at all. To illustrate my point, I will take on two concepts often used in beginning actor-training programs. First is the concept of "neutral," the physical and emotional state from which any character can be built. Actors who cannot be "cured" of their idiosyncrasies to approach neutral may be considered physically and emotionally "inflexible," unable to portray anyone other than themselves or those like them. The second concept is what I am calling the "emotional body," or the belief that physicality develops from past emotional experiences. This belief is put to use in both rehearsal exercises and in the making of acting choices. Uncritical use of the emotional body can humiliate the disabled student in rehearsal and lead to stereotypical choices in performance. Ultimately, unless training programs' very foundations are rehabilitated, current curriculum will dissuade disabled actors from pursuing training.

Evolution of Current Acting Pedagogy

Both "neutral" and "the emotional body" are central metaphors around which current acting curriculum is built. As acting theorist Phillip Zarrilli points out, discourses of acting, like all discourses, are highly metaphorical. Acting theory, though, is particularly invested in hiding its own metaphorical constructions: admitting to a method's constructedness "would reveal the fact that this truth is a particular version authored by a particular person for a particular audience in a particular place and time, and is thereby open to question and revision."[2] In my view, many acting teachers perpetuate their methods as truth by presenting themselves to students as unquestionable authorities. Such self-presentation is often intended to protect students from an ambiguous social situation. In the acting classroom, students often reveal their most personal emotional lives; teachers often touch students' bodies; and students' physicality is available for the most detailed inspection. Given this atmosphere, it is hardly surprising that teachers desire to maintain authority. But the authority asserted often discourages critical thinking about training methods or acting concepts, reinforcing the "truthfulness" of what is, in fact, metaphor.

Most twentieth-century Western training programs, as Alison Hodge points out, draw on metaphors that attempt to explore "the mind and/or body dynamic."[3] These programs developed specifically in response to the needs of psychological realism, a theatrical form in which the differences between actor and character are supposed to be seamless. In other words, the actor is supposed to "disappear" into the role. To achieve such seamlessness, today's university and conservatory programs tend to meld various techniques drawn from both "outside-in" and "inside-out" approaches. *Outside-in* refers to methods in which an actor first develops the character's physicality, which in turn triggers the character's inner state. The term *inside-out*, then, is used to describe methods in which the actor develops the character's inner state, which informs the character's outer physicality. Earlier programs, which tended to take one approach or the other, have been nearly abandoned in favor of those that blend aspects from both.[4] Despite their differences, both outside-in and inside-out approaches are interested in tapping into the pathways that connect the mind and the body, which can sometimes lead to simplistic, causal relationships between body type and a character's emotions and psychology.

While a full genealogy of actor training pedagogy is beyond the scope of this essay, I do want to sketch current methods' roots to explain the assumptions embedded within them.[5] As Joseph Roach has shown, acting methods are closely aligned with their eras' psychological, technological, and medical discourses. Most American training programs are direct descendants of Russian actor and director Konstantin Stanislavski's (1863–1938) "system," which was developed to perform the new realistic works by playwrights such as Anton Chekhov in the late nineteenth and early twentieth centuries. Stanislavski drew on the latest psychological and scientific theories of his day that expounded on the nature of emotions, including the work of Pavlov, Freud, Ribot, and Darwin. Stanislavski developed both inside-out and outside-in techniques as his system evolved. What remained constant, though, was a "holistic belief that the mind and the body represent a psychological continuum" and that in "every physical action there is something psychological, and in the psychological, something physical."[6]

In the United States in the 1930s, actors such as Stella Adler (1901–1992), Sanford Meisner (1905–1997), and Lee Strasberg (1901–1982) at the Group Theatre adapted Stanislavski's system to the needs of the American scene, experiments that led to the development of what is now called the *American method* or simply *the method*. While the Stanislavski system and the American method diverge from one another considerably (and each practitioner develops his or her own philosophy and pedagogy), both teach actors to express genuine emotion on stage, so that their characters will appear to be fully rounded human beings living in the present. To do this, actors must gain access to their own emotional memories or experiences and learn how to use them in creating a character. Unlike Stanislavski, who experimented with both inside-out and outside-in techniques, some early versions of the Method relied almost exclusively on inside-out techniques and tended to pay little attention to the actor's body. Such practitioners believed that once actors generated truthful emotions, character physicality would naturally follow. This assumption led to criticisms that method actors lacked technical movement and vocal skills. That they, in effect, acted "all in their heads."

To rectify this situation, most university training programs since at least the 1970s have augmented Stanislavski-based approaches with specialized training in voice and movement developed from the work of "physical therapists, mind-body specialists, and medical practitioners."[7] Roach explains that such practice is informed by contemporary psychology that teaches us "to see our bodies as damaged by the kind of lives we have lived."[8] This view evolved primarily, but not exclusively, from the work on "character analysis" by early-twentieth-century Austrian psychoanalyst Wilhelm Reich. Reich, a disciple of Freud, believed that spontaneous feelings are blocked by layers of emotional defenses and actual muscular "armor," built up as a result of "stress, trauma, and shame."[9] Reichian therapy involves intense body manipulations intended to release muscular armor that, in turn, releases pent-up negative feelings. One of the ways in which Reich diagnosed psychological disorders was by looking at outward physical characteristics of the patient's body.[10]

In her 1995 textbook, movement teacher Jean Sabatine provides just one example of the continuing influence of Reich's work (though she does not mention Reich). She explains that the first task of training is

> to try to restore the actor's body to the natural grace and ease it was intended to have, before the body developed all the tics, slouches, slumps, and masks that social experience imposes on bone, tissue, and emotions.[11]

To that end, training programs draw on mind-body therapies such as F. M. Alexander's Alexander technique, Moshe Feldenkrais' "body awareness," Rudolf von Laban's "effort/shape," and Alexander Lowen's "bioenergetics," as well as the practices of yoga, tai chi, aikido, and other Eastern martial arts.[12] In addition, programs whose focus is to train actors for naturalistic styles began incorporating training methods derived from physically based, nonrealistic performance practices such as Jacques Copeau–inspired mask work, Vsevolod Meyerhold's biomechanical études, and Jerzy Grotowski's psychophysical techniques. These practices involve intense physical conditioning to improve a performer's balance, rhythm, expressiveness, and flexibility in preparation for highly stylized forms of acting.

Neutral

Despite the differences in these various approaches' styles, exercises, and techniques, they do tend to share an underlying assumption, one that often does not make sense to disabled actors.[13] This assumption is that beginners must first prepare their bodies and minds for the craft of acting by learning to strip away their personal idiosyncrasies: actors should try to achieve a "neutral" body. Although the term *neutral* was first applied to actor training by mask teacher Jacques Copeau (1878–1949) at the beginning of the twentieth century and further developed by a succession of teachers, similar foundational concepts underlie both "body efficiency training" and Stanislavski-based training. Since most current programs draw from all three approaches, it is useful here to delineate the various permutations the concept of "neutral" takes.

Copeau strove to pare the theater down to its essentials to provide a canvas against which to express the condition of humanity. Copeau realized that the "actor would have to be stripped as bare as the stage" so that he could "express himself clearly and simply."[14] To do so, the actor must rid himself of personal markers and habits—become "neutral." Once rid of individuality, the neutral body is "the point of departure of an expression."[15] Sears Eldredge further defines the neutral body as "symmetrical, centered, integrated and focused, energized, relaxed" as well as "economical [and] coordinated."[16] The neutral is also commonly described as intense but relaxed focus, much like the state of a runner before the starting pistol fires.

Copeau and his successors, Etienne Decroux (1898–1991), and Jacques Lecoq (1921–1999), used masks to obscure the individual features of the face so that actors could concentrate on the expressiveness of their bodies. Decroux's training in corporeal mime took Copeau's work to the extreme, demanding a body that could express the sublime in human suffering and struggle.[17] To show the beauty of crisis or revolution, Decroux's mimes moved parts of their bodies in opposing, unnatural ways, a technique that required exquisite control over the body. Former student Deidre Sklar explains, "When the actor moves with harmony, logic and efficiency of the worker or athlete, Decroux finds him *beau*."[18] Herein lies a paradox for the disabled actor that I will return to later: the body in crisis is described as appropriately represented by a symmetrical body in full, even incredible, control. Disabled bodies, whose parts often move in opposing, unnatural ways (think of the person with cerebral palsy), are excluded from representing those whose bodies might most resemble their own.

Other training methods developed. Because they share similar roots and philosophies, I am grouping these techniques together under the term *body efficiency approaches*. In the 1890s, the Australian F. M. Alexander (1869–1955), who was an actor himself, first developed his technique of integrating the mind and the body. Through work on proper posture, breathing, effective movement patterns, and release of tension, actors could discover their "divine neutral."[19] Alexander's philosophy is remarkably similar to Moshe Feldenkrais's (1904–1984), who developed his therapies during the mid–twentieth century in France and the United States. Feldenkrais maintained that the body becomes distorted because of unnatural societal pressures, cultural mores, and work habits, and through therapy could regain its own natural equilibrium. He worked with a wide range of clients, including both actors and disabled people.[20] Central to achieving equilibrium is each person's discovery of his or her own "zero position," which "denotes an absence of personal movement clichés, idiosyncratic ways of standing or tension in a particular part of the body."[21]

I want to include a brief mention of Russian director and actor Vsevolod Meyerhold (1874–1940) and Polish director and actor Jerzy Grotowski (1933–1999). While some would view my categorization of these trainers in a section on the body efficiency movement odd, both men developed techniques to rid their actors of individuality so as to better express the human condition as a whole. Meyerhold developed "biomechanics," an actor training system consisting of sixteen études—or routines—that would prepare actors for the physical and emotional needs of any role. He drew inspiration from the theories of Frederick Taylor (1856–1915), the American inventor who systemized factory worker's movements into the most efficient patterns.[22] While Meyerhold may not have settled on one "neutral" state, his études pare down the body's movements into discrete constituent units. A generation later, Grotowski similarly developed training techniques intended to pare the body down into essential expressive units. Grotowski's psychophysical exercises severely disciplined the body in order to get beyond individual socialization, allowing actors to communicate a supposed elementary psychic language through physical ideograms.[23]

Stanislavski-based acting teachers also make use of a concept similar to neutral, referring to a state of physical relaxation. Stanislavski himself practiced yoga and developed exercises to relax individual segments of the body. Stanislavski-based practitioners see physical relaxation as essential preparatory work to exercises intended to produce authentic emotion and natural, subtle, unstrained physical movement and facial expressions.[24] While method actors are famous for giving their characters meaningful tics, limps, and slouches, Stanislavski emphasized that the actors themselves should be as free as possible of physical defect. In *Building a Character*, Stanislavski's fictional stand-in, Tortsov, tells his students:

> Maybe a body with bulges in the wrong places, legs so spindly that their owner has to totter, shoulders hunched almost into a deformity do not matter in ordinary life. . . . But when we step on the stage many lesser physical shortcomings attract immediate attention. . . . Unless it is his intention to show a character with a physical defect, in which case he should be able to display it in just the proper degree, he should move in an easy manner which adds to rather than distracts from the impression he creates. To do this he must have a healthy body in good working order, capable of extraordinary control.[25]

Without a body able to relax properly, the actor will signify excessively: "Stanislavski said that imperfection in the external expression of a role can disfigure a profound conception of the playwright."[26]

Whether called neutral, divine neutral, zero position, or relaxation, most of today's acting programs spend many hours working with students to achieve this state, since it is considered the absolute foundation of the actor's work no matter what the style of performance. Eldredge explains, "Anything that is not neutral is the beginning of a characterization—a turnout with the left foot, or a cocked-back pelvis, a head tilting down, or a loping walk, a movement center in the chin, or a shallow chest with hunched, curving shoulders."[27] Without finding one's neutral, then, the actor is unable to make clear distinctions between him- or herself and the character. As Anne Dennis remarks, the actor will get lost, be unclear, and mumble.[28] And while most teachers acknowledge that "true neutral" is impossible, they maintain that actors should always strive to attain it.

What I want to stress in this abbreviated genealogy is that the concept of neutral emerged in the late-nineteenth-century industrial age, an age when bodies were studied and trained for efficiency, standardization, and normalcy. Words that recur in this eclectic collection of training methods include *control, efficiency, balance,* and *symmetry.* Whatever the acting style, the notion that actors' bodies should first be stripped of individuality and idiosyncrasy as a prerequisite to creating a role undergirds them all. Bodies are considered damaged physically and emotionally from the process of living, and those bodies capable of cure are suitable actors. Disabled bodies, though, cannot be cured. They may tremor, wobble, or be asymmetrical. Implicit in the various manifestations of the neutral metaphor is the assumption that a character cannot be built from a position of physical difference. The appropriate actor's body for any character, even a character that is literally disabled or symbolically struggling, is not only the able body, but also the extraordinarily able body.

The Emotional Body

Theoretically, once students are able to achieve neutral, they are ready take on the task of creating a character. The neutral body can then begin to signify a character's inner state with each deviation from neutral. But what do certain movements tell us about the inner life of a character? Different teachers have different answers to this question, but most training approaches take for granted that a person's inner, emotional state can be read on the physical body, a concept I am calling "the emotional body." The beginnings of this belief can be traced to late-nineteenth- or early-twentieth-century psychologists such as Freud and Reich, who attempted to read the body for symptoms of disturbed inner states. As with neutral, this concept does not apply neatly to disabled actors and can even be quite offensive and humiliating. The concept of the emotional body pervades actor-training techniques, but here I address only two areas: simulation exercises and physical acting choices.

Simulation exercises in which actors are asked to position their bodies in certain physicalities in order to conjure these bodies' emotions are common fare in many training programs. In *Building a Character,* Stanislavski's Tortsov asks his students whether external distortion affects the actor's inner life:

And what about lameness (Here Tortsov limped) or paralysis of the arms (Instantly he lost all control over them) or a humped shoulder (His spine reacted correspondingly) or an exaggerated way of turning your feet in or out (Tortsov walked first one way and then the other)? Or an incorrect position of the hands and arms holding them too far forward or too far back (He illustrated this)? Can all these external trifles have any bearing on my feelings, my relations to others or the physical aspect of my part?[29]

The fictional students conclude that it is "an undoubted fact that [Tortsov's] inner faculties responded to the external image he had created."[30] Tortsov tells them that in life, people fashion exteriors for themselves that match their inner states.[31] By extension, then, adopting a character's exterior will begin to automatically fashion a character's interior.[32]

Students of Stanislavski's system are not the only ones to use Tortsov's lesson; mask and movement teachers also use similar techniques. In her 1995 textbook, Anne Dennis (former student of Etienne Decroux) emphasizes that actors not merely adopt a physicality for a character, such as a limp or a hunchback, but "become credible" by finding "through his own body, the physical experiences of the character."[33] By adjusting the breath, muscle tension, and posture, actors can begin to "feel" what living in such a body would be like. She encourages students to allow that feeling to influence all the character's movements and to supplement what simulation can teach with the imagination.

While Dennis recommends that students be very specific about a character's physicality (including how age, health, and climate might affect the body), other movement teachers draw directly on broad character types for actors to emulate. These types are considered templates on which to make acting choices. Not surprisingly, these teachers draw on Reichian-based psychology to delineate character types. Actors are instructed first to diagnose their own physical types (which should be corrected as much as possible through the process of finding neutral) and then to experiment with various physical types for their characters. For example, Patricia Relph includes five character types that deviate from the "normal" body based on the research of Reich and Lowen. She illustrates the five types (in addition to normal, oral, masochistic, rigid, psychopathic, schizoid) for the actor using simple line drawings. The line drawings that deviate from normal conjure the physical silhouettes of people with various impairments. Both the "oral" and "masochistic" figures, shown in profile, have "hunched" backs, though the oral type is thin and the masochistic type is stocky. The "schizoid" figure, shown in a frontal silhouette, has an S-curved spine as might someone with scoliosis or cerebral palsy. I was disturbed to discover my own likeness in the swayback profile of the "rigid hysterical."

While Relph acknowledges that no one (actor or character) falls neatly into type, exploring these basic body types is a good place to start, since there is "considerable evidence that the relationships between emotional experience and somatic behavior are very regular."[34] Relph recommends that actors use this information in two ways, "first as a method for finding an appropriate physical characterization, and second as a method of tapping inner feeling."[35] Like Dennis, Relph recommends adopting the breath, muscular tension, and posture of their characters, not just to imitate superficially, but to discover characters' feelings.

Take as a more current example David Alberts's 1997 movement textbook, which also draws on Reichian theories in explaining the relationship between somatic and emotional life. He lays out six basic body types (normal, dependent, self-defeating, self-possessed, self-denying, and schizoid), explains their psychological and physical traits, and then lists characters from the dramatic canon that exhibit those body types. Here, Alberts makes one-to-one correlations between character type and disability. For example, Laura in *Glass Menagerie* is classified under the "dependent" type. These characters exhibit "feelings of loss, helplessness, despair, and inner emptiness. . . . Childlike dependence on others. . . . Feels unloved and unworthy due to lack of love and support as a child, particularly from mother."[36] These emotional traits are manifested physically, according to Alberts, with the following physical traits: "Long, thin body. Weak, underdeveloped muscles, particularly in the legs and arms. . . . Sway back and an inflexible spine. . . . Emotional pain equals physical pain."[37]

Each of the teachers I have discussed in this section has been careful to emphasize that simulating these character outlines is just one step in the process of creating a fully rounded character. These outlines are stereotypes, which the actor must diligently transform into specific characters by discovering their inner emotional lives. Despite this caveat, attributing basic emotional and psychological traits to certain body types encourages stereotypical acting choices. Perhaps these stereotypes become even more pernicious because actors make them appear more fully rounded and lifelike. Additionally, simulation exercises can humiliate the disabled actor on a couple fronts. First, the notion that physicality develops from our inner emotions and psychology does not make sense to a person who was born with or acquired an impairment that causes a limp, a curved spine, muscle spasms, or asymmetrical features. Having to participate in or even observe one's classmates "trying on" disabled or deformed bodies and reporting what emotions are evoked can be painful. Second, simulation exercises in which students are asked to pose as deviant bodies as means of conjuring up their "innate" feelings are not an objective process. Strong value judgments about disabled bodies, such as fear and pity, are ingrained in our popular culture, dramatic canon, and in the acting textbooks themselves. These prejudices cannot help but influence the emotions such simulations will evoke.

Rethinking the Metaphors

It is ironic that contemporary acting theory and methods, some of which came from physical therapy for the disabled and the injured, have ended up excluding them. In a professional theater educator's journal dedicated to movement pedagogy, movement teacher Lynn Norris lamented,

> Those students who are the most difficult, i.e., extreme over- or under-weight, severe psycho-physical manifestations, medical problems like hernias, epilepsy, brain damage, removed organs, spinal malfunctions . . . are left to perish because you cannot spend the time they need. The ones who will sur-vive on their own, the high school athlete and the young women who have been dancing since they were three, will somehow get by on their own. Those in the middle who have posture problems, unconscious physical mannerisms, or mild psychophysical problems will fall to your lot, and if you do not whip them into shape in one year your methods will be challenged.[38]

Norris's frustration is palpable in this quote. Perhaps Norris feels this way because concepts such as neutral are predicated on a cure mentality. Does she feel that she is expected to cure all of her students? That with enough training, students can approach neutral, and if they cannot, they have no sufficient basis upon which to build a character? Where does this kind of thinking leave the disabled student?

It is time to take a critical look at the metaphors foundational to our actor training practices. Zarrilli's observation that acting teachers are reluc-tant to reveal the metaphors embedded in their methods needs to be addressed. We need to use such metaphors consciously and critically as well as develop new metaphors of acting, metaphors that do not "dis" the dis-abled.

Notes

Earlier versions of this essay were presented at the Association for Theatre in Higher Education in 1999, the Society for Disability Studies in 2000, and Florida State University's Film and Literature Conference, 2001. I would like to thank the participants in those presentations for their useful feedback. I want to thank Ben Gunter, Kyle Bostian, Caleb Boyd, James Bell, Leah Lowe, Frank Trezza, Anita Gon-zalez, Victoria Ann Lewis, and Jim Ferris for their comments on earlier drafts. And I would like to acknowledge Jennifer Parker for her assistance with the research and Florida State University for a Committee on Faculty Research Support grant.

1. David T. Mitchell and Sharon L. Snyder, *Narrative Prosthesis: Disability and the Dependencies of Discourse* (Ann Arbor: University of Michigan Press, 2000).

2. Phillip Zarrilli, ed., *Acting (Re)Considered: Theories and Practice* (New York: Routledge, 1995), 8.

3. Alison Hodge, ed., *Twentieth Century Actor Training* (New York: Routledge, 2000), 4.

4. Ibid.

5. See Hodge, *Twentieth Century Actor Training,* and Zarrilli, *Acting (Re)Considered* for more complete genealogies. Also see Joseph Roach, *The Player's Passion: Studies in the Science of Acting* (Newark: University of Delaware Press, 1985); and Claudia Sullivan, *The Actor Moves* (Jefferson, N.C.: McFarland, 1990).

6. Sharon Marie Carnicke, "Stanislavski's System: Pathways for the Actor," in Hodge, *Twentieth Century Actor Training,* 16; the second quotation in the sentence is Stanislavski's words.

7. Sullivan, *The Actor Moves,* 87.

8. Roach, *The Player's Passion,* 218.

9. Ibid.

10. Most acting techniques in this vein draw from Wilhelm Reich's *Character Analysis,* written in the 1920s (3d ed., trans. Theodore P. Wolfe [New York: Orgone Institute Press, 1945]). His later work on "orgone energy" (life energy) in the 1940s and 1950s is widely regarded, however, as quackery. He died in 1957 in a U.S. penitentiary for illegal sales of his "orgone energy accumulator," a box in which patients sat to receive concentrated doses of orgone energy as a treatment for a variety of ailments. See Myron Sharaf's biography *Fury on Earth: A Biography of Wilhelm Reich* (New York: St. Martin's Press, 1983) for a thorough explanation of Reich's work.

11. Jean Sabatine, *Movement Training for Stage and Screen: The Organic Connection between Mind, Spirit, and Body* (New York: Watson-Guptill Press, 1995), 21.

12. Sullivan, *The Actor Moves,* 88.

13. I believe that the concepts of neutral and the emotional body should be revised for able-bodied actors as well, but this contention is beyond what I can cover in this essay.

14. Sears Eldredge and Hollis W. Huston, "Actor Training in Neutral Mask," in Zarrilli, *Acting (Re)Considered,* 121.

15. Copeau quoted in John Rudlin, "Jacques Copeau: The Quest for Sincerity," in Hodge, *Twentieth Century Actor Training,* 70.

16. Sears A. Eldredge, *Mask Improvisation for Actor Training and Performance: The Compelling Image* (Evanston, Ill.: Northwestern University Press, 1996), 53–54, 56.

17. See Deidre Sklar, "Etienne Decroux's Promethean Mime," in Zarrilli, *Acting (Re)Considered.*

18. Ibid., 114.

19. Sullivan, *The Actor Moves,* 95.

20. Ibid., 89.

21. Sullivan, *The Actor Moves,* 94. Rudolf von Laban (1879–1958), like Alexander and Feldenkrais, worked with injured and disabled people, dancers, and actors as well as factory workers. Laban studied various movement patterns, which he described as "efforts." Laban's philosophy seems much more suited to the performance training of disabled people, since it describes in nonjudgmental terms the

ways in which bodies actually move. His focus is less on "cure" or "rehabilitation" than on discovering one's own patterns and how to use one's own body to produce different efforts.

22. Mel Gordon, "Meyerhold's Biomechanics," in Zarrilli, *Acting (Re)Considered,* 88–89.

23. Philip Auslander, "'Just Be Yourself': Logocentrism and Difference in Performance Theory," in Zarrilli, *Acting (Re)Considered,* 64–65.

24. Richard Hornby, *The End of Acting: A Radical View* (New York: Applause, 1992), 154–63.

25. Konstantin Stanislavski, *Building a Character,* trans. Elizabeth Reynolds Hapgood (1949; reprint, New York: Theatre Arts Books, 1964), 36.

26. Sonia Moore, *The Stanislavski System: The Professional Training of an Actor* (1960; reprint, New York: Penguin, 1984), 52.

27. Sears A. Eldredge, *Mask Improvisation for Actor Training and Performance: The Compelling Image* (Evanston, Ill.: Northwestern University Press, 1996), 55.

28. Anne Dennis, *The Articulate Body: The Physical Training of the Actor* (New York: Drama Book Publishers, 1994), 53.

29. Stanislavski, *Building a Character,* 5.

30. Ibid., 7.

31. Ibid., 8.

32. *Building a Character* was translated into English and published in 1949, ten years after Stanislavski's death. American method actors in the 1930s, then, did not have access to the outside-in approaches in this text and instead focused on his earlier inside-out approaches. However, after the publication of this book, Stanislavski's outside-in exercises and philosophy have been explored by American actors and teachers.

33. Dennis, *The Articulate Body,* 28.

34. Patricia Relph, "The Bodily Expression of Emotional Experience," in *Movement for the Actor,* ed. Lucille Rubin (New York: Drama Book Specialists, 1980), 30.

35. Ibid., 47.

36. David Alberts, *The Expressive Body: Physical Characterization for the Actor* (Portsmouth, N.H.: Heineman,1997), 74.

37. Ibid. Alberts also draws on American psychologist William Sheldon's (1898–1977) "constitutional psychology," which delineates three basic body types, each with its own personality traits: the endomorph (round, soft), the mesomorph (muscular, athletic), and the ectomorph (thin, fragile). Alberts suggests that actors study their own physical types and use these types for templates on which to base a character's physicality (48–49).

38. Lynn Norris, "On the Training of Movement Teachers and Related Problems," *Theatre News* 6, no. 2 (1978): 3.

PART V Reading Disability
in Dramatic Literature

The essays in the final part of the volume focus on how the interpretation of plays and performance texts can be inflected by a disability perspective. The texts under examination were not written in order to express the experience or cultural status of disabled people and the issues they face, yet prove to do so in provocative ways when examined closely within the frame of disability studies. Looked at from this point of view, these texts prove implicitly to address vital issues, including the cultural representation of disability, the relationship of those representations to a discourse of "naturalness," and the in/visibility of disability as a strategy of representation.

Although the concept of disability as it is articulated through disability studies did not exist in the eighteenth century, Sharon L. Snyder sees Lord Byron as a literary disability activist *avant la lettre*. In "Unfixing Disability in Lord Byron's *The Deformed Transformed*," a reading of Byron's unfinished last play, she sees him challenging Shakespeare's use of physical disability as a trope for moral corruption and proposing that the equation of disability with iniquity is a social construct, not a biological fact. Byron reverses many of the tropic representations of disability in the Renaissance to suggest that the disabled body is more aligned with nature than is the normative body.

Marcy J. Epstein's "On Medea, Bad Mother of the Greek Drama (Disability, Character Genopolitics)" also addresses the relationship between ideological concepts of the "natural" and disability. Epstein contextualizes media reports on "bad" mothers whose acts of murdering their children are represented as violations of the order of nature rather than the results of mental disability by referring to the myth of Medea and Euripides' play. Epstein hears in Medea's voice a feminist call to consciousness of disability against the social pressure to condemn women who kill their children as beyond the pale.

Stacy Wolf in "Disability's Invisibility in Joan Schenkar's *Signs of Life* and Heather McDonald's *An Almost Holy Picture*" takes up the question of the visibility of disability within dramatic representation in two contemporary plays. Wolf explores how dramatic representation inflects reading disability. She argues that although the two playwrights do not represent their central characters' respective disabilities physically, those disabilities, the experience of them, and their consequences are fully represented through language. Wolf suggests that the strategy of presenting not fully visible characters makes the audience consider its own complicity in constructing images of the disabled.

Unfixing Disability in Lord Byron's
The Deformed Transformed

SHARON L. SNYDER

Transforming Representation

Through a reading of Lord Byron's last and unfinished drama, *The Deformed Transformed*, this essay analyzes disability as a body capable of resignifying the terms of its cultural reception. *The Deformed Transformed* intervenes in disability's repertoire of representations—what Judith Butler calls the "topography of construction" (28)—in order to revalue a denigrated social identity. For Byron, who was born with a condition similar to cerebral palsy,[1] the rewriting of Shakespeare's menacing hunchbacked king of *Richard III*, proved a personal and political necessity. As I have argued elsewhere, numerous productions of Shakespeare's malignant avenger (Mitchell and Snyder 111) heated up the late-seventeenth-century and early-eighteenth-century theatrical stage. As a disabled writer refusing the silence traditionally associated with the cultural outsider, Byron presages the political strategies offered by many contemporary theorists of the body. *The Deformed Transformed* intervenes in the representation of disability to destabilize the historical portrait of Richard III as the "arch-defective in all literature" (Miller and Davis 361).

Byron's *Deformed Transformed* redresses the Shakespearean representation of disability a sign of malignant motivation. Rather than reinscribe this sign, Byron's play severs the relationship between deformity and diabolic intent. Disability is unleashed from its ideological mooring as a sign of personal despair, becoming a malleable source of political, intellectual, and sexual power. In doing so, the play brings the reader to the revelation that the protagonist's disability shields him, however ironically, from the immoralities of the late eighteenth century's version of nondisabled masculinity (and as a norm, standard, and agent of destructive cultural rituals such as war and sexual domination). It also provides the opportunity for Byron to question the meaning of physical difference as a basis for empirical observations about intangible qualities such as "moral character."

Byron recognized that a performance-based art can effectively transform "the deformed" by positing disability as a flexible narrative entity. In doing so, *The Deformed Transformed* does not merely invert cultural meanings about disability by conjuring up an alternative reading; instead, the drama taps into the indeterminacy of bodily appearances by demonstrating that the meaning of disability is tethered to discriminatory cultural ideologies. Consequently, Byron's interrogation of the habitual alignment of disability with undesirability threatens to re-form "biological facts" as linguistically constructed materiality.

The restrictive yoking of disability to an irrefutable, organic, and material deviance provides the site of performative interventions. The objective of disability studies (and performance studies in a larger sense) is not to deny disability its attendant "biological" differences, but rather, to mobilize a more fluid understanding of its meanings. *The Deformed Transformed* articulates a varied universe of narrative potential beyond the horizon of pathological social scripts about the body. Byron takes up this challenge by parodying outsider versions of disability. As a result, the drama poses readings alternative to the pathology of the disabled body itself. For Byron, the key maneuver is to free disability into a performative space (as in Butler's analysis of gender) and to unmoor physical difference from its exclusively debilitating location in inferior corporealities.

Staging Disability

The dramatic structure of *The Deformed Transformed* enacts just such an intervention in the culturally assigned story of disability. Based loosely upon a popular French novel of the time entitled *The Brothers Three,* Byron's play also borrows heavily from Goethe's *Faust.* This appropriation of forms from both low and high culture demonstrates that Byron already recognized his subject matter as a progeny born of two discursive orders. Inherited from the ranks of the literary in works such as Shakespeare's infamous dramatic portrait of Richard III, the story of malevolent disability was disseminated in popular Romantic literature. Consequently, *The Deformed Transformed* strad-dles two related discursive communities—literary art and popular stories—that participate in a mutually debilitating story of disability. This merger of the tragic and the melodramatic delineates a disabled space within drama: one overwrought with bourgeois angst and emblematic of the Romantic belief that suffering is the common denominator of humanity. A signifier for both of these detrimental registers, disability becomes a *master trope of human invalidation*. Byron situates disability as a body multiply displaced from any legitimate site along the normative continuum of human biology.

The Deformed Transformed begins with the excess of affect common to melodramatic and tragic discourses. Byron directly cites numerous scenes in *Richard III* where the duke of Gloucester is castigated by a series of female players who taunt him about the evil implications of his disabilities. The protagonist's mother drenches her son in curses taken from lines borrowed from Lady Anne, Queen Margaret, and the duchess of York in Shake-speare's drama of the malignant avenger: "Thou incubus! Thou night-mare!"; "The sole abortion"; "That monstrous sport of nature"; and "the hedgehog / Which sucks at midnight from the wholesome dam" (477–78). These curses directly allude to Shakespeare's text with the discomforting citation of the protagonist's physical disabilities as evidence for his personal failure. The maternal figure's hyperbolic curses situate the drama within a social context of discrimination.

The distinction between the displays of maternal derision in Shake-speare and Byron is key to understanding the latter's revisionary strategy. In spite of the uncertainty that surrounds courtly interpretations of Richard's disability, Shakespeare establishes that the intimacy of familial knowl-edge—particularly that of the mother's—reveals that Richard's "deformed" outside mirrors an equally malignant interior life (Mitchell and Snyder 108). In contrast, *The Deformed Transformed* uses the mother's figure as a rep-resentative of the injustice that comprises Arnold's life in a denigrated social body. The play portrays the central conflict not as the tragedy of the protagonist's disability, but as the unyielding derision felt by an ableist pub-lic toward bodily differences outside an acceptable range of difference.

The injury Arnold suffers from his mother's slanders upon his physical character cause him to contemplate suicide as the only antidote to ridicule. Whereas Richard strikes out at his tormentors (perceived and actual) with a murderous rage, Arnold turns inward toward a self-destructive impulse. His monologues of melodramatic victimization capitalize upon an able-bodied audience's belief that disability is the ultimate tragedy. While nine-teenth-century audiences could have seen Arnold's interior monologues as a narcissistic wallowing in self-pity, the one topic that might justify such a self-hatred was disability. Consequently, the superfluous angst of Arnold's self-commentaries perform a cultural script of overwrought angst available to the bearer of a deformed body.

Yet this excessive display of emotion is differentiated from Arnold's own beliefs about his "deformity." The opening scene establishes a clear relationship between public stigma and his growing feelings of repugnance toward his own body. The emphasis throughout Arnold's tortured contemplations of his predicament underscores the ability of "one kind word" to reorient his own response to his physical shape. His opening monologue positions the viewer as a witness to an ideological transformation within the protagonist's own consciousness. From human form to satanic parallel, from personal acceptance to public rejection, Arnold struggles to exorcise his own beliefs, based upon internalized normative ideals.

Conundrums of Embodiment

Byron positions the "deformed" Arnold as wholly innocuous within his social setting. Arnold seeks genuine affection from his mother and perhaps the interest of a lover, but no public station. The staging of his internalized sense of public derision in the opening monologues makes moot the question of disability as personal malignancy. Arnold's desires are doomed by social rejections, and the arrival of a Satan-like form in the figure of the stranger suggests that Arnold has conjured up a body akin to the phantom attributed by the community to his own bodily deviance. In this manner, *The Deformed Transformed* indicates that the criminality projected upon disability produces its own subjectivity. As a result, disabled psyches emerge as *split:* somewhere between the desire to commit suicide (as a means to end social ridicule) and fraternization with the monstrous figments of communal imagination.

Shifting the terms of Arnold's participation in his own denigrated form, the arrival of "the tall black man" begins with an interrogation of the binary terms used by Arnold to interpret his sudden appearance. Suspicion are precipitated by Arnold's perception of the stranger's "alien" form:

Arnold: What would you? Speak!
           Spirit or man?
Stranger: As man is both, why not
           Say both in one?
Arnold: Your form is man's, and yet
           You may be devil.
Stranger: So many men are that
           Which is so called or thought, that you may add me
           To which you please, without much wrong to either.

                                                    (1.1.83–91)

The exchange draws out a contrast between responses to the meaning of external deviance. Arnold forgets his physical deformities for the time being in remarking on the stranger's ominous appearance. In the midst of these speculations the stranger begins a banter that blurs Arnold's binary distinction between desirability and external appearance. Arnold has lapsed, ironically enough, into interpretations of deviance in the wake of his own despairing musings about the malignancies ascribed to his disabled form. In this way, Byron remarks upon a lack of identification that determines the subjectivity of disability. If Arnold cannot check his own suspicions with regard to his physically based speculations, then why should he despair over that same suspicion in others toward him?

In the Faustian deal that follows, the stranger continues to challenge the simplistic binary readings offered by the protagonist through hyperbolically performing the malleability of his own material interpretive practices. In a playful rhetorical inversion of disability's social alliance with tragic inability, the stranger offers a panegyric to the promise of physical deviance:

> Were I to taunt a buffalo with this
> Cloven foot of thine, or the swift dromedary
> With the Sublime of Humps, the animals
> Would revel in the compliment. And yet
> Both beings are more swift, more strong, more mighty
> In action and endurance than thyself,
> And all the fierce and fair of the same kind
> With thee. Thy form is natural: 'twas only
> Nature's mistaken largess to bestow
> The gifts which are of others upon man.
>
> (1.1.105–13)

The stranger's declaration to Arnold that his "form is natural" situates the play's redress of the social interpretation of disability within the realm of a discursively produced insufficiency. Although physical differences are presumed to occur in "Nature" as an error of biological programming, the stranger provides an early example of how one might resignify those same "mistakes" as fortuitous rather than calamitous. Deviance becomes the stranger's credo in that he ridicules the culturally wrought language that would create difference as synonymous with undesirability. "Mistakes" of nature produce animal forms that prove the very source of their power. Deviance in this argument is a source of natural innovation that brings into the world the pleasure of diversity—not diversity for its own sake, but rather adaptation that multiplies the capacities of an otherwise narrow biological range.

The stranger opens with this counteressentialist analysis of the difference that disability makes—one that introduces strength rather than weakness, endurance rather than capitulation to restrictive social norms. Arnold, as the disabled subject who has internalized those social meanings, cannot readily hear the stranger's analysis and apply it to his own life. Instead, he becomes drawn into the Faustian offer that he exchange his undesirable form for "the form of heroes" (1.1.143). While the stranger endeavors to tutor Arnold in a more fluid linguistic understanding of his disability, Arnold, as the embodied disabled subject, seeks relief only through a material transformation of his own despised body.

As the stranger conjures up a variety of physical specimens from whose bodies the deformed protagonist can choose—"I can but promise you his form; his fame / Must be long sought and fought for" (1.1.196–97). As this procession of bodies appears, Arnold finds himself in a conundrum: if he bases his choice on historical reputation, the accompanying physical body comes replete with the physical blemishes of a life lived within a vulnerable corporeal container. In addition, the stranger strategically alternates Arnold's choices between those who have accomplished renowned acts with those whose beauty was their sole source of infamy. The historical visages rising up before Arnold's eyes embody this paradox as the stranger continues his efforts to persuade Arnold that his external appearance does not bar him from achieving acclaim. While the disabled protagonist may be disallowed access to meaningful social integration, his tacit acceptance of that fact creates him as complicitous in the ideological aesthetic of bodily appearances.

Just as the stranger exclaims, "Fear not, my Hunchback" (1.1.264), and Arnold begins to despair that there is no pure coupling of beauty with moral accomplishment available (the stranger's point exactly), the figure of Achilles emerges from the pool. As the two marvel over his physical beauty, recall his acts of valor in the Trojan War and his empathetic suffering over the slaying of Hector, the stranger ends with a brief reminder of the exposed ankle that proved his undoing: "Look upon him as / Greece looked her last upon her best, the instant / Ere Paris' arrow flew" (281–83). Arnold misses this reminder of physical vulnerability as he grows increasingly enraptured with the promise of Achilles' near-perfection: "I gaze upon him / As if I were his soul, whose form shall soon / Envelope mine" (284–86). The entrancement with surface beauty ironically exposes Arnold to the flawed nature of his own desires. He who would pursue the enticements of physical symmetry will fail to appreciate the offerings of a diverse universe. Because Arnold invests the empty figure with his own ideas of virtue, the stranger pointedly remarks, "*You both* see what is not, / but dream it as what must be" (290–91).

As the stranger transforms Arnold's body from despised hunchback into classical Achilles, the protagonist's perspective immediately shifts from one of overwrought personal angst about the meaning of his physical appearance to the arrogance that accompanies his possession of an "unblemished" exterior. Arnold immediately applauds his delivery from the "burden of deformity" by seeing his former self through the eyes of an able-bodied masculinity:

> I would
> Have done the best which spirit may to make
> Its way with all Deformity's dull, deadly,
> Discouraging weight upon me, like a mountain,
> In feeling, on my heart as on my shoulders—
> A hateful and unsightly molehill to
> The eyes of happier men.
>
> (1.1.329–35)

The scene seeks to cultivate the audience's skepticism about the ease with which Arnold rejects his previous physical incarnation. The transformation of external physical character precipitates a bankrupt moral perspective. Arnolds' fall, implied by the vulnerable ankle of Achilles, is already anticipated by his willing discrimination against his own rejected form.

As if to emphasize this point, the stranger asks Arnold what he would like to be done with the emptied shell of his former self. The protagonist responds with an indifference related to his newfound embrace of beauty: "Who cares? Let wolves / And vultures take it, if they will" (1.1.428–29).

The final irony of the scene turns upon the stranger's decision to occupy Arnold's rejected former body and go by the name of Caesar. Thus, as Arnold grows narcissistically enraptured with his bodily metamorphosis— "I forget all things in the new joy / Of this immortal change" (450–51)— the "cure" does not obliterate the evidence of his previous state. The stranger dons "[the] hump, and lump, and clod of ugliness / Which late you wore, or were" (426–27), embodying the point that one cannot escape that which influenced one's personal history and life outlook: "Whatsoe'er it may be, / It hath sustained your soul full many a day" (431–32). In resuscitating deformity, the stranger shadows Arnold with the body image of which the protagonist so readily divested himself. In taking up the title of Caesar, he also underscores the possibility that renown and disability may exist in close proximity.

The Deformed Transformed acts out a story of "opportunistic cure" only to demonstrate that the erasure of disability provides no exit from the protagonist's socially produced predicament. Arnold easily steps over into a prejudicial perspective that Byron suggests is the culturally encouraged predisposition of the able-bodied toward those with disabilities. The stranger ironically points out that the evidence of Arnold's entrance into the land of the able-bodied is not his more winsome appearance, but rather his embrace of demeaning attitudes toward physical difference. Within this formulation disability becomes little more than the sign against which the able body will define itself as whole, complete, and functional.

Epistemological Battlegrounds

Reversals of common beliefs about disability abound in the stranger's ironic repertoire of refutations throughout the remainder of the play: "The deeper the sinner, better saint" (1.1.523); "True; the devil's always ugly: and your beauty / Is never diabolical" (524–26). Each inversion of the stranger's logic exposes the shaky epistemological ground upon which disability as a sign of corruption rests. Because the two primary characters have switched bodies, the stranger now supplies his refutations about the meaning of disability from the perspective of one who would serve as the object of such derision.

Numerous examples of the stranger's diminishment based on his disability abound in the drama. As he takes over the role of a disabled Sancho Panza to Arnold's Don Quixote, the stranger's "deviance" becomes the constant subject of social ridicule. As the two approach the encampment of Bourbon's armies awaiting the sack of Rome, the stranger once again encounters his own dehumanization through encounters with the upper echelons of military leadership: "Welcome the bitter Hunchback! And his master, / The beauty of our host" (1.2.219–20). The dehumanizing welcome serves as more than a description of the approach of two seemingly unlike physical companions; the contrast of the bitter hunchback with the host's beauty situates the two terms in a binary relationship. Beauty must have its contrast of deformity in order to secure its own position in aesthetic value.

While the disabled Arnold would have been easily overcome by such overt rejections, the stranger is emboldened to redress each of the accusations with his own countercommentary about excessive physicality. The masculine stage of war becomes the backdrop upon which the "true" life of able-bodied masculinity unfolds. It is this staging that the stranger uses to unravel physical prowess as an inherent cultural value. While Bourbon takes up a habitual diminishment of the stranger's unsightly presence, the derided object, in turn, challenges the unquestioned value of the military leader's own physical valor. Rather than admire Bourbon's militant prowess, the stranger turns this potential strength on its head. He ironically points out that generals entertain little risk by remaining in the rear guard of advancing troops. Every logic, strength, or weakness can be inverted to become its other, and the stranger's linguistic dexterity puts the lie to that which would appear to be otherwise. Such is the nature and necessity of disability, for it must refuse its too easy alignment with disadvantage by inverting that which would pose as inherently advantageous.

The stranger situates himself as a deconstructive force undoing the seemingly fixed material world from its deterministic static definitions: "it answers better to resolve the alphabet / Back into hieroglyphics" (1.2.106–7). Rather than participating in the cultural myth of progress in which the accumulation of knowledge means better understanding, the stranger commits himself only to a theory of the primacy of chaos. To unseat the prejudices of men, one must attack the confidence with which reiterative knowledge gains authority. The stranger's credo, that humanity is most accurately characterized by suffering, weakness, and devolution, resounds with echoes of the anti-Enlightenment stance of the Romantics: the world cannot be empirically dissected from the outside in. Human experience proves more dynamic and mystical in its bearing. Through this artistic challenge to the dictates of scientific empiricism, Byron interrogates the belief that a visually based empirical method could successfully master the unruly dynamism of the body.

Rather than a commitment to a myth of evolution, the stranger unfolds an argument that all matter eventually dissolves into its originary disarray:

> From the star
> To the winding worm, all life is motion; and
> In life *commotion* is the extremest point
> Of life.
>
> (1.2.22–25)

If devolution is the foundational principle of all life, then order proves a ruse of those who believe they can ultimately overcome disorder (bodily or otherwise). Disability, within this philosophy, becomes a "truer" adherent to the essential element of all life because it exposes the falsehood of materiality's absolutism. Its closer cultural alliance with "commotion" disorders the static hold upon normalcy to which able-bodiedness aspires. If life is temporal and parasitic—rather than immortal and independent—then the self-valorizing rhetoric of able-bodied men becomes one more fable upon which the human world precariously rests.

Life is definitively parasitic, reasons the stranger, and disability is no more unnatural than the notion that ability proves inherently desirable. While in cultural registers disability is literally narrated as that which defies a natural order (and thus becomes fixed as a sign of deviance), for the stranger disability represents a necessary rebellion against the illusion of mastery. While disability will be interpreted as that which proves excessively dependent, able-bodiedness preys upon its rejection of difference in order to disguise its own interdependence. Disability becomes ability's own "rule / Of fixed Necessity" (1.2.31–32) because able-bodiedness promotes its livelihood at the expense of its disabled counterpart.

Just as mortality eventually falls prey, sooner or later, to its defining vulnerability in nature, so too does ability give way to the counterthesis of inability. Thus, rather than situate disability as the embodiment of disorder, the stranger uses his dramatic stage to argue that all is commotion, but those with disabilities give up the illusion, that the world is stable and non-chaotic, earlier than most.

> this crooked coffer, which contained
> Thy principle of life, is aught to me
> Except a mask? And these are men, forsooth!
> Heroes and chiefs, the flower of Adam's bastards!
> This is the consequence of giving matter
> The power of thought. It is a stubborn substance,
> And thinks chaotically, as it acts,
> Ever relapsing into its first elements.

$$(1.2.312-19)$$

This monologue sets the stage for the action to come. The stranger argues that his donning of Arnold's deformed body—"this crooked coffer"—means nothing beyond that with which it is invested by language. His rhetorical question to himself about the body as merely a mask for the "principle of life" challenges the Judeo-Christian reading of materiality as a corrupt container for the spiritual aspect of human beings. "Matter" within this reading translates into that which "[t]he power of thought" endeavors to master.

Yet the body proves recalcitrant to such impositions ("it is a stubborn substance") and ultimately eludes the efforts of thinking organisms to fix its meaning. Even the presumed "best" of the species—"Heroes and chiefs"—fail in their efforts to overcome materiality with language, and consequently, the chaos of thought provides nothing more than the illusion of mastery. Disorder proves both foundational to life and the product of thought itself in its eternal effort to organize that which is inherently mutable and dynamic.

Thus, for *The Deformed Transformed* disability gradually becomes the marker of a vulnerable, yet worthy, humanity. Able-bodiedness becomes little more than a temporary masking of a devolutionary principle of life. As the sack of Rome gets under way and the stranger watches as Arnold engages in the violence of war alongside his able-bodied counterparts, the drama conveys the irony of a takeover that destroys the very bodies it so covets as inherently desirable. The riches of the ancient city—its architecture, peoples, art, and material treasures—all fall to ruins under the press of armies and the greed of those seeking to take possession.

As Arnold grows increasingly bold in the wake of his sense of imminent victory and physical prowess, the stranger cautions him against overlooking the need to preserve his body against the violence of men. His cautions to his companion serve as a general commentary against war; military skirmishes act as proof that men undervalue their lives as vulnerable physical beings. But they also emphasize that the experience of able-bodiedness often leads to a haphazard willingness to expose one's physical self to danger. Arnold's becomes undifferentiated from the bodies of other able-bodied warriors in the contest, and, his willingness to expose his newly minted body to the ravages of war proves his physical agility for men. But, as the stranger points out, the press to battle also underscores Arnold's newfound indifference to the value of unblemished embodiment.

After Arnold is wounded in a skirmish, he orders the stranger to dress his wound so he can return to battle, for his "thirst increases;—but / I'll find a way to quench it" (2.3.50–51). This bloodthirsty ethic now driving Arnold proves the substance of life from which his previously disabled incarnation shielded him. The able body demonstrates itself through flirtations with potentially disabling situations, while the disabled body remains unmoved by the need to expose its vulnerability further. Whereas the disabled protagonist was endangered by his increasing sense of alienation from an overdetermined emphasis upon the significance of his physical body, Arnold loses all sense of himself as an embodied, and thus vulnerable, human organism.

Unfixing Disability

These shifting versions of embodied experience are highlighted when the stranger points out to the protagonist that "'tis rarely worth the trouble / Of gaining, or—what is more difficult—Getting rid of your prize again; for there's / The rub! at least to mortals" (2.3.183–86). What is gained in the transformation of a disabled body to an able one proves of dubious value by the conclusion of Byron's drama. While disabled bodily presentation remains physically unaltered over the course of the story, the topography of its representation has shifted dramatically. Disability moves in the course of the work from a socially victimized identity to one that yields insight and exposes the ruse of able-bodied masculinity. Byron sets the representation of the disabled body into motion in order to overwrite its historical signification as an undesirable identity.

The remaining fragment of *The Deformed Transformed* suggests that Byron intended to end his drama of inversions on an ironic note. While Arnold endeavors to win the love of the pope's daughter, Olimpia, the stranger steps into the role of competing suitor. Ultimately the stranger woos Olimpia in spite of (or, even perhaps, as a result of) his visible deformities, and Arnold is left to puzzle over his devotion to the false ideal of unblemished physicality. Here the drama makes its final inversion of audience expectations. The disabled body has come full circle from its opening association with contamination to its concluding position of power. In order to accomplish this representational circuit, Byron inverts the position of the feminine as well. While the mother begins in a position of power with respect to the authority she commands over her son's self-image as a disabled individual, the wooing of Olimpia by the stranger allows disability to regain its lost advantage within a heterosexual model of conquest.

This entrenchment of one denigrated identity at the expense of another demonstrates the conundrum of bodily hierarchies; one regains its cultural advantage at the expense of the other. If the disabled body is to gain a measure of equality, it does so only in the wake of femininity's surrender. The stranger sums up this idea in his concluding monologue on love as the most narcissistic of enterprises:

> you would be *loved*—what you call loved—
> *Self-loved*—loved for *yourself*—for neither health,
> Nor wealth, nor youth, nor power, nor rank, nor beauty—
> For these you may be stript of—but *beloved*
> As an abstraction—for—you know not what!
>
> (3.461–65)

Daniel Watkins argues that Byron rejects ephemeral ideals such as wealth, youth, power, rank, and beauty as the vestiges of an unsatisfying narcissism. In their place the Romantic poet inserts a devotion to the weakness and vulnerability of the body *in spite of* its gross misinterpretation by ideologies grounded in aesthetics: "According to Byron, this abstract controlling belief produces an isolating, spiraling effect because it rests upon the unspoken motivating assumption that material reality is ultimately insufficient" (28). In making this claim on behalf of materiality, Byron recognizes the disabled body not only as worthy of a place on the continuum of human forms, but also as an embodied topography of representation that can be successfully resignified and, ultimately, transformed.

Note

1. In most biographies Byron is noted as having a club foot, a rather amorphous medical classification in the nineteenth century. However, his disability appears to have involved more than this singular congenital impairment. Byron's editor quotes Mary Shelley's observations about his physical demeanor from *Memoirs . . . of Lord Byron* by John Watkins, 1822: "A malformation of one of his feet, and other indications of a rickety constitution, served as a plea for suffering him to range the hills and to wander about at his pleasure on the seashore, that his frame might be invigorated by air and exercise" (474). More recently, Phyllis Grosskurth—following the work of Denis Browne—has laid the groundwork for a more specific diagnosis that we would argue is similar to some forms of what is now labeled cerebral palsy. Byron walked with a "sliding gait" and his "congenital deformity" was confined to his right leg, which "curved inwards, and was so stiff that it impeded the movement of the ankle" (qtd. in Grosskurth 25). This differentiation is not made for the sake of medical accuracy but to establish that Byron's congenital disability had a profound impact on his life as an artist. Whereas most biographers and critics have argued that Byron himself overemphasized it, we foreground its importance for his creative imagination.

Works Cited

Butler, Judith. *Bodies That Matter: On the Discursive Limits of Sex.* New York: Routledge, 1993.

Byron, Lord George. *The Works of Lord Byron.* Vol. 5, *Poetry,* ed. E. H. Coleridge, 467–534. New York: Scribner's Sons, 1901.

Grosskurth, Phyllis. *Byron: The Flawed Angel.* Boston: Houghton Mifflin, 1997.

Miller, Donald S., and Ethel H. Davis. "Shakespeare and Orthopedics." *Surgery, Gynecology and Obstetrics* 128 2 (February 1969): 358–66.

Mitchell, David, and Sharon Snyder. "Introduction: Disability and the Double Bind of Representation." In *The Body and Physical Difference: Discourses of Disability,* ed. D. Mitchell and S. Snyder, 1–31. Ann Arbor: U of Michigan P, 1997.

———. *Narrative Prosthesis: Disability and the Dependencies of Discourse.* Ann Arbor: U of Michigan P, 2000.

Pickersgill, Joshua. *The Three Brothers.* 4 vols. 1803.

Watkins, Daniel P. "The Ideological Dimensions of Byron's *The Deformed Transformed.*" *Criticism* 25 1 (winter 1983): 27–40.

On Medea, Bad Mother of the Greek Drama (Disability, Character, Genopolitics)

MARCY J. EPSTEIN

I have heard of one woman of those of old
one who laid her hands on her dear children
Ino, who driven mad by the gods . . .
stepped over a sea-cliff
and killed herself, dying together with her boys.
After that, what horror could surprise us?

(Morwood 34–35)[1]

Six years after a white South Carolinian housewife Susan Smith drove her two sons into rising waters, spurring the vigil and grief of an entire nation, she reported to the *New York Times* that she had suffered from a suicidal impulse so intense as to have bound her children to her own fate, but in last instant had spared herself from drowning for fear of how her own death would feel. She laid the murders instead on another's shoulders, those of a fictitious black child killer. In the end, interrogation of Smith proved to American readers that the criminalized black male figure of their own imaginations was more credible than its shadow, the figure of a (white) mother who kills.

Medea (*seeking out her children*): Are you indoors?

(Vellacott 44:882)

Susan Smith under arrest

Time magazine followed the demagoguery of prosecution and defense in minute detail, citing Smith's "strange and inappropriate" behavior during the nine-day search for her children, her heart-wrenching lies about their abduction, an uncanny statement about going to the beach in order to learn the shag, the court's minute reenactments of Michael's and Alex's deaths.

> *Medea:* For the wrong, unprovoked . . .
>
> (Vellacott 22:156)

More recently in Houston, Texas, an unhallowed crime scene of five drowned children laid out in a bedroom expressed, according to national press, Andrea Yates's profound postpartum depression, as well as her despondency at being an inadequate mother;[2] once again the image the

Yates had projected as a model family in their suburban, middle-class neighborhood was shattered, and the danger of homicidal mothers lurked beneath the outpouring of grief for husband and children.

Medea: For the wrong, unprovoked . . .

Public sentiment underscores the demise of the natural mother in modernity, especially when white, perfect children are mutilated or killed. Because of the sensationalism of child loss and transgression attached to such reports, however, the real mental illnesses that affect many mothers— psychosis, postpartum depression, bipolarity, manic depression, and object-relations syndromes—rarely acquire substantial press. Like the thousands of women who suffer from more exotic illnesses, like Munchausen syndrome by proxy, a surprisingly common disorder that causes mothers to subject their children to disabling and often life-threatening scenarios in order to gain attention from medical professionals,[3] Yates and Smith become, to borrow from disability performance artist Julia Trahan, "icons of infamy."[4]

The actions of such "bad mothers" extend further into the characterization of infanticidal women than either medicine or journalism can report. In the latest tradition of Electra, Medea, or Clytemnestra, Trahan's "infamy" refers to the objectification of gender, sexuality, and disability. It is the sign we most fear, and to recuperate the experience of disability and womanhood, it must be performed, opened, forced as necessary, not suppressed, rewritten, or recast as a deviation from mores or norms.

Some disabled women indeed re-create their disabilities in their children.[5] Like themselves, the children can lose subjectivity in even Mothers' eyes and become props, even spaces for the performance of their mother's disability dramas. Largely masked in the tight weave of maternity, their disabilities—performed through their progeny—indicate a rift between what the public can be told and what the experience of motherhood is. Media viewers are less interested in the mental disabilities themselves, however, than in an *iconography* of infamy, often hysterical, an iconography that blends together two prevailing myths about disability and gender: primarily, that mothering is a biological act designed from a genetic and social template, inviolable except by women of a bereft, wicked, or counterrevolutionary nature; second, that disability, like gender, is a psychobiological affect that can be made visible and represented dramatically through social and theatrical convention.

In light of this recent outcry over the discovery that race, gender, and ability does not necessarily a good mother make, the stage offers a millennia-old pageantry of perverse maternal icons that warrants closer scrutiny.

The interplay of disability and gender as social conventions reveals that below the speech of tragedy in such circumstances, disabled women break from the sociogenetic template of "able mothers" and "disabled others":

> *Medea:* No doubt I differ from many people in many ways.
> To me, a wicked man who is also eloquent
> Seems the most guilty of them all. He'll cut your throat
> As bold as brass, because he knows he can dress up murder
> In handsome words.
>
> (Roche 34:579–83)

In Euripides' compelling *Medea* (written 430 B.C.E.), the question of a mother's character may be interpolated, performed as a discourse within the drama itself by a figurehead so "bad" as to rival the most pernicious forces winding their ways into the consciousness of audiences from classical Athens to those of our own time. Iconic Medea, who lovingly embraces her two perfect sons, then bludgeons them in their beds, belongs to an ilk of character that speaks out (*muthos* and *logos,* mythologizes) on the compounding of disability, gender, and the politics of hereditary culture. Here is a shift in the madness paradigm, from the mythic past we have created for madness and other invisible disabilities, to the Athenian theater of controversial, mythic mothers falling putatively, untouchable, in the present:

> Seeking for methods of interpretation and techniques of decipherment that will make sense out of what may at first glance appear as no more than a jumble of grotesque tales, scholars have been led to question the concepts of the ancient Greeks and to ponder the true nature of what we call myth. What social and intellectual status does this type of story have? To what extent does it constitute a specific mode of expression, with its own particular language, thought, and logic?[6]

Madness, for Medea, is both affect and effect, providing audiences of any era with a conundrum regarding the psychiatric definition of the revered mother, "disabled" in/by her society. Her madness is not exactly distinct from its visible disability counterpart; since it takes on the whole of Corinth, not just Jason, Medea exposes society's fixation on myth and character, inverting and perverting the status of disabled women, in particular those who provide various, indispensable services to the state: reproduction, caregiving, and the perfection of the species.

> *Medea:* [Corinth,] I would not have you censure me,
> So I have come.
>
> (Vellacott 24:214–15)

Such "bad" women have always attracted me as figures of study, in part because I am intrigued by the moralization of agency in general, and, practically speaking, I often play the foils of such "bad" women in real life. Temporarily able-minded, I am a so-called "good" mother-to-be, more like the Corinthian women who flock to stare at Medea's social demise and possible execution. Euripides positions his audience thus: we cross over regardless of sex (the vast majority of his audience was male), race (few in his audience would share Medea's dark complexion), or disability (the audience would expect that madness is human frailty in the face of forces larger than mere society, Fate or the gods). As Jean-Pierre Vernant points out, in the theater and as intellectuals we still seek in ancient Greek myth a "particular language," "a specific mode of expression," more accessible than ontologies. By application, Medea speaks her mind, but to audience members she is impenetrable, impassive, and confrontational. Her character, or some *characteristic* of her character, is quite real to us. Her infamy, on one hand, is familiar, like Trahan's performances, wrested from the mythos surrounding her, or seen purely in the context of pleasurable madness and debasement attributed to her on the Dionysian stage. Her fame, on the other hand, arguably, is a disability issue.

Her controversy, like Smith's frantic articulations or Yates's laments, has engendered feminist readings. This "speaking across" the divides of time and subjectivity tells us even more about Medea's disability, for her *muthos* and our mythos about her "state of mind" are in fatal opposition. Euripides' text permits interplay between Medea the city-state subject and Medea the objectionable and crazy woman. Abandoned in Corinth by her ambitious husband, Jason, and exiled for her mad articulations, she is mutilated relationally as a function of her motherhood. Bennett Simon has written that maddened characters become so when their world collapses, part of "a frantic hold on to what they know and think right. Their world involves issues of the state, the gods, the family, and the microcosm of their own conflicted ideals and passions."[7]

> *Medea:* [W]rong with worse wrong.
>
> (Vellacott 24:238)

To act out her "maddened" status, Medea exaggerates insanity and ill-use, since her action, however extreme, is the sole apparatus of her beingness on the stage. Delusion is something she uses as theatrical illusion and Corinth as excuse. She must *make* her disability real in a time and place where there is no audience for it. Thomas Szasz purports that to be fully human, one must "possess both the capacity to act and the opportunity to perform before [a legitimating] audience."[8] The stakes are high in Medea's world as in ours:

> Come, flame of the sky,
> Pierce through my head!
> What do I gain from living any longer?
> Oh, how I hate living! I want
> To end my life, leave it behind, and die.
>
> (Vellacott 20–21:143–48)

The Medean character, because of her mutilating madness, should be constructed in abeyance of conventional performance, assuming the "reaction formation" that characterizes mental disability; otherwise, Medea's madness has been infused with erotic cache, like the classical nude and other perfecting tropes.[9] Thus to look upon Medea's beauty and simply imagine her madness as flaw to a perfect space occupied by her is to miss the point. She already occupies her own discursive space. The relation between the audience and the Medean subject is more complex. What appears to be the ability to mother is most open to performance, while the threat that Medea poses to the city-state is covert and harder to capture, linked with the awesome unknowns of evolution and adaptation rather than with its more palatable maternal counterpart. This comes as no surprise when one considers that the theater of Dionysus promulgated the very artistic, social, and juridical ideas intimately linked with Athens's supremacy within a republican empire.

Given Medea's cultural context, making disability visible is quite different from studying visible disabilities. Visible disability in our own time still produces the ongoing stare of those agape at nature's variety. To be visibly disabled in ancient Greece was not uncommon, since injury and postcongenital change of the body were seen in most aspects of civic life. Formal theater was tightly bound with the aesthetics of philosophers and the business elite. As disability scholar Martha Edwards points out, the ideal body was "epitomized by the Greek statuary. . . .[T]he grotesque [was] a necessary counterpoint . . . but the idea of attainable perfection—that a mortal can shape himself to the mathematical perfection of Greek statuary—is modern."[10] While many female and disabled infants were subject to annihilation by exposure, it was also the case that some disabilities were indeterminate at birth, that some mothers raised disabled children, and that the vulnerability of women and children was linked in the determination of disability. The visible space could be flawed, yet still a civic display of the culture's powers; Euripides' theater made use of mask and costume to depict such differences.[11] Likewise, to murder when the other is vulnerable also fits this civic concept of viability, for one's children were considered the extension of the father's lineage and thus the political means to the extension of citizenship within the democracy. To the point, invisible disabilities posed a problem in the polis, one easier ignored. The powder keg of madness was variously attributed to the vengeance of the gods, poor humors, noble wrongs, and other disgraces.

In *Medea* we see the complication of this civic concept. Although she remains beautiful throughout the play, from birth Medea is indeterminately placed in the ancient taxonomy of gods, men, and slaves. The *enfant terrible* of animal, human, and divine forms, she represents a intriguing figuration of moral birth, since she is born from divine roots (granddaughter of Helios the sun god), of Theban royalty, and of Hecate's dominion over animal spirits and magic. She plays both herself cursed and the dark foreigner whom Corinthians imagines the worst of, yet she is also the child of perfection, both statuesque and grotesque. Her "defective" character in slaying her own children (who remarkably pass as the children of the king's fair, perfect daughter, Creosa) in response to Jason's adultery was more likely understood as a political threat rather than a medical condition of mental disability.[12] Largely enforced by playwrights and actors participating in a venerable festival, these complications echoed in some plays like *Oedipus Rex* and *Electra,* while other plays, like *Medea* or *The Bacchae,* reflected uncomfortable messages about indeterminate social order and identity. Staged in 431 B.C.E. and unsurprisingly unpopular, *Medea* posed an important contrast to a prevailing dramatic model, of plot/fate, called *moira,* and earned the famed Euripides second prize.[13]

Certainly Euripides knew the social conventions governing marriage, connubial and extramarital sex, conception, and the civil engineering of children. Athenian women had a more tenuous position in terms of property, social membership, and parentage than even their Hellenistic or Homeric predecessors.[14] In his characterization of a bad mother in *Medea,* reflecting Greek legal, social, and protomedical conventions, though, Euripides composed for Medea the very language that disability critics and performers may use to suggest the social realities of women with mental disabilities, without visible markings of disability or social pathology. The murder of her progeny signifies the *moira* of her faithless spouse rather than her own: her children represent what she doesn't get: rights, justice, and punishment, in Greek parlance, the same word *(dike).* What looks like a scheme of sheer wickedness is a critique. Her voice has been made "useless for honest purposes," muted in a din of Corinthian standards. It is in this madness that she becomes "evil-skilled" (Roche 20).

Unlike Oedipus's mother Jocasta, who unwittingly sleeps with her own son and then destroys herself, Medea plans terrible acts against Jason that result in the death of the innocent. If she seems monstrous for executing her plot against Jason, she is the type of monster that audiences go home with, for wives and other wronged women are aplenty in the Western world.[15] If Jocasta does badly for her shortsightedness, Medea is bad because her mental state permits her to look far into her future. At the surface she is "bad" because she commits heinous acts. She is more "bad" than Jocasta[16] because she subverts the hierarchy of King Creon, and thus perverts her social position as wife, royalty, and mother.[17] She is profoundly "bad" because her mind obeys otherworldly spirits, and she conjures supernatural forces to do her mad bidding. Too simply, Medea is bad *because* of her madness, not in spite of it. Bad to the bone, she thinks herself more than nothing among men. She may tear enemies limb from limb. Her thoughts are both womanly and unwomanly in strength—and she *becomes* the other whom Corinth (and we) fear. Her name, which translates to "cunning" or "knowing," suggests that Medea is a figure of the head as well as a woman of the body. In short, she flexes; she is adaptable. Sociopathic and realistic, Medea is, in most legal senses, psychiatrically unsound in an era before medical psychiatry, a Munchausen's candidate, slaying children to accentuate her self. She is a mutilator, self-mutilating in the sense that her children come from herself.

> Do I not suffer? Am I not wronged? Should I not weep?
> Children, your mother is hated, and you are cursed.
>
> (Vellacott 20)[18]

In another sense, Medea rejects bad conduct while savoring her own wrongs. Her badness is a convention, the villainy of outsidership that is often labeled "outlaw," as explored by Peggy Phelan in *Unmarked.*[18] Medea's brand of rebellion and transgression tells us that she is reacting to her situation in Corinth, doing as the oracles foretold years ago, and also that she "recharacterizes" herself, asserting her voice in all its forms. *Recharacterization,* in dramatic text, appears when a character appraises her own situation as a dynamic of suffering that comes from a conflict between her political reality and the era in which the play is produced. Designed by their authors to transmit conflicts between what the character embodies "then" and what the character embodies for us "now," such characters "recharacterize" throughout the course of dramatic action, past to present, present to past, thus shifting their own plots. Greek dramatists would draw upon *moira* to anchor the paths of their characters. In contrast, Medea's anchor has been lifted, not only by Jason's abandonment, but also by dint of her "evil skills." Most generally, Medea does to her children exactly what the ancient Corinthians and Thebans would do to children of their enemies; we are disgusted not only by her actions, but also by the society that has created the sickness, even done the same. Sheila Acker alludes to recharacterization in "The Monster under the Marriage Bed": it is with "grim irony" that Medea resculpts her world. She laments that she has no family (of humanity), yet she has murdered each and every member of it, past and future. But what appears pathological is indeed sociological, for it tells of what makes Medea ill, and, as Euripides describes her, "diseased" from this intelligence.[19]

> *Medea:* What do you gain from being clever? . . .
> All you fellow citizens hate you. Those who are fools will call you ignorant
> And useless, when you offer them unfamiliar knowledge.
> As for those thought intelligent, if people rank
> You above them, that is a thing they will not stand.
> This I know from experience. Because I am clever,
> They are jealous; while the rest dislike me. After all,
> I am not so clever as all that.
>
> (Vellacott 26:297–305)

Remember, Medea has been left to die from exposure:

> Do you see how I am used—
> In spite of those great oaths I bound him with—
> By my accursed husband?
>
> (Vellacott 22:157–60)

Her boys now occupy the gap between being socially united (in Corinth, in marriage) and being socially cleaved (from her husband, from her fatherland). She must elect instead a "freakish" lineage.[20]

> *Medea:* What pain the future hides from us.
>
> (Vellacott 44:890)

Only now does she corral her own sons into a deathly symbiosis, cursing her own young since they are also filled with Jason's blood: "Death take you all—you and your father: / The whole house wither" (Roche 147). Her sons, played by "perfectly" formed children, are aborted by Medea because she genetically weeds them out.

Medea's children, in this sense, represent her power in her madness to launch a political genocide, a reversal of afflicted birth, against those who value the ties of blood and biology at all. Her ties are with greater powers, not lesser ones.

While we may not agree with the legality or morals of Medea's act, it is crucial, not only as a climax of the play, but as a vicious beginning of revolution without condition, that the death of perfect progeny by their own producer deliver the bloodied flag and message: the untenable will be met with the unforgivable. The polis, with its politics, combats its mothers with maddening effect. She leaves condemned but without retribution. In some versions of the play, Medea strides off stage with the bodies of her children in tow, or she is airlifted to the sky with the corpses in a deus ex machina especially designed for her by Helios, fired by prosthetic serpents so as to escape a sure death sentence.

Perhaps the most fascinatingly "bad" element of Medea's exuent, technically so difficult as to have been elided from most modern interpretations of the play, yet quite common in ancient and pre-1950 production, comes in the form of a flaming, self-propelled sun chariot, a supercharged getaway wheelchair hot rod, her sons' bodies flagged as a warning, "Do not try this at home," or even more radically, "Try this at home." Horribly reminiscent of Susan Smith's crime scene, Medea takes a circuitous path to Aegus, king of Athens, to give him a fertility spell, to turn age and impotence back into parenthood. Linked with deus ex machina, at very least Medea's mental disability assumes theatrical and civic proportions. For giving Medea a country, Aegus will have a super lineage. Aegus's tragicomic fatherhood grossly complements Medea's lost motherhood, posing not only a gruesome portrait of her derangement, similar to Smith and Yates, but also a larger escape from the Sophoclean predicament that Medea's future has already been told. Unlike Oedipus, who blinds himself and wanders in exile at his play's end, nothing is said of Medea's exit: she *goes on.* Yates, Smith, Medea: who kills the mother? Yet who can ignore the rationale? Mythology tells us that she takes up an offer for sanctuary with Aegus and bears him a son, Medus, and, alternatively, she (or her son) comes to avenge her original exile. Sometimes she becomes queen of Media, named for herself, a land of "knowingness." Nothing is known of her thereafter.

Nothing is known of the judgment of her by the chorus of Corinthian women. No mad men or women come to converse with her in some dialectic of disability. Except for their jail cell interviews and suicide watch, little is known about the psyches of Susan Smith, Andrea Yates, or the millions of mothers who occupy the unsanctioned spaces of disability and motherhood. Medea goes *on.* As long as we fail to understand enough of Medea, on Medea goes, the Medean figures in our history stashed away in this country like their counterparts in our institutions, nursing homes, and—dare we reveal the extent of this cultural neglect—next door. With her tendency toward action given as her character flaw and reason for exile, Medea turns tables on the social parasitism of Corinth, and asserts that her character exists according to her experience, not the law. She co-opts and adapts, demonstrating at the end of the tragedy a parallel evolutionary process that

Medea's "deus ex wheelchair," vase painting.

the disability experience documents. Medea evolves while staying on within an unlivable environment. Medea's "evildoing" is a rejection of culture only as extreme as her culture's rejection of her:

> *Medea:* There is no justice in the world's censorious eyes,
> They will not wait to learn a man's true character;
> Though no wrong be done to them, one look—and they hate.
> Of course a stranger must conform; even a Greek
> Should not annoy his fellows by crass stubbornness.
>
> (Vellacott 24:220–25)

This reasoning over the deaths of her son highlights the argument internal to Euripides' drama, for it defines what it means for a woman to reach extralegally and extramorally beyond her "good" place as progenitor and second-class citizen. In an age of euthanasia, genetic modification, and fetal selection, Medea is genopolitical: she kills her own to pronounce sentence on crimes against those who would breed humanity. The force that makes Medea most pathological emanates, to borrow from Fredric Jameson, from the "cultural illogic" of human biologisms and our anxieties over them, especially those concerning viable offspring, viable murders, and the determinations of our own bodies.

In contemporary performances of *Medea,* a mother's vindictiveness has been reconstructed as vengeance for the suppression of women; increasingly we see attention to Medea's mental disability as well. In Miles Potter's 2000 Stratford Festival production, Medea, played by premier Canadian actor Seana McKenna, chides the heightened, journalistic chorus grieving her madness.[21] Potter's *Medea* is classical, dark, unctuous, watery, and weary, undulating between the now and Euripides' time, says the director, "deeper, more mythic . . . but we can still see our faces"; in the foreground, McKenna's character is gorgeous, glittery, powerful, committing murder of kings and kin "according to nature what I was meant to do."[22] In an interview in 2000, McKenna appeared curious about Medea's disability, not having contextualized Medea's madness specifically in the face of modern pathology of mentally disabled women. To the actor, madness was an affect of other complex relations, "contagious," the infanticide a "tearing of one's own heart," culturally horrible, according to McKenna. Her character embodies "the preconceptions we have of the woman wizard," the other of race, gender, and disability who "confronts her own powerlessness . . . linked with the greatest of men." Medea frightens because she will not settle for less than her due, like Greek male heroes, echoed in Christian avengers, eye for an eye, child for an eye, and the modern psychotic (Potter compares her to Hedda Gabler): "[A]m I to look in my son's eyes and see Jason [the man, the citizen] forever? To annihilate the past / is not possible: but its fruit, in the present / can be nipped off. Am I to look in my sons' eyes and see Jason's [the man's, the citizen's] forever? How can I endure the endless defilement, those lives / that mix Jason and me?" (Jeffers 38). Her disability is a product of her racial otherness, displaced class, and unofficial status within the Pantheon, as much as mental disability comes from brain function or humor.

As McKenna and Potter suggest, *Medea* is ripe for telling from within the disability experience, beyond controversy, and not a matter of making child murder right. Instead her performance scripts the interaction among those who would oppress and those already affected by oppression, not only by acts of exile, but from the decimation of character those with mental illness still deal with to this day. The Stratford actor considers her audience as she plays: what do they think a mother will do? What will the mothers they know do? What have their mothers already done? Medea's poignant violence

Seana McKenna as Medea, plotting the death of perfect sons. From the 2000 Stratford Festival of Canada production, directed by Miles Potter, designed by Peter Hartwell, with *(left to right)* Max Besworth and Aidan Shipley as the Children. (Photograph by Michael Cooper, courtesy of the Stratford Festival of Canada Archives.)

takes place off the projected stage, to spare the spectator, perhaps, and definitely to honor the deeds as befitting the doer: says McKenna, "I am playing her as a human being, and letting larger forces speak for themselves."[23]

The Abbey Theatre's production of *Medea,* which toured in Ann Arbor before settling in for a hot run at the Brooklyn Academy of Music, interprets Medea in an equally urbane (Corinth, New York City) context as the Stratford work, but with a subtle reversal of character by reading Medea's mental state as psychiatric, street-damaged, and unstable. Fiona Shaw, whose commanding presence fairly pales director Deborah Warner's large ensemble of underworld wayfarers, is clearly a vehicle for Medea's recharacterization as a person above a wretched mind, wrenched spirit, wrung heart, and womb: she confronts and seduces her audience more generally from the great stages she plays, and enters with damage that seems half wronged-woman and half fucked-up street dweller, with nights spent in the bower of anywhere. Tom Pye's set is back alley and synthetic, a dual vision of a corroded city and a psycho-theatrical ward, with knives and pills buried by Medea's nurse, and an unapologetic chorus of prurient visitors who, like us, want eternity replayed with themselves safely in the scene.[24]

Shaw's Medea is more familiar to the modern audience, the wronged celeb whose curious throngs come nearly hoping blood will be shed, as Ben Brantley reviews in the *New York Times,* in "an age in which private breakdowns, breakups, and humiliations have become public rituals."[25] "Grow . . . tall in the pride of youth," Medea tells her golden children, holding her womb for what comes next, "I must lose you." The reviewer contrasts Shaw with her "toxic jumble" with her icier, classier predecessors, like McKenna or Diana Riggs; let us extend Brantley's sketch of the chorus back to the creature we have come to see, the Medea who fails only at disappointment for her spectators. Squatting in a birthing pool with her perfect son suspended sanguinely between her knees, Medea really exists by dramatic proxy, but turns about to lay the results of genopolitics in our own bloody laps.

> I tore my own heart and laughed:
> I was tearing yours.
>
> (Jeffers 78)

On, Medea. What Medea's infamy tells us is that the politics and diversions explored at the interstices of disability studies, performance studies, drama, and activism require not just new voices of disability playwrights and actor, but old voices as well. Recharacterization may provide theater and performance a radical tool for confronting the vast and complicated structures around or defining disabled characters within and beyond Western society, "confined" to chariots or turned "mad" or "bad" by those who would hate or oppress them. It is also true that Susan Smith and Andrea Yates are performing for the masses, audiences quite different from those of their stage contemporaries McKenna or Shaw. The examination of the counterrevolutionary and counterrevolutionary "voices" in the heads of disabled and disabling mothers, and of mental disability as it is performed and a matter of public record, may provoke questions on behalf of all those who deal with madness as social or genetic construction. Richard Grossinger suggests that it is stigma that perpetuates psychiatric and other "altered" states (pun on internal and civic states intended): remembering Andrea Yates, Grossinger adds, "The goal should not be to confuse such biologically damaged individuals with those undergoing extraordinary experiences, perhaps with a biochemical vector, that can be assimilated and used for psycho-spiritual growth."[26] We do not fully understand Susan Smith's motives or Andrea Yates's background. Certainly we know that many millions of disabled women have existed in a vacuum of knowingness despite the rampage of public inquiry. Medea tells us that while their children do not endure, their stories do, and must be told. The Abbey's director explains, "[T]he tragedy of Medea is that in the end, because of other choices she makes, she has no choice but to kill her sons."[27]

Medea: How my thoughts turn to you now!

(Vellacott 26:307)

It is our thoughtfulness and not our pity that these women deserve as they circumvent life's horrible choices by using death. Thus Euripides' text performs an appropriate, feminist, and disability-experienced polemic on the making of "character" in all so-called democracies, ancient and postmodern, politically real and theatrically imagined.

Notes

1. For this essay, the following translations of *Medea* were used: James Morwood (Oxford: Oxford University Press, 1997), Philip Vellacott (Harmonds-worth: Penguin, 1996), Paul Roche (Boston: Bedford, 2000), and Robinson Jeffers (New York: Samuel French, 1998). I use this variety of translation since it is not my goal to construct historical accuracy in the translation but to capture the range of textual story in editions most often used for theater production and the classroom. Jeffers's, for example, is the translation of choice for Miles Potter's Stratford production. The late Kenneth McLeish and Frederic Raphael translated *Medea* again in the early 1990s (London: Nick Hero Books, 1994), focusing on the "dramatic logic" of Euripides' lines. This version has been used by director Deborah Warner for the Abbey Theatre of Ireland. I am interested in another echo of translation, the "cross talk" of character and audience that is integral to readings of disabled and female

characters once they are offstage and in the hands of critics, academics, and readers. I have chosen to integrate excerpts of Medea's voice without "close reading" for the mental disability and political maneuvering found there. Interesting discussions may spring from this, but my focus here is on the dialogic effects of posing Medea as a disabled woman who must speak on her own behalf without critical intermediation, translating her into my argument about Medean figures without necessarily pretending that her madness is all of Medea. For a fairly solid rendering of Medea's mental illness, see Bennett Simon's chapter on mental life in *Greek Tragedy in Mind and Madness in Ancient Greece* (Ithaca, N.Y.: Cornell University Press, 1978), 89–121. Thanks to Sara Rappe of the University of Michigan, who reviewed translations and argument for cultural accuracy in my comments on Euripides' Greece.

2. "Andrea Yates under Suicide Watch" was the title of over fifty-five news stories, according to a search on Google.

3. See H. A. Schrier, "The Perversion of Mothering: Munchausen Syndrome by Proxy," *Bulletin of the Menninger Clinic* 56, no. 4 (1992): 421–33; and H. Spivak et al., "The Psychology of Factitious Disorders," *Psychodynamics* 35, no. 1 (1994): 25–34, for medical perspectives on this lesser-known condition. To my knowledge, the syndrome has not yet been studied from the perspective of disability studies.

4. From "Nickels from Heaven," performed by Trahan at the Espresso Royale Caffe as part of the This/Ability conference on disability and the arts in Ann Arbor, May 1995. Trahan has not yet interpreted Medea, but her work consistently challenges the social mores connected with a "womanly disability," a womanliness displaying in performance the horror and spectatorship connected to invisible disabilities, the disability that is Trahan's *story.*

5. This is a far more potent statement than space allows. This argument emanates to a wide range of disability issues beyond one essay's scope, such as the importance of sharing the experience of disability with one's children so as to embrace the family's identity, or the inheritance of Deafness/hardness-of-hearing among some families, or even the Goliath of genetic selection issues, one I return to later in the essay.

6. Jean-Pierre Vernant, *Myth and Society in Ancient Greece,* trans. Janet Lloyd (New York: Zone Books, 1990).

7. Bennett Simon, *Mind and Madness in Ancient Greece* (Ithaca, N.Y.: Cornell University Press, 1978), 90.

8. Thomas Szasz, "Action and Intention: Mental Illness and the Problem of Intentionality," in *Insanity: The Idea and Its Consequences* (New York: John Wiley, 1987), 222–23.

9. Joseph Grigely makes a provocative critique of artists who use imagination to fill in cultural spaces for blind people (who already occupy those spaces with their experience); the gaze at disabled people can be a form of colonization. See "Postcards to Sophie Calle," in *Points of Contact: Disability, Art, and Culture,* ed. Susan Crutchfield and Marcy J. Epstein (Ann Arbor: University of Michigan Press, 2000), 25–26.

10. Martha Edwards, "'Let There Be a Law That No Deformed Child Shall Be Reared': The Cultural Context of Deformity in the Ancient Greek World," *Ancient History Bulletin* 10 (1996): 79–92.

11. Sara Rappe has informed me that the Festival of Dionysus began with community pageantry, including the Ephebic dances; in these, the motherless and

fatherless and reconstituted Ephebes were paraded in full martial regalia, demonstrating how the city brought up its most vulnerable children to represent them in battle.

12. Henri-Jacques Stiker's history of disability illustrates the fatal exposure of those persons society deemed defective, revealing the social threat of disabled people as they were expelled. See *A History of Disability*, trans. William Sayers (Ann Arbor: University of Michigan Press, 1999), 39–64.

13. The dominant dramatic figure in fifth-century Athens reflected Oedipus, one who appeared righteous and good, but whose character became real to the audience as he endured *moira*, the unraveling of truth around their identities. Oedipus (swollen foot, marked so from birth by his own father's attempt to murder him) falls from the best ranks of Theban citizenry to its lowest, that of wandering madman, blinded by his own hands, a fate determined by the gods. To a major degree, Athenian viewers at the Dionysian festival celebrated disabled Oedipus, since when the major character would transgress, they could be assured that the civic belief of order, imposed by above, would be enforced. In *The History of Sexuality, Part III, The Care of the Self,* trans. Robert Hurley (New York: Vintage Books, 1988–90), Michel Foucault indicates that public discourse infused and constructed a thematics of privacy in Greek society; this means that concepts of ability and social status were mutually informing, and thus in plays like *Oedipus Rex,* that disability expressed what is immutable, finite, and eternal, *moira* for each man in Athenian society. This idea is easily extended to the stage, for there, acting *Oedipus* would assert a weak transgression from *moira* that would end in the satisfying result of a clear demise. Whereas the Oedipal character reflects simply the post hoc judgment of his immoral acts by a rigidly critical Greek Society, Medea's character thumbs her proverbial nose at society's ways.

14. Stephen Todd and Paul Millett, "Law, Society, and Athens," *Nomos* (Cambridge: Cambridge University Press, 1990), 9.

15. Sheila Acker, in her Stratford Festival production playnotes, "Monster under the Marriage Bed," suggested that the husbands of Athens must have been particularly threatened that evening.

16. Note that Jocasta cannot recharacterize herself within Sophocles' oracular schema; she would need to be performed presentationally, retranslated, her play rewritten, or even her character removed from Oedipus's world to another.

17. From *Trojan Women* to *Stheneboea,* Euripides often referred to adultery as cause for retaliation; the extant law favored men, but also covered former wives and other extramarital relationships. David Cohen argues that this type of antagonist/protagonist embodies the "conflicting normative idealizations of women: desire and fear, dependence and hatred, Medea and Andromache [swing] . . . positive and negative ideals on one hand, and the life of the society on the other." David Cohen, "The Social Context of Adultery in Athens," *Nomos* (Cambridge: Cambridge University Press, 1990), 151.

18. Peggy Phelan, *Unmarked: The Politics of Performance* (New York: Routledge, 1993), introduction.

19. Perhaps we see intelligence of character in *Medea* so prominently since Euripides studied the ethicists of the time, weighing the dramatic effect of actions carefully with the cultural and political mores of the city-state. Euripides' play was

received with interest by dramatic scholars of the ancient and early Roman epoch. The scholia to this play portray Medea as a sort of social critic herself, according to Neophron, the interpreter of oracle pageantry in A.D. 666 as an inevitable act. Among pre-Socratic philosophers, this pathetic expression of pain and mental distortion is not so far-fetched. Advising Euripides, the philosopher Anaxagoras described a cosmology of forces that act on the mind, leading the character to be in control while not acting ethically—a preform of recharacterization. By this token, Euripides' Medea maintains an unusual presence of mind, still heeding the theory that she may act "out of her mind."

20. Medea has a long history of expressing her cultural instability. Previous to the play's events, and probably known to Euripides' audience, Medea butchers her brother Apsurtus into pieces and sets up her father's assassination. In another myth known to the Athenians, Medea defeats Talos, bronze man of Crete, by plucking a nail from the vein of his foot, bleeding him to death from the point of his vulnerability. Filling Jason's father's veins with a potion brewed in a large pot, Medea spellbinds her in-laws into cutting her new uncle into chunks and adding him to the stew.

21. McKenna notes that she has played Medea before, before she had a child, suggesting that playing Medea during her own motherhood amplifies Medea's heroic message.

22. Interview between author and Potter, Stratford, Ontario, May 2000.

23. Interview between author and McKenna, Stratford, Ontario, 2000.

24. This is not the first time Medea has been played within the psych ward (the film *A Dream of Passion*, for example), but Warner's designers, Tom Pye, Peter Mumsford, Jacqueline Durran, Mel Mercier, and David Meschter, worked with the house black space to create interesting psychological limits in the Power Center, for example, a shallow reflection pool that in the final scene surrounds the bloody Medea, sensational sounds effects against city and mother's music, and a translucent screen, one that suggests both the shaky walls of home and those of the clinic.

25. Ben Brantley, "A 'Medea' Fit for the World of Today," *New York Times*, October 4, 2002.

26. Richard Grossinger, "A Phenomenology of Panic," *Sun*, April 2003, 22.

27. Interview and compilation by Leslie Stainton and Kate Remen-Wait, *Speaking of Theater* (Ann Arbor: University Musical Society, 2002). In Remen-Wait's essay, Oxford scholar Fiona MacIntosh, an editor of *Medea in Performance: 1500–2000*, suggests that Medea's power and range, more than her infanticide, account for her longevity in the theater. I would suggest only that powerful acts make Medea's powers known. Were she left unhindered and offered accommodation in her time of trial and twistedness, we might never have glimpsed the depth of human despair, isolation, or anger, a link understood by disabled people (with like power and depth) throughout the same term of modernity.

Disability's Invisibility in Joan Schenkar's *Signs of Life* and Heather McDonald's *An Almost Holy Picture*

STACY WOLF

The mind's eye echoes the mind's ear. Words act. They are elements of the scenic investiture affecting, synesthetically, light space rhythm pattern sound, but they also resound at the deepest level of the *mise en scène*, through self time memory consciousness as well.

—Herbert Blau, *Blooded Thought*

Performance is the art form which most fully understands the generative possibilities of disappearance. Poised forever at the threshold of the present, performance enacts the productive appeal of the nonreproductive.

—Peggy Phelan, *Unmarked*

From the nineteenth-century "freaks" in P. T. Barnum's sideshows, to the early-twentieth-century "deformed" patients in medical theaters, to the late-twentieth-century heroic "cripples" in realist drama, physically disabled bodies have appeared on the stage. Whether stared at with curiosity, gazed upon with titillation, perused with prurience, or studied with admiration, visibly disabled bodies seldom occupy a drama's center stage. Rather they function to allow nondisabled characters to demonstrate their generosity and nondisabled spectators to experience their normalcy. Disabled bodies' corporeal presence creates in nondisabled spectators what David T. Mitchell and Sharon L. Snyder describe as "the double bind of fascination/repulsion with physical difference."[1] Scholars in disability and performance studies have articulated a range of critical and theatrical solutions to undo this double bind. For example, Rosemarie Garland Thomson analyzes the dynamics of "the stare" of presumptively able-bodied spectators at a freak show and how it allows them to buttress their sense of normalcy in relation to the stared-upon disabled body; Carrie Sandahl critiques theater's persistent metaphorization of disability; Victoria Ann Lewis surveys a range of playwrights' dramaturgical strategies that are "aimed at exposing the 'constructedness' of the disability identity in order to eliminate it" and that celebrate " 'disability cool' "; and Chris Strickling demonstrates the importance of disabled performers telling their own stories in their own bodies.[2] Each of these analyses contributes to disability performance studies in significant ways, using the field's theoretical tools and analytical methods to attend to the presence of specific bodies at the site of live performance. This essay will consider a different theatrical manifestation of physical disability: invisibility.

Two plays by contemporary American women feature female characters who have visible physical disabilities that are not seen on stage. In Joan Schenkar's *Signs of Life* (1979), Jane Merritt suffers from multiple neurofibromatosis, or "Elephant Man disease," and she is described as "a monster."[3] But on stage, the actor playing Jane appears as nondisabled. In Heather McDonald's *An Almost Holy Picture* (1995), Ariel is born with lanugo, congenital hypertrichosis lanuginosa, a neurological condition that causes her body to be covered with golden hair.[4] But Ariel is a character in the play only through the protagonist's description of her; she is not embodied on stage at all. These plays differ completely in content and form, in tone, mood, style, and effect. *An Almost Holy Picture* is spare, with one actor, few props, an almost bare stage, and a churchlike atmosphere. *Signs of Life*, in contrast, is like a circus, with numerous actors, a three-sectioned set, and many events happening at once. Still, both plays grapple with the complexity of representing physical disability in theater, and both solve the dilemma in the same way: by eschewing visual representation altogether. Both plays instead use language to evoke the characters' physical disabilities, and they rely on the audience's imagination to conjure characters whose disabilities are rendered solely in speech.

These plays are also similar in how they go about representing the disability unseen on stage, as they employ an extravagant, even excessive vocabulary of the visual and the visible. Both are saturated with visuality in language, with references to vision and seeing, with metaphors and images of sight, with descriptions that are detailed, rich, and evocative. Thematically, each play negotiates questions of visibility, vision, and the visible; each considers what can be seen, by whom, and to what end. Because both plays features characters with visible physical disabilities that are represented aurally rather than visually, the plays construct a particular and particularly active position of listening and imagining for the spectator.

Live performance offers a range of opportunities for the representation and embodiment of characters and of actors with disabilities. Charles Mee, for example, specifies at the end of each of his plays that the roles should be cast across race and ability.[5] Mee instructs a production team to practice "body blind casting," which, like color-blind casting, asks spectators to ignore the specificities of an actor's body in a specific role. In other plays, an actor with a disability might productively complicate a play's meaning, such as actor Lana Dieterich as Lillian in Lisa D'Amour's *Sixteen Spells to Charm the Beast.*[6] Although the character of Lillian is not disabled, she refers frequently to being trapped in her apartment and unable to walk out. In one scene in this imaginative play driven by fantasies of seduction and nightmares of real emotional attachments, Lillian saws off her hands and feet. Dieterich's pronounced limp (from polio), which determined her timing, her blocking, and her energy in the performance, inadvertently heightened the effect of Lillian's literal and emotional immobility.[7] Performers with disabilities have also created autobiographical performances, such as *Actual Lives,* in Austin, Texas, where people with disabilities attest firsthand to how disability constructs their experiences while figuring as only one aspect of their identities. The conjunction of actor and character—they play themselves—accrues the aura of authenticity typical of autobiographical solo performance art and provides important agency and visibility for people with disabilities. A visibly disabled performer's body forces spectators—disabled and able-bodied—to confront their own feelings and knowledges about disability and to see disability's meaning and significance as socially and culturally constructed. More often in theater, though, characters with disabilities are played by nondisabled actors, who sit in wheelchairs, fake a limp, pretend to be blind, or hold a hook under a sleeve.[8]

Whether played by actors with or without disabilities, disabled characters in plays tend to function as caricatures, symbols, emblems, or tropes. Disability scholars in literary, film, and television studies analyze the pervasive use of disability as a metaphor, and the use of the disabled body as a sign against which "healthy" bodies can be marked. "The materiality of metaphor via disabled bodies gives all bodies a tangible essence in that the 'healthy' corporeal surface fails to achieve its symbolic effect without its disabled counterpart," write Mitchell and Snyder.[9] Both *Signs of Life* and *An Almost Holy Picture* use characters' physical disabilities as metaphors. As Sandahl and Ann Wilson each argue, in *Signs of Life* Jane's disfigurement is a metaphor for femininity, the disability that any woman experiences in Victorian society; in addition, her physical disability mirrors Alice's emotional one.[10] In *An Almost Holy Picture,* Ariel's furriness represents Samuel's faith in his own cosmology, which is at once within him and outside of him, beautiful and uncontrollable, natural and freakish. Like many plays that feature a character with a physical disability, *An Almost Holy Picture* is not about Ariel, but rather concerns the protagonist's spiritual crisis and reconciliation by way of her and her disability. Both plays idealize the disabled character, presenting physical disability as a positive metaphor, but, as Sandahl asserts, "Whether used as a negative or positive metaphor, the use of disability as a dramaturgical device tends to erase the particularities of lived disability experience."[11] As Mitchell and Snyder conclude, "Such a history of metaphorical opportunism sits at the heart of the profound ambivalence that disabled populations inevitably feel when faced with the question of disability as a tool of artistic production."[12]

Despite such ambivalence, theater artists strive to represent "lived disability experience" onstage, to productively exploit performance's influence on everyday life. Even as the relationship between representation and reality is, as Mitchell and Snyder write, "inevitably prosthetic in nature—that is, narrative offers an illusive grasp of the exterior world upon which it signifies—disabled people's options are inevitably tethered to the options that history offers."[13] In addition, when able-bodied people see, hear, speak to, interact with, and touch people with disabilities, they gain perspective, insight, and sensitivity. If disability performance studies promotes the theatrical visibility of positive, true, nuanced representations of people with disabilities, then promising images show the experiences of disabled people accurately and complexly. Actors with disabilities appear in situations where they have agency and autonomy and portray well-developed characters rather than dramaturgical devices.[14]

Although representation profoundly affects society and culture, theater is not the same as everyday life, and a body on stage is neither a body in life nor a body in literature or on film. As Herbert Blau writes, "The theater's actuality is . . . in the fluent dimensions of the disjuncture between life and theater, in the vulnerability of the acting body, more specifically coterminous with life and more stubbornly resistant to the implication that they are, despite theater's own propaganda, one and the same."[15] Many foundational arguments in disability studies consider the disabled body as a textual or filmic object, not as an actual performer's body in real space and time. The discursive construction of visible physical disability, when rendered on the page or on film, benefits (or suffers) from the tools of media that have no limits on their abilities to create mimetic effects. Schenkar's and McDonald's dramaturgical choices—not to portray visually the physical disabilities so central to each play's emotional and political project—invoke particular tensions at the site of theater, the cultural form in which "the body" can be neither avoided nor generalized. Elizabeth Grosz notes that "every body is marked with the history and specificity of its existence."[16] Indeed, an actor's presence laminates her specifically marked body onto her role, if temporarily. Amelia Jones writes that the "unique body" of the performer

> has meaning by virtue of its contextualization with the codes of identity that accrue to the artist's name/body. Thus, this body is not self-contained in its meaningfulness; it is a body/self, relying not only on an authorial context of "signature" but also on a receptive context in which the interpreter or viewer may interact with it. This context is precisely the point (always already in place) at which the body becomes a "subject."[17]

In each play, the performance "context" simultaneously produces three bodies: the scripted body-subject who is the physically disabled character, the imagined referent of an actual disabled body-person on whom the character is based (even in the playwright's and audiences' imaginations), and the signifier of the actor's body on stage.

Let's consider, for a moment, a "what if": what if these characters were to be visually represented and realistically so? Blau writes, "When we think of the real in the simplest sense, the movies seem to have the advantage."[18] But, what if? Given that a body on stage is an actor, and most likely, an actor with a disability different from those specified in these plays or without a disability, what, then, is a production team to do? Are these characters whose disabilities cannot be realistically represented on stage? "We hardly think of a suspension of disbelief at the movies, whereas there is always on stage a compromising incompatibility between the corporeal body and the *mise en scène,* which includes touchable objects that seem unreal until you've made some very peculiar mental adjustments to the very dubious but insistent conventions," observes Blau.[19] One option is to find an actor with the same disability, a solution so impractical as to be almost ludicrous. Another is to put her in makeup, hair, plastic, or rubber, which, even in the best of circumstances, would look fake. This practice makes the disability more of a metaphor, more of a performance; it becomes a costume, an external quirk that might help the actor embody the character with more empathy (as with any costume, shoes, wig, makeup, or prop). Even more, such additions suggest blackface, patently offensive as an effort to represent and simulate an identity location via a marked body. Bert States is critical of theater's "sudden display of the virtuosity that is easily achieved in another medium. . . . Any possible audience appreciation of this event . . . will be canceled by disbelief, consternation, and distraction."[20] States explains that theater's "affective power depends on its manipulation of its own material potentials and how at the bottom of a medium's possible art there is a tension between formal limitations and the performance arising from them."[21] The body on stage conveys its own materiality, its own truth.

Instead, these playwrights choose to exploit theater and what theater can do, as they shift the theatrical focus towards aurality. Even in our visual culture, centuries away from Shakespeare's description of a place in lieu of scenery or Aeschylus's description of a violent battle instead of elaborate fight choreography and fake blood, theater still relies on careful listening. Theater audiences know that much of what they experience will be through language and that not everything will be seen. Stanton B. Garner Jr. explains that Shakespeare's evocation of darkness "can be understood equally as a variation played on and within the experiential field shared (differently) by audience, performer, and character—a function, in part, of a dramatic speech capable of evoking and modulating facets of experience."[22] That performed language can evoke bodies not present demonstrates "the ineradicable trace of the body in the word."[23] As Walter Benjamin writes of language and mimesis, "The coherence of words or sentences is the bearer through which, like a flash, similarity appears."[24]

Both Schenkar and McDonald depend on the "flash" that instantly creates a character in a spectator's mind. They refuse to fetishize fake disabled bodies when they block the audience's desire to see and to be empowered by their disembodied stare.[25] McDonald is self-conscious about her choice not to have an actor play Ariel: "It would be terrible—a real letdown—to embody her, because of the way she is described. . . . I wouldn't want to sentimentalize it."[26] Schenkar explains,

> I've actually never ever seen Jane physically made up to look like she has the severe disfigurations of disease. What is generally done—and I approve—is to subtly and not so subtly distort her body and mouth "naturally"—and of course her speech begins as thickened and almost unintelligible and then as the doctor cuts away at her, the speech becomes clearer and she becomes unhappier with herself.[27]

Peggy Phelan speaks of "an active vanishing, a deliberate and conscious refusal to take the payoff of visibility."[28] In this way, these plays take a precisely different tack in representing disability than the freak show and the medical profession. If those fields of representation require the physically disabled subject to be all too visible but silent, these plays render her body invisible but give her a "voice." By shifting the representation of the physical disability from the visual field to the field of language, these playwrights insist on its specificity and the detail of its representation. In this way, disability as portrayed in these plays is less metaphorical than if these characters were portrayed and embodied by actors. Garner writes, "So powerful is this persistence of the actual and its modes of presence that one witnesses its phenomenal effects, curiously, even when the referent is materially absent."[29]

Unlike the freak show, where the performer's body is made into "a hypervisible text against which the viewer's indistinguishable body fades into a seemingly neutral, tractable, and invulnerable instrument of the autonomous will,"[30] the spectator here must work to conjure the images of the unseen character or her unseen disability. By using language to evoke the visual, these plays call attention to different registers of reception, the visual, the aural, and the tactile, or what Laura U. Marks calls "haptic visuality," where "the eyes themselves function like organs of touch," "more inclined to graze than gaze."[31] Schenkar explains, *Signs of Life* "was composed as much as possible as a piece of music . . . [with] movements, developed themes, arias, duets, etc."[32] Each play foregrounds the audience's interpretive labor, turning us back on our own complicity in whatever images we create imaginatively. Rather than facilitate a direct correspondence between image and object, these works exploit a specific hermeneutic, playing "on a feature that characterizes extratheatrical experience as well, where present experience is always subject to variation and displacement by the imaginary in the guise of memories, anticipations, daydreams, fantasies, and other forms of vicariousness and virtuality."[33] In both plays, the physical disability is created in language, can only be heard, can only be conjured in the imagination of the listeners, auditors, audience.[34]

Signs of Life

The virtue of theater remains in the activity of perception.
—Herbert Blau, *The Audience*

Schenkar's *Signs of Life* is a dark comedy of manners, which explores the imagined relationships among Henry James, his sister Alice, her lover Katherine Loring, P. T. Barnum, Dr. Sloper (the name of a character in James's *Washington Square* but based on J. Marion Simms, the "father of gynecology"), and Jane Merritt (a fictitious "elephant woman" based on the real "elephant man," Joseph Merrick).[35] The play alternates between bizarrely raucous scenes of the men having tea and discussing their professional successes, and clever or heart-wrenching scenes in the lives of the two women, Alice and Jane. The men toast repeatedly, "To the ladies," blithely consuming the women, both metaphorically—their professional successes are entirely enabled by them—and literally—they drink their blood and eat their bones—for their own gains. In the first half of the play, the audience witnesses Jane's sentence at a workhouse where "freaks" are taught how to behave, and her valiant attempts to survive Barnum's and then Sloper's physical and emotional brutality. Alice, in the play's second half, tries to resist "the indignity" (51) of being born a girl in the James family by writing incessantly in her journal, cutting herself with knives, needles, and other sharp implements, and enacting hysterical fits during which she speaks a horrific sentence (never heard by the audience) that makes women faint and men blush. The play constructs the women as related: in the scenic design, their rooms are mirror images of each other; their lives are intertwined, as Alice suffers her first fit when she sees Jane's mother giving birth at a circus, and the two women later occupy different floors of the same hospital; and they share a literary preference for Jane Austen's novels. The play's clever equivalencies point to its central metaphor, what Wilson describes as "the monstrous disfigurement of Jane Merritt as a physical emblem for the monster within Alice James."[36]

Signs of Life takes physical disability as its subject, at once using it metaphorically to represent the "disability" of womanhood, and illustrating the historical construction of disabled bodies as sideshow freaks and medical curiosities. Schenkar stresses the politics of sight both in the play's historical setting and as a metaphor for contemporary privileging of vision and the gaze. Barnum and Dr. Sloper work in fields that not only depend on the power of the visual but also fetishize it, the fields that historically catalogued disabled bodies as freaks for entertainment or science. The play presents an alternative perspective on social practices of the late nineteenth century that transformed what and how people see—Barnum's freak show; Dr. Sloper's medical experiments; Henry James's literary portrayal of the American bourgeoisie—by portraying the men as visually obsessed, sickeningly selfish, and bizarrely sadistic. Dr. Sloper says of Jane, "I could never *bear* to take my eyes from her. The at*trac*tions of such repulsiveness" (53). By creating thoroughly reprehensible characters who participate in the social consumption and commodification of disabled bodies, Schenkar encourages the audience's disidentification with their position.[37]

Still, she complicates the audience's position by scripting them as "curiosity seekers" of a preshow freak show that Barnum advertises. Wilson writes, "Schenkar's scheme of equivalencies associates the theater audience with those at the freak show thereby suggesting that watching (in the theater, at the freak show, as part of scientific inquiry) appeals to a base fascination with luridness."[38] Schenkar explains in the opening stage directions, "The scene should induce in those members of the audience who actually listened to Barnum's spiel and therefore expected something salacious, a sharp feeling of disappointment" (50). Schenkar's key critical tactic involves the discrepancy between what is spoken in the play and what is made visible to the audience. She describes the set of Jane's and Alice's rooms as "mostly vacant, clearly confining, and entirely out of the light" (54), reminding the audience of what is obscured. Unlike a realist play in which the audience comfortably empathizes with the protagonist, *Signs of Life* forces the audience to realize their complicity in the construction of physical disability as freakish or medically curable.

Schenkar's choice not to represent visually Jane's physical disability onstage, but rather to express her condition solely through characters' spoken language, places even more responsibility on the audience. As theatergoers, they must pay close attention to what they hear to understand Jane's appearance. They must judge the veracity of those descriptions, told by the men, in relation to their sense of the honesty of the characters who speak them. They must reconcile the cognitive dissonance of an actor who looks nothing like the character who is described. And finally, they must take in the experiences of Jane, which she describes. While the play's theatrical strategy privileges aurality over visuality, vision, as portrayed in language, dominates the script. The language of the play, always evocative and frequently gruesome, invites the audience to produce mental pictures, which are never actually fulfilled on stage.

The temporal process by which the audience receives knowledge about Jane and about Alice and the resulting hermeneutic project structured by theater's relentless ongoingness develop this contradiction between what spectators hear and, then, what they see. Barnum's preshow spiel describes Jane's body in lurid detail: she has "an arm the size of an oak tree! A nose like an elephant's trunk!" (49). The opening scene adds Dr. Sloper, who says she was "born a monster," and Jane's mother, who explains, "At birth her skin was only a little roughened, only a little thick. . . . Her mouth moved a little . . . strangely, that was all. . . . But there was no reason to imagine what she would become" (50). When Jane is taken to the workhouse, the other freaks exclaim "its" ugliness, and block the audience's view of the actor. When they move aside, the actor stands on stage "draped in dark cloth," "an icon center stage" (56). The workhouse warden removes the cloth; Schenkar describes "an awe-full moment" (57). For the audience, the "awe" lies in a certain cognitive dissonance between the visual and the aural, between image and description, in observing an apparently nondisabled body that has been repeatedly described as freakish. Thus the spectator bumps up against her own expectations of what she would see. If she sees Jane as freakish, it is because the spectator produces the image in her mind, not because she sees it on stage.[39]

As the play proceeds, Jane begins to speak, and the audience witnesses her expressiveness, her charm, and her rich, other, elephant life—whether fantasy or real. Schenkar says, "But she's a charismatically awkward and out-of-place figure in this comedy of bad manners and elegant language that cut like knives (that's why Alice only needs words to describe her cuttings) and, in the best productions, Jane always projects a beautiful innocence and what Emerson called 'moral charm.'"[40] If the men are dependent solely on the visible, Jane's language invokes different senses: tactility and sound. She muses, "I'm dreaming I'm with people whose eyes are in their hands" (63). She dreams of "the Blind" sculpting her body, and her body makes music. Schenkar notes in stage directions, "The music, the modalities, should seem to come out of what the hands are touching" (64).

The play's contradictory aural and visual modes, on one level, critique the absurd arrogance of the men and warn the audience to distrust their every word. On another level, they foreground the spectator's own desire to see, frustrating curiosity with visual absence. The repeated references to Alice's "sentence" invoke in the audience an almost perverse curiosity that is never satisfied, serving as a metaphor for the "freakishness" never observed. But *Signs of Life* goes even further to remind the audience that it is *we* who produce the visually disabled body, not the play.

An Almost Holy Picture

Instead of presence, the theater asks to be approached in terms of *presencing;* theatrical phenomena are multiply embodied, evoked in a variety of experiential registers, refracted through different (and sometimes divergent) phenomenal lenses.

—Stanton B. Garner Jr., *Bodied Spaces*

Heather McDonald's *An Almost Holy Picture* is a poetic, meditative one-man play that follows Samuel Gentle from his life as a "gentle" church groundskeeper through the birth and youth of his daughter, Ariel. The play is set on an almost bare stage with a few highly charged objects, including a bag of beans, jars of salsa verde, a white enamel basin of water, some photographs, and various gardening tools. A plot of dirt on stage and the few actual objects used in the performance are, as McDonald specifies, "real and tactile" (37). In the performance of the play at Center Stage in Baltimore, Tim Grimm, who played Samuel, handled the objects with such care and deliberation that a spectator could almost feel their weight, shape, and texture. From the beginning, the play's spare aesthetic narrowly focuses the audience's vision and asks them to listen attentively.[41]

   The play's emphasis on listening sets up a particular dynamic of trust, essential to the performance's success, between character and audience, who are variously scripted as friend, confidante, confessor. What the audience hears in the play—Samuel's extended monologue—is structured around his memories of four faith-testing events, which, as he says, "shaped my personal idea of God."[42] These occurrences, the most significant events of the protagonist's life, are several times removed from the audience's own experiences. First, the audience only hears about these events but does not directly witness them in the play; second, they are distant memories for Samuel and perhaps imperfectly remembered; and finally, they are events that tested his faith and urged him to question his own perceptions. One is a childhood walk with his father when they think they hear the voice of God; another is a school bus crash in his community in which nine children died. The third event is the birth of his daughter, Ariel, his "misguided angel" (40) whom he and his wife shave biweekly from infancy on, performing what he calls "a baptism of water and blood" (44). The fourth episode, the climax of the play, takes place when Ariel is nine. After Samuel inadvertently makes her feel ugly and freakish in her furriness, she shaves herself for the first time, accidentally cutting herself all over. Over the course of the play, the audience watches Samuel garden and plant beans, and he mulls over the significance of these incidents. When he remembers hurting Ariel—his ultimate failure—he comes to understand that no person, God, or external force will intervene to change Ariel's furriness, and that he himself needs to learn to love and value her difference. Trying to maintain some notion of faith in the face of difficult, even tragic events, Samuel concludes his reveries by saying, "And it's my thoughts / Not God / Not faith / Not any religion / But my own thoughts / That give me the greatest comfort" (53).

   The play not only requires the audience to listen closely but its language is saturated with the visual, with images of light and vision and sight, both literal and metaphorical. The play purposefully emphasizes the sense—vision—on which its theatricality least depends. As Samuel says in his typically humble way, "I cannot promise you very much. I'll give you the images I know" (44). In each scene, Samuel notes how the light looks in the desert, by the ocean, at night in the churchyard. His quest throughout the play is to see the light, to gain vision, and to understand how the various events in his life fit into a larger scheme that is structured by faith and by a belief in God. Not unconventionally, then, the play equates light with wisdom, knowledge, and insight, and as in Christianity, associates it with goodness and salvation. Further, the play sets up a vocabulary of the visual through which the audience can imagine Ariel and her physical disability.

   The audience learns everything about the character of Ariel—her appearance, her behavior, her personality—through Samuel's memories of her. His detailed descriptions call up a powerfully visual and tactile image of the girl, through terms that are affectionate but that frequently compare her to an animal. He calls her "a wrinkled cooing bird" (39), "a furry little creature," "a sleeping pup" (40) when she is an infant, and later, when he prepares to shave her, he calls her a "little lamb" (44). His portrayal of Ariel and his frequent, more intellectualized, brief lectures on the topic of hair, from its cultural power and significance to methods of its removal, make Ariel's furry physicality palpable.

Ariel's actions, too, only exist by way of Samuel's stories. He explains, "Ariel skips over cracks in the sidewalk / She demonstrates a cartwheel / Tosses the baton into the air / Spins 'round twice / Catches it" (45). His remarks emphasize her physical ease and her normalcy; she does what other children do. Furthermore, when he quotes her, he conveys her typical childhood curiosity and guilelessness; she says, for example, "Dad / Guess what? / Blue whales are the biggest animals that ever lived. / Their hearts are the size of a Volkswagen. / Their penises are nine to twelve feet long. / And they swim all their lives" (44). In the first section of the play, McDonald creates an evocative image of Ariel; she uses precise language to invoke a clever, sweet, perfectly normal girl with fur from head to toe.

Because Samuel reveals his vulnerabilities and shortcomings (which is the very project of the play), his account of Ariel's trauma reads as true. One summer on Cape Cod, as Samuel explains, he and his wife allow Ariel's hair to grow. Ariel works as a counselor's aide at a summer camp for blind children. Samuel narrates, "Midsummer, and her hair has grown in full by now. She is covered in the lightest golden fleece. She looks like God's first creature. The blind children love her. One calls out to her, 'Oh, my softy.' They love to touch her. She's bought them all sunglasses and is teaching them a Stevie Wonder song, 'For Once in My Life'" (49). In the afternoons, Ariel spends time with Angel Martinez, who also works at the camp. Angel, a solitary, matted-headed, fifteen-year-old "wild child" has "unexpected abilities": he can fix cars, can find lost things, and is a gifted photographer (48). Although he is doesn't speak to anyone except his father, and many people in the town think that he is mute, Angel talks to Ariel, and they become friends. McDonald suggests that the variously disabled children connect with and understand one another.[43]

In the play's climax their connection proves dangerous to Samuel, as Angel truly sees his daughter as an angel, while Samuel sees her through society's eyes as flawed. One afternoon, as Samuel explains, he and Ariel attend the gallery opening of a show of Angel's photography. Upon entering the gallery, Samuel is shocked and horrified to see that all of the photographs are of Ariel and in many she is naked—swimming, sitting on a beach blanket eating blackberries, running through the woods. Samuel recounts his reaction:

> Something fierce in me lurched forward, blocking one photograph with my hands trying to protect my daughter from the eyes of others. I remember how panicked I felt when I saw how many photographs there were. I staggered through the gallery pulling photographs from the walls, letting them smash to the ground behind me. Glass shattered. Ariel screamed. I called Angel Martinez a foul creature. I gathered as many of the photographs as I could carry into my arms, hidden safely away, and I ran from the gallery. (50)

Samuel tries to police the images of Ariel as if they are her and not a representation of her. He occupies the perspective of dominant culture; as Mitchell and Snyder write, "Disability infuses every aspect of his or her social being. This equation of physical disability with social identity creates a tautological link between biology and self (imagined or real) that cannot be unmoored—the physical world provides the material evidence of an inner life (corrupt or virtuous) that is secured by the mark of visible difference."[44]

Following the conventions of a fall-from-grace narrative, the scene tells of Ariel's exile from Eden—the place where she could be furry and free and not a freak—into a place of shame and self-destruction, as she is so ashamed that she runs away and goes home to shave herself. Ariel then returns for a theatrical performance that evening: her mother is starring as Amanda Wingfield in *The Glass Menagerie*—the prototypical disability-as-metaphor play. Samuel has watched numerous rehearsals, fascinated by the young woman who plays Laura "with translucent skin," and obsessively interested in the scene with the young man (49). He imagines Ariel's entry into heterosexuality, assumptively dreading the pain it will cause her, as it does the "crippled" Laura. So preoccupied is Samuel with his own conventional notions about romance that he fails to observe how Angel has come to love his daughter and see her extraordinary beauty, not in spite of her hair but because of it. Still, the damage has been done, when Samuel sees the spots of blood on Ariel's body, nicked and gashed, red bumps and chafing, shaven for the first time all summer and the first time ever with her own hand, he says with remorse, "After years of trying to protect my daughter, I was the one who showed her how the world would see her—ugly and strange" (50).

The audience of the play, "the world" to which Samuel refers, does not imagine Ariel as ugly but as lovely, if tragically betrayed by her father. When he looks again at one photograph, not visible to the audience, Samuel sees that the photographs beautiful:

Ariel is running up a hill, the sea is in the background, and she's trailing a gauzy scarf behind her. It billows in the wind, and it's almost as if she's covered her entire body in sequins because the way the white hot light is all around her, her body shimmers like a highway in the dessert on a hot, hot day, and she is surrounded by a silvery halo. I can see that she is laughing and twirling and is completely unselfconscious and free. I've looked at my daughter all my life and I've never seen her quite this way before, but Angel Martinez has and he captured her and put her on this paper. (50)

Although Samuel initially responds to the photograph with fury, horror, and jealousy, by the end of the play he comes to see it as "an almost holy picture" (54).

Samuel's crises of vision, which thread through the play, remind the audience to question what they see. Although Samuel speaks in images and metaphors of sight and vision, he cannot ultimately trust his ability to see people or to see the truth. He says early in the play, "And so I came to the desert with my longing for vision and light; I had not expected to stumble blind in so much darkness" (38). The school bus (on which he is a passenger) crashes because a child screams when he thinks he see a rabbit in the road. Samuel thinks it's a ball of fire, but it turns out to be a girl whose hair is on fire. That day was, as Samuel recounts, "of clear, blue light and fierce dry heat. Everything shimmered. There were mirages. You could not trust your sight" (38).

The aural representation of Ariel in the play and the audience's dependence on the spoken word to create her requires a degree of imaginative labor unusual in contemporary theater. In its form and content, *An Almost Holy Picture* models a different sensory relationship to the world, one not primarily based on vision. The play argues in theatrical terms for other modes of interaction, for the primacy of hearing and touch, for an alternative register of language and love.

By the end of each play, little is resolved. In *Signs of Life,* Jane kills herself by letting her head fall back, crushing her windpipe—the only way she can take control of her life. Then Dr. Sloper performs a horrific, pornographic autopsy, which he describes in grisly detail, practically orgasmic over what he finds inside Jane: real blood. In *An Almost Holy Picture,* Ariel's last action—shaving herself—is, similarly, her only option for agency. The final image of Ariel is with her arms bloodied from nicks and cuts, seen by Samuel through her summer cardigan. That both plays end with images of the women's disabled bodies marked by blood again exploits the theatricality of theater and the visceral quality of language spoken on stage.

These plays do not offer realistic images of people with disabilities; they traffic in metaphors, using disability as a narrative device. Still, in their utter theatricality, they offer another strategy to represent visibly disabled bodies. By calling on the audience's imagination and attention, these plays make the women whole and complete in their precise detail. So, too, scholars in disability performance studies, while continuing to look to complementary fields for our theories, tools, and analyses, need to continue to develop ways of seeing, listening, and being that are available only in the live, embodied, present-tense theater.

Notes

I would like to thank Jill Dolan and Andrea Levine for their advice and help on this essay.

1. David T. Mitchell and Sharon L. Snyder, "Introduction: Disability Studies and the Double Bind of Representation," in *The Body and Physical Difference: Discourses of Disability*, ed. David T. Mitchell and Sharon L. Snyder (Ann Arbor: University of Michigan Press, 1997), 15.

2. Rosemarie Garland Thomson, "Narratives of Deviance and Delight: Staring at Julia Pastrana, the 'Extraordinary Lady,'" in *Beyond the Binary: Reconstructing Cultural Identity in a Multicultural Context*, ed. Timothy B. Powell (New Brunswick, N.J.: Rutgers University Press, 1999), 81–104; Carrie Sandahl, "Ahhh, Freak Out! Metaphors of Disability and Femaleness in Performance," *Theatre Topics* 9, no. 1 (1999): 11–30; Victoria Ann Lewis, "The Dramaturgy of Disability," in *Points of Contact: Disability, Art, and Culture*, ed. Susan Crutchfield and Marcy J. Epstein (Ann Arbor: University of Michigan Press, 2000), 102; Chris Anne Strickling, "*Actual Lives:* Cripples in the House," *Theatre Topics* 12, no. 2 (2002): 143–62. On autobiographical performance, also see Rosemarie Garland Thomson, "Staring Back: Self-Representations of Disabled Performance Artists," *American Quarterly* 52, no. 2 (2000): 334–38.

3. Joan M. Schenkar, *Signs of Life: Six Comedies of Menace*, ed. Vivian Patraka (Hanover, N.H.: Wesleyan University Press, 1998), 50. Subsequent citations are given in the text. Jane is modeled after Joseph Merrick, whom doctors thought had neurofibromatosis but later was diagnosed with Proteus syndrome. See http://www.proteus-syndrome.org, accessed June 28, 2004.

4. See http://www.emedicine.com/derm/topic811.htm, accessed June 28, 2004.

5. In "A Note on Casting," Mee writes, "There is not a single role in any one of my plays that must be played by a physically intact white person. And directors should go very far out of their way to avoid creating the bizarre, artificial world of all intact white people, a world that no longer exists where I live, in casting my plays." See http://www.panix.com/~meejr/html/cast.html, accessed June 28, 2004.

6. Lisa D'Amour, *Sixteen Spells to Charm the Beast*, dir. Deanna Shoemaker, Salvage Vanguard Theatre, February 2003.

7. Deanna Shoemaker, email to the author, February 26, 2003.

8. On autobiographical performance, see Strickling, "Actual Lives"; Sandahl,

"Ahhh, Freak Out!" Also see Kathleen Tolan, "We Are Not a Metaphor: A Conversation about Representation," *American Theatre* 18, no. 5 (2001): 17–21+.

9. David T. Mitchell and Sharon L. Snyder, *Narrative Prosthesis: Disability and the Dependencies of Discourse* (Ann Arbor: University of Michigan Press, 2000), 64.

10. Ann Wilson, "History and Hysteria: Writing the Body in *Portrait of Dora* and *Signs of Life*," *Modern Drama* 32, no. 1 (1989): 75, 84, 86; Sandahl, "Ahhh, Freak Out!" 15. Sandahl explains that in the production of *Signs of Life*, which she directed without disabled bodies on stage, the metaphor of disability remained unquestioned. She writes, "Without actual visibly disabled bodies, disability in this production could *only* be a metaphor" (26). Both plays are, of course, explicitly about gender's relation to disability, a topic beyond the scope of this essay.

11. Sandahl, "Ahhh, Freak Out!" 15.

12. Mitchell and Snyder, "Introduction," 17. Her difference serves as what Mitchell and Snyder call "narrative prosthesis" (*Narrative Prosthesis*, 52–53); the disability's cause and cure drive the narrative.

13. Mitchell and Snyder, *Narrative Prosthesis*, 9.

14. At the same time, valorizing "positive," "accurate" images necessarily calls up the conundrum of visibility: What exactly is a positive representation? To whom? And who can decide? What is an authentic representation? These questions echo those of other identity-oriented movements that have been preoccupied with the politics of visibility, and that continue to raise similar concerns about representations of women, people of color, lesbians, gays, bisexuals, and transgendered persons, and so on. Proliferating representations can increase understanding, empathy, and tolerance, but they can just as easily delimit identities as expand them. Visibility does not necessarily promote social change. See Peggy Phelan, *Unmarked: The Politics of Performance* (New York: Routledge, 1993).

15. Herbert Blau, *Blooded Thought: Occasions of Theatre* (New York: PAJ, 1982), 127.

16. Elizabeth Grosz, *Volatile Bodies: Toward a Corporeal Feminism* (Bloomington: Indiana University Press, 1994), 142.

17. Amelia Jones, *Body Art: Performing the Subject* (Minneapolis: University of Minnesota Press, 1998), 34.

18. Blau, *Blooded Thought*, 123.

19. Ibid., 123.

20. Bert O. States, *The Pleasure of the Play* (Ithaca, N.Y.: Cornell University Press, 1994), 33.

21. States, *Pleasure of the Play*, 33.

22. Stanton B. Garner Jr., *Bodied Spaces: Phenomenology and Performance in Contemporary Drama* (Ithaca, N.Y.: Cornell University Press, 1994), 41–42.

23. Ibid., 141.

24. Quoted in Laura U. Marks, *The Skin of the Film: Intercultural Cinema, Embodiment, and the Senses* (Durham, N.C.: Duke University Press, 2000), 141.

25. As Thomson writes, "The cultural work of staring is to normalize the viewer by abnormalizing—indeed, spectacularizing—the body on view, fixing it in a position of difference" ("Narratives of Deviance," 82).

26. Charlotte Stoudt, "Stepping into Darkness: An Interview with the Playwright," *American Theatre*, February 2000, 36.

27. Joan M. Schenkar, email to the author, August 31, 2000.

28. Phelan, *Unmarked*, 19.

29. Garner, *Bodied Spaces*, 41.

30. Rosemarie Garland Thomson, "Introduction: From Wonder to Error—a Genealogy of Freak Discourse in Modernity," in *Freakery: Cultural Spectacles of the Extraordinary Body* (New York: New York University Press, 1996), 10.

31. Marks, *Skin of the Film*, 162.

32. Joan M. Schenkar, "Preface: At This Performance. . . ," *Signs of Life*, ix.

33. Garner, *Bodied Spaces*, 42.

34. Spectators of different abilities will, of course, respond to the play's use of aurality differently. Hearing-impaired spectators will note the absence of the physically disabled body being described via sign language. Seeing-impaired spectators who experience a "touch tour" will also find the actor who plays Jane not disfigured and will know that *An Almost Holy Picture* is a one-man play.

35. For additional critical work on this play, also see Vivian Patraka, "Mass Culture and Metaphors of Menace in Joan Schenkar's Plays," in *Making a Spectacle: Feminist Essays on Contemporary Women's Theatre*, ed. Lynda Hart (Ann Arbor: University of Michigan Press, 1989), 25–40.

36. Wilson, "History and Hysteria," 75.

37. Mitchell and Snyder describe a nondisabled reader, which resonates with Schenkar's characterization of the men in the play: "We experience disability through an anticipation of our desire to 'know' the secret labyrinths of difference, without significantly challenging out investment in the construction of difference itself. . . . Readers' experience of the dual pleasures of fascination and repulsion also evolves out of an ability to leave the site of a fiction with our own membership in normalcy further consolidated and assured" ("Introduction," 15). The audience hears this typical perspective on disabled bodies spoken by characters who are themselves freakish and sadistic.

38. Wilson, "History and Hysteria," 75.

39. When Jane arrives at the workhouse, she witnesses a lesson in how to be a freak. The Matron urges the freaks—the disabled—to "look to the *side*, to the *side*, to the *side*," and "laugh accordin' to an audience" (58). The freaks' lesson shifts the hegemonic perspective to demonstrate that their difference is less about their physicalities and more about disciplined behaviors that forbid them to look back. The scene also foregrounds they are well aware of the social constructedness of their otherness.

40. Schenkar, email, August 31, 2000.

41. February 1999, dir. Tim Vasen. Reviews of the New York production note the stage's vast size and the actor's (Kevin Bacon) monumental task of taking up space and holding the audience's attention. See Ben Brantley, "Seeker, Behold: The Answer Is Here, All around You," review of *An Almost Holy Picture*, *New York Times*, February 8, 2002, E3.

42. Heather McDonald, *An Almost Holy Picture*, *American Theatre*, February 2000, 37. Subsequent citations are given in the text.

43. In addition, Angel is marked in the texts as a person of color; he is coded with a physical difference at once as immutable as Ariel's, but that can't be shaven off, even temporarily.

44. Mitchell and Snyder, "Introduction," 3.

Reconsidering Identity Politics, Essentialism, & Dismodernism

An Afterword

PEGGY PHELAN

"For all their merits, the healthy always disappoint" (125). So goes the first sentence of Emil Cioran's remarkable essay "On Sickness."[1] Aphoristic and given to certain lapses in logic, Cioran's essay does not argue so much as gesture toward generative speculation. "As long as one believes in philosophy, one is healthy; sickness begins when one starts to think," he writes. Cioran's notion of sickness interests me as a metaphor for what disability studies does to some of Western philosophy's favorite orthodoxies. Disability studies exposes what we normally take on philosophical faith and sends us to the rougher task of unthinking what we have learned to believe. I am well aware that disability and sickness are not the same, but I want to invoke sickness in Cioran's terms because it helps illuminate the kind of thinking at work in *Bodies in Commotion*. This thinking overturns philosophical orthodoxies about embodiment. Refusing the ideological imperative of the autonomous self, the essays in this volume take seriously concepts of interconnection, the enmeshed nature of the social body, and the complex work of responding to, in all senses, the richness and awkwardness of extraordinary bodies. Employing concepts of disability that range from dementia to Deafness, these essays reanimate and rearticulate the consolidations that have surrounded two decades of critical work on "the body." Much of that work has been written by performance studies scholars who have been extremely attentive to the ways in which race, class, gender, national origin, and sexuality have complicated our approaches to "the body." But it is only in the last few years that issues of ability have been brought into the conversation. Now that they have arrived, the encounter between performance studies and disability enriches both fields immeasurably.

Our usual philosophy no longer works. It held that there are some aberrant bodies among us and those unlucky enough to have such bodies should compel sympathy, compassion, or other more or less paternal and patronizing feelings. But those days, as this extraordinarily wide-ranging volume everywhere demonstrates, are long gone. Indeed, we have emerged on the other side of the rainbow, where the "able" body seems an unusual and increasingly rare occurrence. Morbid obesity, old age, and the side effects of decades of chemical toxicity in the environment have all contributed to the withering away of the "normal" body. Indeed, Lennard Davis, citing a report that between 40 to 80 percent of people over sixty-five are disabled, suggests that the acronym TAB, temporarily able-bodied, might be employed as a way to emphasize "the shaky footing on which normalcy rests" (Davis 2002, 36). This term is useful because it makes health the contingent variable that it truly is, given that all human bodies are (so far anyway) mortal. The human body, in whatever form it takes, is finite, changeable, and destined to die. In this sense, all bodies must come to terms with limits and incapacities. Therefore, how we think about the live body matters, if only because it sheds light on the act we will all undertake before our bodies cease to be, the act of dying. Performance studies, as a discipline, is overtly concerned with what the live is and why it matters. Disability studies is dedicated to understanding how and why these long-ignored—and, therefore, in the philosophical sense "new" bodies—are redefining the substance and force of life and death in the social imagination.

As disciplines explicitly concerned with bodily practice, both performance studies and disability studies have had to contend with the force of identity politics. The Janus-faced first step in new disciplinary efforts of the past thirty years, identity politics affords opportunities to organize around group interests. In the case of disability studies, the importance of collective organizing was in itself revolutionary. Disability activists, many of whom were Vietnam vets in the United States, were actively trying to change the laws restricting access to education, employment, and environments. When this work began in earnest in the 1970s in the United States, disabled people were largely isolated within their own specific communities. The blind socialized with the blind, but rarely with amputees.[2] In this same period in the academy, disability was studied almost exclusively from a medical perspective, a perspective whose foundation was specialization. But activists urged people to find common cause in the oppressive system denying them basic protections and rights in the wider world. These efforts were largely responsible for the passage of the Americans with Disabilities Act in 1990.

As disability activists were organizing and mobilizing diverse communities, the academy was responding to political activism inspired by the civil rights movement. Increased attention to the previously overlooked implications of race, gender, class, and sexuality informed a generation of work in the humanities and social sciences. One of the most striking features of this scholarship was an emphasis on social constructionism. In the 1970s, this emphasis often tangled with activists' success with community building in terms of specific, well-articulated pronouncements about group identity. Eventually, this conflict led to debates about "essentialism."[3] What we have learned from the establishment of women's studies, Asian-American, African-American, Latino/a and gay, lesbian, and transgendered studies is that some version of "strategic essentialism" really and truly works in the academy and in the larger world. But we have also learned that these material victories—getting office space, for example, is easier if you can demonstrate that a specific number of people will use it—are often at odds with the intellectual force of poststructuralism, the dominant mode of contemporary philosophy in the academy for the past thirty years. Poststructuralism, among other things, attempts to reconcile the insights drawn from social constructivism with Western metaphysics' ties to ontological philosophy. Poststructuralist thinking is uneasy about identity politics because it seems to endorse a unified view of the social subject and to posit the individual as an independent agent who mistakes choice for coercion, and free will for necessity.

But it may well be that it is in the realm of identity politics that disability studies makes one of its most incisive claims. This aspect of the field might have the most far-reaching consequences for contemporary philosophy. To date, the critique of identity fostered by poststructuralism relies on a larger argument about the nature of being. The work of Jacques Derrida and Judith Butler, for example, has suggested that Western philosophy's long obsession with ontology has been compromised by insufficient attention to iterative acts—ranging from speech acts to the comportments of gendered performances. Contemporary philosophy's attention to performance has been useful for performance studies because it has put the field within a highly charged, although in recent years somewhat dissipating, argument about being.

Disability scholars have taken up the academy's preoccupation with poststructuralism and minority scholarship. Most disability scholars posit performance as that which occurs with and between widely different bodies. For most scholars of disability, bodily practices and the social-psychological effects such practices produce, illuminate the philosophical and political imagination far more vividly than the abstractions of ontological speculations about the nature of being.

To be specific, disability scholars have rejected the idea that a person who uses a wheelchair "is" disabled. Rather, these scholars quite rightly point out that such people have been made "dis-abled" by environments that lack ramps, elevators, electronic doors and so on. In this aspect of their work, scholars of disability participate comfortably in poststructuralist tropes about performance and identity. As the editors point out in their introduction, it is useful to think of "disability in performative terms—as something one *does* rather than something one *is*." By and large, however, poststructuralists have used such arguments about performance to undermine the stability of ontological essence. This aspect of poststructuralist thinking has not been taken up with the same fervor by disability scholars, and I think this reluctance is worth serious reflection.

What is startling about many of the essays in this volume is how central the connection between the body and the self is. While there are several brilliant riffs on the false orthodoxies of the "autonomous self" here, these are dedicated to proposing the fundamental interdependence of bodies in the social and natural worlds. Surprisingly, there are few questions or comments about the security of the relation between body and self in *Bodies in Commotion*. For disability scholars, it seems almost axiomatic that the social-psychological, political, and artistic force of disability is directly linked to who the disabled person "is." This link is not a repetition of the sometimes unexamined assumptions that led to the essentialist debates within feminism and feminist theory in the 1980s. Rather it appears that in this return to the link between lived experience and subjectivity new thoughts become possible.

To make clear what is at stake in this return to the link between body and self, I want to turn to the work of Lennard Davis, one of the foremost disability scholars writing today. His work is not overtly concerned with issues of performance, but I think this volume helps clarify one of Davis's most interesting claims. Davis is prolific. Among other texts, he has published *My Sense of Silence*, a beautifully evocative memoir about growing up as a hearing child with Deaf parents in the South Bronx; *Shall I Say a Kiss?* a remarkable volume of letters between his parents describing their courtship and complex negotiations to marry; and a collection of essays, *Bending over Backwards: Disability, Dismodernism and Other Difficult Positions.*[4] He is also the editor of *The Disability Studies Reader,* a superb collection of some of the best writing in disability studies between 1963 and 1997.[5]

In *Bending over Backwards,* Davis makes one of his boldest claims. He calls for "the end of identity politics and the beginning of dismodernism" (2002, 9). Arguing that postmodernism and poststructuralism are exhausted, he proposes that *dismodernism* ought to be the new term and concept to replace them. Davis begins by taking the usual argument against the American with Disabilities Act seriously. The usual critique of the act is that it is "overbroad," that it protects too many. At last count (2000), there are more than 54 million people with disabilities in the United States. If so many can claim special protection under the law, the thinking goes, then it is ineffective legislation. Davis turns this argument on its head: he finds the vast size of the protected class to be one of the greatest achievements of the legislation because it, somewhat unwittingly, touches on what basic human rights must offer all bodies. Thus, the ADA does not protect "special interests"; it goes to the core of what universal human rights ought to be. This is a very shrewd and important point. While it has been often pointed out that those at the margins define that which constitutes the center, rarely has this insight been matched to a legal imperative. In making the rights of the disabled the model for all human rights, Davis positions disability as a universal condition and suggests that dismodernism is its principle contemporary expression.

Davis then suggests that serious attention to disability produces a new ethics for all bodies. This ethics is based on three underlying principles: care of the body, care for the body, and caring about the body. These three ethical principles, Davis claims, are at the foundation of a dismodernism that

> argues for a commonality of bodies within difference. It is too easy to say "we are all disabled." But it is possible to say that we are all disabled by injustice and oppression of various kinds. We are all nonstandard and it is under that standard that we should be able to found the dismodernist ethic. (2002, 32)

I find this extremely appealing because in arguing for a bodily ethics, Davis implicitly endorses a performance-based worldview. To take care of the body, to care for the body, and to care about bodies requires a specific ethics—one that takes touch as axiomatic, emotional attachment as a value, and interconnection as constant. As the remarkable essays in *Bodies in Commotion* make clear, such care informs the ethics of performance and disability.

While alert to the risks of endorsing the false platitude, "Everyone is disabled," Davis nonetheless wants disability to become, if not a universal identity claim, a general lens for understanding the world. This apparent contradiction is reminiscent of the dilemmas that still face performance studies: as the argument usually goes, "If everything is performance, why do we need a special field to study it?" It is here that I think performance and disability studies might find common cause. Both fields must continue to insist on the "both/and" endorsed by poststructuralist thinking, and both fields must continue their allegiance to a notion of awakening consciousness that has been so generative for political and intellectual work in the past thirty years.

It was Herbert Blau (1990) who first pointed out that a universal of performance is consciousness that one is in one. This consciousness might be a matter of observing the actions of another, say, a person with a wheelchair. Or performance consciousness might be rooted in the experience of watching how your performance rolling into room influences those observing your journey. Either way, performance consciousness, like disability consciousness, interrupts the co-incidence of self. Just as physicists responded to the vivid transformations in the wave and the particle inaugurated by the observer by inventing quantum theory, so too might we speak of performance consciousness as that which alters and interrupts the seam between performances in everyday life and performances that are larger than life, for any number of reasons. Similarly, consciousness of disability awakens us from our untested beliefs in embodiment; disability consciousness transforms one's worldview because it reorders the invisible and visible frames that illuminate our worlds.

It is possible to see "everything as performance," and it is possible to see everyone as disabled, while also and at the same time recognizing that there are conceptual and perceptual frames that interpret specific events and specific bodies as extraordinary. These "special" frameworks, activities of consciousness and perception, require specific political and material acts; they require specific intellectual focus; and most radically, they require a renewed concentration on the essential connections between the categories of experience we take to be fundamentally human. These categories include the phenomenological experience of embodiment—an experience that is altered by age, drugs, genetics, diet, and a whole host of economic, historical, political, biological, technological, and aesthetic frameworks—and they include the so far unshakable fact of human mortality. This fact has meant that we must see the world in a dialectical fashion: we are simultaneously alive to our death and deadened to aspects of our life. This duality means it is necessary to think of live art, especially performance, as both integral to, and separate from, daily life. Similarly, it is necessary to think of disability as both a natural condition in all human life and as a social interpretation that informs and illuminates the phantasm of normative and "proper" bodies. While new biotechnologies and advances in stem cell research have been both celebrated and criticized for prompting new thinking about the nature of life and the future of disability, performance studies and disability studies have been (far more quietly) revising what it means to have a body and what it means to be alive. These considerations have been undertaken with an eye sharply focused on ethics and aesthetics, the two most significant areas for humanities scholarship in the new century. As a volume dedicated to illuminating how the ethics of differently abled and disabled bodies inform the making of art, *Bodies in Commotion* will be central to the development of this new scholarship. The essays in this volume exemplify an ethics of embodiment alert to the felt connection between experience and subjectivity, and an ethics that places the material performance of physical, intellectual, and political care in the center of our ever renewing and ever dying bodies.

Notes

1. Howard's translation reads, "Whatever his merits, a man in good health always disappoints." I modified the translation slightly.

2. For excellent accounts of the disability rights movement see Shapiro 1994; Linton 1998; and Charlton 2000.

3. For a fuller discussion of the essentialist debates within the history of feminism and feminist theory see Phelan 2001; and Schor and Weed 1994.

4. Davis is also the author of *Enforcing Normalcy: Disability Deafness and the Body*, and *Resisting Novels: Fiction and Ideology*.

5. The 1963 essay is an excerpt from Erving Goffman's *Stigmas*. Everything else was written in the 1980s and 1990s. Interestingly, there is nothing from the 1970s in the book.

Works Cited

Blau, Herbert. 1990. "Universals of Performance; or Amortizing Play." In *By Means of Performance: Intercultural Studies of Theatre and Ritual*, ed. Richard Schechner and Willa Appel, 250–72. Cambridge: Cambridge University Press.

Charlton, James I. 2000. *Nothing about Us without Us: Disability, Oppression and Empowerment*. Berkeley: University of California Press.

Cioran, Emil. 1970. "On Sickness." In *Fall Into Time*, trans. Richard Howard, 125–39. Chicago: Quadrangle Books.

Davis, Lennard. 1987. *Resisting Novels: Ideology and Fiction*. New York: Routledge.

———. 1995. *Enforcing Normalcy: Disability, Deafness, and the Body*. London: Verso.

———. 2000. *My Sense of Silence: Memoirs of a Childhood with Deafness*. Urbana: University of Illinois Press.

———. 2002. *Bending over Backwards: Disability, Dismodernism and Other Difficult Positions*. New York: New York University Press.

Davis, Lennard, ed. 1997. *The Disability Studies Reader*. New York: Routledge.

————. 1999. *Shall I Say a Kiss? The Courtship Letters of a Deaf Couple.* Washington, D.C.: Gallaudet University Press.

Linton, Suni. 1998. *Claiming Disability: Knowledge and Identity.* Cultural Front Series. New York: New York University Press.

Phelan, Peggy. 2001. "Survey." In *Art and Feminism*, ed. Helena Rickett, 14–49. London: Phaidon.

Schor, Naomi, and Elizabeth Weed, eds. 1994. *Another Look at Essentialism.* Bloomington: Indiana University Press.

Shapiro, Joseph. 1994. *No Pity: People with Disabilities Forging a New Civil Rights Movement.* New York: Crown\Three Rivers.

Contributors

Philip Auslander is a professor in the School of Literature, Communication, and Culture of the Georgia Institute of Technology, where he teaches performance studies and media studies. He is the author of numerous essays and four books on theater and performance, including *Liveness: Performance in a Mediatized Culture* (Routledge, 1999), for which he won the 2000 Joe Callaway Prize for Best Book in Drama or Theatre. Most recently, he edited the four-volume anthology *Performance: Critical Concepts in Literary and Cultural Studies* (Routledge, 2003).

Anne Davis Basting is the director of the Center on Age and Community at the University of Wisconsin, Milwaukee, and the founder-director of the Time Slips Project. Basting is both an award-winning playwright and a scholar of performance studies who has written extensively on representation of aging in theater and everyday life. She is the author of *The Stages of Age: Performing Age in Contemporary American Culture* (University of Michigan Press, 1998).

Jessica Berson teaches dance history, Laban movement analysis, and modern dance at Wesleyan University and is pursuing a Ph.D. in theater at University of Wisconsin, Madison. She studied American Sign Language and deaf history at Teachers College, New York University, and New York Society for the Deaf, and has worked as a volunteer interpreter for elderly Deaf and Deaf-blind adults. In New York City, she taught dance to Deaf students at the National Dance Institute and tutored students at the Junior High School for the Deaf. Her research and choreography focuses on community-based dance performance.

Shannon Bradford is the director of the Center for Excellence in Learning and Teaching at SUNY Brockport, where she also teaches courses in dance and theater. Bradford, who is also a Fulbright Scholar, specializes in teaching with technology, including web-enhanced courses, hybrid courses and electronic portfolios. Her multimedia CD-ROM on the Australian Theatre of the Deaf was the first dissertation to be designed in hypertext format at the University of Texas, Austin, where Bradford received both her M.A. and her Ph.D. in theater history/criticism/theory/text.

Brenda Jo Brueggemann is an associate professor of English, women's studies, and comparative studies at Ohio State University, where she coordinates the American Sign Language Program and disability studies minor. She has contributed essays to several edited volumes and to such journals as *Disability Studies Quarterly, College Composition and Communication,* and *College English.* She edits the Deaf Lives series from Gallaudet University Press, and she is coeditor of the Modern Language Association Press volume *Disability Studies: Enabling the Humanities* and author of *Lend Me Your Ear: Rhetorical Constructions of Deafness* (Gallaudet University Press, 1999).

Johnson Cheu received his Ph.D. in English at Ohio State University, where he wrote his dissertation on the cultural and rhetorical constructions of cure in twentieth-century American literature, film, and memoir. He is currently a visiting assistant professor at Michigan State University's department of writing, rhetoric, and American cultures. His scholarly work has appeared in *Disability/Postmodernity: Embodying Disability Theory* (Continuum, 2002), and his poetry is published in *Staring Back: The Disability Experience from the Inside Out* (Plume, 1997), *Disability Studies Quarterly, Progressive, Midwest Poetry Review,* and the anthology *Screaming Monkeys: Critiques of Asian American Images* (Coffee House, 2003).

Maureen Connolly is professor of physical education (disability studies), and a former director of women's studies at Brock University, Ontario. She has published numerous essays and book chapters on phenomenology, dance, movement education, and disability. Recent essays appear in *Narratives of Professional Helping, American Journal of Semiotics, Human Studies,* and *Adapted Physical Activity Quarterly.*

Tom Craig is a fellow in the International Communicology Institute, a sessional instructor in women's studies and communication studies, and a full-time rogue scholar in the politics of stressed embodiment. He has published a book and numerous essays on communication, lived relations, and embodied politics as played out in religious, interpersonal, health care, and educational contexts. Recent essays appear in *Narratives of Professional Helping, Semiotics, Human Studies,* and *American Journal of Semiotics.*

Marcy J. Epstein is a National Institute for Disability Research and Rehabilitation fellow, combining research in trauma and narrative via the department of physical medicine and rehabilitation with teaching in disability studies at the University of Michigan–Ann Arbor. She coedited *Points of Contact: Disability, Art, and Culture* (University of Michigan Press, 2000) and is working on a new book on traumagraphy.

Jim Ferris is a performer, director, scholar, and poet whose work has appeared in the *Michigan Quarterly Review, Ragged Edge, Savvy, Review of Communication, Health Communication, Lowell Review, Lucid Stone,* and *Jeopardy.* He teaches in the Department of Communication Arts at the University of Wisconsin, Madison.

Petra Kuppers is assistant professor of performance studies at Bryant College and artistic director of the Olimpias Performance Research Projects. She is the author of *Disability and Contemporary Performance: Bodies on Edge* (Routledge, 2003) and has edited a double issue of the *Contemporary Theatre Review* on the subject of disability and performance (2001).

Victoria Ann Lewis is an assistant professor of theater at University of Redlands. After twenty-five years as an actor-director-writer in feminist and not-for-profit theater (Family Circus Theater and Lilith, a Woman's Theatre), she earned a Ph.D. in theater from the University of California at Los Angeles. Her published work appears in *Michigan Quarterly Review; Points of Contact: Disability, Art, and Culture* (University of Michigan Press, 2000); *Staring Back: The Disability Experience from the Inside Out* (Plume, 1997); *American Theatre; Disability Rag and Resource;* and *With the Power of Each Breath: A Disabled Woman's Anthology* (Cleis, 1985) As codirector and founder of the Other Voices Project at Los Angeles's Mark Taper Forum, she created and developed a series of documentary plays, among them *Tell Them I'm a Mermaid* (1983), *Teenage Ninja Mothers* (1991–93), and *P.H.*reaks: The Hidden History of People with Disabilities* (1993). She is editor of *Beyond Victims and Villains: Contemporary Plays by Disabled Playwrights* (Theatre Communications Group, 2005).

Lenore Manderson is a medical anthropologist and social historian and is professor of women's health and director of the Key Centre for Women's Health in Society at the University of Melbourne. She is interested in infectious disease in resource-poor communities, sexuality, gender and sexual health, and adaptation to chronic disease. Her books include *New Motherhood* (with Mira Crouch; Gordon and Breach, 1993), *Sickness and the State: Health and Illness in Colonial Malaya, 1870–1940* (Cambridge University

Press, 1996), *Sites of Desire/Economies of Pleasure* (edited with Margaret Jolly; University of Chicago Press, 1997), *Global Health Policy, Local Realities* (edited with Linda M. Whiteford; Lynne Rienner, 2000) and *Coming of Age in South and Southeast Asia* (edited with Pranee Liamputtong; Curzon, 2001). In 2001, she was an awarded an inaugural Australian Research Council Federation Fellowship. She is engaged in research full-time on chronic disease and disability, with particular interest in the social aspects of locomotive impairment, loss of function, and resilience. She is also involved in a collaborative film project on motion, rhythm, and impairment. She is a Fellow of the Academy of Social Sciences of Australia.

Melissa C. Nash earned her Ph.D. in social anthropology in 2002, having studied at University College London with funding from the Economic and Social Research Council. Her research examines cultural intervention by arts practitioners and social activists in the lives of inner-city London adults who have "learning disabilities" (i.e., conditions such as Down's syndrome, autism, or brain damage). The research looks at how artistic activity assists people with learning disabilities adjust to changes in their lives brought about by community care policy, including the issue of the "restoration of the self" postinstitutionalization. She also explores how the disabled can use the arts as a communication channel to express their experiences. Her published work appears in the *Scottish Journal of Religious Studies*.

Jennifer Parker-Starbuck received her Ph.D. from the City University of New York Graduate Center; her dissertation, entitled "Cyborg Theatre: Corporeal/Technological Intersections in Multimedia," deals with contemporary multimedia performance. She is currently a lecturer at the University of Hull's Scarborough School of Arts in England. She is the former managing editor for *Slavic and East European Performance*, and associate editor for *TEATR: Russian Theatre Past and Present*. Her essays and reviews have appeared in *Theatre Journal*, *PAJ*, the *Journal of Dramatic Theory and Criticism*, *Western European Stages*, *Didaskalia*, and *Slavic and East European Performance*. She also works in the theater as a director.

Susan Peake is a doctoral candidate at the University of Melbourne. She is a medical sociologist who teaches in the areas of medical anthropology and sociology of education. Her publications stem from her masters degree research on urinary incontinence in women of middle years and from work related to her doctorate on embodiment, impairment, identity, and gender.

Giles Perring is a working musician, composer, and artist. In 1983 he was a founder of the music project and band Echo City, which has collaborated regularly with performers and artists with learning disabilities in the United Kingdom, Eire, North America, and the European mainland. In Germany, this work has included a long and fruitful partnership with the Bremen-based arts company Blaumeier Atelier. In 1997, Echo City released an album, *Loss of the Church,* written and performed with the Siren Project, an arts project for learning-disabled people based in North London. This led to the instigation of regular London-wide club events under the name The Wild Bunc', and touring performances in the United Kingdom and Germany in 2000. Since the late 1980s he has worked for a number of U.K. arts organizations including Actionspace, Shape, and Artsreach. He is currently involved in the long-term development of a music theater project for Arts-reach in North London. In the mid-1990s, he began to develop his own research into the creative relationship of nondisabled and learning disabled artists, which he then undertook as an M.A. by Independent study under Lea Myers at the University of East London. He completed the degree in 1999, since when he has taught part time at the university in the Department of Education and Community Studies.

Peggy Phelan is the Ann O'Day Maples Chair in the Arts at Stanford University's drama department. She is the author of *Unmarked: The Politics of Performance* (Routledge, 1993) and *Mourning Sex: Performing Public Memories* (Routledge, 1997) and has written the text for the recent catalog *Art and Feminism* (Phaidon, 2001).

Carrie Sandahl is an assistant professor in the School of Theatre at Florida State University. Her artistic and scholarly work focuses on issues of gender and disability representation. She has published in *Theatre Topics, Disability Studies Quarterly, American Theatre, Gay and Lesbian Quarterly, Journal of Dramatic Theory and Criticism,* and *Contemporary Theatre Review.* She is currently writing a book entitled *Americans with Disabilities Act: Disability and Performance since the Civil Rights Era.* Her performance work appears in David Mitchell and Sharon Snyder's video documentary *Vital Signs: Crip Culture Talks Back.*

Owen Smith earned a cultural studies M.A. from the University of East London. He currently works at London Metropolitan University, where he is involved in developing initiatives that seek to improve access to study in higher education. Coming from a background in the performing arts, he has worked with adult learners in a variety of contexts for the past twenty years. Currently, Smith is the outreach manager for the Arts Learning Partnership, an organization, based at and supported by London Metropolitan University, developing new learning pathways with and for arts and community arts organizations in London.

Sharon L. Snyder is the coeditor of *Disability Studies: Enabling the Humanities* (MLA, 2002), coauthor of *Narrative Prosthesis: Disability and the Dependencies of Discourse* (University of Michigan Press, 2001), and coeditor of the first edited collection on disability studies in the humanities: *The Body and Physical Difference: Discourses of Disability* (University of Michigan Press, 1997). She is an assistant professor at the University of Illinois, Chicago's Ph.D. program in disability studies. Her documentary video projects, as the director of Brace Yourselves Productions, include *Vital Signs: Crip Culture Talks Back,* the grand prize winner of Rehabilitation International Film Festival (Auckland, New Zealand, 1996), and Best Film, International Disability Film Festival (Moscow, 2002); and *A World without Bodies,* the recipient of the Corporation on Disabilities and Communication's Superfest Merit Award in 2003. She is currently at work on a new video project, *Out of the Mainstream: The Very *Special* Life of Riva Lehrer.*

Rosemarie Garland Thomson is associate professor of women's studies at Emory University. Her fields of study are feminist theory, American literature, and disability studies. Her scholarly and professional activities are devoted to developing the field of disability studies in the humanities and in women's studies. She is the author of *Extraordinary Bodies: Figuring Physical Disability in American Literature and Culture* (Columbia University Press, 1997), editor of *Freakery: Cultural Spectacles of the Extraordinary Body* (New York University Press, 1996), and coeditor of *Disability Studies: Enabling the Humanities* (Modern Language Association Press, 2002). She is currently writing a book on the dynamics of staring and one on the cultural logic of euthanasia.

Tanya Titchkosky is an associate professor of sociology at St. Francis Xavier University in Nova Scotia. Working in the area of disability studies, from a background in phenomenology and hermeneutics, Titchkosky has published *Disability, Self, and Society* (University of Toronto Press, 2003). Her essays include "Governing Embodiment: Technologies of Constituting Citizens with Disabilities," "Cultural Maps: Which Way to Disability," "Disability—a Rose by Any Other Name?" "Coming Out Disabled: The Politics of Understanding," and "Disability Studies: The Old and the New?" Her current work addresses the ways in which the meaning of disability is enacted within the popular press.

Stacy Wolf is associate professor in the Department of Theatre and Dance at the University of Texas, Austin, and is the author of *A Problem Like Maria: Gender and Sexuality in the American Musical* (University of Michigan Press, 2002). She is the editor of *Theatre Topics.*

Index

333